Divine Justice

Murtaza Mutahhari

Translated by
Sulayman Hasan Abidi
Murtaza Alidina
Shuja Ali Mirza

International Center for Islamic Studies

Book Title: Divine Justice

Author: Murtaza Mutahhari

Translation: Sulayman Hasan Abidi, Murtaza Alidina, Shuja Ali Mirza

Compilation, Editing and Graphics: Abu Yahya al-Hussaini

Publisher: Jerrmein AbuShaba

Year: 2020

ISBN: 9781733028462

CONTENTS

PROBLEM SOLVED 83

DISCRIMINATION 87

EVILS 117

Foreword

The issue of Divine Justice is an important one in the history of Muslim intellectual thought, and it has given rise to important works in different periods of Islamic thought in areas such as theology, law, and Islamic politics.

Because of the importance of the issue to Muslims, Muslim thinkers authored numerous works about the topic and various Islamic schools of thought gave it special importance. Thus, the topic of Divine Justice and researching the various views of different Islamic sects with respect to it have great importance in terms of the history of Islamic thought. In addition, the proliferation of atheistic and anti-religious movements in the modem era have bestowed renewed importance to the topic. Divine Justice can be studied from various dimensions. One of the most important contemporary challenges facing belief in God is the issue of evil, such that some philosophers of religion in the West mention evil as proof of the nonexistence of God. Utilizing the heritage of Islamic philosophers and relying on the transcendental philosophy of Mulla Sadra, the author has striven to present Divine Justice in a logical way; and with attention to the issues of free will and predestination and the ill effects of predestination, he has tried to explain it in a such a way that natural evils-unpleasant things like illness, floods, earthquakes, and so on-find a logical place in the edifice of theist thought and are no longer portrayed as evidence for atheism. In the author's view, Christian and Western theology has weaknesses that render it unable to provide fitting answers to the objections about Divine Justice. Thus, he has dealt with the topic of Divine Justice and its various dimensions and corollaries in numerous works, and by explaining the authentic Islamic belief, he has aimed to prevent intellectual deviation in the young generation. He has dealt with this and related topics such as the Argument from Design in the books *Man and His Destiny* and *Causes of inclination to Materialism* as well as in the *Lessons on "Ilahiyyat" of al-Shifa*. The summation of his efforts in the present work as he himself has said, is to present the issue of Divine Justice in terms of creational or ontological justice in a new and novel way. The issue of Divine Justice in terms of legislative, legal, and also social justice has been discussed in the author's other books, such that by observing his works it can be understood that the issue of Divine Justice had a central role in the late author's thought. In this work, he studies the most fundamental issues related to God's justice. Another point that can be mentioned about the importance of Divine Justice in the author's thought is that in his view, a worthy and coherent solution to the issue can have an important effect on the dynamism of Islamic thought. It is for this reason that the *International Center for Islamic Studies and the World Conference on Mutahhari's Thoughts* requested the able translators Shuja Ali Mirza, Murtaza Alidina, and Syed Sulayman Hasan to take on the translation so as to allow the friends of wisdom and knowledge all over the world to have access to this important work. It is our hope that this effort, in addition to protecting the Islamic faith of the young generation, makes possible the progress and revival of Islamic civilization.

Research Department of the

International Center for Islamic Studies

Preface to the Translation

As a subject of inquiry, "Divine Justice" traditionally falls within the field of theology and *kalam*.[1] Theologians of all ages and religions have had to grapple with this topic, mainly because of its centrality within the ideology and doctrine of religion, and because of the consequences it has for the faith of believers. For, it is held that until the knowledge of God is not spelt out and objectively understood, man cannot correctly place himself in the grand scheme of things, and subjectively stands in danger of losing his bearings and going astray. In this appraisal of things, conceptual knowledge of the truth has direct implications for the human soul and its ability to will the good. To put it differently, it is not until man knows the ultimate truth to be also the absolute good, that he can himself be truly good and perform acts of virtue over and against vice. Hence there is pressing need to absolve God of all evil on the one hand, and to instill man with the freedom of will on the other. It is for this very reason that the "Problem of Evil" and the debate on "Freewill and Predestination" figure so prominently in the discussions on Divine Justice, this present study being no exception.

Having stated that the discussion at hand is the special prerogative of theology, it is important to note that the author of this book is exceptional in that he chooses to approach the subject from an altogether different perspective. He uses philosophy as his base and primarily applies philosophical methods to solve the problems and questions that surround the issue of Divine Justice. This departure from the norm is significant for a number of reasons. Firstly, it shows the level and substance of the author himself-that he was not just an Islamic ideologue, dogmatist, or activist given to fiery apologetics, but beyond that, he was a seeker of truth and a philosopher in the best sense of the word. Secondly, it belies the inadequacy of the theological

---

[1] Short form of *'Ilm al-Kalam* عِلْم الكَلام, literally "science of discourse") also called "Islamic scholastic theology", is the study of Islamic doctrines (*'aqa'id*). A scholar of Kalam is referred to as a *mutakallim*. The Arabic term *Kalam* means "speech, word, utterance" among other things, and its use regarding Islamic theology is derived from the expression "Word of God" (*Kalam Allah*) found in the Qur'an.

approach-something which the author explicitly mentions in his introduction. Thirdly, and as an indication of how and why an inadequacy was perceived in the first place, it bespeaks of the situation cum dilemma of religion in the modem world. This last reason will be briefly explained in what follows, as it is an inherently significant matter and will throw into relief the importance of this work.

Religion is from God and is His special device for mankind by which the greatest number possible are saved. But given the nature of fallen and falling man, religion is obligated to speak to him on his own grounds and at whatever point it finds him on the arc of descent. So, where the former generations had more of a direct access to Revelation and the vision of the prophet through whom the religion was established, the latter due to their distance and the entropic conditions of the Fall have more difficulty in "seeing" the truth. They need to be helped from the outside, so to speak. They require aids to achieve the vision and intellection of the former generations. These aids and "artificial" constructs are providentially provided, and are a part and parcel of the religious tradition as a whole. Thus, while they are in reality the instruments that compensate for the overall decline, they are seen ostensibly as "developments." After the initial vision there is for instance the development in the religious universe and orthodoxy of a doctrine, theology, ideology, sociology, and political system.

Now, as far as the Islamic tradition goes, the problem of evil and the issue of Divine justice-something which from the Qur'anic perspective is not a problem at all and is a non-issue, became the subject of heated debate on the level of theology. For a time, the theological answers, ones that pertain to a discursive and rational understanding of religious truths, were satisfactory and sufficient, as reason was still based on higher levels of the intellect and the sense of the sacred and holy was still alive and strong. Further on this was not the case and reason was increasingly divorced from its higher principle namely the sacred intellect or *al-'aql al-qudsi* and a purely human rationality came to take its place; a rationality that insisted that all aspects of being fall within the pale of its discursive and deductive methods. To complicate matters even more, in the Christian world-which was further ahead in its decline and due to its greater emphasis on the moral and ethical level, the problem of evil took on humanistic connotations and gravitated towards what might be called the justification of "personal" evils and suffering. Evil was now described as "the sum of the opposition ... to the desires and needs of individuals," something very different from the privation of being and goodness that St. Thomas had earlier postulated. With the advent of the modem age, these sentiments found their way into Muslim lands and compounded the existing problems caused by materialist and rationalist tendencies. It is under these complex and trying conditions that the author gave a series of lectures on the topic of Divine Justice and chose to proceed as he did.

To explain, as extreme situations call for extreme measures and further decline and deviation call for greater corrective and compensatory actions, the author consciously chose to up the ante and go the next higher level of intellectuality in his responses to the objections on Divine Justice. Moreover, even within the field of Islamic philosophy, he did not suffice himself with the peripatetic school of thought, but rather employed the firm bases of the transcendental school of Mulla Sadra and its emphatically unitive view of being. Finally, by his constant use of and reference to the works of great Persian poets such as Hafiz and Rumi, he alluded to the further development of the subject at the hands of the 'urafa' and mystics of Islam.

Thus, with the framework of transcendental philosophy in place, the author makes his final argument in favour of Divine Justice by holding that "justice" is a formal Divine attribute that is inseparable from His essence and other Divine attributes such as omniscience and omnipotence. Hence the justice or injustice of Divine acts should not be sought on the level of His operation and efficiency. His justice is as necessary as is His existence. He further holds that evil exists not as an objective fact, but as a subjective notion; things are evil not in and of themselves, but by reason of their relation to other things. All realities are in themselves good. Any perceived evil is subsumed under God's infinite wisdom and is ultimately good. On the question of moral evil and the issue of human free will, the argument takes on a different shape. He states, as is the classical Shia position, that it is not the case that man is totally predestined and under Divine decree and compulsion, nor is it true that he is totally free and beyond the scope of the Divine will. Rather, the reality is something between the two positions. In an attempt to try to locate this "something" the author says that, "the Divine decree and destiny which has willed the human has also willed his freedom of choice." In other words, man is compelled to be free.

This paradoxical way of speaking is the forte of the mystics. It is an attempt to try to get man to go beyond the dualisms of discursive rational thought and to arrive at a unitive understanding-by way of a direct knowledge or "tasting" of the fundamental matters of being. It is to try to overcome the dichotomy implicit in the knower-known paradigm and to achieve a vision of the unity that comprehends and composes all reality. The supra-rational resolution of this paradox is accomplished by the perfect man and it unites him with his Maker in such a fashion that he becomes God's hand, face, and hand on earth, and in short, His vicegerent (*khalifah*) and highest manifestation.

It is appropriate here to quote Imam Khumayni,[2] the author's teacher and perpetual source of inspiration, who writes:

"In conclusion, it is known that both *tafwid* (free will) and *jabr* (compulsion or predestination) are invalid and impossible on the basis of metaphysical reasoning and rational criteria. The creed of the middle position (*amr bayn al-amrayn*) is one which is affirmed by the way of the people of gnosis as well as by transcendental philosophy.... That which is the soundest of views and most secure from controversy and more in consonance with the religion of tawhid is the creed of the illustrious gnostics and the people of the heart. However, this creed, on every topic pertaining to the Divine teachings, stands in the category of "simple and impossible" (*sahl wa mumtani'*) whose understanding is not possible through discursive proofs and arguments and is unattainable without complete piety of the heart as well as Divine succour."[3]

Having said this, Imam Khumayni acknowledges the need to discuss the topic by the way of logical demonstration and philosophical discourse-as rationality, positively seen, is nothing but the shadow of the sacred intellect. What follows is perhaps one of the best attempts at such an explanation and places this book among the classics of contemporary Islamic literature.

* * *

---

[2] See Endnote 1
[3] Sayyid Ruhullah al-Musawi al-Khumayni, *Forty Hadith*, hadith 39

Some notes about the translation are in order here. The translation is unique in that it was done by students of the Hawzah 'Ilmiyyeh Qum, who are is some ways familiar with the theological and philosophical arguments contained in this work. Parts of it were carried out during Muharram of 1425 A.H. while the translators were involved in the commemorative ceremonies of the martyrdom of Imam Husayn (a) in three different continents. This, alongside the time constraints, presented considerable logistical problems which, by the grace of Allah, were overcome. A final editing was done to ensure the consistency of terminology used. The quotes from Persian poets-which occur quite often in the book were researched, and in most cases the references to either the original or published English translations were found and documented in the footnotes. Endnotes were added that contain the lengthy explanatory notes not appropriate for footnotes, biographical material on most of the important personalities mentioned in the text, and the original text in Persian or Arabic, of many of the poems and traditions quoted in the work.

Translations of Qur'anic verses were mostly adapted from the recent translation by Sayyid Ali Quli Qara'i titled The Qur'an with an English Paraphrase. Most of the biographical endnotes are the contribution of Hujjat al-Islam wa al-Muslimin Hamid Parsania. A number of individuals were helpful in finding the references for and explaining the meanings of the many instances of Persian poetry that occur in the book. Among them we may especially mention Aqa Muhammad Hasan 'Arabi and Mahmud Najafi. We would like to acknowledge with gratitude here the help of all these people, as well as those others who have gone unmentioned.

Shuja' Ali Mirza

Qum

8th Safar, 1425/March 29, 2004

About the Author

Martyr Murtaza Mutahhari was born in Fariman, in the province of Khurasan (Iran) in February of 1919. His father Shaykh Muhammad Husayn[1] was a religious scholar and a pious man who spiritually inspired the young Mutahhari. At the age of twelve, he joined the traditional Islamic School at Mashhad where he pursued his studies for five years. Then he proceeded to Qum, the famous theological Centre of Shia Muslims where for fifteen years he pursued his religious education under the supervision of Ayatullah Burujardi in jurisprudence and its principles (who had comprehensive knowledge of Islamic sciences and remarkable insight in socio-political issues), Imam Khumayni[2] in spirituality and principles of jurisprudence, 'Allamah Tabataba'i[3] in Islamic philosophy, and Mirza Ali Agha Shirazi, amongst many other distinguished scholars.

In 1952 he migrated to and settled in Tehran, teaching traditional Islamic philosophical texts in Madrasah-i Marvi and modem Islamic philosophy in the Faculty of Theology at Tehran University. More importantly, he devoted his scholarly research to contemporary challenges to the Islamic faith, creating a rich and profound legacy of original exposition of the Islamic world-view which he presented through lectures, articles, and books to Islamic associations of students, doctors, engineers, traders and in mosques and which covered issues ranging from Islamic philosophy, responses to communist arguments against religion, doctrinal matters such as Divine unity and justice, Predestination, Resurrection, Commentary of the Qur'an and *Nahj al-Balagha*, social issues such as hijab, women's rights, economic issues such as an Islamic economic system and banking without usury, and political topics such as global Islamic movements and revolution in Iran.

Politically, he engaged in covert struggle against the Shah's tyranny and in 1963 was arrested along with Imam Khumayni. After the latter's exile to Turkey and then to Najaf, he maintained close contact with his

---

[1] He was his first guide to his faith, piety and integrity
[2] An important part of my personality was shaped in those spiritual and other classes over twelve years
[3] Author of *Al-Mizan*, the most authentic exegesis of the holy *Qur'an*

mentor for fifteen years and guided the Islamic resistance movement, culminating in the victory of the Islamic revolution. Subsequently, he was nominated as the President of the Revolutionary Council, but his activities were intolerable for the followers of the materialistic schools whose deviation he actively opposed and exposed, who therefore decided to eliminate him. Eventually they assassinated this eminent scholar on May 1, 1979. His martyrdom was a great tragedy for the revolution and the Muslim ummah. When the sad news was conveyed to Imam Khumayni, he could not control his tears (he held his beard and cried "Mutahhari! Mutahhari! Mutahhari!"). In his condolence message he said: "In him I have lost a dear son. I am mourning the death of one who was the fruition of my life."

He was laid to rest in Qum in the precincts of the Holy Shrine of Hazrat Fatima al-Ma'suma, the sister of the eighth Shia Imam, in Qum. May his soul rest in peace.

Murtaza Alidina

Qum

7th Safar, 1425/March 28, 2004

Divine Justice

Introduction

From the perspective of religion, our age is an age of anxiety, ambiguity and crisis-most especially for the youth. The conditions of this age have not only brought with them a recent set of doubts and questions, but they have also taken old and forgotten issues and have tabled them afresh.

Should we become upset and anxious in the face of these doubts and queries-especially as sometimes they are quite extreme?

In my opinion there is no reason to be upset; for doubt precedes certainty, questions are prior to answers, and anxiety is a prelude to tranquility. Doubt is both a good and necessary point of transition, even though it is highly undesirable as a station and final destination. The fact that Islam places so much stress on certainty and calls man to think and deliberate alludes to man's initial state of doubt and ignorance, as well as to the truth that he must reach the station of conviction and certainty by way of connect thought and reasoning. There was a certain philosopher who would say, "If my comments have no greater effect than to throw you into doubt-forcing you to set off in search of [greater] truth and certainty, then it is enough".

Doubt is accompanied by restlessness, but this does not mean that just any type of peace and tranquility should be preferred to it. For animals also don't doubt, but does that mean that they have reached the state of certainty and belief? The type of peace and quiet that they are endowed with can be said to be "lower" than and preceding doubt, whereas the tranquility of the holders of certainty is "above" and a consequence of doubt.

Putting aside those very few who are providentially endowed with certainty, the rest come to it by first crossing the bridge of doubt and apprehension. So just because our age is an age of doubt cannot be seen to be the reason for it being an age of deviation and decline. What is for sure is that this type of doubt is not any less than the simpleminded instances of "certainty" and "peace" that are much witnessed these days.

Now the thing that is a source of sorrow is that the doubt of a person should not lead him to a search for truth; or that the doubts and misgivings of a society should not prompt individuals to answer its needs in this area.

* * *

It has been over twenty years since I took pen in hand and began writing articles and books. During this time and in all of my writings my sole purpose has been to respond to and resolve the questions and problems that have been posed regarding Islamic issues in our time. Even though my works cover such different subjects as philosophy, sociology, ethics, jurisprudence, and history, my purpose and goal in all of them has been one and the same.

Islam has become an unknown religion. Its tenets have steadily been undermined in the eyes of people. The main reason for this fallout of a group of people has been the incorrect teaching that they have been given in the name of Islam. Presently and more than anything else, this sacred tradition is being damaged by those who would make claims of being its helpers. The overt and covert western "imperialist" onslaught on the one hand, and the faults and shortcomings of the would-be helpers of Islam in our age on the other, have led to Islamic thought in all its fields and branches--coming under attack. Hence, I feel that I must perform my humble duty in this regard, to the extent of my capacity, [and defend Islam from these attacks].

Published works on religion, just as I have pointed out in some of my other works, are not systematic. Putting aside those works which are fundamentally damaging and disgraceful, even useful works are not thought out and have not been produced after taking into account the needs at hand. It seems that every author writes and publishes whatever he himself deems useful. Hence there are many useful and necessary subjects that do not even have a single book on them, while there are some subjects that have countless books written on them and more are being written all the time.

We are like a country whose economy is not based on the society at large. In such a country, every person produces goods according to his own taste or imports things according to his fancy, without there being an overseeing authority which regulates these affairs and which sets the levels of production, import, and export according to the needs of the country. In other words, everything has been left to chance. The state of affairs being so, it is only but natural that some goods are produced in excess of their demand and remain unutilized while others are not to be found in the market at all.

So, what is the solution? It's simple. Its seeds lie in coordination and consultation that must take place between the various groups of writers and researchers.

Unfortunately, though, we are usually so enamored by our own way of doing things and our preferences, we think that the only correct way is the one that we ourselves have discovered. I have on occasion put forward this proposal to writers, only to find that they see it as a hampering of their style.

I am by no means claiming that the subjects that I have chosen and written about are the most pressing and necessary subjects. The only thing that is being claimed is that I have stayed within the bounds of the [above] principle-according to my own understanding of it-and have, to the extent of my ability, attempted to untangle and resolve the problems surrounding Islamic matters. In so doing, I have wherever possible, presented Islamic truths as they are; for though it is impossible to eliminate deviant practices, it is in some way possible to fight deviant thoughts and erroneous ideas and specially to expose the stratagems of the enemies of Islam. In this endeavor I have tried to prioritize issues and deal with them in order of importance-at least as I see it.

In the last three or four years I have spent a great deal of my time on Islamic matters pertaining to women and women's rights-with the result that a series of articles on the subject have appeared in magazines and periodicals, or have been printed in book form.

I spent time on this issue because I felt that it was not just a matter of incorrect and deviant practices that have come about as of late [regarding women]-the [real and more pressing] story is that there is a certain group of persons who, in their speeches, school classes, books, and articles, explain the Islamic position on women's rights, limits and duties, in an incorrect manner. These things are then used in propaganda campaigns against Islam. Now it is very unfortunate that the majority of Muslims are not aware of Islam's logic in this-as in many other subjects. As a result of this they have regrettably made many people-both men and women-pessimistic and negative towards Islam. It was because of this that I saw it necessary to demonstrate the logic of Islam on this subject, so that they no longer find faults in the argument, but rather so they start to see that the well-founded and rational arguments that Islam espouses regarding women, women's rights and responsibilities, is the best proof of Islam's truth and supernatural dimension.

* * *

The contents of this book, as was also pointed out in the first print, are the result of the reordering and exposition of a number of speeches that were given at the Islamic Institute Husayniyyeh Irshad. Needless to say, speeches-at least my speeches-are not worthy of being put into print unless they are fixed up beforehand. What's more, when they are put into printed form, the material of the speech on its own is not sufficient. It was because of this that both in the first print and here in the second print, I reviewed the discussions thoroughly and added a lot of new material to the original.

We can say this much about the topics discussed in this book that all of them are carefully "chosen" and that none of them are there by "chance", as it were. They are issues that were taken up with me many times over-especially by the youth. What I have included in this book is in reality a general answer to all those that repeatedly posed questions on the subject. The questions were so many [and similar] that they called for a general and public response.

The arguments presented here have two perspectives or dimensions: intellectual and authoritative[1]. Of course, in respect of the latter, references have been made to verses of the Qur'an and the traditions of the Prophet and the Imams (upon them be Peace). With respect to the

---

[1] Literally "transmitted" or *naqli* - signifying the recourse to traditions and sayings of immaculate religious personalities and saints who are the recipients of Revelation and Divine inspiration.

intellectual arguments though, it was possible to proceed in two ways or "styles": theological and philosophical. Now because I do not endorse the theological methodology in addressing such issues, but rather see the arguments of the philosophers to be correct and convincing, I totally abstained from using the methodology of the former. Of course, wherever it was called for, I did refer to the arguments of the theologians-and even to other arguments such as those of the Traditionalists (*Ahl al-hadith*) and materialists (or sensationalists).

Experts in this field know full well that Islamic philosophers, unlike their theologian counterparts, have not discussed "justice" under a separate heading or category in their works. It is for this reason that the beliefs of the philosophers regarding "justice" had to be derived from their discussions on other topics-presenting me with a formidable task, to say the least.

I have not, as of yet, found any philosophical treatise, article, or even chapter, that deals directly with "Divine Justice" and treats the subject in a philosophical manner. Even though Ibn al-Nadim in his *al-Fihrist* wrote, "Y'aqub ibn Ishaq Kindi has written a treatise on Divine Justice", I do not know if exists at present or not? I also don't know if he wrote it in the manner of the theologians or the philosophers? Some of the philosophers, such as Khwajah Nasir al-Din Tusi for instance, treated the subject in the manner of the theologians. But if their philosophical opinions are any indication, then we must assume that these theological digressions of theirs were for the sake of argument and oratorical prowess, and not formal proofs.

Y'aqub ibn Ishaq Kindi, whose book Ibn al-Nadim mentions, is the oldest of Islamic philosophers and because he was an Arab, he is known as "the Arab philosopher". It is unlikely that al-Kindi would have argued in the manner of the theologians. He most likely used the method of the philosophers.

I have recently been told by a respected scholar that the master of the Islamic philosophers, Abu Ali Ibn Sina (Avicenna)[2] has a short treatise on this subject which was written in response to a question posed to him. Unfortunately, I have not been able to get hold of that treatise.

---

[2] See Endnote 2

In spite of the shortcomings of the philosophers in addressing this issue, theologians-due to certain historical and religious reasons-have made the subject of Divine Justice their focus. It has become such an important subject for theologians that the various groups of theology are measured and differentiated according to their position vis-a-vis this subject.

Predestination and Freewill

Theological discussions made their debut halfway through the first Islamic century-as is discernable from available history texts. From amongst these discussions it appears that oldest one is the discussion on free will and predestination or determinism. The issue of free will and predestination is primarily an issue that concerns man as such and only secondarily involves God and nature. This is because on the one hand, the subject up for discussion is "man" and the question as to whether he is free or predestined? On the other hand, the problem pertains to God and nature-as it is asked whether Divine decree and destiny or the laws of cause and effect in nature have left any room for man's freedom or whether they determine and compel him [to do things]. In any case, because the issue is one that pertains to humanity and has to do with the destiny of man, it is difficult to find a man, with any philosophical or contemplative potential at all, who has not at some point thought of this issue. Similarly, it is not possible to find a society which has entered any of the stages of abstract thought and which has not posed this question for itself.

Islamic society, due to many reasons, entered the stage of scholarly and abstract thought very soon after its inception and one of the very first issues that it grappled with was free will and predestination. It is not necessary to try to trace these reasons as the posing of this question and problem was a very natural development. If it hadn't been tabled and discussed then it would have begged the question that why, in such a society, no attention has been paid to the problem.

Islamic society was a religious one and, in the Qur'an, the religious book of the Muslims-there is repeated mention of free will and predestination, Divine decree and destiny, rewards and punishments .... This, put together with the fact that Muslims put a lot of stress on the intellection and contemplation of Qur'anic verses-something that the

Qur'an itself has called them to invariably leading to the discussions on free will and predestination.

The Issue of Justice

The discussion on free will and predestination automatically led to deliberation on the idea of "justice". This is because there is a direct connection between free will and justice on the one hand, and between predestination and injustice on the other. In other words, it is only when man is presumed to have free will that responsibility, due rewards, and just punishments take on any meaning whatsoever. If man did not have this freedom then his hands would be tied and he would be entirely at the mercy of the Divine Will and the contingencies of natural forces and laws. In such a case, he would no longer be held responsible and rewards and punishments would be meaningless.

From the outset the theologians were divided into two groups. The first, which favoured free will and justice, was called Mu'tazilah. The second, which opted for predestination, was a group of Sunnis which later came to be known as the Ash'arites. Needless to say, that those who opposed justice, did not openly and directly say that they deny Divine justice. This is because both groups claimed adherence to the Qur'an, and the Qur'an strongly negates injustice with respect to God and affirms His justice. What the opponents of justice did do though, is to define justice in a special way. They said: Justice is not a reality in itself that we can describe "beforehand" and set as the standard by which to judge God's acts. In fact, setting such a standard and point of reference for Divine acts is to in some way impose obligations on God and to constrain and limit His will. For can rules and laws be set for His acts which have authority over Him?! All laws are created by Him and fall under His jurisdiction, and He is the ultimate Authority. Any type of "superseding" authority which He must follow is against His absolute Immensity and Dominion. Divine justice does not mean that there are a set of previously defined "just" laws which He must abide by. Rather Divine justice means that He is the source of justice; whatever He does is just, not that He does what is just. Justice and injustice are consequences and derivatives of Divine acts. Justice is not the standard to judge Divine acts by, rather, Divine acts are the standard by which justice is defined.

Mu'tazilites were known for their support of [Divine] justice. They argued that justice is a reality in itself and that God, because He is bound to be just and wise, carries out acts in accordance with this standard of justice. To explain, when we look at the very essence of acts, regardless of whether or not the particular act is associated with God's creative act or His commandments, we see that some of them are different from others. Some of these acts, in their essence, are just-such as rewarding the doers of good deeds; While other acts are in themselves oppression and unjust-such as punishing those who do good deeds. Now because these acts are different on the level of essence and because God is good and absolute in His perfection, wisdom and justice, He chooses acts that are in accordance with the standard of justice.

Essential Goodness and Essential Evil

The next topic that arose as a "development" and expansion of the subject of justice is that of good and evil actions. In general, is it the case that good and evil can be attributed to actions and deeds in their essence? For instance, are deeds such as telling the truth, keeping trusts, generosity and the like, good in and of themselves? While telling lies, treachery, and usurpation and their like, are bad and reprehensible in themselves? Are qualities such as goodness and nobility of the order of the real and essential qualities of actions; implying that any action [having this quality]-regardless of its subject or any other external condition-assumes this quality in and of itself while negating the opposite of this quality?

Rationally Derived Realities

As the previous section talked of essential qualities of actions, it perforce touched upon the intellect, or reason, and its independent role in the perception of these qualities. The argument at hand has been put forward in these terms: Is reason able to perceive the goodness or badness of things by itself unaided and "independently"? Or does it have to take recourse in revelation and the Divine law? It is with this in mind that essential good and evil has been referred to also as rational good and evil.

In this debate, the Mu'tazilites affirmed the existence of the good-essentially, innately, and rationally-and put forward the argument of "rationally derived realities". They said: We obviously perceive that acts are, in their essence, different from one another. We also obviously know that our intellects become aware of these realities without needing to be guided by revelation from the outside, so to speak.

The Ash'arites, in the same way that they previously denied justice being an essential and a priori quality, also denied good and evil being essential, rational, and a priori qualities. They saw good and evil as relative realities that adapted themselves to the conditions of time and space and that were influenced by customs and indoctrinations. Moreover, for the perception of good and evil, they saw reason as being not only in need of revelation, but they even saw reason to be a consequence of revelation.

Because the Ash'arites denied intellectually derived realities, they countered the Mu'tazilite belief in the self-sufficiency of human reason, saying: What's justice? What's injustice? What's good? What's evil? Revelation must speak to these questions; the Islamic tradition-and it only-must be followed in handling these issues. Hence, they referred to themselves as the "People of Tradition". Moreover, the Ash'arites used this name and label to make a social platform and movement for themselves amongst the masses. In other words, this dispute between them and the Mu'tazilah, which was primarily based upon accepting or rejecting the idea of "rationally derived realities"-came to be cast into the acceptance or rejection of tradition (*sunnah wa hadith*) in the popular eye. It was also portrayed as the conflict and opposition between reason and tradition, and for this reason the public platform and popular appeal of the Ash'arites grew, while that of the Mu'tazilah became weaker and weaker.

It is not that the Mu'tazilah disbelieved in tradition, it's more that the Ash'arites chose such a [noble sounding] name for themselves and by placing the Mu'tazilah in the opposing camp, set them up for a fall. What is for certain is that this factor was very effectual in the popular defeat of the Mu'tazilah during the first part of the third century [of the Islamic calendar]. This misunderstanding and error on the part of the masses was so widespread that even some orientalists-knowingly or unknowingly-labelled the Mu'tazilah as "enlightened antitraditionalists". The truth, as is affirmed by those in the know, is that the difference of opinion between these two groups is totally unrelated to their adherence and loyalty to Islam, or lack thereof. In fact, and in practical terms, the Mu'tazilites sympathized and sacrificed more for the Islamic cause than their Ash'arite counterparts.

It seems that usually when there is an intellectualist movement-no matter how sincere-that is opposed by exoteric pietists-no matter how insincere, it comes under these same old attacks and accusations in the public eye.

Even though this dispute between the Mu'tazilah and the Ash'arites started from their disagreement on the rights and scope of human reason and its independence or lack thereof with respect to the issue of justice and essential goodness, it later spread to other topics, such as tawhid.[3] In this latter subject as well, the Mu'tazilah believed that reason had a say on the matter, while the Ash'arites felt that an exoteric and literalist understanding of the traditions was what was necessary. We will expand on this at some later point.

The Motive and End of Divine Acts

Now we turn to the fourth problem, which is also one of the fundamental issues of theology and a consequence of its precursors-namely, are Divine acts the effects of motives and ends?

As we know, and is obvious, human beings have motives and ends for their works and actions. In every action, man has a "for" or "because". Why does he study? "Because" he wants to be knowledgeable. Why does he work? "Because" he wants to make a living. For every "why", there is a "because" or "for". It is these very same "becauses" that give meaning to human deeds. Every act that has a rational end and purpose that is, there is good in it-is counted as meaningful. An act or deed without purpose is like a word without meaning-an empty shell. Now of course every "because" and every "meaning", in their own turn, might themselves have another "because" and "meaning". But the fact is that this chain must end up in a reality which is in its essence an end and a meaning. This reality is what the philosophers call absolute goodness or the Good.

In any case, man has a motive and goal for every rational act of his and in response to every "why?" he posits a "because". If he performs an action but refrains from giving a "because", then that action is considered purposeless, meaningless and absurd.

Philosophers have proven that a completely purposeless and absurd act can never be performed by man, as it is an impossibility. All such absurdities are relative. For instance, an act which issues from an

---

[3] See Endnote 3

imaginative temperament has a purpose and end that is appropriate to that temperament. Now because such an act lacks a rational end, we call it "absurd" and "vain". In other words, with respect to the agent and subject which performed the act, it is not absurd and purposeless. But with respect to any other source that could have performed it but didn't, it is considered absurd.

The opposite of absurdity is wisdom. The wise act is one which is never-even relatively-without a motive and purpose. In other words, it is an act that must have a rational motive which must in all conditions be considered the better option.

Hence, the fact that any action is wise depends upon it having a purpose and end-one that is rationally acceptable and always the better and precedent choice. The wise man is he who firstly, has a purpose and end for his works; secondly, chooses from amongst the many purposes and ends, the best of them; thirdly, chooses the nearest and best and most expedient means to achieve his end. In other words, wisdom or man being wise entails that he, with perfect knowledge, chooses the best possible conditions for the best ends. Once again, wisdom or being wise necessitates that man have a "because" for every "why"-regardless of whether this "why" pertains to his choice of "ends" or his choice of "means."

Why did you do so-and-so?

Because of this-and-that purpose.

Why did you give preference to that purpose and end?

For the reason of this-or-that particularity.

Why did you use such-and-such means?

Because of this-or-that distinction and priority.

Any human act that cannot give a rational answer to "why"-to the degree that it is imperfect in this respect-gives lie to the defective wisdom of the man who carried out the act.

What about God? Are Divine acts, like their human counterparts, the result of motives? Do God's acts also have a "why" and a "because" and involve preponderance and expediency? Or are all these things particular to man-making their generalization to God a type of anthropomorphism and comparison of the Creator to the created?

The Mu'tazilah naturally became the proponents of God's creation having an end and a motive. They saw God's wisdom-something that the

11

Qur'an clearly emphasizes over and over again-to lie in that fact that He has specific motives and purposes for His acts and that He-with perfect knowledge carries out these acts by choosing the best and most expedient means.

The Ash'arites on the other hand, denied motives and ends for God's acts. They explained away the concept of wisdom which appears repeatedly in the Qur'an-in the same way that they had dealt with justice. That is to say, it was their belief that whatever God does is wise, not that He does what is wise.

According to the Mu'tazilah, Divine acts are the result of a series of expedients. According to the Ash'arites, it is wrong to say that Divine acts are due to certain expediencies. For, just as God is the creator of creation, He is also the creator of any such things that are named "expediencies"-albeit, without having created anything because of some expediency and without that thing having an ontological, essential, or causal connection with any expediency.

Lines of Demarcation

When the fact that issues of good and evil are rationally derived and the fact that Divine acts are the result of motives were put alongside the two previous issues of justice and predestination and free will, the lines and trends of theological schools became demarcated and abundantly clear. The Mu'tazilah were die-hard proponents of justice, reason, free will, and wisdom (i.e. Divine acts resulting from motives and intentions). The Ash'arites, who still went by the name of "Sunni" or Ahl al-hadith in that time, adamantly opposed the Mu'tazilah and their method of thinking.

The Mu'tazilah were also called the "justifiers" (*adliyyah*). This word did not just represent their idea of justice. In addition to their doctrine of justice, it also portrayed the ideas of human free will, rational basis for good and evil, and Divine expediency.

Justice or Divine Unity?

The Traditionalists had a criticism that the Mu'tazilah could not properly answer, it was as follows: Justice (in its meaning where it includes human free will, rational or natural morality and Divine expediency) is not compatible with the unity of God-neither in His acts or even in His essence. This is because the freedom that the Mu'tazilah give man is a type of delegation of authority on God's behalf which negates His own essential freedom. Moreover, it is opposed to the doctrine of the unity of God's acts-something which has been conclusively proven and which is seen throughout the Qur'an. With the excuse of exonerating God from certain acts that you deem ugly, how can you possibly ascribe a partner for Him in His acts? For by positing agents who are independent of Him you are in effect ascribing a partner to God; whereas the Qur'an clearly states:

لَمْ يَتَّخِذْ وَلَدًا وَلَمْ يَكُن لَّهُ شَرِيكٌ فِي الْمُلْكِ وَلَمْ يَكُن لَّهُ وَلِيٌّ مِّنَ الذُّلِّ ۖ وَكَبِّرْهُ تَكْبِيرًا

Allah, who has neither taken any son, nor has He any partner in sovereignty, nor has He any *wali* out of weakness,' and magnify Him with a magnification [worthy of Him]..

[Qur'an, 17:111]

So the wisdom and expediency that the Mu'tazilah *posit* for Divine acts, runs counter to His essential unity and self-sufficiency as well as conflicting with His incomparability and causal transcendence. This is because when a man performs acts towards certain ends and purposes, he in fact becomes influenced and motivated by those ends. For is it not the case that the final cause is the cause of the efficient cause. That is to say, the final cause is what causes the efficiency of the agent; in its absence the agent is no longer an agent. Now the man who has a motive, purpose and end in his actions is in reality governed by the determinism called for by that purpose and end. But God is free from any form of determinism and limitation, even the one that is caused by a purpose or motive.

The Ash'arites claimed that the issue of innate or rationally derived good and evil and the verdict that Divine acts must conform to this standard of good and evil was like setting rules for God to follow. It was like saying, "God is obliged to make His acts conform to the framework that our human brains have setup." Now of course, the absolute nature of the Divine Will refuses to accept any such limits.

In short, the Ash'arites claimed that what the Mu'tazilah propounded under the name of justice, reason, freedom, wisdom and expediency was firstly, a form of anthropomorphism and confusion between Creator and creation, and secondly, a negation of the unity of Divine essence and acts.

The Mu'tazilah, on their part, held that the beliefs of the Ash'arites were in opposition to the principle of incomparability that is oft repeated in the Qur'an. They argued: Ash'arite positions necessitate that we ascribe qualities to God that He is absolved of-the Qur'an being very clear on this matter. Things such as injustice, caprice, and vice become ascribed to Him. This is because if we don't accept Divine justice and human free will, then we must hold that God is unjust; for He has created and made created beings totally obliged [and compelled to do only His will], whereas at the same time he has made them responsible for their actions and goes on to punish them when they sin. So whatever deed man-God's handiwork does, in reality it is not he who does it but rather it is God. So, then it follows that it is God who becomes implicated in vices and crimes, not His creation and vassal. What's more, because the Ash'arities hold that Divine acts are not goal-oriented, God is seen to act capriciously and without purpose. Hence the logical consequence of Ash'arite beliefs is to ascribe qualities to God, such as injustice, capriciousness, and vice-that both reason and revelation clearly absolve Him of.

Each one of the two schools of thought, the Mu'tazilite and the Ash'arite, had a strong point and a weak point. Their strong points came to the front when they found fault with the opposing school; and their points of weakness were revealed when they tried to defend their school as a complete self-contained system.

The followers of each of these schools wanted to prove the truth of their school by proving the invalidity of the other school-without necessarily having properly defended their own school and without having answered the criticisms made regarding it. Each school knew the weak points of the other school quite well and hence they fiercely attacked one another.

There is a well-known anecdote that goes like this: One day Ghilan Damishqi, an advocate of the free will argument, happened to meet Rabiat al-Raiy, an opponent of free will, and said to him: "You are the one who thinks that God likes to have people sin and rebel against Him." (That is to say, the necessary conclusion of the belief in determinism and predestination is that the sins of mankind are willed by God Himself, and hence He prefers that people should rebel against Him).

Upon hearing this and without defending his own position, Rabiat al-Raiy homed in on Ghilan's vulnerable point and said: "You are the one who thinks that God is obligated to like what people like." (That is to say, you think that God wills something and man wills something else and in conclusion, God is subjugated by the whims and wishes of free man).

One day Qadi 'Abd al-Jabbar, a Mu'tazalite was in the audience of Sahib ibn 'Abbad. Just then Abu Ishaq Isfarai'rii made his entrance. Abu Ishaq was an Ash'arite who believed in predestination, while Qadi Abd al-Jabbar was a Mu'tazilite who held that man had a free will. As soon as Qadi saw Abu Ishaq, he said: "Holy God, the One who is clear of all vice". (Meaning that, you hold that all things, including vices, are from God.)

Abu Ishaq, without bothering to defend his own belief, immediately retorted, "Holy God, the One in whose kingdom nothing transpires but by His Will". (An allusion to that fact that you, Qadi, with your belief in total freedom and delegation of power, have effectively accepted the existence of a partner alongside God in His kingdom; you believe that man is independent in his acts and that he has been left on his own having no need of God now.)

The Mu'tazilah called themselves "the People of Justice and Unity". "Unity" or *tawhid* here refers to the unity of the Divine Attributes. The Ash'arites were of the belief that there were Divine Attributes external to the Divine Essence. For example, they held that knowledge, power, or life were attributes that in reality resided outside of the Divine Essence and like it, were eternal. The Mu'tazilah held the opposite and did not see the Attributes to be apart from the Essence.

The Mu'tazilah saw this belief of the Ash'arites to be a type of shirk and ascription of partners to God. They argued: The logical consequence of the beliefs of the Ash'arites is that there exist a series of Eternals alongside God. Now being eternal means that they have no cause and are not created and are essentially self-sufficient. Hence the belief of the Ash'arites leads a person to believe that there are as many Eternals and self-sufficient beings as there are attributes of God; meaning that there are as many "gods" as there are Divine attributes. As the Mu'tazilah themselves did not agree to the separation of the Divine attributes from the essence, they believed that there was only one Eternal.

We have seen why the Mu'tazilah called themselves the People of Justice and Unity-meaning the Unity of Divine attributes. But when it came to the Unity of Divine acts, they fell short of the mark and it was the Ash'arites who outdid them calling themselves the "People of Unity."

The truth is that while the Mu'tazilah found valid criticisms with the Ash'arite doctrine of the Unity of Divine attributes, their own position respecting it was also flawed. For while the Mu'tazilah did not believe in any disparity between the attributes and the essence, they were not up to the task of proving their identity. Instead, they resorted to the introduction of the idea of the essence "representing" the attributes. This idea was a major point of weakness in their school of thought.

Over and beyond their not being able to properly place the concepts of justice, reason; free will, and wisdom, the Ash'arites had other weak points as well. They found themselves extremely frustrated on the issue of Divine unity-an issue over which they showed great sensitivity. For instance, with the excuse of defending the Unity of Divine actions, they were forced to deny the order of essential and formal causality and held that everything was the direct and unconditional effect of the Divine will. Now, the experts in the field know that such a belief is in opposition to the simplicity, sublimity, and eminence of the Divine Essence.

Both these schools of thought saw themselves as having to take sides between Divine justice and the Unity of Divine acts. The Mu'tazilah imagined that they had to sacrifice the Unity of Divine acts to save Divine justice, while the Ash'arites thought that they must forfeit Divine justice to salvage the Unity of Divine acts. The fact is though that, on the one side, the Mu'tazilah could not properly expound Divine Justice, and on the other side, the Ash'arites could not profoundly explain the Unity of Divine acts.

Although the points of contention between the Ash'arites and the Mu'tazilah are plentiful, the major ones are Divine unity and justice. As was previously shown, the theological discussions took justice as their point of departure and ended up in the arguments over Divine unity. Divine unity has stages. There is Unity of the Divine essence, Unity of the Divine attributes, Unity of Divine acts, and Unity of acts of worship. The Unity of the Divine essence means that the Sacred Essence is One and incomparable.

لَيْسَ كَمِثْلِهِ شَيْءٌ

Nothing is like Him.

[Qur'an, 42:11]

Nothing is on par with His essence. All things are His creation and in need of Him. He is the Creator of all things and independent of everything. With regard to this stage of Divine unity there is consensus among all Muslims.

When it comes to the next stage, the Unity of the Divine attributes, there is a difference of opinion. The Ash'arites denied unity on this level and believed in multiplicity [of attributes].

On the level of the Unity of Divine acts, the situation was reversed; the Ash'arites believed in unity and the Mu'tazilah in multiplicity.

In the case of the Unity of acts of worship, once again there was not the slightest difference of opinion among Muslims. That is to say, no one from among the Muslims was of the opinion that there is "multiplicity" involved on the level of the acts of worship [in principle]. Some Muslim scholars though, chiefly Ibn Taymiyyah, came to hold the opinion that many common beliefs and practices of the Muslims [today] were opposed to the Unity of acts of worship. For instance, they held that "intercession" (shifa'ah), or beseeching and using the saints as mediums [to God] was in violation of this Unity. These ideas later led to the formation of a sect known as "Wahhabiyyah".

The Effects of Islamic Theology on Islamic Philosophy

Though the debates of Islamic theology (kalam) remained inconclusive, they did much to help Muslim philosophers on issues of theology. One of the reasons why Islamic philosophy was able to open up new frontiers in theology and increase its distance from Hellenic and Alexandrian philosophy, had to do with this impetus that it received from traditional theology (kalam), Hence theologians can make claims to helping philosophers reach new horizons and posing unique problems even though they themselves were not capable of resolving any of them.

In addition to paving the way for philosophers by tabling a series of new questions, theologians performed other important services. In particular, theologians were opposed to Greek thought and did not "give in" to it. They attacked and tarnished the image of philosophy and philosophers whenever they could. They wrote books criticizing and denouncing philosophy and philosophers-refuting their arguments. It was the theologians who opened the door of doubt and uncertainty with respect to philosophical ideas. This friction and locking of horns between traditional theologians and philosophers and the resultant vigorous attempts of the latter at trying to escape deadlocks and [conceptual] dead-ends, initiated a certain movement and development in Islamic philosophical theology. Such exertions and efforts lead to flashes of inspiration, revealing new ground and uncharted territory.

The Shia Intellectual School

Among the various schools of theology, the Shia school of theology and philosophy is worthy of attention. The two schools of theology-Ash'arite and Mu'tazilah-that have so far been mentioned pertain to the Sunni world. The Shias, in the same way that they maintained independence in matters of jurisprudence and the "branches" of faith, were also independent in the "roots" and principles of religion: theology, philosophy, and what is termed as Islamic Scholastics (ma'arife Islami).

The issues of Divine justice and unity were also tabled in the Shia school of theology and philosophy, and the opinions expressed in their regard in this school were some of the most profound. On the four famous issues of justice, reason, free will, and wisdom, the Shia school supported the Mu'tazilah stance and consequently also came to be called "justifiers" (adliyyah). But in the Shia school, the concept of each one of these four was different from that of the Mu'tazilah. For instance, in the Shia school the concept of free will was not posed as absolute delegation of authority and freedom-which would amount to a type of negation of Divine freedom and an affirmation of the pure independence of human actions; a type of deification of man, naturally implying polytheism or shirk. Instead, and for the first time, the immaculate Imams of the Shia (may Peace be upon them) who were the source of inspiration for the Shia school, put forth the principle of "an affair between the two affairs". Their statement in this regard became famous:

لا جبر ولا تفويض بل أمر بين الأمرين

Not determinism, not delegation-rather an affair between the two affairs.

Also, in this school, the concept of justice-in its most comprehensive form came to be accepted without compromising in the least the principle of the Unity of Divine acts or Unity of the Divine essence. Justice was put alongside unity and it was rightfully said:

العدل والتّوحيد علويّان، والجبر والتّشبيه أمويّان

Justice and unity are Alawi (Shia); determinism and anthropomorphism are Ummayad.

In the Shia school, fundamentality of justice, sanctity of human reason, dignity of human free will and sagacious ordering of nature were established without any detriment to the principle of Divine unity-in essence or acts. Man's free will was demonstrated without him becoming a partner to God's dominion and power and without God's will becoming subservient to the human will. Divine decree and destiny were also proven to encompass all of Being without it leading to man being determined in his actions and subjugated to predestination.

All the tendencies in the Shia school of theology were unitive or *tawhidi*. To explain: in the debate over the unity or multiplicity of attributes, the Shia sided with unity. In so doing, they denied the Ash'arite belief in this regard and agreed with the Mu'tazilah-with this difference that the Mu'tazilah denied the [independent existence of the] attributes and spoke of the essence "representing" [and performing the functions of] the attributes. The Shia though, held a belief-one of the most profound beliefs in the divinities-in the unity and identity of the essence with the attributes. When it came to the Unity of Divine acts, the Shia sided with the Ash'arites, but with this discrepancy that they did not deny causality. Hence the doctrine of the Divine unity of the essence, attributes

19

and acts was propounded by Shia theology at a height and intensity not yet witnessed in the world.[4]

In the introduction to the fifth volume of *Principles of Philosophy and the Method of Realism* we dealt with how Islamic philosophers and divines took their inspiration from Qur'anic sciences as well as all other Islamic sources-including traditions, speeches, supplications, etc. and hence we do not see the need to expand any further on the matter here.

Because Islamic philosophers were aware of correct principles of demonstration on the one hand, and had recourse to the intuitions of Islamic sciences on the other, they were able to establish-after a millennium of toil-a sound system of philosophical theology (*Ilahiyyat bi al-ma'na al-akhass*).

From the perspective of Islamic philosophers, justice was seen to be a reality, without this leading to God being subjugated to any determinism or any law, and without it tarnishing in the least His absolute dominion and might. Rationally based good and evil was also explained in a different fashion. It was no longer defined within the parameters of intellectual speculation-such as were worthy and capable of revealing reality. Instead, the issue was brought within the domain of arbitrary and necessary practical notions. Hence it could no longer be accepted as the standard for Divine acts. In consequence and unlike the traditional theologians, the. philosophers did not make use of these concepts when speaking on the level of the divinities and about God.

The issue of final causes, ends and purposes [being attributed to God] was also resolved by dividing final causes into final ends of the action and final ends of the agent or actor and by equating the concept of wisdom as it pertains to the Divinity with the concept of Providence and the arrival of things to their final ends. In the view of the philosophers, every action has a final end and purpose and God is the ultimate End-that is, He is the final end of all ends. All things are from Him and go towards Him.

وَأَنَّ إِلَى رَبِّكَ الْمُنْتَهَىٰ

---

[4] We have dealt with this subject in our work, *Glimpses of the Nahj al-Balagha* and in volume 5 *Principles of Philosophy* and *the Method of Realism*. We have also discussed Divine decree and destiny in our book, *Destiny of Man.*

and that the terminus is toward your Lord.

[Qur'an, 53:42]

Of course, there is much more to all of the above-mentioned subjects, but it cannot be covered here in this introduction.

The Idea of Justice in the Field of Jurisprudence

The roots of the issue of justice in the Islamic world must not be sought only amongst its theologians. It has other roots as well and they are to be found in Islamic jurisprudence (*fiqh*).

From its inception, Islamic society was founded on the basis of the Book and Tradition (*sunnah*). This community obtained its laws and regulations-whether personal, commercial, civil, penal, or political-from Revelation. Religious responsibilities were clear at the outset because the Qur'an was explicit in its rulings on matters and because Tradition was established and there was easy access to the Prophet or the Imams (according to the Shia). But where there was no explicit verse or evident tradition on a matter and recourse to an Immaculate (*ma'sum*, meaning Prophet or Imam) was not possible, laws were derived and deducted from available sources (*ijtihad wa istinbat*).

As to exactly when the method of *ijtihad* was instituted and what developments it went through in the Shia and Sunni worlds requires a long and involved discussion whose place is not here. There is no doubt that *ijtihad* existed at the time of the Prophet, or at least from the time of his death. But whether or not it was correctly carried out at that time or not is another question. We have covered this topic in another place.[5]

Islamic jurisprudence, like other sciences, quickly developed and evolved leading to the formation of different systems. Among the Sunnis, two main systems or schools of jurisprudence developed: The Traditionalist system (*ahl al-hadith*) which was popular amongst the jurisprudents of Medina, and the Analogist system (*ra'y wa qiyas*) which was influential amongst the jurisprudents of Iraq.

---

[5] See the book by the author entiled, *Ten Discourses*

The methodology of the Traditionalists was that at the first they would refer to the Qur'an, and if they did not find the ruling on the issue that they were looking for there, they would turn to the Prophetic traditions. If they found the traditions to be different from one another, they would give preference to one depending upon the chain of transmission. But if they either did not find a tradition on the issue, or if they could not give preponderance to any single tradition among a group, then they would turn to the opinions and rulings of the Companions of the Prophet. If this latter way was also to no avail then they would try to find useful hints and intimations in the texts at hand. Hence it was very rare that they would take recourse in analogy or baseless opinions (*qiyas wa ra'y*).

The methodology of the Analogists was different from that of the Traditionalists. If they did not find the ruling on an issue in the Qur'an or in categorical and definitive Prophetic traditions, they would not so readily turn to and trust the transmitted (*manqul*) traditions-for they held them to be for the most part made-up and doctored. They were of the belief that a Muslim jurisprudent, due to his command over and experience of categorical Islamic rules and regulations, was in tune with the spirit of the Law and could come to the ruling on any particular issue by way of analogy and comparison.

Along these lines, the Analogists were of the opinion that "justice" and "expediency" were good guidelines for jurisprudents to follow. Hence it was incumbent on the jurisprudent to ponder and deliberate on the "dictates of Divine justice" and the "callings of expediency." It was due to this that terms such as *istihsan* and *istislah*; were coined.

The Traditionalist-Analogist Dispute

The Traditionalists saw the method of the Analogists to be somewhat extreme in its referral to reason and faulty in its recourse to traditions. In other words, they saw their method to be a type of short sightedness with respect to the discovery of true expedients. They would say: The [Divine] Law is founded upon collecting and bringing together differing elements and variegated collectivities-something that is beyond the scope of normal intellects. Reason, by an act of simplification, presumes that it has arrived at the root and spirit of the Law, while this is not the case. For their part, the Analogists would accuse the Traditionalists of being backward and rigid.

Introduction

In the field of the Principles of Jurisprudence (*usul al-fiqh*) there is a rule known as the Rule of Correspondence (*qa'idah mulazimah*) or the correspondence of the rulings of reason with the Law. This rule is put forward in this way:

كلّ ما حكم به العقل حكم به الشّرع

و كلّ ما حكم به الشّرع حكم به العقل

The Law dictates what reason dictates

and reason dictates what the Law dictates.

What this means is that whenever the intellect categorically realizes something to be good and beneficial or to be bad and harmful, by way of reasoning from causes to effects we conclude that Islamic Law must have a ruling that promotes this expedient good or repels this corruptive bad, even though we do not find such a ruling in the transmitted sources [of Law]. Likewise, whenever we come across a ruling of the Law whether prescriptive, proscriptive, or preferred-by way of reasoning from effects to causes we conclude that there is some good and benefit or some bad and harm involved, even though we may not be currently, consciously, and intellectually aware of its existence.

From the perspective of Islamic jurisprudents, especially those who were more inclined towards analogy or unfettered opining (*qiyas wa ra'y*), there exists perfect harmony and correspondence between reason and the Law. Islamic laws and rules are not a set of cryptic, hidden, and unknowable laws which demand only [blind] obedience. Rather, intellection and rationality also have a role to play in the understanding and derivation of these laws.

These scholars took the issue of rational good and evil which was previously discussed in theology-and introduced it in the subject of the principles of jurisprudence and saw those goods and evils as the *manatat* and *malakat* (*i.e.* the bases and criteria) of laws. They said: Among the bases and criteria, reason perceives the goodness of justice and benefaction and the evil of injustice and vice more evidently than anything else. It was in this way that justice and injustice began to play the role of a standard and criterion in Islamic jurisprudence.

The Traditionalists held that there were three sources of jurisprudence: the Book (Qur'an), Tradition (*sunnah*), and consensus. The Analogists on the other hand held that there were four sources of jurisprudence: the above mentioned three in addition to analogy (*qiyas wa ra 'y*).

The Traditionalists found fault with the Analogists and by bringing forth a series of examples, they made it clear that depending upon analogy led a person to making mistakes and deviations in apprehending the Law. The Analogists on their part accused the Traditionalists of trusting a series of transmitted reports and traditions whose correctness and validity was not clear.

The Shia Jurisprudential Method

Shia jurisprudence (*fiqh wa ijtihad*), just like Shia philosophy and theology, developed in an independent way. In the jurisprudence of the Shia, the principle of the subordination of the Law to actual expediencies and the Rule of Correspondence (*qa'idah mulazimah*, or the correspondence of the rulings of reason with the Law) was accepted and the rights of reason in the process of *ijtihad* were maintained. The principle of analogy (*qiyas wa ra 'y*) though was refuted by the Shia even more so than by the Traditionalists amongst the Sunnis.

The Shia refutation of analogy was not due to the argument used by the Traditionalists among the Sunnis-namely, reason lacking the authority to be one of the sources of the Law. It was rather due to two other reasons: firstly, the fact that analogy is based on supposition and not on certain knowledge-it is the preference of imagination over the intellect; secondly, turning to analogy or unfettered opinions is tantamount to saying that the general principles of Islam are insufficient; and this is either an injustice to Islam or an ignorance of it. While it is true that not all the rulings of all issues are spelled out in detail-something which is not even possible because particulars are unlimited, the general principles of Islam are laid out such that they meet the demands of these endless particular instances and the differing situations of various times and places. Accordingly then, the responsibility of a jurisprudent is not to be pedantically stuck on literal words-wanting the particular ruling for each and every event from the Qur'an and traditions; nor is it his obligation-with the excuse of not having a ruling for a particular issue-to let his imagination go wild and make liberal use of analogy [to come up with a ruling]. On the contrary, the mandate of a jurisprudent is deduction (*tafri'*) and inference by reasoning from the general to the specific (i.e. weighing particular facts or instances against general principles). Islamic principles already exist in the Book and Tradition; only one skill is necessary, and that is *ijtihad* or the skillful correlation and application of general Islamic principles to transient and changing particulars.

In the book *Usul al-Kafi*, there is a chapter heading which reads, "There is no issue but that its principle is to be found in the Book and Tradition."

Hence, the principle of justice, the principle of subordination of the Law to actual expediencies, and in consequence the principle of essential good and evil along with the validity and authority of reason made up the foundations of Shia jurisprudence. In the end, the principle of justice regained its place within the edifice of Islamic jurisprudence.

Shia jurisprudence made distinctions between reason and imagination-in other words, between logical proofs and irrational (*zanni*) analogies (which are the same as the "analogies" of formal logic). It was affirmed that the sources of jurisprudence are four in number: The Book, Tradition, consensus, and reason. Hence, while analogy was rejected in this school of jurisprudence, in its stead reason and formal proofs were given credence.

The Idea of Justice in Society and the Political Forum

What has been said so far had to do with the scholarly debate on the subject of justice in intellectual and academic circles within the Islamic world. It all had to do with understanding how it is that the issue of Divine justice-whether on the ontological or the legislative level-was introduced into the Islamic sciences from the earliest times and how it gained such importance that some groups actually named themselves the "justifiers" (*adliyyah*)-counting "Divine justice" as one of their pillars of belief and the distinguishing factor between themselves and other factions. In a similar vein when we Shias recount the pillars of faith, we make mention of "Divine justice" as one of them.

In addition to these academic debates, this issue was prevalent and popular in another form from the dawn of Islam: the application and practice of justice. For in the most rudimentary and basic thinking of any given Muslim, it was abundantly clear that the leader and head of a community must be just, a judge must be just, a legal witness must be just, a witness to a divorce must be just, and according to the Shia, the leader of the Friday and daily congregational prayers must also be just. Consequently in lieu of these positions and posts which called for justice, each and every Muslim felt a certain sense of responsibility. For instance, the following tradition of the Prophet (s) had become a commonly used figure of speech:

إِنَّ أفضَلُ الجِهادِ كَلِمَةُ عَدلٍ عِندَ إمامٍ جائِرٍ

The best [way of] holy war is [true and] just speech in front of an unjust ruler.[6]

It is remarkable to note what acts of courage and bravery this short sentence gave rise to.

The issue of justice, as practiced and applied in society, has a long and involved history which, because it is beyond the scope of this book, will not be followed up here.

The Real Origin

After deliberating upon the theoretical developments and practical aspects that were referred to above, one fundamental question still remains unanswered: Why did Islamic theology treat of Divine justice more than any other subject? Why did Islamic law and jurisprudence table the issue of justice more extensively than any other issue? Why is the word "justice" more widely used in the world of Islamic politics than any other word? The fact that in all of these fields, currents, and levels there was talk of justice, points to the reality that there must be one single root and particular source in the works.

Was there an original current which was the source of these offshoots or which fed and gave rise to these minor streams?

In our opinion the provenance and real origin of the theoretical and practical facets of the issue of Divine justice in the Islamic world must, first and foremost, be sought for in the Qur'an. It is the Qur'an that sowed the seed of justice in the hearts of men and cultivated its growth-causing

---

[6] *Al-Kafi*, vol, 5 p. 60

them to be preoccupied with the issue, whether intellectually and philosophically, or practically and socially. It is also the Qur'an that put forth the issue of justice and injustice in their various forms: ontological justice, legislative justice, moral justice, and social justice.

The Qur'an explicitly states that the existential and created order is based upon justice and balance-on rights and potentials. If one was to overlook the many verses that explicitly and emphatically negate injustice from the Divine; or overlook the verses that put forth the conclusive argument against man by recounting those modalities of Providence whose existence is a type of justice and man's certain extinction by virtue of their non-existence is a type of injustice; or overlook those verses which explain that creation is founded on truth-the complement of justice; overlooking all of these, in some verses Divine agency and expediency itself is known as the station of sustentation (*qiyam*) and justice.

شَهِدَ اللَّـهُ أَنَّهُ لَا إِلَـٰهَ إِلَّا هُوَ وَالْمَلَائِكَةُ وَأُولُو الْعِلْمِ قَائِمًا بِالْقِسْطِ

God bears witness that there is no god except Him-and [so do] the angels and those who possess knowledge-maintainer of justice

[Qur'an, 3:18]

In other verses justice is called the balance of God in the created order:

وَالسَّمَاءَ رَفَعَهَا وَوَضَعَ الْمِيزَانَ

He raised the heaven high and set up the balance

[Qur'an, 55:7]

It is with regards to this verse that the Prophet (s) said:

بالعدل قامت السّموات والأرض

27

The heavens and the earth are maintained with justice. [7]

"Legislative justice" means that the principle or idea of justice was-and is-always taken into consideration in the legislative process or lawmaking. This has been explicitly referred to in the Qur'an. For instance the Qur'an mentions that the wisdom behind the sending of prophets is the establishment of justice in the human order.

لَقَدْ أَرْسَلْنَا رُسُلَنَا بِالْبَيِّنَاتِ وَأَنزَلْنَا مَعَهُمُ الْكِتَابَ وَالْمِيزَانَ لِيَقُومَ النَّاسُ بِالْقِسْطِ

Certainly, We sent Our apostles with manifest proofs, and We sent down with them the Book and the Balance, so that mankind may maintain justice

[Qur'an, 57:25]

Now it is quite obvious that the establishment of the principle of justice in the social order depends upon the legal system being just in the first place and the practice [or legislative] enactment of the law in the second.

In addition to this general principle regarding all prophets, the Qur'an speaks to the Islamic legislative order in this way:

قُلْ أَمَرَ رَبِّي بِالْقِسْطِ

Say, 'My Lord has enjoined justice.

[Qur'an, 7:29]

Or with regards to some laws, the Qur'an has this to say:

ذَٰلِكُمْ أَقْسَطُ عِندَ اللَّـهِ

That is more just with Allah

---

[7] *Tafsir al-Safi*, vol 2, p.106

[Qur'an, 2:282]

The Qur'an sees leadership to be a Divine covenant and a position [intrinsically] against injustice and attended by justice. For instance, when the Qur'an speaks of Abraham's suitability and worthiness for leadership it says to the effect: When Abraham was tested and came out successful from all of them, it was said to him that We have chosen you for leadership (*Imamah*). At that point Abraham requested or asked whether this Divine bounty would continue in his progeny. He was told that leadership is a Divine covenant which is never made with the unjust.

لَا يَنَالُ عَهْدِي الظَّالِمِينَ

My pledge does not extend to the unjust.

[Qur'an, 2:124]

In the Qur'an, the moral man is called a "just man". In a number of places in the Qur'an where there is talk of the judgement or witness status of men who are morally and spiritually trustworthy, they are called by the above-mentioned title. For instance, in one verse:

يَحْكُمُ بِهِ ذَوَا عَدْلٍ مِنكُمْ

as judged by two fair men among you

[Qur'an, 5:95]

Or in another verse:

وَأَشْهِدُوا ذَوَيْ عَدْلٍ مِّنكُمْ

and take the witness of two honest men from among yourselves

[Qur'an, 65:2]

Following the translation of Greek texts in the Islamic world, the Platonic maxim "Justice is the root of all moral virtues" became popular. But approximately two centuries before this saying of Plato was ever known among the Muslims, they had already heard it from the Qur'an.

Most of the verses on justice have to do with collective or group justice-whether familial, political, legal, or social. I have estimated that there are sixteen verses in this category.

From *tawhid* or Divine unity, to eschatology and the End; from prophethood to imamate or leadership; from personal ideals to social goals, all of these are founded upon and revolve around the principle of justice. Qur'anic justice is among other things: the counterpart to tawhid; the cornerstone of Resurrection and Judgement day (*ma'ad*), the objective of the Law of the prophets, the philosophy behind leadership and imamate, the criterion of personal success and perfection, and the barometer of social wellbeing.

When Qur'anic justice pertains to *tawhid* or *ma 'ad*, it offers a unique perspective on being and creation; in other words, it gives shape to a certain "world view." Now when justice is applied to the level of revelation (or prophecy), legislation, and the law, it plays the part of a "criterion" or "standard" in legal matters; in other words it forms a foundation upon which reason can stand and be counted as a source of jurisprudence alongside the Book and Tradition. When justice is used for matters of leadership and imamate, it is seen as a "worthiness" and "propriety." When it is used in moral matters, it is seen as a human ideal and aspiration. Finally, when justice is applied to society, it becomes a "social responsibility."

So how could the Muslims have remained indifferent to the issue of justice when the Qur'an, something to which they gave utmost favour and attention-gives it such importance; to the extent that it sees it as a world view, the frame of reference for knowing the law, the criterion of a leader's merit and suitability, a human ideal, and a social responsibility? It is for this that I believe that we need not tire ourselves in search of other reasons and causes for the pervasive presence of the word "justice" in all the intellectual and practical endeavours of the Muslims from outset.

The ultimate reason for Muslim sensitivity on the issue of justice and its outreach into the fields of Islamic theology, jurisprudence, and society was without a shadow of a doubt the Qur'an. The taking up of different and conflicting positions on this issue-in that some have accepted it in its bare and unadulterated form, while others have watered it down and neutralized it by means of a series of excuses and interpretations-goes back to a number of factors, some of which are psychological, some sociological, and others political. This then was my opinion regarding the real origin and source of the issue of justice in the Islamic community. Other people, depending on their particular perspective, may analyze and deduce things in a different way. For we know as a fact that the followers of certain schools of thought analyze social currents in a different manner. The followers of these schools have readymade moulds into which, by hook or by crook, they try to force or fit all phenomena.

In such schools of thought class conflicts and social stratifications based upon haves and have-nots, play the fundamental and major role in all movements and uprisings. According to them, all manifestations of human intellectuality, spirituality, emotionality, and art are just reflections of material needs and economic factors; all things are superficial and that which is fundamental and the basis is economy and economic realities. Hence the intellectual, imaginative, emotional, and artistic characteristics of any person must be sought for among his particular class stratifications. If Sa'di has said, "The essence of human pleasure lies in the stomach," then according to this group it is not only the essence of pleasure, but also the essence of thought, feelings, emotions, imaginations, and in the end anything that can be called sacred. In short, it is as if all paths lead to the stomach.

In the opinion of the followers of this school, if we see that there is talk of justice in a society, then we much search for its roots in economic and social imbalances, and nowhere else. Moreover if we see two groups-in the guise of jurisprudence or theology-opposing one another: a group which seriously supports the principle of justice as a valid world view or a legal criterion and standard, and the other one which denies all of these principles, then we must understand that the intellectual, theological, or legal opposition here actually shows that there is a behind-the-curtains struggle going on. In this opposition, there is a group that is connected with the have-nots and the other with the haves or well to do class. Human thought is but a slave of the stomach. It is impossible for a well to do person to defend the cause of justice, just as it is impossible that a needy person should deny the ideal of justice. Now, in our opinion this is a one-sided and myopic accounting of history. No doubt, material needs are a very important factor in man's interests and tendencies-and sometimes it is even possible to find traces of economic causes in some Islamic intellectual, social, and political debates. But it is not possible to reduce all human tendencies and effects, and all the fundamental elements of human history, to economic needs. Though it may be too soon to give a categorical judgement on the sum total of the fundamental elements and factors that govern man's individual and social life, what is for sure is that material needs cannot be accepted as the sole and most basic need.

With these rigid yardsticks and moulds, I don't know how one would explain away the fact that, for instance, Ma'mun, Mu'tasim, and Wathiq were diehard supporters of the Mu'tazilah and accepted the doctrine of justice, whereas on the other hand, Mutawakkil-who was from the same class and lineage as they were-had opposing tendencies and behaved with the supporters of justice in the same way as his predecessors did with the opponents of justice.

Or for instance, how would one explain the case of Sahib ibn 'Abbad who despite the fact that he was one of the richest men in the world, was a strong advocate of the doctrine of justice; while almost all of the religious scholars of his time, who were also poor, denounced the ideal of justice and were followers of the Ash'arite school.

Sahib ibn 'Abbad was a government minister of means who had few peers as he, in contrast to the majority of ministers [of his time] who did not die peacefully and were much hated, remained a minister until his final days and was given an historical funeral-both numerically and qualitatively. Ibn Khalkan writes of him, "No one was like Sahib ibn 'Abbad in being able to combine success and prosperity during his life and after his death."

Sahib ibn 'Abbad was both a minister in the government as well as being a religious scholar. He lived his life much like the people of his class, the ministers, did-in perfect prosperity. But unlike those other ministers who left the world being despised and whose names were quickly forgotten, he was liked and had made a name for himself. His death was like that of the people of the other class that he belonged to-the 'ulema' or religious scholars-with this difference that they usually live their entire lives in anonymity and poverty and only gain fame and acclaim after their deaths.

In addition to the fact that he kept his ministerial post until the end and gained a good name like that of *'ulama'* for himself, Sahib ibn 'Abbad had another unique characteristic: they say that he was the only minister in history whose father and grandfather were also ministers. Three generations, one after the other, passed on the ministerial post as an inheritance. Sahib ibn 'Abbad's name was Isma'il, his father's name was Abbad, and his grandfather's name was Abbas. Poets have written the following about him:

> Notable after notable inherited the ministry,
> Muniment linked to muniment;
> Abbad obtained ministerial authority from Abbas,
> And Isma'il [acquired it] from Abbad.

Even with all these endowments and holdings, Sahib ibn 'Abbad was an obstinate defender of the doctrine of justice and saw this as a source of honour and pride. He wrote[8]

> If my heart were rent asunder, in its midst would be seen,
> Two lines inscribed without a scribe;
> On one side "Justice and *Tawhid*,"
> On the other, "Love of the People of the House."

We see the same phenomena with regards to the justice of the law or the level of jurisprudence. For instance, Abu Yusuf, the Haruni Head Judge, was a rigid supporter of the justice doctrine, while Ahmad ibn Hanbal categorically denounced it, despite being imprisoned and tortured [on account of it].

In my opinion then, analyzing and explaining away human intellectual and dogmatic predilections exclusively with this criterion of economy and material needs, is too simplistic.

The main reason for having broached this topic in this introduction is double fold: Firstly, we wished to highlight the role of the Qur'an in the elevation of human thought and intellectual endeavors; secondly, to shed

---

[8] See Endnote 4

light on the importance and principality of [the doctrine of justice] from the vantage point of the Qur'an.

We do not claim that this book has investigated the subject of justice from all of its angles and in an exhaustive manner so as to be worthy of Qur'anic sanction. But what can perhaps be claimed here is that, to some degree, this book has looked at it from the perspective of Divine or "ontological" justice-one of the issues in the overall field of justice that the Qur'an takes into consideration-in a new and novel fashion.

29 Khordad, 1352 S.H.

17 Jamadi al-Ula, 1393 A.H.

Murtaza Mutahhari

Conceptual Outline of the Subject

Human vs. Divine Justice

When we humans take into consideration another individual of our species who: does not have bad intentions towards others, does not transgress their rights, is not biased or racist, is extremely impartial in exercising his authority, and who supports the cause of the oppressed and is an enemy to the oppressor in any conflict, we believe him to have a certain type of perfection and hold his actions to be praiseworthy, and call him "just."

On the contrary, when we see a person who: violates the rights of others, is biased in his extent of authority, supports the oppressor and treads on the weak-or at least remains neutral in struggles and disputes between the oppressed and the oppressors, we know such a person to have a type of defect called "injustice" and we label him as an "oppressor" and hold his actions to be blameworthy.

What about God? Is justice a perfection and injustice a defect for God just as it is for man? Or are justice and injustice, as commonly understood, just moral terms applicable to human societies? In other words, are they conventional concepts which pertain to the realm of practical philosophy and ethics (*hikmat-i 'amali*) and not to theoretical philosophy (*hikmat-i 'ilmi*)-meaning that they do not extend beyond the human realm and man's voluntary actions?

Now assuming that justice and injustice apply to God in the same human and moralistic sense, that is to say moral justice is counted as a perfection and moral injustice is counted as an imperfection for God, can injustice have any actualized referent with respect to the Divine agent? The question is not being posed from the standpoint in which it impossible for God to do an unjust act. Nor is it being asked from the perspective that sees good and evil, justice and injustice, to be all legal and canonical terms and concepts instead of inherent intellectual ones-as is the opinion of the Ash'arites. These two aspects are another matter altogether and will be discussed later on. So irrespective of whether it is

35

possible or impossible for God to carry out injustice, and assuming that we have accepted the fact that the goodness or badness of acts is essential to them, or the fact that justice and injustice have actual and concrete meanings, we pose the question from this perspective that justice entails observing the rights of others and injustice is the transgression of those rights. This is to say, in the case where we can speak of rights and there exists an entity which has a greater claim to those rights than others, any infringement of those rights by others will be considered an act of injustice and an incident of oppression of the primary holder of the rights.

It follows, as is obvious, that it is meaningful to speak of priority and lack of priority or ownership and absence of ownership in the interaction and relationship between created beings. For instance, Daniel has priority and ownership with respect to his own life, his personal freedom, and the wealth that he has produced. Likewise, Adam also has precedence with respect to his life, freedom, and income. For Daniel to impinge upon the domain of Adam's priorities and privileges is an act of injustice, just as Adam's transgression of Daniel's privileges is an incident of oppression.

Now what about the relation that exists between the Creator and the created? Whatever the created being possesses is from the Creator. The created being's priority, privilege, and ownership falls under and within the vertical hierarchy of the Creator's precedence and ownership. That is to say, there is no ownership or priority on par with that of the Creator. For illustrative purposes we can compare God's and man's ownership to that of a father and his children. The father procures a toy for each of his children. Every child believes that he has the right of ownership and precedence with respect to the toy that he has been given. Hence, if another child uses his toy, he sees this as a hostile action and one which infringes on his personal rights. But the question is, does the precedence and ownership of the child negate the priority and ownership of his father? Or is it the case that the former ownership is vertically subordinate and subsumed under the latter and there is no contradiction at play here-meaning that if the father were to make use of the toys, he would in actuality be using his own possessions? God is the absolute owner and has no partners whatsoever. In complete honesty and without a glimmer of allegory it must be said of Him:

$$\text{لَهُ الْمُلْكُ وَلَهُ الْحَمْدُ}$$

36

To Him belongs all sovereignty and to Him belongs

[Qur'an, 64:1]

وَإِلَيْهِ يُرْجَعُ الْأَمْرُ كُلُّهُ

and to Him all matters are returned

[Qur'an, 11:123]

Accordingly, God's disposal of all things and affairs is in actuality a free right of disposal of things that are His to begin with. In comparison to God, no one has any right of ownership or precedence with respect to anything whatsoever. Hence injustice is negated from and does not apply to God; not because it is evil and God does not carry out evil actions, nor because good and evil have no meaning in the case of God and do not apply to Him-for even if the evil of injustice was innate and essential to injustice and essential good and evil were to govern Divine acts in the same way that they govern over the acts of man-but because a concrete and actual referent for injustice cannot possibly exist in the case of God (as no one has any right over anything relative to Him for injustice to actually take place).

It is said that Sayf al-Dawlah Hamdani, a monarch of the Hamdan dynasty, was a well-read man whose court was frequented by the literati. On one occasion and speaking to the literary intelligentsia, which included Abu Faras the pedantic Shia Arab poet, he said: "I have composed a couplet that I deem no one can complete other than Abu Faras."

فدمي لا تطلُّهُ   لك جسمى تعلّهُ

My body is yours, you torment it repeatedly,

But you do not spill my blood [once and for all].

Abu Faras retorted:

فلي الأمرُ كلُّهُ   قال إن كنتُ مالكاً

[the Beloved] said: If I am a sovereign,

Then all things are at my disposal.

Now of course if we take justice and injustice in their common meanings, as moral concepts based upon the doctrine of essential goodness, and go on to explain Divine acts in their light-that is, if we wish to assay Divine acts by reference to the "rights of others"-then we must conclude that in this meaning, God is neither just nor unjust. This is because there is no "other" who has priority or primacy over God with regard to anything, so that by comparison we could label the observance of those rights as "justice" and a transgression of them as "injustice."

Now if we disregard the common meaning of justice or injustice, and instead take it to be a conventional concept limited to the sphere of human social activity, the question arises: is there a concept higher and greater than the common one that would justify the placement of the idea of justice among the ideas of theoretical philosophy and hence taking it out of the sphere of practical philosophy and ethics-which deal with conventional or agreed-upon concepts? If such a higher concept existed then would "justice" become a positive Divine attribute or perfection on par with attributes such as "knowledge" and "power", or at least similar to the attributes of "creator" and "sustainer"? Would "unjust" then be a negative attribute such as "composite", "material", or "limited"? On this basis, would the events and phenomena of the external world be explicable given such a conception of justice, or would it have to be taken on faith? A further point of inquiry pertains to the Qur'an. The Qur'an depends on the ideas of justice and injustice quite a lot. Just what does the Qur'an mean by these two ideas? It is necessary to find the correct and detailed answers to these questions. What is for certain is that in all religions, man's relation with God rests on knowing Him to be the "Enjoiner or Establisher of Justice." For while it is true that the God of the philosophers-like the "Prime Mover" of Aristotle-pertains solely to man's rational faculty and does not speak to his heart, emotions, and feelings, and is not seen from the perspective of justice or injustice; the God of the prophets on the other hand has dimensions over and beyond the logical, rational, and intellectual. He has an intimate connection with the inner heart and emotions of man. Naturally, man engages Him with these aspects and with love-the relationship being one of human need for a God that is without needs, omniscient, omnipotent, benevolent, and merciful. Most definitely one of the attributes of such a God is justice. The question is: how are we to understand this Divine justice?

Justice in its sociological sense is the purpose and goal of prophethood, and in its philosophical sense it is the basis of eschatology or *ma'ad* The Qur'an says of the purpose of prophethood:

لَقَدْ أَرْسَلْنَا رُسُلَنَا بِالْبَيِّنَاتِ وَأَنزَلْنَا مَعَهُمُ الْكِتَابَ وَالْمِيزَانَ لِيَقُومَ النَّاسُ بِالْقِسْطِ

Certainly, We sent Our apostles with manifest proofs, and We sent down with them the Book and the Balance, so that mankind may maintain justice

[Qur'an, 57:25]

With regard to eschatology and the accounting and accountability on the Day of Resurrection, the Qur'an says:

وَنَضَعُ الْمَوَازِينَ الْقِسْطَ لِيَوْمِ الْقِيَامَةِ فَلَا تُظْلَمُ نَفْسٌ شَيْئًا ۖ وَإِن كَانَ مِثْقَالَ حَبَّةٍ مِّنْ خَرْدَلٍ أَتَيْنَا بِهَا ۗ وَكَفَىٰ بِنَا حَاسِبِينَ

We shall set up just scales on the Day of Resurrection, and no soul will be wronged in the least. Even if it be the weight of a mustard seed We shall produce it and We suffice as reckoners. [Qur'an, 21:47]

In many verses of the Qur'an, God has been exonerated from any and all kinds of injustice and oppression.

For instance:

فَمَا كَانَ اللَّـهُ لِيَظْلِمَهُمْ وَلَـٰكِن كَانُوا أَنفُسَهُمْ يَظْلِمُونَ

So it was not Allah who wronged them, but it was they who used to wrong themselves.

[Qur'an, 9:70]

The Qur'an has not sufficed itself on just exonerating God from injustice, it has gone further and in some verses it has explicitly affirmed His justice.

شَهِدَ اللَّهُ أَنَّهُ لَا إِلَهَ إِلَّا هُوَ وَالْمَلَائِكَةُ وَأُولُو الْعِلْمِ قَائِمًا بِالْقِسْطِ ۚ لَا إِلَهَ إِلَّا هُوَ الْعَزِيزُ الْحَكِيمُ

Allah, maintainer of justice, the Almighty and the All-wise, besides whom there is no god, bears witness that there is no god except Him, and [so do] the angels and those who possess knowledge.

[Qur'an, 3:18]

Hence, it is abundantly clear from the Islamic perspective that "Divine justice" is a reality in itself and that "justice" is an attribute that must be ascribed to God.

Various Lines of Approach

Generally speaking, there are various methodologies and lines of approach used in the subject of eschatology (*mabda'* wa *ma'ad*). Traditionalists, theologians, philosophers, mystics and the adepts of the natural sciences-each have their own particular approach.

The Traditionalists' approach to the roots and fundamental principles of religion is similar to their methodology in the branches and laws of religion, in that they support a strictly exoteric and pietistic approach and are opposed to any type of deliberation, contemplation, demonstrative proofs and logic. According to this group, when it comes to matters of the faith-whether general beliefs or the Law, one must not bring forth demonstrative arguments or ask why. One must be only silent. In the Qur'an and Tradition, we read that God is alive, omniscient, omnipotent, and willing, as well as just. Hence, we must trust the speech of the prophets and must accept all of these attributes without asking any questions. There is no need whatsoever to think about what justice is or by what logical reason we speak of God as being just. In fact, to deliberate on these matters is an innovation in the religion [tantamount to heresy] and hence is forbidden.

For them justice is a non-issue. They do not see it as at all necessary to answer the questions and doubts that sometimes arise with respect to Divine justice.

Now according to us, the opinions of this group are unfounded. We have dealt with the baseless claims of this faction in the introduction to the fifth volume of *Principles of Philosophy and the Method of Realism*, and hence do not feel that it is necessary to repeat the discussion here.

Aside from the Traditionalists, the other remaining groups permit thought and deliberation and proceed along these lines using various methods of research.

On the subject of justice, the theologians are divided into two groups. One group (the Ash'arites) has come to this conclusion that the attribute of justice is derived from the Divine act qua act. They hold that, essentially, any given act is neither just nor unjust. An act is only just if it coincides with a Divine act. Moreover, they insist that there is no agent or actor whether independent or otherwise-other than God. Putting these two together, they conclude that injustice is meaningless. They have no other definition for justice than this, *i.e.* to say that it is what God does. Hence all acts, because they are God's acts, are just, and not that God does something because it is just.

For this group, there is no principle or rule in the works. For example, we cannot use the principle of justice to categorically claim that God will reward the doers of good and that He will punish the evildoers. Moreover, we cannot even make the claim that God has made such a promise in the Qur'an and that He will live up to the promise. On the contrary, if God rewards the good and punishes the evil, it is just; and if He punishes the good and rewards the evil, it is still just. If He carries out His promises, it is justice; and if He doesn't, it is also justice. This is because whatever God does is just. As the poet says:

آنچه آن خسرو کند شیرین بود

Whatever Caesar does is savory.

While it is true that the Ash'arites do not denounce "justice", their exposition of the issue is for all practical purposes a negation of the doctrine. It is for this reason that their opponents-that is the Shia and the Mu'tazilah came to be called the "justifiers" (*adliyyah*). As for the

41

Ash'arites, in so far as their arguments do not justify the doctrine of justice, they are tantamount to a denial of it.

According to this group, just like the first, one cannot speak of the issue of Divine justice. But unlike the first group, they are freer and, in some sense, feel a greater sense of duty when it comes to answering the doubts and questions that arise vis-a-vis justice.

This group tried, as they saw it, to go the route of purity and exoneration. They wished to exonerate God not only from partners and associates in His capacity as Creator, but also from injustice and oppression. It is due to this that they, on the one hand, effectively negated the agency of all things other than God and, on the other hand, they situated the attribute of justice posterior to the Divine act. In this way, they denied the very existence of the essential goodness or evil of acts. They said, the meaning of an act being just depends on the act being attributed to God. In this way, they concluded that God has no associates in His agency, nor does He do any injustice.

In reality, this group did not exonerate God as much as they exonerated human oppressors. This is because the first and most obvious conclusion that can be drawn from this line of thinking is that the acts of any given oppressor are not his acts, but God's! Moreover, because God does those acts, they are not counted as injustice-they are rather the embodiment of justice itself. The concept of justice was for them nothing other than acts-and acts are only the acts of God. Now because the acts of other-than-God were by no means even existent, there was no such thing as "injustice." Perhaps the reason why oppressors such as the Abbasid Mutawakkil supported the Ash'arites, lies in the fact that this conclusion was to their liking.

Given this logic and this conclusion, what is the role that the oppressed must play in defending their rights and in carrying out their religious duties? The answer is glaringly clear.

But as to what these theologians say with respect to all those verses in the Qur'an that attribute injustice to a host of oppressors and the corresponding duty of the believers that it outlines in response to injustice and oppressors-this is a question that must be asked from the Ash'arites themselves.

The other theologians-who happen to be in reality the outstanding figures of theology-categorically rejected the Ash'arite arguments and logic. Unlike the Ash'arites, they neither negated the prerogative of agency from actors other than God, nor did they-with the pretext of [safeguarding] the unity of Divine acts-abolish human injustice and oppression from the scene. What the non-Ash'arite theologians, the Shia and the Mu'tazilah, did do is confer validity on the doctrine of justice by seeing it as an actual and concrete reality in the phenomena of existence, irrespective of whether the phenomena are attributed to God or not. It is in this way that this group of theologians came to hold the belief that good and evil are essential, rational, and *a priori* qualities.

These theologians believe that the principle of [essential] goodness can be applied to the Divine affairs and function as a criterion in the same way that it is for human ones. It is for this reason that they always turn to this principle and use it as an authority in the divinities. By using this principle and the self-evident nature of the goodness of justice and the badness of injustice, they transform the issue of justice into a moral principle and proceed to apply it on the level of the Divine. They argue: justice is essentially good while injustice is essentially evil. God, who is infinite intelligence and intellectuality and who is in fact the benignant bestower of human reason, can never forgo an act that the intellect knows to be good and can never carry out a deed that reason knows to be bad.

As for the philosophers, they took another route-one which we will shed light on at some later point. For now, it can be said that the philosophers, on the level of Divine acts, negated the existence of associates in the creative process, while at the same time they did not hold that agency was restricted to God. Moreover, while they believed that good and evil were posterior to the Divine act and were derived from existence, they also exonerated Him from injustice. This does not mean that they denied the doctrine of essential good and evil-as they considered the Ash'arite doctrine in this regard to be invalid. What they did do is to limit the scope of these concepts to the sphere of human life and activity. In their view, the concepts of good and evil do not have any place in the Divine realm and cannot be used as criteria or standards in the interpretation of Divine acts.

According to the philosophers, God is just, but not because justice is good and the Divine will is engaged in only good acts. They hold that God is not unjust, but not because injustice is bad and God does not do bad things. The criterion of God's justice, and even the concept of Divine justice, is something else and will be mentioned later on.

In the philosophical perspective, the ideas of good and evil and the goodness or badness of human acts-which are the substance of human morals and conscience-are considered as conventions and not as real and concrete ideas. The value of conventional ideas lies in the domain of practice and application and not in the realm of knowledge. In other words, the instrumentality of the notions gives them their sum total value. For it is the agent in potency, seeking to actualize its end with respect to volitional acts, which needs to create and make use of such ideas as "instruments of the act." God, who is absolute being, all perfection, and pure actuality, does not need such mediating-agencies and ideas or any sort of "instruments" whatsoever.

What is the difference between conventional (*i'tibari*) concepts or ideas and real or concrete ones (*haqiqi*), and how does the mind construct concepts such as good and evil? This is an advanced and intricate discussion in Islamic philosophy and one which we cannot enter into here.

The philosophers do not negate the efficiency of agents other than God-at least not in the way that the Ash'arites do. In consequence, they admit to the existence of human injustice and the responsibility that man has in trying to remove it from society. On the other hand, because the philosophers do not accept the principle of essential good and evil to be a criterion for appraising Divine acts, they have never applied it anywhere in Islamic philosophy or theosophy; For to apply it would in some sense be to "dictate responsibilities and duties" for God.

The philosophers, just like the non-Ash'arite theologians, feel that the set of doubts and questions on the subject of Divine justice, which will be listed here later on, must be faced and solved.

There was yet another group who claimed the invalidity of the approach of both the philosophers and the theologians, on grounds that their methodology was purely rational and mental and that it was not supported by any real or experimental observation. They were of the opinion that even in matters of the fundamental beliefs and doctrines of religion, one must follow the methodology of scientists. Moreover, they held that the outstanding questions on the issue of Divine justice should be solved by a study of natural phenomena and the hidden order within creation.

We have dealt with the claims of this faction in the introduction to the fifth volume of *Principles of Philosophy and the Method of Realism*, and hence do not feel that it is necessary to repeat the discussion here. The interested reader may refer to that work.

The outstanding problems and questions regarding Divine justice-which will be dealt with later-were also important for this group and were presented as issues which must be resolved. In fact, they were more important for them because they only had a single line of approach to the issues at hand, namely the argument from design. The philosophers and theologians on the other hand had recourse to a number of approaches. Even if they were not able to resolve the issues of justice and injustice by the methods of logic and demonstrative proofs, they still managed to salvage belief in God based on their faith and the other methods available to them. Due to this certainty, they were able to maintain a general belief in the workings of God's justice in creation, even if they could not give details and specify the exact causes. Such was not the case with the group under question. They were restricted to just one way. Hence if they came face to face with points of contention arising from the created order which their perspective on justice or their assumptions regarding the argument from design found problematic, they fell prey to a weakening of faith and were beset by doubts about God. For them, God's reflection was to be found in creation and in creation only. So, if the mirror which was to reflect the image of Divine justice was in any way discoloured or if it was to show something other than the reality, then this would shake their faith to its foundations.

According to this group, it was not possible to speak about God in a categorical fashion without first having resolved the paradox of Divine justice. This is because the outstanding criticisms on the issue of Divine justice present problems in the proof of God's existence. They do this by disfiguring the picture and argument of a perfect and complete created order from design. Hence, we see that Allamah Hilli in his *Sharh e Tajrid*, under the discussion on Divine knowledge, asserts that unless the problem of evil and the blemishes of creation are not solved and explained, it will be counted as a defect in God's knowledge and wisdom.

What is Justice?

One of the first matters that must be addressed is the question: What is justice? What is injustice? Until the concept of is justice is not clearly and exactly defined, all of our efforts will be futile and we will be prone to error. Generally speaking, the word "justice" has been used in four senses or for four situations. These will be dealt with in what follows.

A. Balance

If we take a system or collectivity into consideration that is composed of various parts and that is made for a specific purpose, certain conditions-such as the amounts of the component parts and the way that they are put together-must be met before the desired effect is reached and the system subsists and continues to play the role that it was meant to. For example, if any given society wants to subsist and endure, it must be balanced. That is to say, everything in it must be to the extent required, but not necessarily in equal amounts. A balanced society needs various specialties and fields-political, cultural, legal, and educational. These must be divided up among the people and every field must have appointed to it the right amount of manpower. To be a balanced society, it is necessary that the right level and scale of needs is taken into consideration and the appropriate resources-human and material-are allocated. It is exactly here that the ideas of "good policy" and "expediency" come into play; or rather the idea of the "general good", meaning the good that involves the subsistence of the "generality" or "society" and its goals. According to this perspective, the part or individual is but a means and is not taken into account independently.

Much the same can be said about balances of the physical world. For example, if a machine that is made for a particular purpose and requires various components for its structure is to be in a steady state, it must have the necessary amounts of those components and elements.

Chemical balances are also like this. Every chemical agent has a particular formula and there is a particular relationship between the elements that compose it. It is only by following the formula and the various quantities that it calls for that a certain balance reached and the agent produced.

The world is balanced and in an equilibrium. If it wasn't, then it would not subsist; there would be no particular order, economy, or continuity. The Qur'an says:

$$وَالسَّمَاءَ رَفَعَهَا وَوَضَعَ الْمِيزَانَ$$

He raised the heaven high and set up the balance

[Qur'an, 55:7]

The commentators have said that the meaning of this verse is that a certain balance has been taken into account in the structure of the world. Each and every thing has been made using just the right amounts of the elements composing it and the right distances. In a tradition from the Prophet (s) it is said:

$$بالعدل قامت السّموات والأرض$$

The heavens and the earth are maintained with justice.[1]

The opposite of "justice" (adl) in this meaning of the word (i.e. balance) is "imbalance" or "inexpediency", not "injustice" (zulm). Hence, justice in this first sense of the word is not the subject of our discussion and is outside its scope.

Many of those who wanted to address the criticisms of the Divine justice doctrine related to the problem evil, discrimination, and disasters, did so by recourse to the balance-imbalance paradigm of justice. They did this by sufficing themselves with the explanation that these evils, differences, and disasters are necessary for the general and overall order of the world. There is no doubt that from the perspective of universal order and the checks and balances required in its maintenance, the existence of all that subsists is necessary. But this does not answer the problem of evil and injustice.

---

[1] *Tafsir al Safi*, vol. 2, p.638 or vol. 5, p. 106

The discussion of justice in its meaning of balance and propriety is with reference to the entire and total world order, whereas in the meaning where justice is opposed to injustice (and not imbalance or impropriety) the arguments pertain to each and every part or individual in isolation from others. Justice in the first sense talks about expediency and good of the whole, while justice in the second sense speaks to the issue of individual rights. If someone was to take the first meaning, an antagonist could argue in the following manner: I do not deny the existence of a balance and propriety in the world as a whole, but what I say is that the implementation of this balance and the observance of this propriety necessarily brings in its wake a series of inequalities and discriminations. These inequalities and partialities are justifiable in the big picture and according to the whole, but they are inexplicable in relation to the individual or part.

Justice in its meaning of propriety and balance corresponds to the Divine attributes of wisdom and omniscience. For it is the wise and omniscient God who, due to His comprehensive knowledge and eternal wisdom, knows what component elements are needed and in what amounts and commissions those exact same amounts.

B. Equality and Non-discrimination

Sometimes they say that a certain person is just. What they mean is that he is not partial and does not differentiate between people. Hence justice is made to be the same as equality.

This definition needs to be explained. For if what is meant is that justice requires all merits to be set aside and that all are to be regarded in one way by an act of levelling, then this "justice" is actually injustice and oppression. If an equal bestowal is justice then an equal retention is also justice. The famous figure of speech, "Oppression given out equally to everyone is justice," comes from such a perspective.

But if what is meant by this second sense of justice is the application of equality in cases of equal merit, then this is correct. For justice calls for such equal treatments and these equalities are the corollary of justice. But it must be noted that this meaning is based on the third meaning that will be presented next.

C. Rights-Giving to Each Thing its Due

The third sense of justice pertains to giving to every holder of rights, his rights. Injustice then becomes transgressing, withholding, or disposing of the rights of others. This meaning is the true meaning of social justice-the justice which must be observed in human legal codes and which must be honoured by all individuals. This type of justice is based on two things: First, rights and priorities. In other words, individuals acquire certain rights and priorities with respect to one another. For example, the person who produces a product with his labour has priority with respect to that product. The source and basis of this priority is his work and activity. Similarly, a baby that is born of a mother has certain rights and priorities over the mother's milk. The basis of this priority is Mother Nature who in its purposefulness created the milk for that child.

Another example pertains to an innate character trait of man, who has been created in such a way that he makes use of conventional ideas or concepts as instruments and a means to achieve his natural ends. These notions are imperative and are specified by "musts" or dos and don'ts. One of these is: If the individuals of a society are to be personally successful, they must observe rights and priorities. This is the concept of human justice that the conscience of every person recognizes and accepts. It is this meaning of justice which has as its opposite the reprehensible qualities of injustice and oppression. Mawlana Rumi[2] says in his famous poem:

What is justice? To put (a thing) in its (right) place.
What is injustice? To put it in its wrong place.[3]
What is justice? Giving water to trees.
What is injustice? To give water to thorns.[4]
(If) you put the king in the rook's place, 'tis ruin;

Likewise, (if you put) the elephant (rook) in the king's place, it's ignorance.[5]

---

[2] See Endnote 5
[3] Reynold A. Nicholson, *The Mathnawi of Jalalu 'ddin Rumi* (Delhi, Adam Publisher,1992), vol .6, p.402, vr. 2596.
[4] Nicholson, vol. 5, p.67, vr. 1089
[5] Nicholson, vol. 6, p.401, vr. 2594

This meaning of justice and injustice, because, on the one hand, it is based on the principle of precedence and priority, and on the other hand, it is due to an innate human predilection forcing man to make use of conventions, fabricate do's and don'ts, and abstract good and evil, it is peculiar to man and does not apply to the Divine realm. For just as we previously saw, God is the absolute owner and sovereign and no existent has precedence over Him in any manner whatsoever. However, God wishes to dispose of a thing, He has a total right as that thing is dependent on God for its very being and is in His ownership. It is for this reason that injustice, in this meaning of transgressing on another's rights or violating his person or property, is inconceivable in God's case and is impossible in actuality.

D. Emanation or Bestowal of Being on Merits and Not Abstaining from This in Respect of That Which Can Possibly Exist or Be Further Perfected

We will see later on that the differentiation of existents is due to their varying potentials and abilities in receiving grace and emanations from the source and origin of being. Every existent, whatever its level, from the point of view of its potential for receiving grace, has certain merits and rights for itself. God, who is all-Perfect, all-Good, and the absolute bestower of grace, gives to each thing its possible existence and perfections. Hence justice is onto logically defined according to this perspective as: every existent acquiring the degree of existence and perfection that it merits and is possible for it. Injustice then lies in preventing an existent from receiving such grace as it merits and is its due. According to the philosophers and sages, the attribute of justice that is worthy of God and is affirmed of Him as a perfection is in this very meaning. In a similar way, the attribute of injustice that is an imperfection and is negated of God is also in the meaning mentioned above.

The philosophers believe that there is no existent that has any rights over God, so that we could speak of God being responsible for giving those rights to it; and then go on to call God "just" because He has performed all of His duties towards others to a tee. This is not the case and God's justice is His graciousness and is identical with His being. That is to say, God's justice lies in not withholding His grace from any creature that has any capacity whatsoever for receiving it. This is the meaning of the words of Imam Ali (a)[6] where he says:

فَالحَقُّ ...لَا يَجرِي لِأَحَدٍ إِلَّا جَرَى عَلَيهِ وَ لَا يَجرِي عَلَيهِ إِلَّا جَرَى لَهُ وَ لَوْ كانَ لِأَحَدٍ أَنْ يَجرِيَ لَهُ وَ لَا يَجرِيَ عَلَيهِ لَكانَ ذَلِكَ خَالِصاً لِلّهِ سُبْحَانَهُ دُونَ خَلْقِهِ

A right ... does not accrue to any person unless it counts against him also, and it does not count against a person unless it also accrues in his favour. If it were to accrue (only) in favour of a person without (in turn) counting against him, then this (situation) would be solely for Allah, the Glorified, and not for His creatures.[7]

Now with this the only correct yardstick of justice in hand, we must look among the many examples of so called "evil", "injustice", and "discrimination", to see if there really is in these instances an existent among existents that could have existed in the total order but did not acquire existence; or could have had a particular perfection in the grand scheme of things but did not receive it; or perhaps it was given something that it should not have. In other words, did God give such an existent something that is evil and a defect in place of something that is good and a perfection?

In the second volume of his book Astir, during the discussion of specific forms, Mulla Sadra[8] has a chapter entitled, "What is the Existential Modality of Contingent Existents?" In this chapter he refers to the concept of justice in the meaning and style of the philosophers. He writes:

You previously saw that matter and form are the proximate co-causes of material things. From their mutual dependency it was concluded that there must be an efficient cause beyond the material and physical one. We will later prove in the discussion on "General Movement" that each and every motion has a metaphysical end. The metaphysical agent and the metaphysical end are two remote causes of material existents. If these two

---

[6] See Endnote 6
[7] Imam Ali ibn Abi Talib (a), *Nahj al-Balagha*, Sermon 216
[8] See Endnote 7

remote causes were sufficient in the existence of material things then material things would subsist forever and annihilation or non-existence would not apply to them. Moreover, they would have all the perfections they merit from the start, their first state being the same as their last. The two remote causes are not sufficient and the two proximate ones (matter and form) are also effectual. There is on one hand opposition between forms, and the initial states of forms are prone to decay-on the other hand, every matter has the potential for accepting opposing forms. Hence every existent acquires two opposing merits and aptitudes, one due to the form and the other due to the matter. The form calls for subsistence and maintaining the present state of the existent, whereas matter calls for change in state and taking on a form other than the first one. Because it is not possible for these two opposing "rights" or precedences to be fulfilled simultaneously, as it is not possible for matter to have simultaneous opposing forms ... Divine benefaction causes the completion and perfection of the matter of this world-the lowest of all the worlds-by means of forms. It is for this reason that God in His Divine wisdom ordained perpetual motion and unending time. He also destined matter to be perpetually in flux-constantly changing with different forms through time, one replacing the other out of necessity and every state or form having a specific period so that it can in its turn take advantage of existence. Now because matter is common to these forms, each form has certain rights over the others and demands rights from them. Justice dictates that the matter of this form be given to the other and the matter of the second one be given to this one. In this way matter is passed on hand to hand between the forms. It is because of this "justice" and the observance of the innate merits and rights of things that we see in the world the continuity and subsistence of species and not individuals.

Another question comes up at this point If all things are equal before God, there is no such thing as "merits" or "rights" for there then to be "justice" as the observance of these rights. So, if we speak about justice in the case of God, it can only be as the observance and application of "equality". This then means that justice in its meaning of the observance of rights and merits, and justice in its meaning of the observance of equality, both give the same results in the case of God. Hence Divine justice must dictate that there cannot be any differences and discriminations between created beings. But in reality, we see that there are scores of differences-whatever there is comprises contrasts, differing types, and oppositions.

The answer to this is that the concept of the rights of things in relation to the Divine revolves around the need and possibility, or perfection, of existence. Because God is the agent par excellence and the necessary bestower, He bestows existence or perfections on every existent that can possibly exist or has the possibility for any type of perfection whatsoever. Divine justice then-as we saw in the quote from Mulla Sadra is the bestowal of universal grace to all existents that have the possibility of existence or further existential perfections, without the least bit meanness or discrimination.

Now as to the question of the ultimate source of differences in merits and potentials: Given God's universal and infinite grace, how is it that things are essentially different - different in their potentials, possibilities, and merits or rights? We hope, God willing, to take up this discussion in the next section.

Objections and Criticisms

Let's see what questions have been posed in this regard.

The first question is: Why are there distinctions and variety in the world? Why is one person white and another black, one ugly and another handsome, one healthy and another ill? Or why, for that matter, is one being a human and another being a goat or a worm? Why are some things mineral and others plants? Why are some people angelic and some others devilish fiends? Why aren't all things the same? Why aren't all people white, or all people black? Why aren't they all ugly or all beautiful? Assuming we accept that there should be differences, why is it that the white man wasn't made black, or the black wasn't created white? Why wasn't the ugly man made handsome or the beautiful woman ugly?

Another set of questions pertain to annihilation and nonexistence. Why do things come into existence and then become non-existent? Why has death been ordained? Why does man come into this world and then leave it before he has tasted the pleasures of this life or before having found faith in an eternal afterlife?

To throw light on the connection between this question and the issue of justice, one can quote the saying: "Utter nonexistence is better than an imperfect existence." To explain: nobody and nothing has any rights while it is non-existent. But as soon as it comes into existence, it gains the right to subsist and perpetuate. If it didn't exist at all it would have been better off and at ease as that is better than being created and being taken away as a loser; hence such a coming into being is injustice.

Another question is: Setting aside the temporal limitations of created beings, what is the reason for such imperfections as ignorance, incapacity, weakness, and poverty?

This question pertains to the issue of justice in the following manner: It is imagined that the withholding of graces such as knowledge, power, and wealth from creatures that need them is injustice. In this objection it has been assumed that the thing that has not come into being yet has no rights, but as soon as it comes into being it naturally gains the rights that accompany life and existence. Hence ignorance, incapacity, weakness, poverty, hunger, and the like, are a type of deprivation from rights.

Granted the existence of differentiation and discrimination and the fact that all things must at one point cease to exist, and given the reality that some things come into this world while not being given some of the necessities and accessories of life, the question remains: what is the purpose of disasters, plagues, and calamities that exterminate an existent half the way down the road, or that make its existence full of unease, pain, and suffering? What is the rhyme and reason behind killer-viruses, diseases, oppressions and repressions, robberies, floods, storms, earthquakes, separations, calamities, wars, oppositions, Satan, the carnal soul…?

These then are the types of questions that are posed surrounding the issue of justice and injustice. No doubt these very same questions or ones resembling them with minor variations could be asked with regard to other theological topics. For instance, topics such as: ends and final causes, cause and effect, providence, and the Divine attributes. It is said, if creation had a purpose and end or some type of overruling wisdom in the works, then all things would have some use. Hence, a useless or harmful creature should not have been created; or a possibly useful one should not have been left uncreated. But the existence of discrimination, contrast, annihilation, ignorance, impoverishment and incapacity, shows that certain phenomena should have been created and present. Phenomena such as: equality, subsistence, knowledge, power, and the like, should have been there but were not created. On the other hand, things which are either useless or harmful were created-things such as diseases, earthquakes, etc. When all of these things are put alongside God's supreme wisdom and justice in its meaning of equality and balance, it just doesn't add up.

These questions and issues, with slight variations, can also be posed with regards to the subject of *tawhid*, in the discussions on "good and evil." In this case the objection put forth is: There is a double standard at play in the universe, hence there must be duality at the root of the matter. Philosophers discuss the topic of "good and evil" sometimes in the subject of *tawhid* when arguing against the theory of "Duality," and sometimes in the subject of Providence where they speak of God's overruling and encompassing wisdom. In the latter discussion it is said that Providence dictates that all that exists must be good and perfections-the existing order and design must be the best one possible-hence evil and imperfections, things which ruin the best order scenario, must not exist; while we see that they do exist.

We are going to approach the issues and questions here from the perspective of justice and injustice, but whether we like it or not, other aspects will come into the scene and will also be resolved along with the rest. We have previously stated that the idea of justice as the opposite of injustice is to be taken in its meaning of the observance of innate merits and capacities and not in the meanings of balance or equality. Moreover, as has already been pointed out, the observance of merits and rights in the case of God corresponds to what the philosophers have seen and understood and not to what others have assumed or thought.

Justice as a Pillar of Faith and Principle of Religion

Doubts and objections regarding theological issues normally pertain to theologians, philosophers, and experts of the field. The substance of these debates is usually beyond the scope of laymen and both the objections and the responses are discussed on a level higher than that of the laity. But the outstanding objections and problems surrounding the issue of Divine justice are not like this, and they are current even on the lower and popular level of the masses. Both the illiterate villager and the erudite philosopher think about this topic in some form.

It is because of this that the issue of justice is situated so strategically and has special importance. This also could be a possible explanation as to why Islamic scholars (the Shia and Mu'tazilah, not the Ash'arites) have placed justice alongside the "principles of religion" and have counted it as the second root or principle out of the five principles of religion. In any case, "justice" is also one of the Divine attributes; but if the Divine attributes were to be among the principles of religion, then it would be necessary to include other attributes such as knowledge, power, will.... But the real reason why the Shia have counted justice as one of the principles of religion is something else. To explain, the Shia and Sunni do not differ on most of the Divine attributes. And even if they do differ, it is not something that has received much consideration. But with regards to justice, there are serious differences and these differences have received considerable attention and airing. To the extent that, they have become the criteria and distinguishing marks of the various schools of thought. It is by use of these criteria that we can tell a Shia from a Sunni and within the Sunnis, a Mu'tazili from an Ash'ari. The doctrine of justice by itself was the sign of not being an Ash'ari. Justice along with Imamate were considered as the marks of the Shia. This is why it was said that the principles of religion or pillars of faith in Islam are three in number and the principles of the Shia sect are those three with the addition of the principle of justice and the principle of Imamate.

Justice and Wisdom

As we have seen previously, among the Divine attributes, there are two which bear a resemblance to each other when the doubts and objections with regard to them are considered: justice and wisdom.

By God's justice what is meant is that He does not leave the merits and capacities of any existent unattended to and hanging in the air, as it were. On the contrary he gives to everything its due. By God's wisdom what is meant is that God's creation and design is the best possible. Khwajah Nasir al-Din Tusi[9] writes in verse:

Other than the judgement of truth which is the judgement,
There is no judgement which outstrips the judgement of the Truth.
Whatever there is, must be so;

---

[9] See Endnote 8

That which must not be so, is not.

Divine wisdom and providence imply the existence of a purpose and meaning for the world. Whatever exists is either itself good or is a means to goodness. Wisdom is an aspect of both knowledge and will. It is the reality that throws light on the final cause of the world. Justice, on the other hand, is not directly connected with the attributes of knowledge and willpower. Justice in the meaning that was given for it, pertains to God's efficiency and role as agent. In other words, it is an attribute of act and not an attribute of essence.

The objection common to both Divine justice and Divine wisdom is the problem of evil. The issue of evil can be raised as an objection under the heading of "injustice" when it comes to justice, and under the heading of "purposeless or meaningless creations" in the case of wisdom; it is due to this that this issue is counted as one of the reasons for the inclination towards materialism. For instance, when the natural defense mechanisms of living creatures are given as an example of God's order, design, and wisdom, the question is immediately posed that why must there be dangers in the first place for there then to be a need for defense mechanisms? Why do harmful viruses even exist so that there should be a need for white blood cells to fight them? Why were sharp toothed predators created for animals of prey to require legs to escape from them or antlers to defend themselves against them? In the animal kingdom, the weaker animals of prey have been given instincts of flight from danger and fear, while the stronger predators have been given fearless voracity. For man the question arises that why do ferocity and attack instincts exist in the first place for there then to be a necessity for clever defense mechanisms?

These questions and objections, whose solutions and answers call for detailed and thorough analysis, are like a tremendous vortex that has swept up destroyed many groups and schools of thought in its path. We must agree with the poet who said:

In this vortex a thousand ships have gone under,
Such that not even a single plank was cast ashore.

Materialist and dualist philosophies, as well as pessimistic or nihilist schools of thought usually took form in such vortexes.

Dualism

From time immemorial man, especially the Arian race, has divided worldly phenomena along the lines of two poles, good and evil. Light, rain, sun, earth, and many other things have been counted as among the good, and darkness, drought, floods, earthquakes, disease, savagery, and aggression-to name a few-have been called bad and identified with the pole of evil. Of course, man has made himself the criterion of division and has known those things which are useful to him as "good," and those things which harm him to be "bad".

For men of former times the following thought occurred: Is the creator of the evil and bad things the same as the creator of the good and beneficial? Or are good things produced by one source and bad things by another? Is the creator of good and evil one and the same, or does the world have two sources and two creators?

A group from among them figured that the creator himself can either be good or he can be bad. If he is good, then he doesn't create evil or bad things. If he is bad, then he doesn't make good things. From this they reached the conclusion that the world has two sources or two creators. This belief became known as "dualism."

The belief of ancient Iranians in a god of good and a god of evil-which were later called by the names Ormazd and Ahriman-took form in a similar way.

According to historical records, after the Arian race inhabited the land of Iran it began to worship natural objects, albeit good ones, such as fire, sun, rain, earth, and air. The historians report that Iranians did not worship bad things but that there did exist a non-Arian people who worshiped bad and evil objects with the aim of placating evil spirits. What existed in the Iran of antiquity was the belief in two origins, sources, or creators, and not a two-faced type of worship. That is to say, Iranians held that there were associates and partners in the act of creation, but did not hold that they should worship things other than god.

It was later on that the prophet Zoroaster made his appearance. Historically speaking, it is not clear whether the Zoroastrian religion was originally monotheistic or dualistic. The extant Avesta does not resolve this ambiguity as parts of this book are drastically different from one another. One part, the Vendidad, is explicitly dualistic, whereas the

Gathas do not really put forward the dualist argument and, according to the claims of some researchers, they champion monotheism. It is these great discrepancies that have led researchers to believe that the present Avesta is not the work of one man, but of more than one individual.

Historical researches in this field are not definitive, but according to our Islamic beliefs we can maintain that the Zoroastrian religion was originally a monotheistic creed. This is because the majority of Islamic scholars hold the belief that the Zoroastrians belong to the category of "the People of the Book." Specialists in history also bear this out as they say that the entry of dualist thinking into the Zoroastrian religion was due to the dualism of the Arian race before its advent.

Having said this we must add that it is only on the basis of religious authority that we can call Zoroastrianism a monotheistic religion. This is because from the historical perspective the one that we obtain by a purview of works attributed to Zoroaster-and even if we take into account only the Gathas, we cannot accept Zoroastrianism to be a monotheistic creed. Basing themselves on the Gathas, the best that the researchers and experts have said with regard to the monotheism of Zoroaster is that he believed in the essential unity of the Divine. That is, he believed that there was only one being that was self-existent and uncreated, namely Ahura Mazda, and that all other existents-including Ahriman-were creations of Ahura Mazda. In other words, Zoroaster was of the opinion that the tree of being had only one root. But based on the saying of some other researchers we can hold that Zoroaster believed in the unity of worship. That is, he believed that only one entity should be the object of worship. But for any religion to be monotheistic, over and beyond a belief in the unity of the Divine essence and the unity of worship, a belief in the unity of creation is necessary. On this latter count the Zoroastrian religion, according to historical records, was totally dualistic. It appears that these documents teach that the opposite pole of Angra Mainyu (Destructive Spirit) is Spenta Mainyu (Bounteous Spirit). Spenta Mainyu is the source of good things-that is, those things that are good and must be created. On the contrary, Angra Mainyu (or Ahriman) is the source of bad and evil things-that is, those things that should not be created and Spenta Mainyu or Ahura Mazda are not responsible for their creation. According to these ideas, even though being does not have two "roots," it certainly does have two "branches." That is to say the existence that begins with Ahura Mazda forks off into two branches: the branch of goodness or Spenta Mainyu and his good works, and the branch of evil or Angra Mainyu and all his bad creations. If we make the Gathas-the most original, authoritative, and monotheistic scripts that have been left by Zoroaster-the criterion for judging Zoroaster then we are still left with a problem. For where there is talk of six goods and five evils, or the fact that the existing order is not the best and does not embody wisdom, we must on this account set Zoroaster aside from the other prophets of God.

Due to this ingrained problem, the Zoroastrian religion could not hold out against the doctrine of dualism and in consequence this doctrine was once again revived after the death of Zoroaster among the Iranian people. Hence the Zoroastrians of the Sasanian period, the Manichaeans and the Mazdakites, who are considered to be offshoots of Zoroastrianism in Iran, were extremely dualistic.

In reality it must be said that the Zoroastrian religion was unable to remove the roots of dualism and pantheism from the hearts of Iranians in practice, and from the teachings of the Gathas in theory. It eventually gave in to these heretical beliefs and itself became a heterodoxy.

Islam alone was able to purge this thousand year old heresy from the Iranian mind. This is just one of Islam's shows of strength-where it was able to deeply affect the Iranian spirit and in consequence bring them salvation. This is no small feat given the fact that dualism had become the flesh and blood of the Iranians-to such an extent that some orientalists are of the opinion that it forms the basis of the Iranian psyche. Iranians were so caught up with this doctrine that they even allowed their religion to be affected by it. Hence, it was Islam that made monotheists out of these diehard Iranian dualists. Once the Iranian people acquired the truth of:

الْحَمْدُ لِلَّهِ الَّذِي خَلَقَ السَّمَاوَاتِ وَالْأَرْضَ وَجَعَلَ الظُّلُمَاتِ وَالنُّورَ

All praise belongs to Allah who created the heavens and the earth and made the darkness and the light.

[Qur'an, 6:1]

And once they came to also believe in this verse:

الَّذِي أَحْسَنَ كُلَّ شَيْءٍ خَلَقَهُ

who perfected everything that He created

[Qur'an, 32:7]

And then when they had understood this meaning:

رَبُّنَا الَّذِي أَعْطَىٰ كُلَّ شَيْءٍ خَلْقَهُ ثُمَّ هَدَىٰ

'Our Lord is He who gave everything its creation and then guided it.'

[Qur'an, 20:50]

When all this took place, Iranians were so overwhelmed by God, creation, the world, and being, that every fiber in their bodies burned with love and they were then able to praise the design in being in the following way:

My pleasance with the world is, 'cause the world is His Pleasance.

I am in love with the whole world, 'cause the whole world is His.

I drink with pleasure the bitter cup of poison, 'cause perhaps the cup-bearer is He.

I forbear with affection the pains, 'cause the cure is also from Him.[10]

After the advent of Islam, the Iranians stopped believing in a source or force of evil. They went on from there and with a mystical outlook they obliterated evil from the total universal order. They said: "Fundamentally evil does not exist," or alternatively, "Evil is that which is not." Ghazali[11] (who was an Iranian) says:

لَيْسَ فِي الإِمْكَانِ أَبْدَعَ مِمَّا كَانَ

There isn't in the realm of possibility anything more marvellous than what exists.

---

[10] Shaykh Muslih al-Din Sa'di
[11] See Endnote 9

61

It is such men, trained and nurtured by Islam, who are able to foster such sublime thoughts. They realize that calamities, pains, and sufferings are ugly and unwanted from one perspective, and that from a higher perspective and with a deeper insight, they are all graces and beauties. Hafiz,[12] who was appropriately given the title "the Expounder of the Unseen," eloquently explained many deep philosophical and mystical concepts by way of allegories, metaphors, and parables. In one poem he explains the difference between the two perspectives-the superficial, limited, and common perspective, and the deeper, comprehensive point of view from above, as it were, which he calls the opinion of the *pir* or shaykh meaning the perfect man or mystic. He does this by using puns and a play on words.

آفرین بر نظر پاک خطا پوشش باد　　　پیر ما گفت خطا بر قلم صنع نرفت

Said our *Pir*: "On the Creator's pen, passed no error:"

On his pure sight, error-covering, plaudits be![13]

In other words, from the point of view of the *Pir*-one that is not alloyed or sullied by limitations and superficiality-the world is seen to be a single manifestation of God. All mistakes, lapses, and unseemly things, which appear to people of limited vision, are obliterated for him. The world is the shadow of God. God in His essence is absolute perfection and absolute beauty. The shadow of beauty cannot be but beautiful. In the case of a beautiful body, if we look at a single part or limb by itself and without taking into consideration the fact that that limb has a certain place in the body and that along with the other parts it makes up one single body, we will not perceive the body's correctness and perfection. We might even end up thinking that if it was some other shape, it would have been better. But as soon as we look at it comprehensively and as a part among parts of a beautiful whole, our perspective will change, and that

---

[12] See Endnote 10

[13] Henry Wilberforce Clarke, trans, *Ghazal of Hafez Shirazi, In Persian with English Translation*, Ghazal 105.

which we previously thought to be incorrect and unseemly will have entirely disappeared.

In another couplet, as is generally and usually his habit in every ghazal, Hafiz explains the reasons and methods behind his use of metaphors, allegories, parables, and various plays on words.[14]

Of the number of mirror-holders of [the Beloved's] line and mole, my eye became:

Of the number of the kiss-snatchers of [the Beloved's] bosom and back, my lip be.[15]

In the first line of this couplet, he speaks of the station of "the essence of certainty" (*'ayn al-yaqin*), where seeing everything as good in itself, he sees in the world reflections of His eyebrow, mole, and eye. In the second line he hopes to attain the station of "the reality of certainty" (*haqq al-yaqin*).

Other ghazals of Hafiz repeatedly refer to this truth that after having arrived at the station of Reality, the mystic does not see anything other than perfection, beauty, and grace. For instance, he says:[16]

By its grace, Thy beautiful face explained to us a verse of the Koran:
For that reason, in our explanation, is naught save grace and beauty.[17]
To the world's work, never was attention mine;
In my sight, Thy face its happy adorner thus is.[18]

Hafiz was a man whose world view was essentially mystical. He put unity in place of the multiplicity of the philosophers; manifestation and emanation in place of their causality; and love and beauty in place of their reason and necessity. He saw the world to be the "the unique manifestation of absolute beauty." How could such a man think along the same lines as say Khayyam'[19] or Abu al-'Ala'[20]? Hafiz takes the three elements which compose his mystical vision of the world-unity,

---

[14] See Endnote 11
[15] Clarke, Ghazal 105
[16] See Endnote 12
[17] Clarke, Ghazal 10
[18] Clarke, Ghazal 22
[19] See Endnote 13
[20] See Endnote 14

manifestation, and beauty-and puts them to verse in the most poignant and eloquent manner:[21]

> When, into the mirror of the cup, the reflection of Thy face fell,
> From the laughter of wine, into the crude desire of the cup, the Arif fell.
> With that splendor that in the mirror, the beauty of Thy face made,
> All this picture into the mirror of fancy fell.
> All this reflection of wine and varied picture that have appeared
> Is a splendor of the face of the Said that, into cup fell.[22]

The use of the word "error-covering" in the first verse of Hafiz quoted has misled some people into making a mistake. They have not taken into consideration that the devices of equivocality, ambiguity, and plays on words are often used by mystical poets. They sometimes use a sentence or word that has two senses, or even use a word in the opposite meaning from its apparent one-these being some of the beauties of rhetoric. Other verses and poems of Hafiz provide contextual support for understanding the real meaning of this couplet. Moreover, assuming we accept the fact that he had complaints against creation, is it possible that he would discredit the *Pir* given all the respect that he has for this term and bearing? For in this case his purport would be that the *Pir*'s claim that no error passed on the Creator's pen is either a lie or that the *Pir* is a simpleton who does not know what he is saying.

In some of his other couplets, Hafiz has expounded the real story behind evil-in that it does not imply the division of creation-in the best of manners. We will recount this matter in the appropriate place. Hence, the supposition that Hafiz, in the verse under question, was finding fault with creation and was disparaging the *Pir* is a layman's supposition.

Satan

It can be argued that Zoroastrianism has the dualist conception of Ormazd and Ahriman, and that Islam for its part has the beliefs of God and Satan as two opposing poles. What is the difference between the Ahriman of Zoroastrianism and the Shaytan or Satan of Islam?

---

[21] See Endnote 15
[22] Clarke, Ghazal 111

There is a world of difference between the conception of Ahriman in the Zoroastrian or Mazdakite creeds and the idea of Satan in Islam. This calls for some explanation.

According to the teachings of the Avesta, there is an entity known as Angra Mainyu or Ahriman who is responsible for the creation of all evils, calamities, and bad or harmful things; things such as disease, ferocious beasts, stinging and biting animals, snakes, scorpions, and even barren lands, droughts, and the like. These things are not attributed to the great god Ahura Mazda, or to Spenta Mainyu, the arch rival of Angra Mainyu.

From some segments of the Avesta it appears that Ahriman is an ancient and eternal being like Ahura Mazda himself and is not created by him. Ahura Mazda discovered Ahriman but did not create him. But from other parts of the Avesta, especially the Gathas which are the most authoritative part of the Avesta, it comes to light that Ahura Mazda created two beings: Spenta Mainyu or "Holy Wisdom" and Angra Mainyu or "Unholy Wisdom" (Ahriman).

In any case, what is apparent from the Avesta and has been, and is, the belief of the Zoroastrians is that created things in the world are divided into two groups of good and bad. The good are those that exist and must exist and it is good that they exist-their existence being necessary for the world order. The bad are those things that exist, yes, but should not exist-their existence being the cause of the imperfection of the world. These latter things, the bad or evil things, are by no means the creation of Ahura Mazda. They are rather the creation of Ahriman, regardless of whether Ahriman himself is the creation of Ahura Mazda or not.

Hence no matter how you look at it, Ahriman is the maker and creator of a great many of the things in the world. A whole section of the created order is his realm and he is an eternal entity-an Ancient. He is either Ahura Mazda's counterpart or associate. on the level of essence, or is Ahura Mazda's creation but his associate and partner on the level of creation.

In the Islamic world view though, the world or created things are not fundamentally divided into two groups or categories-good and bad. There is in this perspective no created thing that "should not have been created" or "was created badly." On the contrary, all things are created beautiful-everything being in its right place. In addition, all things are the creation of God in His essence.

In Islam, the realm of Satan is the legislative level (of human volition and act) and not the ontological level. That is to say, Satan can only affect human existence and cannot influence anything outside the human realm. Even within the human realm, Satan's range and free scope is limited to influencing human thought, not the body. In affecting human thinking, Satan is limited to temptation, suggestion, and the portrayal of false ideas in the imagination or fantasies of men. The Qur'an speaks of these Satanic devices by using terms such as *waswasah* (whispering or temptation), *taswil* (seduction or enticement), and *tazayyun* (to make to seem beautiful and a part of decorum). Satan has these methods, but he cannot create anything, nor can he have any type of existential control over man. That is to say, he cannot be an irresistible force which overpowers man and makes him do bad things. Satan's authority and control over man is limited to the situation where man himself desires to give himself over to him.

إِنَّهُ لَيْسَ لَهُ سُلْطَانٌ عَلَى الَّذِينَ آمَنُوا وَعَلَىٰ رَبِّهِمْ يَتَوَكَّلُونَ. إِنَّمَا سُلْطَانُهُ عَلَى الَّذِينَ يَتَوَلَّوْنَهُ

Indeed, he does not have any authority over those who have faith and put their trust in their Lord His authority is only over those who befriend him....

[Qur'an, 16:99-100]

In reply to those people who hold Satan responsible for their misguidance, the Qur'an quotes Satan on Resurrection Day saying:

وَمَا كَانَ لِيَ عَلَيْكُم مِّن سُلْطَانٍ إِلَّا أَن دَعَوْتُكُمْ فَاسْتَجَبْتُمْ لِي ۖ فَلَا تَلُومُونِي وَلُومُوا أَنفُسَكُم

I had no authority over you, except that I called you and you responded to me. So do not blame me, but blame yourselves.

[Qur'an, 14:22]

The philosophy and wisdom behind even this amount of dominion that Satan has over man can be found in man's free will. Man's ontic level dictates that he be free. A free being must always be at a proverbial fork in the road and in the position to choose between two options for his freedom to be fully realized and actualized.[23]

From the World are coming two cries in opposition to each other; (bethink thyself) for which (of them) thou art adapted.

It's one cry is the (means of) quickening the devout with (spiritual) life; and its other cry is the (means of) cajoling the graceless.[24]

In the Islamic world view, no existent has any independent role in the creative act. The Qur'an does not attribute independence to any existent whatsoever. All existents play only mediating roles and act as the instruments through which the Divine will and Providence act. The Qur'an gives credence to the intervention of angels in the application of God's will on earth, but it does not allow even this for Satan. Hence by all the more reason, it repudiates the existence of independent creative powers for him-setting him apart from the Avestan Ahriman who possessed such powers alongside Ahura Mazda.

From this we can conclude that the translation of the word "Satan" or *Shaytan* [in Persian literature] as "Ahriman" or "*div*", is totally wrong and a great mistake. The word "Satan" or "*Shaytan*" does not have an equivalent in Persian and hence it must not be translated and must be kept as is in any translated text.

According to the Qur'an, Satan is not by any means a "pole" that is contrasted with and antipodal to the Divine pole. He is not even a pole or antipode to the angels who are, by Divine sanction, the intermediaries of creation and the executors of the Divine will in its creative aspect.

Generally speaking, the notion of jinn that our people have is different from the picture that the Qur'an presents. In the Qur'an, jinn are like men in that they are morally responsible and answerable for their actions, but unlike men, they are "unseen" and "spirits". Lay people think them to be of the rank of angels, but the Qur'an puts them alongside mankind. The Qur'an explicitly states that Satan is of jinn. According to the Islamic world view, angels have executive powers in the existential world order; as opposed to jinn who have no such powers. Putting jinn and angels on the same footing, as is done in [Persian] Islamic literature, is due to a

---

[23] See Endnote 16
[24] Nicholson, vol. 4, p. 362, vr. 1622

historical mistake that was made by Muslims and is attributable to the cultural baggage and ideas of the Zoroastrian tradition.

Now, to return to the discussion at hand, it must be said that in opposition to the Zoroastrian, the Manichaean, and the Mazdakite world views which can be said to be bipolar, the Islamic perspective is unipolar. In the perspective of the Qur'an, Satan is the embodiment of:

الَّذِي أَحْسَنَ كُلَّ شَيْءٍ خَلَقَهُ

who perfected everything that He created

[Qur'an, 32:7]

And he is also the example of:

رَبُّنَا الَّذِي أَعْطَىٰ كُلَّ شَيْءٍ خَلْقَهُ ثُمَّ هَدَىٰ

'Our Lord is He who gave everything its creation and then guided it.'

[Qur'an, 20:50]

Satan's existence, as well as his evil and misguidance, are all based on and according to wisdom and expediency. It is due to this very wisdom and experience that Satan is a relative evil and not a real or absolute evil.

What is even more amazing is that according to the Qur'anic logic, God Himself gave Satan his position and post as the "misguider". God addresses Satan in the Qur'an and orders him:

وَاسْتَفْزِزْ مَنِ اسْتَطَعْتَ مِنْهُم بِصَوْتِكَ وَأَجْلِبْ عَلَيْهِم بِخَيْلِكَ وَرَجِلِكَ وَشَارِكْهُمْ فِي الْأَمْوَالِ وَالْأَوْلَادِ وَعِدْهُمْ ۚ وَمَا يَعِدُهُمُ الشَّيْطَانُ إِلَّا غُرُورًا

Instigate whomever of them you can with your voice; and rally against them your cavalry and your infantry, and share with them in wealth and children, and make promises to them!' But Satan promises them nothing but delusion..

[Qur'an, 17:64]

It appears as if Satan was ready to accept his post of misguidance, for we find him saying:

فَبِمَا أَغْوَيْتَنِي لَأَقْعُدَنَّ لَهُمْ صِرَاطَكَ الْمُسْتَقِيمَ ﴿١٦﴾ ثُمَّ لَآتِيَنَّهُم مِّن بَيْنِ أَيْدِيهِمْ وَمِنْ خَلْفِهِمْ وَعَنْ
أَيْمَانِهِمْ وَعَن شَمَائِلِهِمْ ۖ وَلَا تَجِدُ أَكْثَرَهُمْ شَاكِرِينَ

As You have consigned me to perversity 'I will surely lie in wait for them on Your straight path... Then I will come at them from their front and from their rear, and from their right and their left, and You will not find most of them to be grateful.

[Qur'an, 7:16-17]

For certain, the meaning of "misguidance" and the scope of Satan's influence and authority in his position is just as we have already mentioned. That is to say, there is no obligation or coercion in the works. All that there is, is *waswasah* (whispering or temptation), *taswil* (seduction or enticement), *da'wah* (invitation), and *tazayyun* (to make to seem beautiful and a part of decorum).

A word of caution and necessary reminder is in order here. In saying that Satan does not have recourse to the existential and ontological level of the world, we do not mean that he has no role whatsoever on this plane. For is it even possible for there to be an existent existing on this plane and not having any effects or role in it?! What we do mean though, is that Satan is not an independent creator of any part of creation; he is not an antipode to God; he does not have any part to play in the vertical hierarchy of existence like the angels who have been given executive and managerial duties with respect to created beings; and finally, his authority and command over man is not of such a level and extent that he could force or coerce him to do his bidding. The Qur'an believes in an existential role for Satan and jinn, but generally not any greater than the role of man.

The real intention behind this discussion is to show that the Qur'an has approached the question and issue of Satan[25] in such a manner that it does

---

[25] See Endnote 17

not harm its basic principles in the least bit. For instance, the principle of the unity of the Divine Essence, as exemplified in the verse:

لَيْسَ كَمِثْلِهِ شَيْءٌ

Nothing is like Him

[Qur'an, 42:11]

Or the principle of the unity of Divine creation, as in the verses:

لَيْسَ كَمِثْلِهِ شَيْءٌ

Look! All creation and command belong to Him.

[Qur'an, 7:54]

قُلِ اللَّـهُ خَالِقُ كُلِّ شَيْءٍ

Say, 'Allah is the creator of all things,

[Qur'an, 13:16]

وَلَمْ يَكُن لَّهُ شَرِيكٌ فِي الْمُلْكِ

nor has He any partner in sovereignty

[Qur'an, 17:111]

Philosophical Pessimism

Another consequence of the issue of evil is the philosophy of pessimism. Pessimistic philosophers usually come from a materialist background. That there is a causal link between materialism and the philosophy of pessimism cannot be denied. Why? Clearly, it is because materialism is impotent and helpless when it comes to the problem of evil.

According to the perspective of transcendental philosophy, existence is equal to the good and evil is relative. From this point of view, underlying every apparent evil is a good. For the materialist school, there is no such thing.

A pessimistic outlook on the world brings with it distress and suffering. It is a source of sorrow that a man should think that the world is without feeling, sentiment, and purpose. Once a man, who sees himself as a small insignificant issue and child of the world and has a goal in life, understands that the very world which created him and his thoughts and which taught him to have a goal, itself doesn't have a purpose, he is shaken to core. Moreover, if a man, who thinks that there is no justice in the world and that discrimination and oppression exist in nature, were to be given all the blessings and treasures that the world has to offer, he would still be pessimistic and unhappy.

The efforts of such a person for his personal happiness and for the prosperity of mankind are marred by a sense of hopelessness and heavy heartedness. For, if the world itself is based on injustice and oppression, man's struggles for justice become meaningless. And when the cosmos is without purpose, our having a goal and purpose is both inconsequential and idiotic.

The fact that believers and people of faith have calm demeanours and peace of mind is due to their perception of the world as an ordered and purposeful whole based on wisdom and knowledge. They do not see it as being senseless, chaotic, and without purpose. They firmly believe in its justice-that it supports the cause of truth and the people of the truth; they don't see it as being intrinsically unjust and either supporting the oppressors or remaining neutral on the issue. With regard to evil and the bad things that take place in the world, the monotheists know that nothing is by accident and chance and that there is a rhyme and reason to everything. They believe that these bad things are either just punishments or purposeful tests that lead to rewards.

What about those that don't have faith? What placates them? They turn to suicide [as their final placebo]. As one of them put it, they "embrace death with ultimate bravery."

The World Health Organization recently published some statistics on suicide and found that its incidence was on the rise among intellectuals. According to their report, the suicide rate has reached high proportions in eight European countries. One of these eight countries happens to be Switzerland-a nation that we think to be the example of prosperity. The report goes on to say that suicide has become the third most important factor of death-meaning that its casualties outnumber the victims of cancer-and that its incidence among the educated class is greater than in the uneducated.

The same report states that the suicide rate is greater in developing nations [then the underdeveloped]-the very nations that are currently going through a crisis of faith. In West Germany, twelve thousand people lose their lives annually due to suicide, while sixty thousand are saved while attempting it.

This is the state of affairs of those who have lost their faith in God, the all-knowing Lord of the worlds.

Many factors or causes for the phenomena of suicide have been mentioned: attracting attention, breakup of lovers, defeat in financial rivalries, losing social standing or competitions, poverty, drug addiction, feeling smothered, and nihilistic attitudes. These have been mentioned as causes, but the cause of these causes is just one thing: lack of faith. William James in the second chapter of his book *The Varieties of Religious Experience-A Study in Human Nature*[26]. has this to say about a materialist author, Marcus Aurelius, and also about Schopenhauer and Nietzsche:

"... melancholy, according to our ordinary use of language, forfeits all title to be called religious when, in Marcus Aurelius's racy words, the sufferer simply lies kicking and screaming after the fashion of a sacrificed pig. The mood of a Schopenhauer or a Nietzsche ... though often an ennobling sadness, is almost as often only peevishness running away with the bit between its teeth. The sallies of the two German authors remind one, half the time, of the sick shriekings of two dying rats. They lack the purgatorial note which religious sadness gives forth.[27]

Nietzsche,[28] whom William James counts among the philosophers of pessimism, was famous for his philosophy based on might-or the "will to power". He is known for claiming the following:

---

[26] This book is the text of William James' lectures which he gave at the prestigious Gifford lectures on natural religion at the University of Edinburgh at the turn of the twentieth century and was translated into Farsi under the title, *Din wa Rawan*.

[27] William James, *The Varieties of Religious Experience – A study in Human Nature*, Lecture 2.

[28] See Endnote 18

'Kindness and tender-heartedness must be put aside. Kindness is from weakness. Humility and obedience are debasement. Patience, forbearance, forgiveness, and sufferance is due to a lack of ambition and laziness ... killing the [carnal] self, for what? The self must be encouraged. What is worshiping others for? One must will the self and must worship the self. The weak and feeble must be left to die ...' [29]

By adhering to such ideas, Nietzsche had effectively turned the world into a jailhouse for himself. In the latter part of his life he saw these sentiments bear their just fruits. In a letter that he wrote to his sister during his final days, he says:

'Every day that passes bears heavily on me. Though I have been ill for many years and have experienced the extreme limits of depression and affliction, I have never been so desolate and hopeless as I am now. What has happened? Exactly what should have happened. The differences that I had with all and sundry has made me lose their trust. Now we both sides see that we were in error. God how lonely I am! There is nobody with whom I can have a laugh and a cup of tea. There is no one who will admit to be my friend.'[30]

Schopenhauer[31], whom William James also mentions, believed:

The principle motif of human life is suffering and vulnerability. Pleasure and happiness, and indeed the avoidance of pain, are not positive but rather negative realities. The higher a living existent is in the hierarchy of life, the more it suffers. This is due to its greater sensitivity and the fact that it remembers the pains of yesterday and better predicts the sufferings of tomorrow ... momentary pleasures are followed by a life of sorrows. If you don't marry you suffer, if you do you have a thousand woes. One of the biggest tribulations is falling in love. People think that procuring a wife is one of the greatest delights, whereas in reality it is source of many miseries. If you socialize you are beset with troubles, if you remain aloof from people you come to loath life. No longer any need to worship, no divinities in the works. In short, while there remains any life in the body, there is no release from suffering and difficulties. Life is through and through just dying. Rather, life is just a death that is being

---

[29] Muhammad Ali Farughi, *Sayr e Hikmat dar Urupa* (The story of philosophy in Europe) (Tehran: Kitabfurushi e Zawwar Publications, 1966), vil. 3, ch. 5, p.201-202.

[30] Furughi, vol. 3, ch.5, p. 205

[31] See Endnote 19

postponed moment to moment. In the end death occurs while life is seen to have been of no use whatsoever.[32]

The Islamic world also had, and has, figures that saw the world as gloomy. Their reactions vis-a-vis nature and natural phenomena were characterized by sullenness, gloom, and even anger-or in the words of William James by "peevishness." The famous Arab philosopher and poet Abu al-'Ala' al-Ma'arri, as well as the poet Khayyam belonged to this group. We say, "the poet Khayyam" here because scholars do not believe that the pessimistic poems could have been written by Khayyam the philosopher and mathematician. This is because the reasons for complaining and crying that Khayyam the poet espouses, are matters that Khayyam the philosopher would have already solved and put behind him.[33]

In our time and following in the footsteps of the West (and for other reasons not appropriate to mention here) a group of pessimistic writers has appeared that is poisoning the youth and making them apathetic and indifferent to life, and sometimes even leading them towards suicide. This group is being encouraged and ushered on by overt and covert powers. Their numbers are increasing daily. Sadiq Hidayat belongs to this group. His writings bear resemblance to-as in the words of William James-the "kicking and screaming ... a sacrificed pig", or the "sick shriekings of ... dying rats." In stark contrast to figures such as Nietzsche, Schopenhauer, Abu al-'Ala', and Khayyam, are the "optimistic" philosophers and sages. The sages of the Divinities are usually from this latter group. The great mystic Mawlana Rumi is the representative, par excellence, of this group. All of his utterances give evidence to an incredible love, rapture, and spiritual presence. According to this mystic, man is the thriving centre of pleasure and felicity in this world, but with this condition that he consciously takes advantage of this centre. For, there is no sorrow in the world that cannot be converted into a beatitude or pleasure. Rumi disparages those who seek to derive pleasure exclusively from wine, women, and song. He addresses man in these terms.[34]

---

[32] Furughi, vol. 3, ch.1, pt. 4, p. 85
[33] See Endnote 20
[34] See Endnote 21

The wine that is bubbling invisibly in the jar bubbles thus from longing for thy face.

O thou who art the whole sea, what wilt thou do with dew?

And O thou who art the whole of existence, why art thou seeking non-existence?

Thou art lovely and beautiful and the mine (source) of every loveliness: why indeed shouldst thou lay thyself under obligations to wine?

The tiara of *We have honoured (the sons of Adam)* is on the crown of thy head; the collar of *We have given thee* hangs on thy breast.

Thou seekest knowledge from books-s-oh, ridiculous! Thou seekest pleasure from *Halwa* (sweetmeats)-oh, ridiculous!

What is wine or music or sexual intercourse that thou shouldst seek delight and profit therefrom?

('Tis as though) the sun sought to borrow (light) from a mote, (or) a *Zuhra* begged for a cup (of wine) from a small jar.[35]

Rumi also says:[36]

I am exceedingly enamoured of His violence and his gentleness

'tis marvelous (that) I (am) in love with both these contraries.[37]

The other mystical poets such as Sa'di and Hafiz also take this route. It is true that words with double meanings are found in the poems of Hafiz and others, but those who are familiar with their parlance and idioms know full well that there is nothing other than goodness in their ideas.

Now all this is not limited to mysticism (*irfan*) and Sufism. This way of seeing things is a feature of faith in general. Disbelief and faithlessness are types of deficiency which in its own turn brings about an imbalance. It is this imbalance that creates suffering. Faith on the other hand, has this ability to transform sorrows and suffering into pleasure and happiness.

---

[35] Nicholson, vol. 5, p. 214, vrs. 3570-1, 3573-74, 3578,3580-1.
[36] See Endnote 22
[37] Nicholson, vol. 1, p. 86, vr. 1570

When those who have been nurtured by Islam come across a difficulty or a calamity, they pay attention to the following truth:

الَّذِينَ إِذَا أَصَابَتْهُم مُّصِيبَةٌ قَالُوا إِنَّا لِلَّهِ وَإِنَّا إِلَيْهِ رَاجِعُونَ

those who, when an affliction visits them, say, 'Indeed we belong to Allah and to Him do we indeed return.

[Qur'an, 2:156]

As a real-life example of what such nurturing can do, we will quote an incident that took place to a Muslim couple-Abu Talhah and his wife Umm Salim-who were companions of the Prophet (s).[38]

Abu Talhah loved his son very much. His son fell ill. When the child's death was imminent, Umm Salim feared that Abu Talhah would be greatly troubled and anguished [by the death of their son], so she sent him off to the Prophet (s). When Abu Talhah had left the house, the child died and Umm Salim shrouded him with a cloth and put him away in some corner of the house. She then approached the house members and told them to not tell Abu Talhah anything [of what took place]. Then she prepared a meal and put on some perfume. Just then Abu Talhah returned from his visit to the Prophet (s). He asked, "What's my son doing?" She replied, "He's resting." He said, "Do we have something to eat?" She got up and brought the food for him. Then, [a while later] she made advances to him and he lay with her. Once he was assuaged, she said to him, "Abu Talhah, would you be angry if we had somebody's belonging with us for safekeeping and we returned it to him?" He said, "Glory be to God, no, not at all." She said, "Your son was a trust with us that God has taken back." Abu Talhah said, "I have a greater obligation to be patient than you." He got up from his place, performed his ghusl (ritual bath), prayed two cycles (rake 'j, and then went off to see the Prophet (s). He informed him of what she did. The Prophet (s) said to him, "May God bless you both in your [fruitful] coition." Then the Prophet (s) said, "Praise

---

[38] See Endnote 23

be to God who has placed in my nation a person like Sabira of the Sons of Israel...."[39]

These then are the workings of faith and religion in the smoothing of difficulties and hardships, and even in transforming them into pleasures and felicities.

William James, in the book that was previously mentioned, writes about the different sects and groups of religion and pure morality in the following way:

'At bottom the whole concern of both morality and religion is with the manner of our acceptance of the universe. Do we accept it only in part and grudgingly, or heartily and altogether? ... Morality pure and simple accepts the law of the whole which it finds reigning, so far as to acknowledge and obey it, but it may obey it with the heaviest and coldest heart, and never cease to feel it as a yoke. But for religion, in its strong and fully developed manifestations, the service of the highest never is felt as a yoke. Dull submission is left far behind, and a mood of welcome, which may fill any place on the scale between cheerful serenity and enthusiastic gladness, has taken its place .... The *anima mundi*, to whose disposal of his own personal destiny the Stoic consents, is there to be respected and submitted to, but the Christian God is there to be loved; and the difference of emotional atmosphere is like that between an arctic climate and the tropics, though the outcome in the way of accepting actual conditions uncomplainingly may seem in abstract terms to be much the same.' [40]

Coyness or Objection?

Discussions on the problem of evil, and sometimes objections to the very existence of evil, take up an important part of our literature. Poets in particular, whether in jest or in all seriousness, frequently apply themselves to this subject. But of course, that which has been said on this topic must be taken with a pinch of salt-as it is not all a serious objection and complaint against creation, and there is usually a tongue in cheek

---

[39] Majlisi, *Bihar al-Anwar*, vol. 79, p. 151
[40] William James, *The Varieties of Religious Experience—A Study in Human Nature*, Lecture 2.

attitude at play. Some poems contain what may be called the "dissimulation of mystics." Many quatrains attributed to Khayyam are of this type. To repeat, it is not known for certain whether these poems are the work of Khayyam the philosopher. All that which has been brought under questioning and objected to in the poems of Khayyam the poet, are things that Khayyam the philosopher would have already solved and put behind him. Hence these poems are either not from the pen of Khayyam the philosopher, or they are and must be considered as either tongue in cheek and satirical jabs at exoteric religious puritans, or as the dissimulations and "coquetry" known to exist among the mystics. In any case, Khayyam says in the quatrains attributed to him'.[41]

> The stars, who dwell on heaven's exalted stage,
> Baffle the wise Diviners of our age;
> Take heed, hold fast the rope of mother wit.
> These augurs all distrust their own presage.[42]

> Heaven multiplies our sorrows day by day,
> And grants no joys it does not take away;
> If those unborn could know the ills we bear,
> What think you, would they rather come or stay?[43]

> Since all man's business in this world of woe
> Is sorrow's pangs to feel, and grief to know,
> Happy are they that never come at all,
> And they that, having come, the soonest go![44]

> Ah! wheel of heaven to tyranny inclined, '
> It was e'er your wont to show yourself unkind;
> And, cruel earth, if they should cleave your breast,
> What store of buried jewels they would find![45]

---

[41] See Endnote 24

[42] Edward Henry Whinfield, trans, *The Quatrains of Omar Khayyam. The Persian Text with an English Verse Translation* (London: The Octagon Press, 1980), first published 1883, quatrain 214.

[43] *Ibid*, quatrain 240

[44] *Ibid*, quatrain 387

[45] *Ibid*, quatrain 25

This objection to and censure of the heavens that be, is in fact a criticism of something higher. This is because the astrological heavens are not anything in themselves for them to be possibly accused of wickedness or delinquency. This is perhaps why it is said in a tradition:

قال رسول الله(ص): لا تسبّوا الدّهر فإنّ الدّهر هو الله

Do not curse Time, for surely Time is God Himself.[46, 47]

Khayyam also says:[48]

The Master did himself these vessels frame,
Why should he cast them out to scorn and shame?
If he has made them well, why should he break them?
Yea, though he marred them, they are not to blame.[49]

Behold these cups! Can He who deigned to make them,
In wanton freak let ruin overtake them,
So many shapely feet and hands and heads
What love drives Him to make, what wrath to break them?[50]

There is a chalice made with wit profound,
With tokens of the Maker's favor crowned;
Yet the world's Potter takes his masterpiece,
And dashes it to pieces on the ground![51]

Nasir Khusraw[52] is a poet who should in reality be called a philosopher. He was on one hand, intellectually meticulous and philosophically beyond such diatribes, and on the other hand, his strong religious convictions did not allow him to complain about Providence. This said, we do find couplets in his Diwan which are of this type. We can put this down to either tongue and cheek humour, or to the

---

[46] Taj al-Din Sha'iri, *Jami' al-Akhbar* (Qum: Radi Publications, 1984), p.161
[47] See Endnote 25
[48] See Endnote 26
[49] Whinfield, quatrain 126.
[50] *Ibid*, quatrain 42
[51] *Ibid*, quatrain 290.
[52] See Endnote 27

dissimulation current among mystics. As examples of this we can quote some verses.[53]

O God, if by your Divine mandate you made the substance of man beautiful all,

What then in the Roman countenance and African face, is the reason for beauty and ugliness? Why the Indian appearance and the Turkish countenance-one [dark as] the depths of hell and the other, the face of heaven?

Why is one felicitous, the other a wretch--one an ascetic, the other a priest enrobed?

Why these contrasts in creation-for You were the mother and embellisher of all?

Accepted then, due the world's disloyalty, a group you exalted, and another made abject,

Why still, are the affluent given loads and loads, And the poor have nothing but troubles and troubles?

Nasir Khusraw has a lengthy and famous poem which starts with the following couplet:

توانی در دل موری کشیدن   الهی طول و عرض عالمت را

In this poem he says.[54]

All my pains are from the Bulgarian [beauties], what endless longing must be endured.

It is not the fault of the Bulgarians, I will tell all, if you could only listen.

O God, to tell the truth, sedition is from You, but I speak not out of fear.

The elegant lips and teeth of the Turks of upper China, You should not have made so fine;

---

[53] See Endnote 28
[54] See Endnote 29

Because upon [seeing] their hands, lips, and teeth--one bites [his]
teeth, hands, and lips [in astonishment] .

By clamour you put the deer to flight; while the hound you strike
[and incite] to [take up the] chase.

Some experts in the field have claimed that this poem has been
changed, and that it is not the work of Nasir Khusraw.

About forty years ago, a poet from Shiraz wrote a ballad on this
subject. In response to this ballad, Sarhang Akhgar wrote an open letter
in *Akhgar* magazine, inviting the literati to give their opinions on the
poem. Many people-clergymen, lay people, men, and women-from all
parts of the country wrote back with their replies. Some of these replies
were in verse and some in prose; some of them were in support of the
Shirazi balladeer and some against. All of these letters were collected and
published in a book with the title, *Asrar e Khilqat* (Secrets of Creation).

As to the worth and importance of these replies-this is a topic which I
don't want to get into at present. It must be noted though that some
scholars made noteworthy points in their letters.

Problem Solved

Islamic Philosophy

The issue of the best world order, or order from design, as well as the problem of evil, are some of the most important philosophical questions extant. As was shown in the previous section, this issue led to the appearance of such ideologies as dualism, materialism, and pessimism in both the east and the west. Few indeed are those who have not made comments on this issue and given it their due attention. Philosophers of both the east and west have considered the problem of evil but, to the extent of my knowledge, western philosophers have not found a conclusive solution to this problem. The philosophers and sages of Islam, on the other hand, have analyzed this issue in detail and have met the challenge that it poses in an admirable fashion-unravelling an important enigma in the process.

It would not be out of place if at this point, and by way of appreciation, we said some words on the transcendental philosophy of the east. This sacred wisdom, hailing from eastern lands, is a great blessing and boon that has blossomed by virtue of the advent of Islam and has been given to humanity as a precious gift. But unfortunately, only a handful fully and deeply understands this rich body of knowledge and it is for the most part promulgated by those ignorant of it and by its avowed enemies. A group of those who lack sufficient understanding of traditional philosophy and who do not know much more than the theory of the "nine heavenly spheres," and the "ten intellects," judge texts of Islamic philosophy by this grossly imperfect measure. Upon glancing through such a text, if they do not understand anything in it, they conclude that Islamic philosophy is not anything in excess of the nine spheres or ten intellects and because this cosmology has been "proven" wrong today, they have the right to hold their head high and consider themselves to be higher than Farabi,[1] Ibn Sina, or Mulla Sadra, This group imagines that Islamic philosophy is just the same thing as Hellenic philosophy and does

---

[1] See Endnote 30

not have anything extra to offer. Moreover, they add that this Greek tradition was illegitimately brought into Islam.

Knowingly or unknowingly, this group has done a great disservice to Islam and Islamic teachings. Islamic philosophy differs from Greek philosophy to the same degree that the physics of Einstein differs from the physics of Antiquity. There is evidence to support the argument that even the theology of Ibn Sina has not been fully transferred to the west and that westerners are still uninformed with regards to it. The following is an example of this assertion.

In the footnotes of the second volume of *Principles of Philosophy and the Method of Realism* we mention the fact that the Cartesian[2] maxim, "I think, therefore I am," which is taken to be a brilliant innovation and valuable contribution to philosophy in the west, is an insubstantial and senseless idea that Ibn Sina explicitly and formally invalidated in the third section of his *Isharat*. If the Avicennian corpus had been correctly translated and transferred to Europe, this saying of Descartes would not have been heralded as an "innovation" and "new idea" and would not have gone on to become the basis for a new philosophy. But what are we to do in a world where, for now, everything that is labelled as European or western is warmly received, even if it be an old and worn out idea which we have left behind many years ago?'

Now we will turn our attention to the questions that were posed in the preceding section. We will answer those questions under four different headings: Discrimination, Annihilation and Non-existence, Imperfection and Defectiveness. From these four, the first one will be discussed in the following section on Discrimination. The remaining three will be addressed in the section on Evil. We feel that it is necessary to briefly go over the various methodologies and approaches that have been used to answer the questions and objections at hand.

Methods and Approaches

There are various methods and approaches to Divine justice. Believers who have faith in God and religion usually satisfy their conscience in this regard by giving a general answer to the problem. They think like this: Definitive proofs have been given for the existence of a wise and all-

---

[2] See Endnote 31

knowing God, hence there is no reason for such a wise and omniscient God to do injustice. Why should He? Does He have any enmity with anyone that He should, out of animosity, want to deprive him of his rights? Or does He have need of something, so that he would want to deny someone of their rights and take them for Himself? The inclination to oppress is either due to a psychological complex, or it is due to certain needs and wants. As such an inclination does not exist in the case of God, oppression or injustice has no meaning for Him. God is omnipotent, omniscient, and all-wise-He knows the best possible order and design for the world and has the ability to create it. So, there is no reason for God to make the world other than with the best order and design. Surely, those things which are called bad or evil-as they are opposed to this best order-would not be created. Even if this group sees things which they cannot explain away, they put it down as some type of wisdom and expediency-something which is hidden from them and which only God knows the secret of. In other words, they see it as a part of the secret of destiny [and the mystery of creation].

No doubt this type of thinking and deduction is in itself a type of proof, and a correct one at that. The people who think like this can argue that even if some evils are unexplainable, it is due to the weakness of the human mind in understanding the secrets of the universe. When man sees himself in a world full of mysteries and hidden reasons, he must not doubt the basic facts, even if he cannot decipher a particular incident and see the wisdom behind it.

Let's assume that a person reads a book that throughout shows the mental acumen and meticulousness of the writer. If he comes across a couple of passages in this book that are ambiguous or inexplicable, he naturally thinks that, "I don't understand what the writer meant in these few cases." He in no way thinks that, "Just because I could not understand the meanings in these cases, the author is careless and lacks a proper intellect and that all those places which made sense came about accidentally." It would be a very selfish and ignorant thing to do if somebody were to say that because of a few ambiguous parts of a book, that otherwise is stock full of evidence of the erudition of its author, the writer is ignorant or that the wisdom that the book contains is entirely fortuitous.

Whenever the average believer comes across such issues, he solves them for himself in the manner suggested above.

As was previously seen, the Traditionalists are exoteric pietists who choose to remain silent in the face of such questions and refrain from giving their opinions. But in reality their [personal] way of solving these issues is the way of the average believer and majority. The Ash'arite theologians have taken a route that avoids the question altogether-meaning that the question doesn't even arise for them. But as for the rest of the theologians, and also for those who favour an empirical approach to theology, the resolution to the problems involved in the doctrine of Divine justice lies in researching the secrets, uses, and expedients of existents.

The philosophers approach the problem in an *ilmmi* way that is to say they proceed from the cause to its effect attempting to formalize the above-mentioned solution of the average believer. They argue that the world is an effect of God. It is effectively a "shadow" of God who is all-beauty. The shadow of the beautiful must naturally also be beautiful. They also argue that evil, in its essence, is non-existing and is accidental. They go on to speak of the necessity of evil and the fact that it can never be separated from good-or in other words, the fact that creation can not be divided and partitioned off into segments. Finally, they discuss the effects and uses of evil.

We will not examine in detail the philosophical proof (from causes to effects) here as it is beyond the level and scope of this present study, but we will discuss some other pertinent areas.

As we have previously stated, the questions and objections surrounding the subject at hand will be covered under two general headings: Discrimination and Evil. We will first turn our attention to the discussion on Discrimination and then will go on to analyze the subject of Evil in a separate section.

Discrimination

The objection of discrimination was that if created beings have an equal relationship to the Divine Essence, why then have they been created with differences and distinction? Why is one black and another white? One ugly and the other beautiful? One perfect and the other defective? Why is one an angel, another a human, a third an animal, a fourth a plant and a fifth inanimate? Why was it not the other way around? Why did the animal not become an angel and the angel an animal? Why among the created beings was only man created as man with the capacity for accepting responsibility, reward and punishment but other creatures were not? If it is good, then why aren't all created like this? And if it is bad then why have only humans been created thus?

The answer to this question is possible on two levels: brief and detailed. The brief response is what was pointed out earlier in the discussion on schools of theology. We said there that usually believers satisfy themselves with a brief explanation. Their argument is: These questions are only posing some unknown issues, not presenting fundamental contradictions. The most we can say in these cases is that we don't know the answer.

We have recognised God with attributes like Omniscient, All-Wise, Independent, Perfect, Just, Generous; and since we have known Him with these attributes, we are certain that whatever happens is according to some 'wisdom' and 'purpose', though we may not be able to comprehend all those wisdoms and higher purposes. We are not privy to the so called 'secret of destiny'. It would be very selfish and boastful for man whose collective efforts for several millennia has not yet enabled him to fully understand all the secrets of his own physical body, to now aspire to understand the 'mystery of creation' and the 'secret of destiny'. When man witnesses all this mind-boggling wisdom and design in creation, he ought to confess that his failure to appreciate the wisdom of one issue is based, not on some defect in creation, but rather, on his own shortcoming and inability.

This group never engages itself in such questions and reasoning; instead of spending time on such issues they would rather spend it in research on issues which they can understand and which have some practical implications.

There is no doubt that this response is correct; believers are not required to delve into the depths of these issues; the laity does not even have the capacity to engage in these discussions; in fact, they have been prohibited from engaging in such discussions. In fact, this argument is a type of reasoning whereby we are convinced of an effect's perfection through the perfection of its cause.

But there is another issue here. The majority of people recognize God through His effects, i.e. through the design in the Universe. Such a comprehension will turn out to be a defective comprehension. Obviously when they come across unknowns in their basis of comprehension they will be more or less uneasy, and there is no way to solve their problem except by responding to the objection. They have not recognized God independently of the world and created order, such that their belief in God as the absolute, all-perfect, independent, and infinitely beautiful being or cause would imply the most beautiful creation as an effect. They have only one means of access to the universe, this being the ordinary one through the physical senses. They see God as reflected in the image of the universe; obviously any defect visible in the mirror would affect their view of the image; if they had the capacity to view the universe as a reflection of God, or in other words, if they could view the universe from above, then all the defects and ugliness seen below would disappear, as it would be clear that all of it is due to a faulty perception. This type of view is the one which we said has been termed by Hafiz as "*nazar e pir tariqat*."[1]

Said our *Pir*: "On the Creator's pen, passed no error:
On his pure sight, error-covering, plaudits be!"[2]

Those people whose basis of perception is confined to the world and created order, know God and His being All-Wise, Omniscient, All-Just, Independent and Perfect, through the image they see reflected only in that

---

[1] See Endnote 32
[2] Henry Wilberforce Clarke, trans, *Ghazals of Hafez Shirazi in Persian with English Translation*, Ghazal 105.

88

world; hence any unknowns or ambiguities they come across in the universe will show up as defects in this image, preventing the perception of a proper image and honest reflection.

On the other hand, in our times, such objections and questions are frequently posed, particularly in the discussions and writings of those inclined toward materialism. I frequently encounter people who pose such questions. Such people are either those who basically do not believe in God at all, or those who have not been given arguments strong enough to satisfy them of that there is a greater wisdom and higher purpose at play. Hence it is essential that we discuss some issues pertaining to the root of this question in order to solve this problem.

Another issue is that there is an important objection regarding the argument from wisdom and purpose which is seldom raised, and if it is not addressed, then even the aforementioned brief explanation will lose its value. The response to this objection depends on us laying down the foundations of a fundamental principle-which will also prove to be the basis of the future detailed response and which most Divine sages and philosophers use in answering the question at hand. It is based on this principle alone that we will be able to give value both to the brief response and the future detailed response. The objection is this:

Can the concept of 'wisdom' and 'higher purpose' essentially have any relevant meaning in God's case? Can one say that God has done so and so work for so and so higher purpose or that the wisdom behind a given Divine act is so and so? Is it not that such concepts about God stem from the comparison of God to His creation?

Someone can possibly claim that essentially 'higher purpose' and 'wisdom' has no relevance and meaningful application to God, and all this has come from comparing the Creator to His creation. This is because the meaning of a higher purpose dictates 'so and so' is that in order to reach a particular goal one ought to use a particular means. This implies that the selection of a particular means is expedient since it enables one to reach the goal, and that the selection of means other than the particular one is not expedient since it will keep one from the goal. For instance, we say expedience dictates that there should be pain and suffering so that pleasure becomes meaningful and relevant; or wisdom requires that a mother ought to have breasts so that a newborn can have access to readymade food; wisdom and expedience dictates that a particular animal ought to have horns in order to defend itself from a predator's attack. Cannot one say that all these are simply comparing God to man and other imperfect creatures?

Wisdom and experience have relevance and meaning for man and every other imperfect creature, since man or any other imperfect creature is located in a system which is, after all, a system comprised of a series of causes and effects. That creature, in order to achieve an effect, has no option but to seek the help of a cause. When such a creature aspires to reach a goal, if it selects as a means the same thing which is actually a cause for that goal in the creative realm, then it has performed an act according to wisdom and expediency. Otherwise it has acted contrary to wisdom and expediency.

Wisdom and expediency then, apply to a creature who is part of the existing order and whose abilities are limited, and has no option but to recognize and work within the limits of the world around it. Hence, the limitation in power and ability forms an integral part of the idea of wisdom and expediency.

But a Being who is above this order and who is the Creator of the order-what relevance or application can the concepts of wisdom and expediency possibly have for Him? What need does He have to seek the help of specific causes in order to reach a particular goal, such that we may designate a particular act of His as corresponding to wisdom and another act of His as devoid of wisdom? Hence, it is incorrect to say that God, for instance, created pain and suffering so that pleasure assumes relevance and meaning; that He created mother's breasts so that a child should not remain without nutrition. God has the power to satiate the child without it ever having the need for breast milk. Likewise, the Almighty has the ability to allow man the perception of pleasure without ever exposing him to pain and suffering.

Causality is of great consequence to us, but for God it is nothing more than a formality. Thus, we qualify to become wise, not God; our acts can be described as wise when they conform to the contingencies of the existent order, but not God's acts which are the very order itself. The order has not been created to conform to some other order. God is the Creator of the order which, after the fact of its creation and at a lower level, acts as a criterion for wisdom-depending on whether a created being acts in conformity with it or not.

If it is argued that God has decreed the world to be organized according to causes and effects, means and ends, so as to display His knowledge and wisdom to His creatures, whereby they could gain knowledge about Him (since if the world were to have no design and order, that is, if it were to be haphazard and accidental such that any cause could produce any effect, then there would have been no way of knowing God); the response is that this matter itself- *i.e.* the creatures' knowledge being dependent on the study of the orderly design of the universe-implies that a definite and necessary order governs the universe. Whereas based on the aforementioned principle, to seek help of causes to reach one's goals is the predicament of creatures not the Creator; for God, it is possible to create some knowledge for His creatures without employing these means.

Based on the above explanation, an objection can be possibly raised against the argument of one who explains discrimination and evil based on Divine wisdom and expediency. The objection is: discrimination and evil cannot be justified based on Divine wisdom and expediency, since God could have created all the benefits and advantages which discrimination and evil have without seeking recourse to such discomforting means.

This is the great objection which must be addressed beforehand so that we can then discuss the issue of wisdom and expediency in response to the objection.

Is the Order in the Universe Inherent?

Now we will address the main answer. The main task is to understand the order of the universe. Is the universe's order an artificial one or is it essential? What is the meaning of creation from this perspective? Does it mean that God creates a set of things and events such that there is no real inherent relationship between them, then He arranges them in a particular order and from this arrangement there emerges an order and pattern, means and ends, cause and effect? Or does it mean that the relationships between causes and effects, and the connection between means and ends, and the interdependence between preliminaries and their results is such that the placement of every effect and consequence after its specific cause and reason, the entailment of every end through its specific means and the appearance of every result after its specific preliminary is its actual existence; in philosophical terms: "the level and state of every existence in the vertical and horizontal hierarchy of being is inherent to the essence of that existence". This is similar to the levels and states of numbers. For instance:

In numbers we see number one is before number two, and number two is before number three, and after number one; likewise, every number other than number one is after the preceding number and before the succeeding number. Every number occupies a specific grade or level, and in that level, it has specific effects and rules. The totality of numbers, which are unlimited by any limit, create a system or order.

What is the existential status of numbers? Is the existence and quiddity of a number distinct from its level and station, meaning that every number has a distinct existence and essence of its own independent of its level and station of existence, and hence has the potential for occupying any other level and station. For instance, the number five is number five in all cases and it makes no difference whether it occurs between number four and number six or between number six and number eight-meaning that which occurs between number four and number six is the number seven. Is it like this? Is it possible for any number to occur in any level or position whatsoever and still maintain its essence and quiddity? Just like humans in society who occupy posts and those social positions have no effect on their true identity and essence; their identity and essence is also unrelated to their social status; or is the reality contrary to this? Is it not the case that number five has an essence of being five, and being five for five is contiguous with its level and position, *i.e.* inseparable from its being between four and six? This would mean that the number five is not two (realities) and that the supposition of number five occurring between six and eight is equivalent to five not being five, but rather seven. That is, the supposed and imagined five is not really five, rather it is actually the number seven which occupies its own position and we, by an error in supposition, named it five. In other words, the supposition of number five to occur in the position of number seven is merely a nonsensical meaningless and illogical imagination-being no more than a figment of our imagination.

Now let's turn to the sequence of causes and effects, means and ends, preliminaries and results. Have they been created beforehand and then, in the next phase, designated to specific levels and positions? Or is their very existence contiguous with the very level and position they occupy? For instance, Sa'di occupies a specific level and position (in existence) as far as his temporal and spatial conditions are concerned. Clearly, he is temporally precedent to us. The question is, was Sa'di created then placed in those specific conditions? Or is it that Sa'di's creation is inseparable from the specific level of existence with all its accompanying conditions of space, time, level, position, etc. and that the relationships which Sa'di developed with things around him are a part and parcel of Sa'di's existence? To answer, Sa'di's existence means the existence of the totality of all those specificities. Thus, to separate Sa'di from his own time and place is to separate Sa'di from himself; that is Sa'di should not be Sa'di, rather we have assumed someone else, e.g. Jami who lived after Sa'di, to be Sa'di and have mistakenly named him as Sa'di.

Any discussion on order in the universe is an intriguing discussion and some surmise that if we hold the created order to be repaired and fixed. so that every effect occupies its specific position out of necessity, that this would be tantamount to somehow limiting God's unlimited Power. They do not realize that the issue is not the existence of something else in the universe other than existents themselves, (for such a thing must exist and it is nothing other than the order and hierarchy of being); the issue is that this order and hierarchy is inseparable from the essence of the existents, and has emanated from the absolute Being; it is the Will of the Almighty to bestow them with this order but not in the sense that with one will He creates them and with another will assigns them into a particular order, such that one could assume that if this order were to be lifted the will of their original creation would still remain intact. Since the existence of creatures is inseparable from their position in existence, the will to create them is also the will to bestow them an order, and the will to grant them order is the same as the will to grant them existence.

From this perspective, the Divine will to create anything takes shape only through the will to create the cause, and it is impossible otherwise; and the will to create the cause is through the will to create the cause of the cause, and it is impossible for it to be otherwise. In the vertical hierarchy, existents end up at an ultimate cause which is the direct result of the Divine will to create. Hence the Divine will to create any particular existent, is the very will to create everything and order.

وَمَا أَمْرُنَا إِلَّا وَاحِدَةٌ

and Our command is but a single [word]

[Qur'an, 54:50]

Thus, wisdom and expediency can apply in a meaningful way to God, the Exalted One, even though His power and Will is unlimited, and even though He is not subject to the system that He creates. The meaning of God's wisdom is that He enables creatures and everything to reach their goals and existential perfection. But in the case of human acts, wisdom means to perform an act to enable oneself reach a given goal and perfection.

As we saw, the existence of a cause and its connection and relationship to its effect is one and the same and not two entities. A duality and separation cannot be postulated into it. Thus, God's willing it means willing the specific relationship between it and its specific cause. This causal chain can be followed until it reaches a cause whereby willing that cause is equal to the relationship with the Absolute Being, and God's willing it- *i.e.*, the proximate cause-is equal to willing of everything and all relationships and all order.

A Pleasant and Lasting Memory

I recall when I was studying in Qum, I took time one day to sit and assess myself, my studies and the path that I had chosen in life. I thought to myself that instead of these studies, would it not have been better if I had taken up one of the modern disciplines? Obviously with the mentality that I had and the value I placed on faith and spiritual teachings, the first thing that came to my mind was what in that case would have happened to my spiritual and intellectual state? I thought that now I believe in the principle of Unity, Prophethood, Resurrection, Imamate, etc. and I am extremely attached to them, but if I had taken up a career in natural sciences or maths or a literary field, what would have been my state?

The answer I came up with was that the belief in these principles and basically to be a true spiritual person is not dependent on one studying the classical studies. There are many who are deprived of these studies but in practice are pious and God-fearing and sometimes even defenders and propagators of Islam and have more or less done some reading on Islamic subjects on the side. I thought that perhaps if I had studied what they had specialized in, I would have attained a firmer and more scholarly grounding in matters relating to my faith and that I would be better off than I am at present.

Those days I had just gotten familiar with Islamic philosophy and T used to study from a teacher who unlike most other claimants and teachers of this discipline was not merely well informed but had actually experienced Islam divinities and had reached the depths of the most profound teachings of Islam and also taught it in the most eloquent and sweet manner. Some of the unforgettable memories I have of those days is the joy I experienced especially from the beautiful, profound and subtle explanations of the teacher.

In those days I had just learnt this issue with its complete preliminaries; I had comprehended the famous law of *al-wahid la yasduru minhu illa al-wahid*[3] the way a true philosopher comprehends it, or so I thought. I was seeing the definite inexorable order of the universe with the eye of the intellect, and was observing all my questions and objections being melted away? I could understand there was no contradiction between this definite law that placed everything in a definite order and between the principle of *la mu'aththir fi al-wujud illa Allah*,[4] and how I could place both side by side; I could comprehend the meaning of the statement *al-fi'l filu Allah wa huwa fi'luna*[5] and I would see no contradiction between the two parts of this statement. Moreover, the issue of *amrun bayn al-amrayn*[6] was completely solved, and was immensely influenced and ecstatic by the special explanation offered by Mulla Sadra about the nature of the relationship between effect and cause and especially using this principle to prove the law of *al-wahid la yasduru minhu illa al-wahid*. In short, a fundamental paradigm was set up in my mind which became the basis to solve many issues in an ever-expanding worldview; it was the consequence of comprehending this matter and similar issues of this nature that I was convinced of the authenticity of the lofty teachings of Islam. I reached new heights with regards to the sublime teachings on Divine unity of the Qur'an, *Nahj al-Balagha*, and certain narrations and supplications of the Holy Prophet (s) and holy Infallibles of Ahl al-Bayt (a).

---

[3] See Endnote 33
[4] See Endnote 34
[5] See Endnote 35
[6] See Endnote 36

At that moment I thought that if I had not been in seminary and had not had the opportunity to enjoy the presence of such a great teacher, all my other things both materially and psychologically would have been perhaps better than what they are now, would have had all the things I have now or at least something similar to them, and perhaps even better. However, the only thing really missing would have been this paradigm of thought with the fruits and conclusions that it has produced; and even now I am of the same view.

The present discussion on Divine Justice, which was originally supposed to be presented in a simpler manner, has dragged on and we have touched on some of the higher philosophical issues that pertain to it. If we wish to travel further, we must be prepared to ascend even higher peaks, but I do not think that we have that readiness. It is better if we analyze the matter in a simpler language and at a lower level. The readers who I think will be reading this book would be better able to understand the issues with a simpler explanation.

The brief response to the objection of discrimination and evil is based on the argument that there exist a series of higher purposes for "evils" and because advantages, benefits, and profits accrue from them, their existence is not pure evil, it is rather evil mixed with goodness. Now since the goodness is greater than the evil, it is judged overall to be good, not evil. This argument is based on the principle that the causal chain is a definite and essentially necessary order, not an artificial or conventional system. To acknowledge this matter prepares the ground for the next discussion; namely, that that which actually exists is 'differences' not 'discrimination' and 'bias.'

Differentiation not Discrimination

What exists in creation is 'difference' not 'discrimination'. 'Discrimination' occurs when given equal conditions and similar potentials, a distinction is made between things. But 'differentiation is when conditions are unequal a distinction is made between things. In other words, discrimination is in the province of the agent making it while differentiation fundamentally resides within the objects being distinguished.

The matter can be illustrated with a simple example: if we place two containers, each with a ten liter capacity, under a tap and fill one with ten litres and the other with five litres of water, here we have discrimination taking place. But if we had two containers, one with a ten liter capacity and the other with a five liter capacity, and to fill them we immerse both in the ocean, again a distinction occurs, but the source of distinction is the difference in the capacities and potentials of the containers themselves and not in the ocean or the pressure of water.

Another example: If a teacher awards different grades to pupils who are all in the same class and have performed the same work, this would be discrimination; but if the teacher were to look at all pupils equally, teach all in the same manner, examine them in the same way, then some pupils due to their poor mental ability and intellectual deficiency or due to lack of hard work fail in the exams or perform poorly whereas some other pupils due to their greater potentials, and hard work, respond to the exam questions correctly and the teacher awards all according to their responses in the exams, which will necessarily be different grades, here there would not be discrimination, rather differentiation. Justice does not mean that the teacher should total all marks and divide equally among the pupils; justice means that everyone is awarded what he deserves. In such cases, to differentiate is true justice and fairness, and not to differentiate is injustice and discrimination.

If an objection is made to the effect that we cannot compare God to a teacher, as God is the Creator of all beings, and every distinction that exists emanates from Him; but a teacher is not the creator of the pupil. If one is clever and another dumb, that is not related to the teacher; if one is full of potential and worked hard whereas another lacks potential or failed to put in the necessary hard work, this has nothing to do with the teacher. In the case of God and creation we must admit that all, the differences and distinctions are actually in the hands of God. God works on two levels. On one level, He has created beings with differing potentials, and on the second level, has dealt differently with the beings of differing potentials, giving everyone according to his potential. In reality, the objection is directed at the first level, and asks why didn't He create everyone equal right from the outset? We must see what is the secret of these differences?

The Secret of Differences

The secret of differences is one statement:

"The differences between beings are innate and essential and a
necessity of the system of causes and effects"

It is a profound statement, but there is no option, it must be explained.
Here we are compelled to repeat with a different explanation what we
had said earlier, and somehow reduce the complexity of the discussion;
and in the hope of reaching a lofty and interesting conclusion we must
carry on our previous discussion and out of necessity we must become a
little philosophical.

As was pointed out earlier, in Divine philosophy, this discussion is
posed under the title "the manner in which beings emanate from the
Absolute Being". The subject of discussion is this: Does God's will
engage the creation of beings separately? For instance, He wills and
creates X; and then with a separate act of the will He creates Y, and with
a third will say, creates thing Z. In this manner, He creates everything by
a separate will specific for that being? Is it like this, or does He create
everything with one single and simple will?

A group of theologians who think superficially in matters of divinity
and theology support the first interpretation. But it is the second
interpretation which is proved by solid logical proofs, firm philosophical
reasoning, and supported by evidence from the Qur'an. According to this
interpretation, the whole universe from its beginning till the end, has been
created by a single act of Divine will. That is, infinite things come into
existence, all created by the Divine will, but not by separate wills for
every being, rather through one single act of will, that is also a simple
will. The holy Qur'an states,

إِنَّا كُلَّ شَيْءٍ خَلَقْنَاهُ بِقَدَرٍ و مَآ أَمْرُنَآ إِلَّا واحِدَةٌ كَلَمحٍ بِالبَصَرِ

Indeed We have created everything in a measure, and Our command is
but a single [word], like the twinkling of an eye.

[Qur'an, 54:49-50]

According to this view there is a specific order, hierarchy and law for
creation and that God's will for the existence of individual beings is
exactly His will for the total order. This is where the chain of causation,
or the sequence of preliminaries and results emanates from. The sequence

of causes and effects means that every effect has a specific cause and every cause has a specific effect; neither can a particular effect result and come into existence from just any cause and without any intermediary, nor can a particular cause bring into existence any effect without any intermediary. In reality, everything in the sequence of causes and effects has a specific station and known position *i.e.,* the effect is an effect of a specific thing and a cause of a specific thing; and this is the profound meaning of "Indeed We have created everything in a measure". In order to clarify this matter, we will discuss the order of the universe in two parts: the vertical order and the horizontal order.

The Vertical Order

The meaning of the vertical order or hierarchy of cause and effect is the hierarchy in the creation and existence of things. In philosophical terms, there is a hierarchy in the activity of God in relation to creation and the emanation of things from Him. The exaltedness and purity of the Divine Essence dictates that the beings are related to Him in a hierarchical way one after another; a first emanation, a second emanation, a third emanation, and likewise, one existent after another is created such that each one is the effect of the previous one. Of course, it should be realized that we do not mean first, second, third in time since time does not apply to that realm of existence, in fact, time itself is one of the created entities.

What has been mentioned in the religious language in terms of angels, Divine hosts, messengers (working in the creative realm not the legislative realm), distributors of affairs, executor of affairs, and concepts like Throne, Seat, Tablet, Pen, which refer to a series of immaterial and Divine entities related to God, are actually all a description of this same reality that God the Almighty, has willed and runs creation with a specific order and a particular hierarchy. This matter has been explained by the Divine philosophers in their specialist language and has been mentioned in the sublime teachings of Islam in a different language. We will choose the Islamic language since it is sweeter and more eloquent:

In this order and hierarchy of being, God is situated at the apex. The next level pertains to the angels who are executors of His orders. Among the angels themselves there also exists a hierarchy: some are heads and commanders while others are helpers and workers. Mika'il is the angel in-charge of provisions, 'Izra'il is the angel of death entrusted with the task of separating souls from bodies, and each of the two have myriads of supporters and helpers, each angel occupying a specific position:

وَمَا مِنَّا إِلَّا لَهُ مَقَامٌ مَّعْلُومٌ

There is none among us but has a known place.

[Qur'an, 37:164]

We should not forget that the relationship of God with creation and the created order is that of genesis, creation, and origination. We should not imagine His order and organization to be like the social systems and artificial human organizations prevalent in human societies. The system of command and obedience in the Divine scheme between God and the angels is creative and real not conventional and virtual. God's command is not a literal word, it is creation-the very act. The appropriate response of the angels to such a command is utter obedience. When we say He ordered the angels to do something, it means that He has created them such that they should be the cause and creative agent for the particular effect and act. Hence the meaning of the angels' obedience is this same creative causality and efficiency. This afore-mentioned order is a creative and ontic order.

It is thus that the holy Qur'an sometimes attributes administration of creation to God and sometime to angels; in one instance it states:

يُدَبِّرُ الْأَمْرَ مِنَ السَّمَاءِ إِلَى الْأَرْضِ

He directs the command from the heaven to the earth

[Qur'an, 32:5]

In another instance it asserts:

فَالْمُدَبِّرَاتِ أَمْرًا

by those who direct the affairs [of creatures]:

Sometimes it attributes to the angels the separation of the human souls at the time of death, sometimes to the chief angel of death, and at other times to God, the almighty. Sometimes it attributes revelation to one angel:

نَزَلَ بِهِ الرُّوحُ الْأَمِينُ ﴿١٩٣﴾ عَلَىٰ قَلْبِكَ

brought down by the Trustworthy Spirit, upon your heart

[Qur'an, 26:193-4]

and sometimes it attributes the same function to God:

إِنَّا نَحْنُ نَزَّلْنَا عَلَيْكَ الْقُرْآنَ تَنزِيلًا

Indeed, We have sent down to you the Qur'an in a gradual descent

[Qur'an, 76:23]

The secret to understanding all this is to know that God's act has an order and hierarchy and that God's will to create and govern the world is the same one which gives it that order and hierarchy.

In the scenario of the absence of any specific order between created beings many outcomes are entailed. Such a scenario entails the outcome that every being can create everything, and also entails the possibility of everything being created from everything. For instance, it should be possible for a great explosion, which requires a great amount of energy, to result from a small amount of energy. Or the opposite scenario, whereby a great amount of energy produces a disproportionately small burst. It should be possible that a flame from a small match should equal in illumination the whole sun. It should be possible for an effect to take the position of its cause and for a cause to take the position of its own effect; and based on this reasoning, it should be possible for God to be like a created being and a created being to be God.

101

The necessity of the Necessary being and the possibility of the possible being is inherent and essential to them. It is not such that the possible being could be a Necessary being and the Necessary being could be a possible being. This can never take place, either accidentally or through an external cause. The possible being is possible by necessity and the Necessary being is necessary by necessity.

The situation is similar in the case of the hierarchy between possible beings. Every state of being and level of existence that these contingent existents occupy has the same rule. For instance when one considers the being in-charge of delivering provisions to creation, or the one in-charge of returning and receiving the created beings, one comes to the conclusion that the position which has been entrusted to them is a necessary consequence of the nature and ontic level of the existence which has been bestowed on them. It is not such that, for instance, a mosquito by one decree could take up the position of Mika'il and an ant through another decree could become 'Izra'il, and a human become Jibra'il.

All these errors, that a perfect being can occupy the position of an imperfect or an imperfect can occupy the position of a perfect, stem from people who do not realize the necessity, essentiality, and inherency of relationships existing among created beings. They assume that the hierarchy between beings in creation is similar to the conventional and unreal hierarchy of human societies. All these errors spring from comparison of God to man and comparison of the inherent hierarchy of the universe to the artificial hierarchy in human society. Such people think to themselves that if there is no objection to some ruler possibly becoming ruled or a ruled one becoming a ruler, then why cannot a sheep become human or a human become sheep? Why did He make that a sheep and this a human?

They do not realize that such a thing is impossible, because the causality of a specific cause for a particular effect, and the efficiency of a specific effect related to a particular cause, is not conventional and unreal. If 'a' is a cause for 'b', it is due to a characteristic existing in the essence 'a' which qualifies it to become a cause for 'b'; and if 'b' is an effect of 'a' it is because of a characteristic existing in it which makes it dependent on 'a'. And this characteristic is nothing but their nature of existence and modality of being; and it is for this very reason, that the characteristic is a real existent entity, not something unreal, conventional, and hence transferable. Thus, the relationship of every effect to its cause and the relationship of every cause to its effect originates from the essence and nature of the cause and essence of the effect. An effect, by the totality of its essence, is dependent on the cause and the cause also, by the totality of its essence, is the source of the effect.

Based on this, as was pointed out earlier, it becomes clear that the level of every existent is inseparable from its essence and inexorable. Just like the order of numbers. In a bus queue one can move individuals forward or backward, but the position of numbers cannot be moved above or below; number five whose position is after number four, cannot possibly be positioned before it. Before number four nothing but number three can be positioned, even though we may name it number five, we would have only changed the name but it is impossible to change its reality.

Such a necessary and profound system operates between created beings. This statement of the holy Qur'an about the angels wherein it asserts:

$$\text{وَمَا مِنَّا إِلَّا لَهُ مَقَامٌ مَّعْلُومٌ}$$

There is none among us but has a known place i

[Qur'an, 37:164]

is actually applicable to every created being. Everything has a specific position, and to transpose it to a position elsewhere other than its own is tantamount to having it abandon its own essence, which is a contradiction.[7]

The Horizontal Order

In addition to the vertical system which allocates the hierarchy of beings according to creativity and activity, there is another order which governs especially the material world and which specifies the material and preliminary conditions for the existence of a phenomenon. This order is termed as the horizontal order; and it is based on this system that world history acquires a definite and specific pattern. Every event transpires in

---

[7] For details refer to the book *Usul e Falsafeh wa rawishe Realism*

a specific time and space; and every particular time and space becomes the receptacle of a specific event.

Normally when we enquire or investigate an event we focus our attention on that event alone, we do not take into account what status or position that event occupies in the created order. Whereas in fact every event, whether good or bad, is an effect of a series of specific causes and connected to particular conditions. A fire never starts without a previous and particular relationship to other factors and events. The prevention of the fire also rests on a series of other causes and factors, material or immaterial. There is no event in the universe which is 'unique' and totally 'independent' of other events; all parts of the universe are interconnected and interrelated. This connectivity and interrelation pervade all parts of the universe, and brings about a comprehensive all-encompassing unity. The principle of interrelatedness of things to each other, or in other words, the principle of true unity in the universe, "organic unity" as it were, is a principle frequently invoked by Divine philosophers. The principle of interrelatedness of things assumes a profound meaning in Divine philosophy and that is the principle of indivisibility of the universe. We will elaborate further on this principle later.

It is stated in philosophy that:

$$ كلُّ حادِثٍ مَسبوقٌ بمادةٍ ومدَّةٍ $$

i.e. every event occurs in a framework a of specific time and a specific place. Every event has a specific time and specific place. It is impossible for all times and all places to be indifferent for an event.

Our physical observations also support this fact. When a fire bums somewhere in the world, it does so in a specific time, particular place, and through a specific material. The fire is dependent on conditions which specify its time and place. The conditions themselves in turn have a specific time and place and are dependent on particular causes and factors. If we continue tracing the origins, we would reach the conclusion that the series of events is interconnected like the rings in a chain; every event is connected to an event preceding it and an event succeeding it, or in other words, everything is connected to its past and future. And this connectivity creates an eternal and endless chain of events.

More interesting is the fact that emerges on an even deeper study. We discover there is interrelatedness even between events which are parallel and contemporaneous to each other.

A carpet worker weaves a carpet and a surgeon operates on a patient. On a superficial plane there seems to be no apparent connection between these two events. But if upon taking a deeper look we found for instance that a fire had caused the burning of both the carpet and the patient, we would be convinced that both the carpet-weaver and the surgeon's work originate from a single source; a single event, which if it had not occurred, neither of these two would have become busy in their work.

The works of all humans who originated from one forefather are connected to the existence of that forefather in his own specific time and place, and as a result the works of all human beings are interconnected.

The event of the separation of the proto-planet that became the earth from the sun, is the common point of all actions and movements which occur on the face of the earth. The occurrence of that event is the cause of all subsequent events.

In philosophy there is a term named 'relative necessity' and another called 'possibility-in-relation to something'. These terms are used to describe an event in comparison to another event. If by assuming the existence of the first event the existence of the second event becomes necessary then we describe the second event to be 'relatively necessary' to the first event. But if by assuming the first event the existence or nonexistence of the second event is both equally possible then we describe the second event to be connected to the first by 'relative possibility'.

By a superficial glance at some events one may get the impression of a 'relative necessity' between them and in other cases where there seems to be less of a connection between them, one would think that a 'relative possibility' is what presides. But on deeper study we discover that between every two events there is in fact the connection of 'relative necessity', and relative possibility has no real external existence. So, because all events ultimately share one 'primary cause', and because there is a relation of necessity between every cause and its effect, we reach the conclusion that an all-pervasive necessity governs all events.

The principles based on which this necessary and universal interconnectivity can be established are as follows:

1. The principle of universal causation.

2. Necessity of cause and effect [in particular].

3. Correspondence between cause and effect [in their modalities].

4. Ultimate termination [of the causal chain] of all created beings at the Cause of all causes and the Prime Mover.

The first principle is the fundamental and axiomatic law which forms the basis of all sciences and its denial entails denial of everything and plunging into the abyss of skepticism.

The second law enunciates the fact that every effect can only come into existence when, not only its cause is existent, but also only when it attains necessity from its cause. So long as an effect does not attain necessity from its specific cause it is impossible for that effect to come into existence; and vice versa. If the complete and sufficient cause of a thing materializes, it necessitates the existence of the effect, in which case the non-existence of the effect becomes impossible.

The third principle, guarantees the specific relationship between the cause and effect, and hence no cause can create an effect other than its own specific effect; and no effect can possibly emanate from a cause other than its own specific cause.

From these three principles we can conclude that the universe has a definite unalterable order and in association with the fourth principle which is the principle of 'Unity of Origination', we can conclude the definite and universal interrelatedness and interconnectivity of all events.

In the third section under the subject of 'differences in potentials' we will give further elaboration on this issue.

Divine Precedent or Way

What is known in philosophy as 'order or design of the universe' or 'causation', is termed in religious language as the "Divine precedent". The holy Qur'an states in several places:

وَلَن تَجِدَ لِسُنَّةِ اللَّهِ تَبْدِيلًا

you will never find any change in Allah's precedent.

[Qur'an, 33:62, 48:23]

i.e. God's acts have a particular style and fixed pattern which is unalterable. In surah Fatir this theme has been repeatedly emphasised:

فَلَن تَجِدَ لِسُنَّتِ اللَّهِ تَبْدِيلًا ۖ وَلَن تَجِدَ لِسُنَّتِ اللَّهِ تَحْوِيلًا

you will never find any change in Allah's precedent, and you will never find any revision in Allah's precedent.

[Qur'an, 35:43]

(*i.e.* "Change": God's ways do not change to other ways, like a law being abrogated and replaced by another law. "Revision": like a clause being added to a man-made law, or part of it is abrogated, or changed without the original law being changed)

It is an amazing statement from an amazing book! How great is the Qur'an! Guide to scholars, companion to the pious. The philosophers thinks and meditates for years to discover the universal law of causality and order of the universe; he wants to boast and take pride in this great achievement that he has managed to discover such a great secret, and recognize such a great law when he suddenly sees the holy Qur'an in front of him stating the same secret in simple but eloquent language: **you will never find any change in God's precedent**.

Who can speak more clearly? Which statement could be firmer and more eloquent than this? **you will never find any change in God's precedent**

The holy Qur'an does not only generally expound on creation having a system and law but also in some cases specifies some of those laws.

Regarding the prosperity or misfortune of a community it states:

إِنَّ اللَّهَ لَا يُغَيِّرُ مَا بِقَوْمٍ حَتَّىٰ يُغَيِّرُوا مَا بِأَنفُسِهِمْ

Indeed Allah does not change a people's lot, unless they change what is in their souls.

[Qur'an, 13:11]

This holy verse explains the secret of progress or backwardness of a community. No people can reach prosperity from misfortune but through repelling from themselves the factors which cause misfortune, and vice-versa, a prosperous community will not be rendered backward by God except if they themselves cause their own degradation.

We complain how can God allow a group of Jews, the police of America, to dominate seven hundred million Muslims in different military, cultural, economic, and intellectual ways? Why did one hundred million Arabs face defeat in the 5th June War? Why does God not grant Muslims honour? Why doesn't He turn the natural laws in favour of the Muslims? We get angry, lose nights of sleep out of grief, we suffer pain and complain, beseech and supplicate to God, but our prayers are not answered. The response the holy Qur'an gives is one statement:

إِنَّ اللَّهَ لَا يُغَيِّرُ مَا بِقَوْمٍ حَتَّىٰ يُغَيِّرُوا مَا بِأَنْفُسِهِمْ

Indeed, Allah does not change a people's lot, unless they change what is in their souls.

[Qur'an, 13:11]

God will not change His laws. We must change ourselves. We are immersed in ignorance, swimming in moral decadence, have no unity or co-operation, but still hope God should help and support us! We will make a thousand rumours for a small incident, lying and dishonesty is our working style, we have distanced ourselves from every virtue yet expect to enjoy presiding and ruling over the world! This can never be.

According to the sacred scriptures of the past the Jewish people-who because of their sinfulness and impurity, had more prophets sent to reform them than other peoples-will undergo two social movements, two revolutions and upheavals. Both of these have occurred and the holy Qur'an mentions both the prediction and the upheavals which took place in Jewish history. The prediction mentions that they will do corruption on earth twice and God will punish them for it.

Then the Qur'an enunciates a general law. That law is that every corruption is a prelude to defeat and affliction; and every revival and traditional reform renews God's mercy. Now consider the text of the verses:

وَقَضَيْنَا إِلَى بَنِي إِسْرَائِيلَ فِي الْكِتَابِ لَتُفْسِدُنَّ فِي الْأَرْضِ مَرَّتَيْنِ وَلَتَعْلُنَّ عُلُوًّا كَبِيرًا ﴿٤﴾ فَإِذَا جَاءَ وَعْدُ أُولَاهُمَا بَعَثْنَا عَلَيْكُمْ عِبَادًا لَنَا أُولِي بَأْسٍ شَدِيدٍ فَجَاسُوا خِلَالَ الدِّيَارِ ۚ وَكَانَ وَعْدًا مَفْعُولًا ﴿٥﴾ ثُمَّ رَدَدْنَا لَكُمُ الْكَرَّةَ عَلَيْهِمْ وَأَمْدَدْنَاكُم بِأَمْوَالٍ وَبَنِينَ وَجَعَلْنَاكُمْ أَكْثَرَ نَفِيرًا ﴿٦﴾ إِنْ أَحْسَنتُمْ أَحْسَنتُمْ لِأَنفُسِكُمْ ۖ وَإِنْ أَسَأْتُمْ فَلَهَا ۚ فَإِذَا جَاءَ وَعْدُ الْآخِرَةِ لِيَسُوءُوا وُجُوهَكُمْ وَلِيَدْخُلُوا الْمَسْجِدَ كَمَا دَخَلُوهُ أَوَّلَ مَرَّةٍ وَلِيُتَبِّرُوا مَا عَلَوْا تَتْبِيرًا ﴿٧﴾ عَسَىٰ رَبُّكُمْ أَن يَرْحَمَكُمْ ۚ وَإِنْ عُدتُّمْ عُدْنَا ۘ وَجَعَلْنَا جَهَنَّمَ لِلْكَافِرِينَ حَصِيرًا ﴿٨﴾

We revealed to the Children of Israel in the Book: 'Twice you will cause corruption on the earth, and you will perpetrate great tyranny So when the first occasion of the two [prophecies] came, We aroused against you Our servants possessing great might, and they ransacked [your] habitations, and the promise was bound to be fulfilled. Then We gave you back the turn [to prevail] over them, and We aided you with children and wealth, and made you greater in number[saying,] 'If you do good, you will do good to your [own] souls, and if you do evil, it will be [evil] for them.' So when the occasion for the other [prophecy] comes, they will make your faces wretched, and enter the Temple just as they entered it the first time, and destroy utterly whatever they come upon Maybe your Lord will have mercy on you, but if you revert, We [too] will revert, and We have made hell a prison for the faithless.

[Qu'ran 17:4-8]

In fact, these verses are an expansion of that same overall formula:

إِنَّ اللَّهَ لَا يُغَيِّرُ مَا بِقَوْمٍ حَتَّىٰ يُغَيِّرُوا مَا بِأَنفُسِهِمْ

Indeed, Allah does not change a people's lot, unless they change what is in their souls

[Qu'ran 13:11]

What is the Law?

From the discussion so far, we have come to know that events in the universe are governed by a series of fixed and unalterable Divine laws. In other words, God has some fixed and unchanging ways of operating.

Now let us consider what is the law? What does "fixed way" mean? Is the Divine law and way similar to man-made laws, like social contracts, agreements and commitments? Or is it a special creation made by God? Or none of these two statements are correct about Divine law and practice? And in any case, is it possible for God not to create or design a law? Why is alteration in Divine law impossible?

In response we say: Law and practice is not something which has to be created separately and designed distinctly. Law is a general concept and a mental construct and in the external world does not exist with its universality and as Law. What exists in the external world is the causal order and the multiple states and levels of being. These then are made abstract in the mind, intellectualized, and represented as the concept or idea of law. Existence has levels and every level has a fixed and defined position. It is inconceivable that a cause should transfer its own specific position to another, or that an effect should transfer from its specific position. This reality is expressed in these terms: the universe has a law.

Hence, the law of creation is not an artificial virtual entity, since it is derived from the very nature of the existence of things, and for this reason there is no change or alteration possible in it.

Exceptions

Are the laws of creation subject to exceptions? Are miracles and supranatural acts a violation of the Divine law?

The answer in both cases is negative. Neither are the laws of creation subject to exceptions nor are miracles and supranatural acts an exception in the Divine law.

If there are alterations witnessed in the laws of creation then those alterations are actually the result of changes in conditions.

For it is but obvious that any law is applicable in specific conditions and with a change in conditions another law springs into operation, and that the original law always remains applicable in its own specific conditions. Hence, an apparent alteration in Divine law and practice is actually within the law and according to established practice, but not in the sense that an older law is abrogated by another newer one, rather, in the sense that the conditions of a law change and new conditions come in its place. And in those new conditions a new law operates. In the universe, there is nothing but the unalterable Divine laws, precedents, and rules. If dead are brought back to life miraculously, that has its own set of laws and rules. If a son is born, like Jesus son of Mary, without a father, it is not contrary to Divine law and practice in creation.

The fact is that man does not know all the laws of the universe, and when he sees something contrary to the laws and rules that he is familiar with, he feels that this "anomaly" is absolutely contrary to (Divine) law and practice and a violation of the principle of causality. Of course, in many cases what he considers as law is actually just the appearance of law but not the actual law. For instance, we think that the law of creation for life is that a living being always results from the marriage between a father and mother, but this is only an apparent law, not the real law. The birth of Jesus son of Mary has violated only the apparent law not the real law. That the laws of creation are unalterable is one matter, and whether the laws we have recognized are the actual laws or just the apparent laws is another matter altogether.

The meaning of a miracle is not that it is without a law or it is above the law. The materialists fell prone to the error that those natural laws of the universe discovered by science were the only real laws and hence miracles were a violation of the laws. We say that whatever has been explained by science is applicable only under specific and limited conditions but when a Prophet or saint wills to perform a super-natural act, conditions change, since in such a case a powerful and pure soul has found recourse to the Unlimited Power of the Almighty, and this changes all the conditions. In other words, a specific factor and new player has entered the scene. Obviously in new circumstances created by the presence of the new actor *i.e.* the powerful and pure will of a saint, another set of laws become operational.

In the case of the effects of supplications and charity in warding off afflictions and the like, the same process applies. There is a narration that the Holy Prophet (s) was asked that if every event that occurs in the universe is according to the predetermination and unalterable will of God what effect can a supplication or medicine have? He replied: supplication also is part of God's predetermination and plan[8]

In another tradition it is narrated that Imam Ali (a) was seated near a wall. He noticed that the wall was broken and it could possibly fall. He immediately stood up and distanced himself from there. Someone objected that, "Do you flee from Divine decree?" Meaning that if it is decreed you should die it would make no difference whether you avoid the wall or not, death will catch up with you; and if it is decreed that you suffer no affliction, then again you will be protected. Hence, what does it mean to distance yourself from the wall which is about to fall? In response, Imam explained:

أَفِرُّ مِنْ قَضَاءِ اَللَّهِ إِلَى قَدَرِ اَللَّهِ عَزَّ وَ جَلَّ

I flee from God's decree to His plan.[9]

The meaning of this statement is that every event that occurs in the universe is subject to God's decree and plan. If a person exposes himself to danger and suffers injuries, it is Divine law and decree, and if he escapes danger and is saved, that too is God's decree and plan. If a man enters an environment full of microbes and gets infected, it is (Divine) law, and if he takes drugs and gets cured from the infection, that too is (Divine) decree. Thus, if a person stands up from a beneath a wall about to fall, he has not done anything contrary to Divine decree and plan. In such circumstances the Divine law is that he is protected from death; and if continues sitting under a wall about to fall and perishes under the crushing wall, that too is a law of creation.

The holy Qur'an explains this reality in an interesting manner. In *surah al-Talaq* (65:2-3) we read:

وَمَن يَتَّقِ اللَّـهَ يَجْعَل لَّهُ مَخْرَجًا ﴿٢﴾ وَيَرْزُقْهُ مِنْ حَيْثُ لَا يَحْتَسِبُ ۚ وَمَن يَتَوَكَّلْ عَلَى اللَّـهِ فَهُوَ حَسْبُهُ ۚ إِنَّ اللَّـهَ بَالِغُ أَمْرِهِ ۚ قَدْ جَعَلَ اللَّـهُ لِكُلِّ شَيْءٍ قَدْرًا ﴿٣﴾

Whoever is wary of Allah, He shall make for him a way out [of the adversities of the world and the Hereafter] and provide for him from

---

[8] *Bihar al-Anwar*, vol.5, p. 78
[9] *Saduq al-Tawhid*, p. 369

whence he does not count upon. And whoever puts his trust in Allah, He will suffice him. Indeed, Allah carries through His commands. Certainly, Allah has ordained a measure [and extent] for everything.

[Qur'an, 65:2-3]

In this verse apparently the law which is above all laws and governs all of them is mentioned, and that is the law of God-consciousness and reliance.

From this verse, one can derive the fact that, with reliance, God's special grace is definite and confirmed; whosoever truly relies on God will certainly attract special Divine grace, and Divine support and grace which itself has a special process, is a Divine law which involves a series of causes and effects, reaching one's goals becomes inevitable. This is a law which overrides all other laws. At the same time, so as not to forget that God's act has an order and laws, the verse states "Certainly God has set a measure for everything," and also states, "And whoever is wary of God, He shall make a way out for him." That is to say, His acts are not without rules or means, even though those means may be of a nature which are not accessible and knowable but rather "from whence he does not reckon".

Divine Decree and the Issue of Compulsion

If we keep in mind that Divine decree and predestination implies that the universe works in accordance with definite laws and precedents, the objection of compulsion in relation to Divine decree and predestination is also solved. In our book *Man and His Destiny,* we have discussed this matter in detail and those wanting details can refer to that book. Here we will only briefly touch on the topic:

This objection arises from the fact that a group believes the meaning of Divine decree is that God wills every event directly and outside the framework of the law of creation.

It has been attributed to Khayyam:[10]

True I drink wine, like every man of sense,

---

[10] See Endnote 37

For I know Allah will not take offense;
Before time was, He know that I should drink,
And who am I to thwart His prescience?[11]

The composer of this poem thinks man's will regarding any act is pitted against and contrary to the Divine will and hence assumes if man decides not to drink wine, it is impossible, since God's will was that he ought to drink wine, and since the Divine will and knowledge is inviolable, man has no choice but to drink it.

This is a very weak argument and is based on sheer ignorance, and hence it is difficult to believe it was composed by Khayyam the philosopher. Every philosopher and pseudo-philosopher knows at least this much that God neither directly wills the wine-drinking of someone nor does any act in the universe happen outside the framework of the Divine order and law. In as much as no natural event can occur without its natural cause, so also voluntary human acts cannot occur without man's will and choice. God's law regarding human actions is that man should possess freewill, ability and choice; he should select either good or evil acts himself. Freedom to choose is an inseparable part of the human essence. A man without freedom is impossible; that is, the supposition that there is a human without choice is just a supposition not a reality and implies in actuality a non-man. So, if there is no-man, then he is not dutybound; like the case of a cow or a donkey putting its head into a vessel of wine and drinking some of it. Thus, the Divine decree and predestination which has willed the human has also willed his freedom of choice. Hence, drinking wine by a man without his choice and freedom but just on Divine compulsion is contrary to eternal Divine knowledge and if man were to drink wine by compulsion that would mean God's knowledge is ignorance.

Experts today doubt whether Khayyam the poet is the same as Khayyam the philosopher. There is a possibility, in fact they have proof, that there may have been two or more people and history has confused between them. Anyhow, whether it was two different people with the same name, or one person with two differing personalities, this argument that Divine knowledge and decree is the cause of committing sins such

---

[11] Whinfield, quatrain 197

that it robs man of his responsibility and freedom of choice is false and in response it has been aptly put:[12]

To pose Divine knowledge the cause of sins;
Is to the wise ultimate ignorance.

Summary

From the lengthy perhaps tiring discussion which we had in this section, the response to the argument of discrimination and differentiation can be summarized as below:

1. The world of creation is governed by a series of essential unalterable laws and order, according to which every being and every event has a specific position, level and state; no alteration or change is possible therein.

2. The corollary of the world having an order is the existence of multiple states and varying levels in being, and this is the basis of the appearance of differences and variations, and the appearance of defects and nonexistences.

3. Difference and variation is not created, rather it is the inherent necessity of created beings, and it is an erroneous assumption that someone presumes the Creator has discriminated between his creatures.

4. What would be contradictory and an invalidation of justice or wisdom is discrimination not differentiation and what exists in the universe is differentiation not discrimination.

---

[12] See Endnote 38

Evils

Three Aspects of the Discussion

What we have discussed so far has been about disparities and discriminations. As we mentioned previously, the objections and problems related to "Divine Justice" are of several types: discriminations, annihilations and non-existences, faults and defects, and afflictions.

Earlier we promised that out of these four types of objections, we would discuss the first under the heading "Discriminations" and the remaining three under the heading "Evils." Now that we have completed the discussion about discriminations, we will begin the discussion of evils.

The answer that philosophers have given to the issue of evils includes three parts:

A. What is the essence of evils? Are evils real, existential things, or are they non-existential (*adami*) and relative?

B. Whether evils be existential or non-existential, are good and evil separable or inseparable? In the second case-that they are inseparable-is the entirety of the universe, with all its goodnesses and evils, good or bad? That is, do goodnesses predominate over evils, or do the evils of the world predominate over its goodnesses? Or does neither predominate over the other, with them being equal.

C. Whether evils be existential or non-existential, and whether they be separable from goodnesses or not, is that which is evil actually evil, without there being any aspect of goodness in it; that is, without it being a preliminary or basis for one or several goodnesses? Or is there one or rather several goodnesses hidden in every evil, every evil producing one or several goodnesses?

In the first part, an answer will be given to the dualists, who maintain two types or sources of existence. And with the addition of the second part, an answer will be given to the objection of the materialists, who consider evils to be an objection to Divine wisdom, and also the objection of those who, by mentioning the problem of evil, find fault with Divine justice. The third part of the discussion reveals the beautiful and unique order of the world of existence, and it can be considered an independent answer-albeit sufficient-or a useful complement to the first answer.

Our Method

Using the same material that Islamic philosophers have mentioned in this discussion, we have engaged in answering the problem of evils in a new fashion. The answer we present in this book contains the same elements that are mentioned in books of Islamic philosophy especially the books of Mulla Sadra and both answers are essentially the same. The difference between our answer and theirs is in the particular method we have followed, and this is because we are studying the issue of evils from the perspective of "Divine Justice," while the custom of Islamic philosophers was to cover it in the discussion of Divine Unity while refuting the objection of the dualists, or in the issue of "Divine providence and knowledge" and how Divine decree (*qada*) relates to evils. And since they have studied it from that particular perspective, their answer pertains directly to refuting the question of the "duality of origin" or the manner of relation of Divine decree (*qada*) to evils, and can only be used indirectly in the discussion of "Divine Justice."

The Issue of the Duality of Existence

The basis of the objection of the dualists and their supporters-as have also indicated previously-is that if existing things in their essence are of two types-good and evil-they must necessarily originate from two types of sources, so that both goodnesses and evils relate to a separate creator. In reality, the dualists wished to exonerate God of evil, and ended up charging Him with having an associate. In the view of the dualists, who have divided the world into two divisions, good and evil, and consider the existence of evils to be extraneous, or rather detrimental, and naturally consider them to be from not God but rather a power in opposition to God, God is like a well-intentioned but weak human being who is tormented by existing conditions and is not pleased with them, but is faced with a wicked and ill-intentioned rival who, in opposition to His desire, creates evils and vices.

The dualists have been unable to harmonize belief in the unlimited power and unchallenged will of God and His uncontested decree with belief in His Wisdom, Justice, and Goodness. But Islam, at the same time as it considers-God to be the origin of all existence and possessor of unending mercy and supreme wisdom, it doesn't find fault with His supreme will and uncontestable power; it relates everything to Him, even Satan and his leading astray.

In Islam's view, the issue of evils is solved in a different way, which is that Islam says that while in one reckoning the affairs of the world are divided into the two categories of good and evil, in another reckoning, there is no evil in the order of creation; what exists is good, and the existing order is the best order. Nothing more beautiful than what exists is possible.

Intellectually, such an answer to the issue of evils relies on a particular philosophy in which the issues of existence and nonexistence are studied in depth. The answer this philosophy gives to the dualists is that "evils" are not real and actual existent things for them to have need of a creator and an origin. This point can be elucidated in two ways: that evil is nonexistential, and that evil is relative. By explaining this point, the objection of the duality of existence is eliminated in its entirety.

Evil is Non-existential

A simple analysis shows that the essence of "evils" is nonexistence. That is, all evils are of the form of non-existence and non-being. This point has a long precedent. The roots of this idea go back to ancient Greece. In books of philosophy, this idea is attributed to the ancient Greeks and specifically to Plato. But later philosophers have analyzed it better and to a greater extent; and since we consider this point to be correct and fundamental, we mention it here to the extent appropriate to this book. As an introduction, while asking our readers' pardon on account of the difficulty of the material, we request them to persevere and try to understand the intent. We think the matter is important enough to be given attention, and of course we will try to explain the matter as simply as possible.

The intent of those who say "Evil is non-existential" is not that that which is known as "evil" does not exist, for it to be said that this is obviously false; we see clearly and with our senses that blindness, deafness, sickness, oppression, injustice, ignorance, inability, death, earthquakes, and so on exist. Neither can we deny the existence of these things, nor their being evil. And [their intent] is also not that since evil is nonexistential, therefore evil does not exist; and since evil does not exist, human beings have no obligation, since the obligation of man is to combat evils and evil people and acquire virtues and support good people. And since every condition is good and not evil, one must always be satisfied with the current situation, and must rather consider it the best possible condition.

Don't be quick to judge; neither do we want to deny the existence of blindness, deafness, injustice, poverty, sickness, and so on; nor do we wish to deny their evilness; nor do we wish to deny the obligation of human beings and ignore the role of man in changing the world and perfecting society. The overall ascent of the world-and especially humanity-and the mission of humanity in managing that which has been placed on its shoulders is a part of the beautiful order of the world. So it is not these things that we are talking about; what we are talking about is that all of these are forms of "non-existential things" and "imperfections," and their existence is of the form of the existence of "deficiencies" and "vacuums," and they are evil because they are themselves non-being, deficiency, and emptiness, or are the source of non-being, deficiency, and emptiness; the role of humanity in the necessary ascending order of the world is to compensate for deficiencies, fill up the vacuums, and eliminate the sources of these vacuums and deficiencies.

If this analysis is accepted, it is the first step and the first level; its effect is that it drives from one's mind the question, who created evils? Why are some beings good and some evil? It makes clear that that which is evil is not of the form of being, but of the form of emptiness and non-being, and it eliminates the background for dualist thought, which claims that existence has two branches, or rather two sources.

As for the aspect of Divine justice and infinite Divine wisdom, there are still other levels which we have to pass after this one.

Good and evil things in the world are not two separate and differentiated types from one another in the sense that, for example, inanimate objects or minerals are separate from plants and plants are separate from animals and create particular groups. It is a mistake to assume that evil things are a specific group of things whose essence consists of evil and in which there is no good; and good things in their turn are another category separate and differentiated from bad things. Good and evil are mixed together; they are inseparable. In nature, where there is evil there is also good, and where there is good there is also evil. In nature, good and evil are bound and mixed together in such a way that it is as if they have been compounded together, not a chemical compound, but a deeper and more subtle compounding, of the type of the compounding of being and non-being.

Being and non-being do not comprise two separate groups in the external world. Non-being is nothing and emptiness and cannot occupy a particular place side by side with being. But in the natural world, which is the world of potentiality and actuality, movement and evolution, and contradiction and opposition, wherever there are forms of being, forms of non-being also apply. When we speak of "blindness" we should not think that "blindness" is a specific thing and a tangible reality that exists in the eye of a blind person. Instead, "blindness" is nothing but the lack of "sight" and it itself has no reality.

Good and evil, too, are like being and non-being; in fact, fundamentally good is the same as being and evil is the same as non-being. Wherever we speak of evil, there is definitely a non-being and lack [of something] involved. "Evil" is either itself of the form of non-being, or it is a being that necessitates a form of non-being; that is, it is a being that, inasmuch as it is itself, is good, and it is evil inasmuch as it necessitates a non-being; and it is only evil because it necessitates a non-being, not for any other reason. We consider ignorance, poverty, and death to be evil. These by their essence are non-being. We consider poisonous and dangerous animals, bacteria, and afflictions to be evil. These are not non-being by their essence, but they are beings that necessitate non-being.

"Ignorance" is the lack and non-existence of knowledge. Knowledge is a reality and an actual perfection, but ignorance is not a reality. When we say, "An ignorant person lacks knowledge," it doesn't mean that he possesses a particular quality called "lack of knowledge," and knowledgeable people don't possess that quality. Knowledgeable people, before they acquire knowledge, are ignorant; when they acquire knowledge, they don't lose anything; they only acquire something. If ignorance were an actual reality, acquiring knowledge-since it would be alongside a loss of ignorance-would simply be the changing of one attribute for another, just as a body loses one form and quality and acquires a different form and quality.

"Poverty" too is non-possession, not possession and being. One who is poor lacks something called wealth; it is not the case that he in turn possesses something called poverty and, like a wealthy person, has a type of possession, except that a wealthy person possesses wealth and a poor person possesses poverty.

"Death" too is the loss of something, not the acquiring of something. This is why a body that loses the attribute of life and turns into an inanimate object has descended, not ascended.

As for poisonous and dangerous animals, bacteria, floods, earthquakes, and afflictions, they are evil because they cause death or the loss of an organ or ability, or prevent abilities from reaching perfection. If poisonous animals did not cause death and sickness, they would not be evil; if plant afflictions did not cause the annihilation of trees or their fruits, they would not be evil; if floods and earthquakes did not result in human and material losses, they would not be evil. Evil is in those casualties and losses. If we call a beast of prey evil, it is not because its peculiar essence is the essence of evil, but because it is a cause of death and loss for something else. In reality, what is evil by essence is that loss of life itself. If a beast of prey were to exist but not to prey [on other things], that is, if it were not to cause loss of life for anything, it would not be evil, and if it exists and loss of life takes place, it is evil.

In terms of the relation between cause and effect, usually those very actual deficiencies, meaning poverty and ignorance, become causes of things like bacteria, floods, earthquakes, war, and so on, which are evils of the second type, meaning that they are beings that are evil inasmuch as they are a source of deficiencies and non-being.

In order to combat these types of evils, we must first combat the first type of evils and fill vacuums such as ignorance, inability, and poverty, so that evils of the second type don't come about.

The same applies with regard to moral actions and ugly qualities. Injustice is bad because it destroys the "right" of the oppressed. A "right" is something which a being deserves and which one must receive. For example, knowledge is a perfection for a human being which the innate human capacity demands and moves toward, and, for this reason, deserves. If someone is denied the right to learn and is prevented from gaining knowledge, that is oppression and evil, since it prevents a perfection and causes a deficiency. Similarly, oppression is evil for the oppressor as well since it contradicts his higher potentials; if the oppressor possessed no higher power and potential than that of anger, oppression would not be bad for him, or rather it wouldn't have any meaning with respect to him.

Now that it has been established that evils are all of the form of non-being, the answer to dualists becomes clear. The objection of the dualists was that since there are two types of beings in the universe, the universe must necessarily have two types of origins and creators.

The answer is that there is no more than one type of being in the universe, and that is the existence of good things; evils are all of the form of non-being, and non-being is not a created thing. Non-being is from a "not creating," not from a "creating." One cannot say that the universe has two creators: one is the creator of beings and the other is the creator of non-beings. The example of being and non-being is like that of the sun and shadow. When a pole is put up in the sun, the area that remains dark because of the pole and doesn't become lighted by sunlight is called a "shadow." What is a shadow? A "shadow" is darkness, and darkness is nothing but the non-being of light. When we say that light emanates from the originating centre, one cannot ask where the shadow has emanated from and what the centre of darkness is. Shadow and darkness have not emanated from anything and have no independent source and centre of their own.

This is the meaning of the words of the philosophers when they say that "evils" are not created in themselves, but are created subordinately and figuratively.

Evil is relative

Attributes by which things are described are of two types: real and relative. If an attribute applies to a certain thing in all conditions and irrespective of everything else, it is called a "real" attribute. A real attribute is one for which it is sufficient to posit a thing and that attribute in order for it to be possible for that thing to be described by that attribute. In contrast, a relative attribute is one in which supposing [the existence of] a thing and an attribute is not sufficient in order for that thing to be described by that attribute, unless some third thing is supposed that can serve as a basis for comparison and relation. Thus, whenever the affirmation of an attribute with respect to a thing depends on the keeping in mind of some third thing and comparing this with that, such an attribute is called "relative."

For example, life is a real matter. A being, irrespective of whether it is compared to something else, either possesses life or doesn't possess it. Similarly, whiteness and blackness (assuming that colours are actual things) are real attributes. A thing that is white is white without it having to be compared to anything else, and a thing that is black is black in itself, and it doesn't need to be compared to something else for it to be black. And many other attributes are the same way, such as quantity and dimension.

But smallness and largeness are relative attributes. When we say that a body is small, we have to see in comparison to what thing or relative to what thing we call it small. Everything can be both small and large; it depends what thing we make our base and standard [of comparison].

For example, we say that an apple or a pair is small, and another apple or pair is big. Here, the standard is the size of other apples and pairs; that is, the apple or pair in question is either smaller or larger in size compared to other apples and pairs that we are familiar with. We also call a particular watermelon small. This too is in comparison to other watermelons.

This same watermelon which we view and call very small is bigger than that big apple, but since we compare it to watermelons and not apples, we call it small.

Consider the size of a large ant which is so large that you put your finger to your lip in wonder and the size of a very small camel whose small size you wonder at. You will see that the small camel is many millions of times the size of that very large ant. How can "very small" be bigger than "very big"? Is this a contradiction? No, it is not a contradiction. That "very small" was very small for a camel, and is very small compared to the standard and mould the mind has created in accordance with its familiarity with camels; and that "very big" was very big for ants, and is very big compared to the standard and mould the mind has created in accordance with its familiarity with ants.

This is the meaning of our statement: "Largeness and smallness are relative concepts"; but quantity itself-meaning number and dimension-are real things, as was indicated. If we have a number of apples, for example, one hundred, this "onehundredness" is a real attribute, not a comparative one; the same is true of their size, for example, if it is half a cubic meter.

Number and dimension are of the category of quantity, and smallness and bigness are of the category of relation. Being one, two, three, four, and so on are real things; but being first, second, third, fourth, and so on are relative things.

For a societal law to be good or bad depends on it keeping in view both the individual's interest and society's interest together, giving precedence to collective rights over individual rights, and ensuring individual rights to the extent possible. But to ensure all individual freedoms one hundred percent is impossible, and thus whether a law is good from this perspective-that of ensuring freedoms-is relative, since only some of them can be ensured. A good law is one that ensures the maximum number of freedoms possible, even though it may necessitate the denial of some freedoms. Thus, the goodness of a law with respect to ensuring freedoms is relative to other supposable laws which are less able to protect and ensure freedoms than it is.

Here it is necessary to mention a point to prevent a misunderstanding, which is that, as was noted, the intent of the statement "Evil is relative" is relative as opposed to being real; "It is relative" means it is comparative. Sometimes relativity is used in opposition to absoluteness; in this case it means that the actuality of a thing depends on a series of conditions; and absoluteness means freedom from a series of conditions. If we take relativity in this sense, all natural and material things, inasmuch as they are contingent and dependent on a series of limited temporal and spatial conditions and only possess their particular reality under those conditions, are relative. Only nonmaterial beings have absolute being. Rather, the ultimate and real absolute, which is a reality free of every condition, cause, and limitation, is the Divine Essence, and it is from this perspective that the necessity of His Essence is a pre-eternal necessity and not an essential necessity in its conventional meaning. The point is that here, where our discussion is about the relativity of the evilness of beings from which essential evils-meaning non-beings-originate, the intent is relativity as opposed to reality and actuality, not relativity as opposed to absoluteness, in which sense many good things are also relative.

Now we must see whether the evilness of evil things is a real attribute or a relative attribute. Previously we said that evil things are of two types: evils that are themselves nonexistential, and evils that are existential things but are evil because they become causes of a series of non-existential things. Evils that are themselves non-existential, such as ignorance, inability, and poverty, are real (non-relative) attributes, though [they are] non-existential; as for evils that are existential but are evil because they are a source of non-existential things, such as floods, poisonous animals, beasts of prey, and sickness-causing bacteria, without doubt their evilness is relative. In such cases, what is evil is evil with respect to one or several specific things. Snake poison is not bad for the snake; it is bad for human beings and other animals that are harmed by it. A wolf is bad for a sheep, but not for itself or for a plant [for example]; just as a sheep, with respect to a plant that it eats and destroys, is bad, but with respect to itself, human beings, or a wolf [for example], it is not bad.

Rumi says,[1]

Snake-poison is life to the snake,
(But) it is death in relation to man.
Hence there is no absolute evil in the world;
Evil is relative,[2] know this (truth) also.[3]

---

[1] See Endnote 39

[2] In this verse, Rumi has confused two issues. One is thst evil (meaning evil of the second type) is in the relational and comparative being if things, not in their real and in-itself being. That is, everything in itself is good for itself; ifit is evil, it is evil for something else, just like snake poison is good for the snake and bad for other things. Here, it must be said that the evilness of snake poison is in its for-other being, not in its in-itself being. The other issue is that something whose being is good with respect to all things is called "absolute good", like the being of the Necessarily Existent:and if something is postulated whose being is evil with respect to all otherthings,it would be called "absolute evil".Relative good and evil, as opposed to absolute, mean that something is good or evil with respect to some—not all—things, likemost things in the world. What Rumi mentions in this verse is a combination of the two issues; the first verse mentions the first issue, and the second verse the second one.

[3] Nicholson, vol. 4, p. 276, vr. 68 and 65

On the other hand, real existence-anything which is created and originated and has actual existence-exists for itself, not for other things. The existence of everything for another thing or things is a suppositional and non-real existence and is not subject to being created and originated.

In other words, everything possesses an innate existence and an extrinsic existence (i.e. an existence for some other existence), and more precisely, the existence of everything has two aspects: "in-itself" or innate, and "for-other" or extrinsic. Things, inasmuch as they exist for themselves, are real, and in this sense are not evil.

Everything is good for itself; if it is evil, it is evil for something else. Can it be said that a scorpion is evil for itself? A wolf is evil for itself? No, without doubt the being of a scorpion or wolf is good for itself, they are for themselves just as we are for ourselves. Thus, the evilness of a thing is not in its innate being; it is in its relational being. But without doubt that which is real and actual is the innate and essential existence of everything; relative existences are and suppositional and conventional things, and since they are relative and suppositional, they are not real, meaning that they do not actually have a place in the order of existence or possess actual being for it to be debated why this existence-meaning relative existence-has been given to them. In other words, things have not come into being twice or been given two beings, one in-themselves and the other in-relation.

Suppose that you explain a point for some students. Then you repeat it once, and again for a third and fourth time. Each time, you explained the same point without adding or subtracting anything. That is, your explanation which came into being through you is the same in all four instances, but each of those instances has an attribute peculiar to itself. One is "first," another "second," another "third," and the last is "fourth." In each instance, did you do two things: one, explaining your point; and two, giving your explanation the attribute of "first," "second," "third," or "fourth"? Or are these attributes a series of relational attributes-that are at the same time suppositional and derivational-that come about through your repeated action, which took place in all four instances in the same form, and through a comparison of those four instances with one another? It is obvious that the second case is correct. These types of attributes, which are suppositional and derivational attributes, are at the same time necessary and inseparable corollaries of their objects, which are real and actual things.

Thus, such things cannot be discussed as independent things. The question cannot be asked in the form, "Why did the Creator and Originator create these relational and suppositional beings?" since in the first place, these beings are not real for their creation to be discussed, and in the second place these suppositional and derivational beings are corollaries of actual beings and cannot be discussed independently; and if they are discussed non-independently, it will be in the form of why actual beings were created of which these are the inseparable suppositional and derivational corollaries. And this is the issue that will be broached and answered in the next section.

Incidentally, let us also point out that what we said about firstness, secondness, and so on being suppositional and derivational things and not possessing actual being, and thus not being subject to creation, should not be confused with another issue, which is the issue of precedence, meaning that a person or other free and self-conscious agent choose one of two things or actions over the other and place it first. This is another issue, and we will discuss it later. Paying attention to the example above will clarify the matter.

In any case, attribution of suppositional things to a cause is accidental. This is why philosophers have said that evils are not created by essence; in their essence they are not effects or created. Their being effects or being created is accidental. As we said previously, it is precisely as if we were to say, "The sun is the cause of the existence of shadow." Of course, without the sun, there would be no shadow as well, but the causality of the sun with respect to shadow is different from its causality with respect to light. The sun actually and really emanates light, but it doesn't really create shadow. Shadow is not a thing for it to be originated. Shadow comes about from the limitation of light; rather it is the limitation of light itself. With respect to evils, whether of the first or the second type, the same is the case. Evils are suppositional and non-existential. Blindness in a blind person is not an independent reality for it to be said that one source created the blind person and another source created his blindness. Blindness is non-being, and every evil is nonbeing. Non-being has no origin or creator.

Evils from the Aspect of the Principle of Justice

In this way, the objection of the dualists and the fallacious idea of the duality and dual origin of being is eliminated, since it was demonstrated that being is not of two types for there to be a need of two origins.

But as we indicated earlier, the issue of the nonexistentiality of evils alone is not sufficient to solve the problem of "Divine Justice"; it is [only] the first level and step. The conclusion that can be reached from this discussion is only that being is not of two types: one type those beings that, inasmuch as they are existent, are good; and the other type those beings that, inasmuch as they are existent, are evil. Instead, being, inasmuch as it is being, is good; and non-being, inasmuch as it is non-being, is evil; beings can be evil inasmuch as they are coupled with non-beings or are the sources of non-beings. Thus, in being itself there is no overruling duality for the idea of two sources of being to take root. And [in tum] non-being, inasmuch as it is non-being, does not require a separate origin and source.

But in terms of Divine Justice, the problem of evil takes a different form. From this aspect, the issue isn't the duality of things; the issue is-whether things are of two types or not-why deficiency, lack, annihilation, and non-being have a place in the order of being to begin with. Why is one person blind, another deaf, and why does a third have a physical deformity? For blindness, deafness, and other defects to be non-existential is not enough to solve this problem, because the question remains as to why being hasn't taken the place of this non-being? Isn't this a form of holding back of Divine bounty and grace? And isn't the holding back of Divine grace a form of injustice? In the world, vacuums and deficiencies exist which are themselves the sorrows of this world. Divine Justice requires that these vacuums be filled.

There is also a series of existential things that-as indicated previously-are born of non-beings like ignorance, inability, and poverty, and in their tum are causes of a series of deficiencies, annihilations, and non-beings. Illnesses, storms, fires, and earthquakes are of this type. Divine Justice demands that such things not exist so that their effects, which are deficiencies, also not exist.

When we look at the problem from this aspect, we have to look into two issues:

First, is it possible to separate these deficiencies and lacks from the affairs of this world, or not? That is, is this world possible without these deficiencies, or are they inseparable corollaries of this world, with their non-existence being equivalent to the non-existence of the world?

Second, are those things that are called deficiencies and lacks absolute evil with no good hidden in them, or they are not absolute evil, with many benefits and effects following from them, and without which the order of the world will be destroyed and good things won't be able to exist [as well].

These two points comprise the second and third part of our discussion regarding evils, which we indicated earlier. The second part has become clear in the course of the first part and will become clearer in what follows, and the third part requires greater discussion, and we will discuss it in depth in the next section.

Benefits of Evils

Our discussion in the course of the previous section was a philosophical discussion and a rational analysis of the problem of evil. In this section, we look into the issue from another point of view.

Usually people who consider the problem of evil in the world with a view to criticizing it do not stop to calculate how the world would be if it were bereft of these evil? They only say, simply and generally, if only the world were filled with enjoyment and felicity, and if only everyone would attain his wishes, and no pain or failure ever existed... The following verses are attributed to Khayyam:[1]

If I had control over the universe as God does,
I would destroy it all together
And make anew a universe in which,
All would attain their heart's desire with ease.

Now let us see how it is possible to create a world better than the present world, as the poet wished. When we want to start making the "world", "destroying the roof of the universe and putting forth a new design", we must definitely set aside limited thoughts and childish ideas that are appropriate for the limited life of a human individual and contemplate a large and vast design. I don't think this engineering will be an easy task, and we may not be able to make a decision.

In any case, it is best that first, we look into the existing situation and get to know it better; then we can tire our minds thinking about a "better order." Perhaps, after a serious study, we would prefer the current state. To study the present world, it is necessary to discuss the phenomena of tragedy and tribulation from two points of view:

1.   What place do evils have in the order of the entire world?

2.   What is the value of evils in their own right?

In the first part, the discussion is about whether, in the entire order of the world, evils are dispensable. In other words, is a world without evils

---

[1] See Endnote 40

possible? Or, contrary to what might first come to mind, is omitting them from the world impossible, and is the non-existence of calamities equivalent to the destruction of the world? In other words, are the evils of the world inseparable from its good things?

In the second part, the discussion is whether tragedies are solely harmful, and so to speak, have negative value? Or do they also have benefits and positive effects, with their negative effects actually being as nothing next to their beneficial and positive effects.

The Issue of Separation of Good and Evil

From what was said in the discussion of "discrimination" and in the discussion "evil is relative", to a large extent it became clear that evils are inseparable from good things, since evils are of the form of lacks and non-beings. In other words, vacuities like ignorance, inability, and poverty that exist in creation, to the extent that they are related to the ontic order, are absences of potential and limitations of possibility. That is, in the creational order, whatever level of deficiencies exist for every being is due to a deficiency in the capacity of the recipient [of Divine grace], and not due to the holding back of Divine grace, for it to be considered oppression or discrimination. Now in these things, the one thing that doesn't [essentially] pertain to the lack of potential and limitation of possibilities is what lies in the domain of human freewill and responsibility. Man, by virtue of his freewill and role in the formation of both himself and his society, must needs be attend to them-filling the vacuums as it were. This is one of the dimensions of man being God's vicegerent. That humanity has been created in this way and has such a responsibility is a part of the design of the ideal order [of the universe]. And as for evils that are existential and are good in their in-itself being and evil in their for other being, as mentioned their evil aspect, in that it is relative and relational and one of the inseparable corollaries of their real being, is inseparable from their good aspect.

What we must add here is another point, which is the principle of interdependence and the facts that the parts of the universe are as a single "body." For we know that, the universe is an indivisible unit.

An important issue in philosophical and intellectual worldviews is how the different parts of the world relate and connect to one another. Do they take the form of a series of separate and scattered things? If a portion of the universe were not to exist, or if it were to be supposed that some beings of the universe were to annihilated-what does this mean in terms of the remaining parts of the universe, is this possible [or not]? Or are the parts of the universe somehow all related and connected to one another.

In the fifth volume of *Principles of Philosophy and Method of Realism* we have discussed this issue. Here we suffice it to say that this issue has been the subject of debate from the time of the earliest philosophical inquiries. Aristotle supported the unity and "body-likeness" of the universe. In the Islamic world, this principle has always been affirmed. Mir Findariski, the well-known philosopher and gnostic of the Safavid era, says in the language of poetry.[2]

Truth [God] is the soul of the world, the world like a body. The hosts of angels are as powers of this body; Heavenly spheres, elements, and all that is born are organs; This is tawhid, all else is trivia.[3]

Hegel,[4] the well-known German philosopher, notes this principle in his philosophy. The dialectical materialism of Marx[5] and Engels, which is strongly influenced by the philosophy and logic of Hegel, accepted this principle under the name of "mutual influence."

Right now, we can't enter this issue in detail. Of course, all of those who have spoken of the "body-likeness" and interdependence and relatedness of the parts of the universe have not spoken at the same level.

What we mean by this principle is that the universe is an indivisible unit; that is, the relation between the parts of the universe is not such that it is possible to suppose that some of them are removable and some retainable. Removing some parts necessitates, or rather equals, removal of all parts, just as retaining some equals retaining them all.

Thus, not only are non-beings inseparable from beings and relational and relative beings inseparable from real beings, real beings themselves are also inseparable from one another. So, evils too, in addition to the two above-mentioned aspects and regardless of those two aspects, are

---

[2] See Endnote 41
[3] This poem has also been attributed to Baba Afdal.
[4] See Endnote 42
[5] See Endnote 43

inseparable from good things. In the words of Hafiz, "the Prophetic lamp" is together with the "Abu Lahabic flame".[6]

In this parterre, none plucked a rose without a thorn.
So the lamp of Mustafa and the flames of Abu Lahab is.[7]

And he also points to the indivisibility of the parts of the universe where he says.[8]

In the workshop of love, infidelity is unavoidable;
Who will the Fire consume, if not for Abu Lahab?

The Total Order

So far, the discussion has been about the relation and connectedness of things in existence and the indivisibility of the universe. Over and beyond this aspect, another point must be kept in mind; namely, in terms of goodness and evilness if things are looked at alone, separate, and independently of other things they have one ruling; and if they are looked at as part of a system and as an organ of a body they have another ruling, which occasionally may be opposite to the first one. It is obvious that if things that are in reality separate are looked at as a system, their actual being will be separate and their organic and body-like being will be suppositional; and in the same way if things that are actually and ontologically parts and organs of a system are looked at separately, their actual being will be organic and body-like, and their separate being will be suppositional. Now, we say:

If we were to be asked whether a straight line or a curved line is better on its own, we might say that a straight line is better than a curved line. But if the line in question is part of a complete system and order, we have to take the balance of the whole system into consideration in our judgement. In a complete and total order, in an absolute sense neither a straight line is desirable nor a curved line; just as in a face, it is good for the eyebrows to be curved and for the nose to be taut and straight; it is good for the teeth to be white and for the pupil of the eye to be black or

---

[6] See Endnote 44
[7] Clarke, Ghazal 64
[8] See Endnote 45

blue. It is as someone said: "The curved eyebrow, if it were straight, would be off mark."

In a complete system and total order, every part has a particular status in accordance to which a particular quality is appropriate for it:

"For a lion it is good to attack; for a gazelle, to flee."

In a painting, there have to be different types of shading and various colours. Here, it is not right for there to be one colour and no variation. If the entire painting were to be monotonous and undifferentiated, it wouldn't be a painting.

When we look at the universe as a whole, we must accept that in the entire system and to maintain its balance, the existence of lows and highs, valleys and mountains, level and unlevel places, darknesses and lights, pains and pleasures, successes and failures, are all necessary.

The world is like an eye, curve, mole, and eyebrow;
Everything in its place is good.

Fundamentally, if variation and differences did not exist, there would be no such thing as multiplicity and variety; variegated beings would not exist; and there would be no meaning to there being a system or order (neither a beautiful order nor an ugly one). If there were to be no difference and variation in the world, all of being would have to be composed of a [single] simple matter, say carbon. The dignity and beauty of the world is in its vast variety and colourful differences. The Qur'an counts the existence of differences among the signs of Divine power and wisdom: differences of colour, differences of language, difference of night and day, differences of people, and so on.

Ugliness as the Manifester of Beauty

Uglinesses are necessary not only in that they are a part of the complete system of the universe and the total order depends on them, rather their existence is also needed to manifest and bring to light beautiful things. If beauty and ugliness were not compared to one another, neither would the beautiful be beautiful nor the ugly be ugly; that is, if ugliness were not to exist in the world, neither would beauty. If all people were to be beautiful, no one would be beautiful, just as if all were to be ugly, no one would be ugly. If all people were as beautiful as Yusuf (a)[9], beauty would cease to exist; and likewise, if everyone was like Jahiz,[10] there would be no more ugliness. Similarly, if all people had heroic powers, there would be no more heroes. The expressions of emotion and praise that heroes receive are because they are few in number. In reality, the sensations and perceptions that man has of beautiful things are only possible if ugliness exists alongside beauty. The fact that people are pulled toward and attracted by beautiful people, and in other words attraction and stimulation is the natural response to beauty, is because they see ugly people and are repelled by them. In the same way, if mountain ranges and plateaus did not exist, plains would not exist and water would not fall from high to low.

In reality, the attractiveness of good-looking people is strengthened by the repulsiveness of ugly people. The magic and spell of beauty exists courtesy of the gracelessness of ugliness. The ugly have the greatest of rights over the beautiful. If not for them, the beautiful would not have had the glitter and shine that they do. The meaning of beauty comes from ugliness. If all were the same, there would be no appeal, nor attraction, nor movement, nor love, nor passion, nor pain, nor burning, nor warmth.

It is a simpleminded idea to say that if everything in the universe were the same, the universe would be better. They suppose that the demand of Divine justice and wisdom is for all things to be at the same level. Whereas it is precisely by such a levelling out that all goodnesses, beauties, and all energies and passions, movements and evolutions towards perfection are destroyed. If mountain and valley were the same level, neither would mountain remain nor valley. If there weren't low points, there would be no high points either. If not for Mu'awiyah, Ali (a) with all his dignity and goodness would not exist. "In the workshop of love, infidelity is unavoidable."

Of course, one shouldn't think that the All-Wise Creator, in order to make the existing order the best [possible] order, and because His eye was to the entirety of the system, randomly made things beautiful or ugly even though it was possible for those beautiful things to be ugly or for those ugly things to be beautiful, choosing each being for its post by lottery or on a whim.

---

[9] The prophet Joseph (Yusuf), who was the epitome of human beauty.
[10] A medieval literate known for his ugliness.

We said earlier that the order of the universe, horizontally and vertically, is a necessary order. God gives every being the very existence and the level of perfection and beauty that it is able to accept; deficiencies come from the essences of those beings themselves, and not from [a shortcoming in] Divine grace.

The meaning of saying that evil has, for example, such-and-such a benefit is not that so-and-so, who could possibly have been made beautiful, was specifically made ugly in order for the value of the beauty of some other person to become clear, for it then to be asked, "Why didn't the opposite happen?" Instead, the meaning is that at the same time that every being has the greatest degree of perfection and beauty possible for it, good effects also exist for this variation, such as beauty gaining value, the coming into being of attraction and motion and so on. The comparison we mention in the following part may make the issue clearer.

Society or Individual?

Scholars have a discussion under the title "Principality of the individual or society" about whether the individual is principle or society? Sometimes the discussion has a philosophical aspect and the point is whether the individual is a real entity and society is a conventional and derivational one, or on the contrary, society is a real entity and the individual is a suppositional and derivational one. Of course, here a third case can also be postulated, which is that both are principle and real; and in our view only this last case is correct. And sometimes the discussion is from the legal aspect and the aspect of "philosophy of law" and the point is whether the goal of law should be the "felicity of the individual" or the "empowerment of society." Supporters of the principality of the individual say that to the extent possible the lawmaker must take in view the ease, welfare, pleasure, and liberty of individuals; the happiness of the individual has first priority. The happiness and felicity of individuals should not be hindered with the pretext of societal interest, except where there is a risk of the destruction and dismemberment of society; only in such a case should the interest of society take precedence over the interest of the individual, since if society comes apart, the individual will naturally be destroyed as well. And in reality, here too it is the condition and interest of the individual that has been observed. As for the supporters of the principality of society, they say that what is most important is the strength and honour of society;

lawmakers and politicians must focus their energies on the strength, honour, and pride of society. The pride of the individual, the comfort and happiness of the individual, the felicity of the individual, the freedom of the individual, and everything that relates to the individual should be sacrificed for society; society must stand tall, even if all of its individuals are in a lowly suffering and wretchedness.

To compare these two systems of thought, we take a look at the national budget. If the leaders of a country think in terms of the principality of the individual, they will strive to spend their country's budget in programs that are responsible for the comfort of the people of the nation and improvement of the economic standing of the general public, even if the pace of national progress is to slow down. But if they think in terms of the principality of society, they will not attend to the needs of individuals and will strive to put forward programs that ensure the ever-greater progress of society in the future and its glory and honour among other societies. The space programs that the powerful countries of the world have originated are in line with this way of thinking. As we know, these programs are given priority over programs of health and public education and training. For the designers of these programs it isn't important that individuals in their country live in hunger, disease, and ignorance; what is important is the honour and glory of their country. The expense of these programs is so great and burdensome that it has weighed down the people of these countries, and in spite of the fact that these governments steal more than fifty percent of the wealth of the world through hook and crook, they still suffer from budget deficits.

The issue is that if the national budget were to be spent in an economic, health, or cultural program designed for the benefit of the general public, it is possible that it could bring about a good amount of welfare, comfort, and liberty for the people of the nation. But if the budget is spent on these programs though it constricts all the individuals [of the country], it is a cause of pride and honour for that society.

Supporters of the principality of society say that the power and glory of society should be given the greatest degree of importance; and supporters of the principality of the individual say that the interests, comforts, and freedoms of the individuals must be given the greatest degree of attention.

The aim of presenting this topic is to draw attention to the point that the rule of the part is different from the rule of the whole. It is possible that something which is harmful and ugly for the part is beneficial and beautiful for the whole.

Differences of Capacities

With regard to human societies, as we said sometimes there is a conflict between the part and the whole; that is, sometimes for the good of society, it is necessary for an individual to be deprived of his rights. But with respect to the natural order of the world, this is not the case. Here, no part has been oppressed in order for the entirety of the universe to be beautiful.

From what we explained in the second section under the title "the secret of differences" it became clear that the differences and variation that have made the universe similar to a perfect and beautiful painting are essential differences. The positions and levels specified in creation for beings are not like social posts, which are changeable and alterable.

These positions and states, similar to the attributes of geometrical shapes, are essential to the beings. When we say that the peculiar attribute of a triangle is that the sum of its angles is equal to two right angles and the peculiar attribute of a square is that the sum of its angles is equal to four right angles, it doesn't mean that the former has been bestowed the attribute of having two right angles or the latter has been bestowed with the attribute of having four right angles. Thus, it is baseless to ask why the triangle has been dealt with unjustly and not given the attribute of having four right angles. No, a triangle can have none but its own specific attribute. No one has made the triangle a triangle; that is, it is not the case that the triangle previously had some other state with differing attributes, and then someone came and turned it into a triangle. Nor is it the case that the triangle, square, and so on in one stage of their existence and actuality lacked all attributes, and then some overruling power came and distributed these attributes among them, and he desired to give the sum of a triangle's angles the attribute of equivalence to two right angles and give the sum of the angles of a square the attribute of equalling four right angles, in which case the question would arise as to why there has been discrimination. Meaning that it would be appropriate for the triangle to wordlessly object to the injustice done to it and demand an attribute like the attribute of a square.

The differences among the creatures of the world is also the same way. The fact that inanimate objects do not have growth and perception, that plants have growth but not perception, and that animals have both growth and perception is essential to the level and state of being of inanimate objects, plants, and animals respectively. It is not that they were initially all equal, and then the Creator gave one, both perception and growth, another, only one of the two, and a third, neither of them. Ibn Sina has a well-known statement that expresses this reality; he says,

ما جعل الله المشمشة مشمشة بل أوجدها

God did not make the apricot an apricot; He merely created it.

The apricot was mentioned as an example; what is meant is all existents. God created things, and they are different in their essence. God created the apricot, the apple, the pomegranate, and so forth; but it is not that they were formerly all equal and God established differences among them after the fact, so to speak. God created time. Time has a particular characteristic; it incorporates the past, present, and future. How did God create time? Did He initially create time like a ball of thread in the form of a collection with all of its parts being together, and then stretch and open it and make it in its current form? He also created the body. Did He first create the body without dimension and size, and then give it size and dimension? Or is the creation of the body equivalent to creation of dimension, length, size, precedence and antecedence, there being no duality between the creation of the body and the creation of size and dimension? The Qur'an has a very subtle and fine expression here; it relates from Prophet Musa[11] (a) that when Pharaoh asks him and his brother Harun[12] (a), "Who is your lord?" Musa (a) replies,

رَبُّنَا الَّذِي أَعْطَىٰ كُلَّ شَيْءٍ خَلْقَهُ ثُمَّ هَدَىٰ

'Our Lord is He who gave everything its creation and then guided it.

[Qur'an, 20:50]

---

[11] The prophet Moses
[12] Aaron of the bible

What is interesting is the use of the expression "its creation," from which we can deduce that everything has a peculiar creation that is its own; that is, everything can accept only one particular manner of being and no more; and God bestows it with that particular being. One shouldn't think that things used to be some other way and God changed them to their present form; or at least it was possible for them to be different or have a manner of creation different from what they have, better or worse, and God chose this particular form of creation in spite of those possibilities. The reality is that the universe was possible only in this form in which it presently exists, and for every one of its parts as well only a specific form of creation was possible, and God bestowed it with that very creation.

The Qur'an expresses this point with a sublime simile. The Qur'an brings the simile of rainwater which falls from above and gradually creates floods and water in the beds of various rivers and streams; it says:

أَنْزَلَ مِنَ السَّمَاءِ مَاءً فَسَالَتْ أَوْدِيَةٌ بِقَدَرِهَا

He sends down water from the sky whereat the valleys are flooded to [the extent of] their capacity

[Qur'an, 13:17]

That is, the mercy of the Lord does not deprive any able existent, but the potential and capacity of existents also is not equal; potentials and capacities are different; Divine mercy fills every container to the extent of its capacity.

This point is what we expressed in the second section under the title "the Secret of Differences"; it was repeated here because, in addition to the benefit of completing [the discussion], it would not be fallaciously supposed that in the creation of the universe, the principality of the whole was kept in view, and for the beauty of the whole, some of the parts were dealt with unjustly. Instead, a beautiful whole has come about that owes its beauty to differences and variation [among beings], and at the same time those differences do not take the form of discrimination and injustice, and both the right of the part and the interest of the whole have been observed.

141

Those who, in responding to the problem of evil, have paid attention solely to the necessity of differences in the entire order, provide an incomplete answer, since the deficient part [of the system] has the right to object and say, "Now that it is necessary that in the whole order, some be perfect and others be deficient, why was I created deficient and another created perfect? Why wasn't it the other way around?" Similarly, it is possible for the "ugly" to object and say, "Now that it is necessary in the total order of creation for both the ugly and the beautiful to exist, why should I be ugly and another be beautiful? Why not the other way around?" When there are two things, one of which must get a lesser share of being and the other a greater share of being, what basis is there to give precedence to, say, A over B?

Thus, simply for us to say that in the total order, the coexistence of ugly and beautiful, perfect and deficient is necessary does not solve the objection. It must also be added that at the same time, every being and every part of the universe has received its right and the share it was possible for it to receive.

In other words, the issues of "benefit," "interest," and "wisdom" that are mentioned with respect to evil things are all subordinate to our understanding of reality-i.e. our understanding the fact that the relation of causes to their effects and the relation of premises to their conclusions is a necessary one, and the Divine pattern or precedent is unchanging.

Calamities, the Source of Felicities

Apart from the fact that evils have an important role in manifesting beauty and bringing about a wonderful whole, there is also another basic point in the relation of evil and good. Between that which we call calamity and evil and that which we know as perfection and felicity, there is a causal relationship. Evil things are the source of and give birth to things that are good. This is the third beneficial effect of evil.

The first effect was that the existence of evil and ugliness is necessary in bringing about the beautiful whole of the universe. The second effect was that beautiful things as well are manifested by ugly things, and if ugliness and evil didn't exist, beauty and good would have no meaning, in the sense that the beauty of a beautiful thing in [one's] senses is because ugly things exist to which they can be compared.

Here, we discuss the third effect of evil and wretchedness under the title that ugliness is a preliminary for and originator of the existence of beauty. Felicities and happiness are hidden in the belly of afflictions and calamities, just as sometimes tragedies are formed inside of happiness; and this is the formula of this world:

يُولِجُ اللَّيْلَ فِي النَّهَارِ وَيُولِجُ النَّهَارَ فِي اللَّيْلِ وَأَنَّ اللَّـهَ سَمِيعٌ بَصِيرٌ

He makes the night pass into the day and makes the day pass into the night ...

[Qur'an, 22:61, 31:29, 35:13, 57:6]

The well-known parable that says, "At the end of every dark night there is light" expresses the definite mutual link between the bearing of troubles and attaining of felicity. It is as though illumination is born of darkness, just as in instances of deviation whiteness produces blackness.

Hegel, the well-known German philosopher of the nineteenth century, has a statement that is worthy of note in this regard. He says,

"Conflict and evil are not negative things originating in the mind; instead, they are entirely real things, and in the view of wisdom they are stages of good and development. Conflict is the law of progress. Attributes and characteristics are originated and perfected in the battlefield of chaos and turmoil of the world, and one can only reach the peak of elevation through suffering, responsibility, and hardship. And suffering is a comprehensible thing, a sign of life, and a motive for reform. Passions, too, have a place among comprehensible things; no great thing has reached its perfection without passion, and even the ambition and self-centeredness of Napoleon contributed, without his intention, to the progress of [various] nations. Life is not for felicity (ease and the contentment resulting from it). Rather, it is for evolution and development. The history of the world is not a scene of happiness and felicity; periods of felicity comprise its soulless pages, since these periods were periods of agreement, and such a costly contentment and happiness is not appropriate for a man. History was made during periods in which the contradictions of the real world were solved through progress and development."

To explain the mutual link between comforts and hardships, the Qur'an says:

فَإِنَّ مَعَ الْعُسْرِ يُسْرًا ﴿٥﴾ إِنَّ مَعَ الْعُسْرِ يُسْرًا

Indeed, ease accompanies hardship. Indeed, ease accompanies hardship.

[Qur'an, 94:5-6]

The Qur'an doesn't say that after hardship there is ease; the Qur'anic expression is that with hardship, there is ease. That is, ease is within the confines of and together with hardship; and in the words of Rumi,[13] "One opposite is hidden within its opposite."

> Life depends on dying (to self) and on suffering tribulation
> The water of Life is the (Land of) Darkness.[14]

There is a delicate point here, the understanding of which depends on quoting all of the verses of this chapter:

بِسْمِ اللَّـهِ الرَّحْمَـٰنِ الرَّحِيمِ

أَلَمْ نَشْرَحْ لَكَ صَدْرَكَ ﴿١﴾ وَوَضَعْنَا عَنكَ وِزْرَكَ ﴿٢﴾ الَّذِي أَنقَضَ ظَهْرَكَ ﴿٣﴾ وَرَفَعْنَا لَكَ ذِكْرَكَ ﴿٤﴾ فَإِنَّ مَعَ الْعُسْرِ يُسْرًا ﴿٥﴾ إِنَّ مَعَ الْعُسْرِ يُسْرًا ﴿٦﴾ فَإِذَا فَرَغْتَ فَانصَبْ ﴿٧﴾ وَإِلَىٰ رَبِّكَ فَارْغَب ﴿٨﴾

This chapter is addressing the person of the Prophet (s), and it is peculiar to the Prophet (s):

In the Name of God, the All-beneficent, the All-merciful.

Did We not open your breast for you and relieve you of your burden which [almost] broke your back? Did We not exalt your name? Indeed, ease accompanies hardship. Indeed, ease accompanies hardship. So, when you are done with, appoint, and turn eagerly to your Lord.[15]

[Qur'an, 94:1-8]

---

[13] See Endnote 46

[14] Nicholson, vol. 6, p.524, vr. 4830

[15] The word *"fansab"* can mean either "appoint" or "make effort"; in this discussion, the author relies on the latter meaning

This chapter, with a tone full of kindness, reassures the mind of the Prophet (s), which was as though it had been troubled by hardships. It speaks of how God lightened his heavy load from his shoulders and changed his difficulty to ease; then, in the manner of experimental sciences, from an event which has occurred and been observed, it draws the conclusion: "Ease accompanies hardship"; that is, from the fact that in the past there was a burden on your shoulders and we lifted it and elevated your name and gave you perseverance and tolerance, you should conclude that "Certainly, with every difficulty is ease."

Then, to strengthen the conclusion and assure that it is definite, the chapter repeats that certainly, "Ease accompanies hardship."

The interesting point is that after concluding this general formula, the chapter also specifies the future path to follow on this basis; it says,

"So, when you become free, make effort."

That is, since ease has been placed within fatigue and hardship, whenever you find leisure, make efforts anew and once again put yourself to work.

This peculiarity relates to living beings, especially humanity: hardships and difficulties are a preliminary for perfections and progress. Blows destroy inanimate objects and reduce their power, but they motivate living beings and make them powerful.

"How often abundance is within deficiencies!"

Calamities and hardships are necessary for the development of humanity. If not for hardships and sufferings, humanity would be destroyed. The Qur'an says,

لَقَدْ خَلَقْنَا الْإِنسَانَ فِي كَبَدٍ

Certainly, We created man in travail.

[Qur'an, 90:4]

Man must tolerate hardships and suffer difficulties to attain his appropriate level of being. Conflict and turmoil are the whips of development. Living beings traverse their path towards perfection through this whip. This law applies to the world of plants, animals, and especially human beings.

Imam Ali (a), in one of his letters to Uthman ibn Hunayf, his appointed governor of Basrah, made mention of the biological law that living in ease and comfort and avoiding difficulties causes weakness; and conversely, living in difficult and disturbed conditions makes a person strong and fit, strengthening the essence of his being and making it experienced. In this letter, this great leader rebukes his governor for participating in an evening gathering of the nobles and setting foot in an assembly that had room only for the rich and not for the destitute. And in this connection, he explains his own simple life and asks his followers and especially the members of his government to follow the example of his conduct.

Then, to close the door of pretexts, he explains that disturbed conditions and simple nutrition do not reduce a person's powers or weaken one's strength.

أَلاَ وَإِنَّ الشَّجَرَةَ الْبَرِّيَّةَ أَصْلَبُ عُوداً، وَالرَّوَائِعَ الْخَضِرَةَ أَرَقُّ جُلُوداً، وَالنَّابِتَاتِ الْعِذْيَةَ أَقْوَى وَقُوداً، وَأَبْطَأُ خُمُوداً

Remember that the tree of the forest is the best for timber, while green twigs have soft bark, and the wild bushes are very strong for burning and slow in dying off:[16]

God says in the Qur'an:

وَلَنَبْلُوَنَّكُم بِشَيْءٍ مِّنَ الْخَوْفِ وَالْجُوعِ وَنَقْصٍ مِّنَ الْأَمْوَالِ وَالْأَنفُسِ وَالثَّمَرَاتِ ۗ وَبَشِّرِ الصَّابِرِينَ

We will surely test you with a measure of fear and hunger and a loss of wealth, lives, and fruits; and give good news to the patient.

[Qur'an, 2:155]

That is, calamities and afflictions are beneficial and have good effects for people who combat them and persevere; therefore, if they are steadfast, they should be given glad tidings.

---

[16] *Nahj al-Balagha* Letter 45

God, in order to train and rear the soul of human beings, has two programs: creational and legislative; and in each He has placed difficulties and hardships. In the legislative program, He has mandated acts of worship, and in the creational program, He has placed adversities in humanity's path. Fasting, pilgrimage, holy war, charity, and prayer are hardships that have been placed [on people's shoulders] by making them obligatory, and patience and perseverance in carrying them out are a cause of perfection of the soul and evolution of the lofty human abilities.[17] Hunger, fear, and loss of property and life are hardships that have been placed in creation and naturally have sway over people.

Tribulations for Divine Friends

This is why when God shows special grace to one of His servants, He places him in hardships. The well-known sentence "البلاء للولاء" ("Tribulations are for God's friends") expresses this principle.

In a tradition from Imam Muhammad Baqir (a), we read,

انّ الله عزّ و جل ليتعاهد المؤمن بالبلاء كما يتعاهد الرّجل أهله بالهدية من الغيبة

"Verily God seeks out the believer with affliction as a man seeks out his near ones with gifts when he is away from them."[18]

In another tradition from Imam Jafar Sadiq (a) we find:

إن الله إذا أحب عبدًا غتّه بالبلاء غتّا

"Verily God, when He loves a servant of His, drowns him in tribulations. [19]

That is, just like a swimming trainer who puts his young trainee in the water so that he will make an effort, flail his hands and feet, and thus gain practice and learn to swim, so too God places in affliction those whom

---

[17] This point does not contradict the negation of hardship in religion, which is an established principle, because the meaning of hardship is not that training and duty do not exist in religion. Instead, the meaning is that commands that prevent human advancement and conflict with proper activity do not exist in religion. Religious laws have been written so that they neither encumber nor encourage laziness.

[18] *Bihar al-Anwar*, vol. 15, part one, p. 56, from *al-Kafi*

[19] *Bihar al-Anwar*, vol. 15, part one, p. 55, from *al-Kafi*

He loves and wishes to convey to perfection. Even if a person reads for his whole life about swimming, until he goes in the water, he will not become a swimmer; he will learn to swim only when he actually goes in the water, practices struggling against drowning, and occasionally sees himself in danger of drowning if he isn't careful. Man must see hardships in the world in order to learn how to escape from them; he must face difficulties in order to become experienced and complete.

Regarding some birds, they have written that when their young grow wings, in order to teach them how to fly, they take them out of the nest and into the heights of the air, and then let go in the middle of the sky; the young bird, out of necessity, struggles and makes uncoordinated movements, flapping its wings until it gets tired and is about to fall; at this time, its merciful mother grasps it and places it on her own wing until its fatigue goes away, and as soon as it has had a little rest, she once again lets it go in the air and forces it to struggle until it gets tired and she again grasps it. She repeats this until her young one learns to fly.

The Prophet (s) was invited to the house of one of the Muslims. When he entered the house, he saw a hen that had laid an egg on top of a wall, but the egg didn't fall, or fell and didn't break. The Prophet (s) was amazed at this. His host said, "Does this amaze you? By God Who raised you as a prophet, I have never seen affliction." The Prophet (s) stood up and left that man's house, saying, "Someone who has never seen an affliction is not a recipient of God's grace."

It has been narrated from Imam Sadiq (a) that:

$$ إِنَّ أَشَدَّ اَلنَّاسِ بَلَاءً اَلْأَنْبِيَاءُ ثُمَّ اَلَّذِينَ يَلُونَهُمْ ثُمَّ اَلْأَمْثَلُ فَالْأَمْثَلُ $$

"Verily, the most severely tried people are the prophets, then those who follow them [in their level of virtue], and so on in order of [people's level of] virtue."[20]

In books of traditions, a special chapter has been dedicated to the severity of the trial of Imam Ali (a) and the Imams of his progeny.

---

[20] *Bihar al-Anwar*, vol. 15, part one, p. 56, from *al-Kafi*

For the friends of God, adversity is a Divine grace that has the face of wrath, just as blessings and ease for those who are astray and far from God's favour may possibly be punishments with the apparent form of a blessing, and wrath disguised as grace.

Pedagogical Effect of Calamities

Difficulty and hardship are both an instructor for individuals and awakener for nations. Hardship awakens and makes more alert those who were asleep and motivates people's decisions and determination. Like a polish given to iron or steel, the more hardships touch a person's soul, the more determined, active, and sharp they make him, since the peculiarity of life is to combat hardship and, knowingly or unknowingly, become prepared to face it.

Hardship, like alchemy, has the attribute of changing the essence of things; it changes the soul of a person. The elixir of life is two things: love and tribulation. These two create genius, and from depressed and lusterless matter make lustrous and shiny gems.

All his life Sa'di has faced bitterness,
For his name to be known as sweet-tongued[21]

Individuals who live in the heart of difficulties and hardships become strong and determined. A leisure-seeking and pampered person is condemned and wretched.

It is within nature that disgrace must come
To every nation that becomes used to ease and leisure

How beautifully has Rumi expressed the story of the imprisonment of Yusuf (a):[22]

The loving friend came from the ends of the earth and became the guest of Joseph the truthful,
For they had been well acquainted in childhood, reclining (together) on the sofa of acquaintance.

---

[21] See Endnote 47
[22] See Endnote 48

He spoke to him (Joseph) of the injustice and envy of his brethren:
Joseph said, "That was (like) a chain, and I was the lion.

The lion is not disgraced by the chain: I do not complain of God's destiny.

If the lion had a chain on his neck, (yet) he was prince over all the chain-makers."

He asked, "How wert thou in regard to the prison and the well?"
"Like the moon," said Joseph, "in the interlunar period (when she is) on the wane."

If in that period the new moon is bent double, does not she at last become the full moon in the sky?

Though the seed-pearl is pounded in the mortar, it becomes the light of eye and heart and looks aloft.

They cast a grain of wheat under earth, then from its earth they raised up ears of corn;

Once more they crushed it with the mill; its value increased and it became soul-invigorating bread;

Again, they crushed the bread under their teeth; it became the mind and spirit and understanding of one endowed with reason;

Again, when that spirit became lost in Love, it became (as that which) rejoiceth the sowers after the sowing.[23]

In another place, to convey this reality he relates the state of an animal that, however much it is beaten, becomes fatter:[24]

There is an animal whose name is ushghur (porcupine): it is (made) stout and big by blows of the stick.

The more you cudgel it, the more it thrives: it grows fat on blows of the stick.

Assuredly the true believer's soul is a porcupine, for it is (made) stout and fat by the blows of tribulation.

For this reason, the tribulation and abasement (laid) upon the prophets is greater than (that laid upon) all the (other) creatures in the world,

---

[23] Nicholson, vol. 1, p.172, vr. 3157-68.
[24] See Endnote 49

So that their souls became stouter than (all other) souls; for no other class of people suffered that affliction.[25]

Then he compares the effect of tribulation in purifying the soul to the mixtures used to purify skins when tanning them:[26]

> The hide is afflicted by the medicine (tan-liquor), (but) it becomes sweet like Taif leather.
> And if he (the tanner) did not rub the bitter and acrid (liquor) into it, it would become fetid, unpleasant, and foul-smelling.
> Know that Man is an untanned hide, made noisome and gross by humours.
> Give (him) bitter and acrid (discipline) and much rubbing (tribulation), that he may become pure and lovely and exceedingly string;
> But if you cannot (mortify yourself), be content, O cunning one, if God give you tribulation without choice (on your part),
> For affliction (sent) by the Friend is (the means of) your being purified: His knowledge is above your contrivance.[27]

Ali ibn Jahm was a poet during the era of the 'Abbasid caliph Mutawakkil; he was an able poet. He fell into imprisonment and has very sublime verses about the benefits of prison, its character-building, its being a matter of pride for people who are free, and finally about what virtues imprisonment represents and fosters. Mas'udi relates them in *Muruj al-Dhahab* and we relate them here:[28]

> They said, you have been jailed; I said it matters not;
> What sharp sword isn't put in its scabbard?
> Have you not seen the lion, how it keeps to one side?
> While the lowly beasts roam about?
> And the fire, hidden inside its stones,
> Not flaming up unless stirred by iron
> Prison, if not entered on account of a crime
> Is a wonderful abode to be in

---

[25] Nicholson, vol. 4, p. 277, vrs. 97-101.
[26] See Endnote 50
[27] Nicholson, vol. 4, p. 277, vrs. 102-7.
[28] See Endnote 51

Contentment with Divine Decree

It is in view of the valuable benefits of tribulations that the quality of contentment with Divine decree and pleasure at what God brings about is born.

Sa'di says[29]

> Let the shortsighted seek comfort
> And the gnostic, affliction; for his ease is in tribulation
> Leave all that you have and pass by, for it is nothing
> This five days of life behind which is death
> All who were killed by the sword of love
> Say grieve not, for their blood-money is the Eternal Kingdom
> Whatever you get from the hand of a friend, give thanks
> Sa'di, seek not your own pleasure, for this is His pleasure

In some of the prayers narrated from the Imams, we read:

اللّهم إنّي أسألك صبر الشّاكرين لك

"O God, I ask of You the patience of those thankful to You."

The patience of the thankful is not a bitter patience; like honey, it is sweet. Those who know that tribulations are what build the soul of a human being are not only happy to face them and welcome them with open arms, they even occasionally put themselves in the claws of tribulation and create troubles for themselves; they create seas and whirlpools for themselves to swim in and become well-practiced.

Rumi, after the verses we related, says[30]

The affliction becomes sweet (to the sufferer)

---

[29] See Endnote 52
[30] See Endnote 53

when he sees happiness: the medicine becomes sweet (to the sick
man) when he regards health.
He sees victory for himself in the very essence of
checkmate; therefore, he says, "Kill me, O trusty ones!"[31]

Sa'di says[32]

They bring precious stones from the mouths of whales
While he who fears for his life avoids the sea

Adversity and Blessings are Relative

We should not be inattentive to the point that tribulations are only a
blessing if a person makes use of them and makes his soul reach
perfection with patience, perseverance, and by facing the hardships that
create tribulations. But if a person chooses to flee and complain in the
face of hardships, in such a case, afflictions are truly an affliction for him.

The reality is that the blessings of the world, like tribulations, can be a
source of ascent and felicity, and they can be a source of wretchedness
and helplessness. Neither is poverty absolute wretchedness, nor is wealth
absolute good felicity. How often has poverty caused the development
and perfection of human beings, and how often has richness been a source
of ill-luck and misery! Safety and insecurity are the same way. Some
individuals or nations, in times of security and luxury, fall victim to
worldliness and gluttony, and as a result fall into abasement. And many
other nations, through the whip of hardship and hunger, get into motion
and achieve power and honour. Health and sickness, honour and
lowliness, and all other natural gifts and trials are also included in this
law. Blessings, and likewise trials and tribulations, can be a gift-because
each of them can be put to great use-and they can also be considered an
affliction and misery-since it is possible for each to become a cause
misery and descent. One can reach felicity both through wealth and
through poverty; and through both it is also possible for a person to reach
wretchedness.

Thus, for a blessing to be a blessing depends on how a person reacts
to it, whether he or she is thankful or ungrateful. And similarly, for an

---

[31] Nicholson, vol. 4, p. 278, vrs. 108-9
[32] See Endnote 54

adversity to be an adversity depends on how a person reacts to it, whether he or she is patient and forbearing or weak hearted and indecisive. In this way, one thing acquires two varying states with respect to two people; that is, it is a blessing for one and an adversity for another. This is the meaning of the statement, "Blessing and adversity are both relative."

What should be called a calamity is that which is a nonmaterial Divine punishment; that is, the evil consequences of human actions. These are actual afflictions and adversities in that first, they are an effect of the intention and free will of man himself, and second, they are not a preliminary for any type of good or perfection. For example, hardheartedness is an affliction for a person, as has been said in a tradition:

ما ضرب الله عبدًا بعقوبة أشدّ من قسوة القلب

God has not struck any [of His] servants with a punishment worse than hardheartedness.[33]

In the stories of the prophets, it is related that a man said to Prophet Shu'ayb (a), "Why is it that I commit all these sins, but God does not punish me?" He replied, "You have been subjected to the worst of punishments without you knowing it." Rumi explains this story in these words:[34]

In the time of Shu'ayb a certain man was saying,
    "God hath seen many a fault from me.
How many sins and trespasses hath He seen me commit!
    And (still), God in His kindness does not punish me."
In answer to him God most High by the mysterious way spoke clearly
    into the ear of Shuayb,
Saying, "(Tell him), Thou hast said, 'How many sins have I
    committed! And (still) God in His kindness hath not punished
    me for my trespasses.'
Thou art saying the opposite and reverse (of the truth), O fool, O thou
    that hast abandoned the road and taken to the wilderness!

---

[33] *Irshad al-Qulub*, al-Daylami
[34] See Endnote 55

How oft, how oft do I chastise thee, and thou unaware! Thou art lying
(bound) in chains from head to foot.

Thy rust, coat on coat, O black pot, hath marred
the visage of thy heart.

Layers of rust have collected upon thy heart, so that it hath become
blind to (the spiritual) mysteries.[35]

That is, your thinking is backwards. If God had involved you in an
apparent punishment, which you would have felt to be a punishment, and
if you were worthy of such a requital, it would be possible for that
punishment not to actually be a punishment, but a Divine grace and
mercy; for it might be a cause for you to wake up and take heed. But the
punishment which you are currently involved in and which is a corollary
of your actions is one which is entirely a punishment and nothing else.

Actual afflictions are the results and effects of a person's actions, and
it is with regard to these very effects and results and punishments that the
Qur'an says,

$$وَمَا ظَلَمْنَاهُمْ وَلَكِن كَانُوا أَنفُسَهُمْ يَظْلِمُونَ$$

and We did not wrong them, but they used to wrong themselves.

[Qur'an, 16:118]

Rousseau[36] has a book called *Emile* which is about raising a child. It
is an interesting book. Emile is the name of a fictional child whom he
places under his care in the book and looks after from all aspects, physical
and emotional. In all cases, Rousseau's idea is to put Emile in contact
with and in the grasp of nature and to raise her in the lap of hardships.

He believes that the most unfortunate children are those whose parents
pamper them and don't let them taste the heat and cold of the world or
feel its highs and lows. Such children become oversensitive to hardships
and are indifferent towards pleasures. Like the narrow trunk of a small
tree, they shiver in the face of every breeze, and the smallest bad event
upsets them, to the extent that a small incident may make them

---

[35] Nicholson, vol. 2, p. 396, vrs. 3364-71
[36] See Endnote 56

contemplate suicide. And on the other hand, whatever pleasurable things they are given, they do not get excited or aroused. Such people can never perceive the taste of blessings; they have not tasted hunger for them to appreciate the flavour of food. The best foods are for them of less value and less satisfying than the barley bread that a village boy or girl may eat.

Why did Sadiq Hidayat commit suicide? One of the factors in his suicide was that he was an aristocrat. He had more pocket money than he needed but lacked a proper and methodical way of thinking. He was devoid of the gift of faith. He thought of the world as being pleasure-seeking, pointless, and foolish like himself. The pleasures that he knew and was familiar with were the dirtiest of pleasures; and of those pleasures nothing worthwhile remained for life and existence to have the value of waiting for them. He could no longer derive enjoyment from the world. Many others like him lack systematic thought and are devoid of the gift of faith, but unlike him are not satiated and highborn, and life is still attractive for them, and so they are not pushed to commit suicide.

If the likes of Hidayat complain about the world and view it as ugly, they have no other choice; their luxurious lives demand as much. They are unable to sense the agreeable taste of Divine gifts. If they had taken Sadiq Hidayat to a village, thrown him behind an ox and plough, and made him taste hunger and nakedness, lashing him with a firm whip when necessary, and then when he was famished with hunger placed a piece of bread in front of him, then he would well understand the meaning of life; and water, bread, and the other material and nonmaterial conditions of life would have value and meaning for him.

In the first chapter of the *Gulistan*, Sa'di mentions the story of a man who sat with his servant on a boat. The servant had never seen the sea and was distressed and uneasy, to the extent that his agitation disturbed the other passengers of the boat. There was a wise man aboard; he said that he knew the solution and told them to throw the servant overboard. The servant, seeing himself face-to-face with death in the crashing and merciless waves of the sea, strove hard to reach the boat and save himself from drowning. After some fruitless struggling, and when he was about to drown, the wise man told them to rescue him. After this the servant was calm and said nothing. They asked the wise man about this; he said, "It was necessary for him to fall into the sea to know the value of the boat."

Without doubt, familiarity with sufferings is the condition of benefiting from pleasures. Unless a person goes to the depths of the valley, he doesn't perceive the might of the mountain. The fact that suicide is more common among the leisured class is partly because normally faithlessness is more common among them and partly because the wealthy class doesn't perceive the pleasure and value of life. Too much pleasure and comfort make a person callous and turn him into a numb and foolish being. Such a person commits suicide over insignificant things. The "philosophy of nihilism" in the west is partly a result of the loss of faith, and partly an effect of too much luxury. The west is sitting on the tablecloth of the east and sucking its blood; why shouldn't it speak of nihilism and emptiness?

Those who attribute suicide to sensitivity should know what kind of "sensitivity" this is. Their sensitivity is not of the form of taste and perception; it does not mean that they have a finer understanding and perceive things that others don't. Their sensitivity means they are unfeeling and numb towards the beauty of the world, easily lose heart in the face of difficulties, and are unable to face them. Such people may as well commit suicide, and so much the better that they do. They are a disgrace to humanity, and so much the better that human society be made pure of their unclean existence.

I once had a distant familiarity with someone and used to think he was among the luckiest of people. Every sort of material object was available to him. Money, wealth, position, fame, he had everything. We spoke about having children. He said, "I never wanted, and don't want, to have children." I asked why. He said, "It's enough that I came into this world. Why should I bring about the suffering of another being? For him to suffer as I have?" This surprised me at first, but later as I became more familiar with him, I realized that he was being honest. In all his comfort and luxury, he saw nothing but pain and suffering. Usually people who we think have freed themselves of all suffering are in greater suffering than everyone else.

Yes, adversities and tribulations are great blessings for which one should be grateful; they are blessings in the apparent form of wrath. Similarly, sometimes wrath is manifested in the form of a blessing. One must, in turn, be grateful for these manifestations of wrath. But in any case, one must bear in mind that for a blessing to be a blessing or an adversity to be an adversity depends on our reaction to it. We can change every adversity into a blessing, let alone those things that also happen to have the apparent form of a blessing. And we can turn every blessing into an adversity and misfortune, let alone those things that are in the clothing of misfortune and adversity.

Reconciliation of Contradictories and Opposites

From the discussions we have had in this section, we reached the conclusion that the basic formula of the creation of the universe is the formula of opposition, and the world is nothing but a collection of opposites. Being and non-being, life and death, continuance and annihilation, sickness and health, youth and old age, and finally felicity and perdition in this world are together. In the words of Sa'di,[37]

"Treasure and snake, flower and thorn, grief and happiness are together."

Rumi says, page 172

Pain is a treasure, for thee are mercies in it: the kernel becomes fresh
 when you scrape off the rind.
O brother, (to dwell in) a dark and cold place, to endure patiently
 sorrow and weakness and pain,
Is the Fountain of Life and the cup of (spiritual) intoxication, for those
 heights are all in lowliness.
That Spring is implied in autumn, and that autumn is (fulfilled) in the
 Spring: do not flee from it.
Be a fellow-traveller with grief, agree with desolation, seek long
 (lasting) life in thy death (to self).[38]

The changeability of the matter of the world and the occurrence of development originates from conflict. If not for conflict, there would be no variety and evolution, the world would not play a new role in every instant, and new pictures would not take shape on the pages of the world.

If we wish to give the issue a philosophical color, we should say that the ability of matter to accept various forms, and the mutual conflict of forms with one another, is a factor in both destruction and creation;

---

[37] See Endnote 57
[38] Nicholson, vol. 2, p.396, vrs. 2261-5.

destruction of the past and creation of the future; removal of the old forms and bringing in new ones. Both destruction and abandonment on one hand and variety and evolution on the other are an effect of conflict, because if a thing were not to be destroyed, there would be no meaning for its parts to be composed anew or evolve. Unless the parts and elements fight and influence each other, a middle composition and new compound will not come into being. So, it is correct for us to say, "Conflict is the source of good, and the pillar of the world and the order of the universe are based on it." In the first section of this book, when we spoke of the essence of justice, we related the meaningful words of Mulla Sadra in the second volume of *Asfar* about how two demands exist in matter (*mawadd*) and forms and how those very conflicting demands necessitate the continuous change of images. Now we relate another of his statements.

Elsewhere, Mulla Sadra says,

لو لا التّضاد ما صحّ دوام الفيض عن المبدأ الجواد

"If not for conflict, the eternal grace of the Benevolent Origin [God] would not exist.[39]

The world of nature is full of links and breaks, cuts and stitches, and this is a corollary of the peculiar make of the universe. The matter of the universe is like capital that circulates, and the profit it generates is due to its circulation. If the universe were fixed and unchanging, it would be like stagnant capital which neither produces profit nor results in loss.

A specific capital that circulates within a market sometimes results in profit and sometimes in loss; but if we look at the total of capital, then no longer is there any loss, and the circulation of capital definitely results in gain and increase.

In the order of the world as well, for all its matter to be put to use, which takes place through the formula of the potentiality of matter and the conflict among forms, is without doubt profitable and conveys the world towards perfection. In dialectic logic, the issue of "conflict" has been given extraordinary importance and became the basis of the

---

[39] *al-Asfar*, vol. 3, p.117

dialectic worldview. But much before the appearance of this philosophy, the philosophers and gnostics of Islam paid attention to the principle of conflict and expressed interesting views in this regard; and even from some quotations from Greek philosophy it appears that attention to this principle had precedent in Greece as well.

Tantawi relates in *Tafsir al-Jawahir* [a commentary on the Qur'an] from Socrates that he used the "principle of conflict" as a proof of life after death.

Tantawi writes: When they wished to put Socrates to death, in the last moments of his life, he reasoned as follows to prove that there is life after death:

"We see that in the world opposites are constantly created from one another: beauty from ugliness, justice from injustice, wakefulness from sleep, sleep from wakefulness, strength from weakness, and so forth ... everything comes into being from its opposite. Death and life and non-being and being as well will be within this general law; and for this reason, out of death, another life must come into being, or else, the general law of nature will be contradicted."

About the development of opposites within each other, Rumi says:

> (When) he came to himself, he said, "O Sea of bliss, O Thou who has stored (transcendental) forms of consciousness in unconsciousness.
> Thou hast stored a wakefulness in sleep, Thou hast fastened (attached) a dominion over the heart to the state of one who has lost his heart.
> Thou dost conceal riches in the lowliness of poverty, Thou dost fasten the neckless of wealth to the iron collar of poverty.
> Contrary is secretly enclosed in contrary: fire is enclosed in boiling water.
> A (delightful) garden is enclosed in Nimrod's fire: revenues grow from giving and spending;
> So that Mustafa (Muhammad), the Kind of prosperity, has said, "O possessors of wealth, munificence is a gainful trade.
> Riches were never diminished by alms-giving: in sooth, acts of charity are an excellent means of attaching (wealth) to one's self.

The sweet fruit is hidden in boughs and leaves: the everlasting life is (hidden) under death.[40]

At the bottom of the sea there are pearls (mingled) with pebbles: glories are (to be found) amidst shames.[41]

From the day when thou earnest into existence, thou wert fire or air or earth.

The Transmuter did not leave thee in thy first (state of) existence: he established a better (state of) existence in place of that (former one);

And so, on till (He gave thee) a hundred thousand states of existence, one after the other, the second (always) better than the beginning.[42]

When you consider, this world is all at strife, mote with mote, as religion (is in conflict) with infidelity.

One mote is flying to the left, and another to the right in search.

War of nature, war of action, war of speech-there is a terrible conflict amongst the parts (of the universe).

This world is maintained by means of this war: consider the elements, in order that it (the difficulty) may be solved.

The four elements are four strong pillars by which the roof of the present world is (kept) upright.

Each pillar is a destroyer of the other: the pillar (known as) water is a destroyer of the flames (of fire).

Hence the edifice of creation is (based) upon contraries; consequently, we are at war for weal and woe.

My states (of mind and body) are mutually opposed: each one is mutually opposite in its effect.

Behold the surging armies of my "states," each at war and strife with another.[43]

Ibn Khaldun, as quoted by Ali al Wardi in the book *al Mahzala*, says,

---

[40] Nicholson, vol. 6, p.454, vrs. 3567-73,3576.
[41] Nicholson, vol. 3, p.50, vr. 866.
[42] Nicholson, vol. 5, p. 49, vrs. 789,791-2.
[43] Nicholson, vol. 6, p. 260, vrs. 36-7,46-51, 53.

إنّ التَّنازع عنصر أساسيّ من عناصر الطّبيعة البشريّة.

Conflict is a fundamental element of human nature."

Hegel, the well-known German philosopher, a portion of whose words we quoted earlier, has a particular view about opposites which is known as "Hegelian dialectics" and is excessively relied on by those with claims to philosophy. He says,

"Every condition of thought or of things, and every concept or state in the world is strongly pulled towards its opposite, and then merges with it to form a greater and more complex whole ... Every state and every effect necessitate an opposite which evolution must conciliate and convert to unity." [44]

Imam Ali (a) has indicated the law of opposition in numerous places in his sermons. In sermon 184 [of *Nahj al-Balagha*] he says,

بِتَشْعِيرِهِ الْمَشَاعِرَ عُرِفَ أَنْ لَا مَشْعَرَ لَهُ وَ بِمُضَادَّتِهِ بَيْنَ الْأَشْيَاءِ عُرِفَ أَنْ لَا ضِدَّ لَهُ وَ بِمُقَارَنَتِهِ بَيْنَ الْأَشْيَاءِ عُرِفَ أَنْ لَا قَرِينَ لَهُ ضَادَّ النُّورَ بِالظُّلْمَةِ وَ الْوُضُوحَ بِالْبُهْمَةِ وَ الْجُمُودَ بِالْبَلَلِ، والحرور بالصّرد، مؤلف بين متعادياتها، مقارن بين متبايناتها، مقرّب بين متباعداتها، مفرّق بين متدانياتها

Here, the Imam (a) makes use, in recognition of God, of the principle "He is like nothing else" and makes a negative comparison between God and the world.

The translation and meaning of the passage are:

From the fact that God created the sensory organs it becomes known that He has no sensory organs. (In other words, the fact that He has placed a means and a place for perception in His creations is proof that His own perception is not through any means or any place.) From the opposition He has placed between existent things it is known that He has no opposite. From the parity He placed between things it becomes known that He has no peer. He placed opposition between light and darkness, clarity and ambiguity, dryness and wetness, hot

---

[44] Durant

and cold. He conciliates conflicting natures, brings together things that are separated, brings near things that are far from each other, and separates things that are near each other.

In the first sermon of *Nahj al-Balagha*, he says of the creation of Adam (a):

مَعْجُوناً بِطِينَةِ الْأَلْوَانِ الْمُخْتَلِفَةِ وَالْأَشْبَاهِ الْمُؤْتَلِفَةِ وَالْأَضْدَادِ الْمُتَعَادِيةِ وَالْأَخْلَاطِ الْمُتَبَايِنَةِ

Here, after explaining that God formed Adam's dust from various parts of the earth and then blew a spirit into him, the Imam (a) describes the created human:

"admixed with various natures, harmonious and similar parts as well as conflicting opposites and separate components."

The Philosophic Basis of Opposition

In a world formed by movement, opposition must necessarily predominate, since as philosophers have said, "Motion is not possible without the existence of obstacles."[45] Motion is effort and struggling, and effort takes place when there is friction and collision.

To explain this in another way, it can be said that no natural motion is possible without force. A body will only move towards its natural place if it is not in its natural place; but when it is in its natural place, it will be inert and motionless. The human being as well rushes towards perfection when he lacks it. Human felicity is always in wanting something, and want occurs when there is lack and deprivation.[46]

Dialectic logic, to the extent that it relies on the principle of opposition and the principle of the interconnection of the parts of nature, is acceptable. These principles were given attention by Divine philosophers from the earliest days. What separates our path from theirs, and in reality, is considered the basic kernel of dialectic thought from Hegel onward consists of other issues; among which is that thought, like matter, is under

---

[45] *Tabi'iyyat al-Shifa*, section 1, article 4, chapter 9. Also *al-Asfar*, "al-Umur al-Amma," level 8, chapter 14

[46] Refer to the article "*Asl al-Tadadd dar Falsafe-ye Islami*" by the author, in the periodical *Maqalat va Bar-rasiha*, ed. 1 (found in vol. 1 of the author's book *Maqalat-e Falsafi*)

the sway of the law of motion and opposition and so on. The laws of motion, opposition, and mutual influence are correct to the extent that they relate to nature, and they are philosophical principles. But when they wish to make knowledge subordinate to these laws-and it is for this reason that they call it "logic"-it is not acceptable, though this is not the place to discuss this point.[47]

Summary and General Conclusion

This concludes our discussion of evils from the aspect of Divine justice. We discuss the issue of death in a separate section with a special view. Here, we consider it necessary to summarize and state the general principles that have been mentioned so far in addition to what was said at the end of section four.

1. The attribute of "wisdom," or "being wise," with regard to God and man is true in two different senses. For a human to be wise means that he or she has a reasonable aim in every action, and in every action chooses the highest and most worthy goals and the best tools. But God is the absolutely free of need and seeks no goal; no perfection can be conceived which He lacks, for Him to seek it. For Him to be Wise means that He conveys beings to the perfections appropriate to them, to the extent possible for them. His action is to originate-which means to convey things to being, which is a perfection-or to plan and make complete and lead things to their secondary perfections, which is another form of conveying things to their perfections.

Some questions and objections come about because of a false comparison of God's being Wise with a human being's being wise. Usually when it is asked, "Why has such-and-such a thing come into existence?" the questioner has thought to himself, "What aim did God have in doing this?" without realizing that if we consider God to have goals like people do, it means that, like people, God compensates with His actions for His shortcomings and perfects Himself. If one realizes from the beginning that God's being Wise means that His actions have a goal, not His Essence, and the wisdom of every created being is the goal

---

[47] Refer to vol. 1, 2, and 4 of *Usul-e Falsafe va Ravish-e Realism* and the epistle "The Rising and Revolution of the Mahdi (a) from the viewpoint of the Philosophy of History" by the author

hidden in its creation, and God's Wisdom entails Him leading created beings to their natural goals, the answer will be clear from the start.

2. Divine bounty, meaning the bounty of being that incorporates the entire universe, has a peculiar order; that is, antecedence and posteriority and cause and effect are supreme in it. And this order cannot be contravened; that is, it is not possible for any being to stay back from its own position and occupy another's position. The evolutionary course of beings, and especially the evolutionary path of the human being, does not involve a turning away from one's own position and occupying another's. Instead, it denotes the "existential breadth" of man. The corollary of having levels and degrees is that a form of difference in terms of deficiency and perfection and strength and weakness exists among them, and such differences are not discrimination.

3. The works of God are general, not particular, and necessary, not coincidental.

The other source of mistakes in this area is a comparison of God's actions with human actions in terms of it being thought that it is possible for God's actions, like people's, to be particular and coincidental.

The human being, by virtue of being a creation among God's creatures and a part of the overall order with his intention being a plaything of particular and accidental causes, decides, for example, to make a house in a particular time and place-and of course, under particular conditions. He collects an amount of bricks, cement, iron, sand, and lime, which have no natural connection with each other, and with a series of artificial compounds links them together in a particular form and makes a house.

How about God? Is God's firm work of the form of making an artificial and temporary link between two alien things?

The creation of artificial and temporary links is appropriate for a creature like the human being, who first, is a part of the existing order and is subject to its laws; second, who wishes to make use of the existing powers and properties of things; third, whose intention is a plaything of particular causes (such as protecting oneself from heat and cold by means of a house); and fourth, whose causation is limited to causation of motion, not creative causation. That is, he doesn't create anything, but instead links existing things by means of moving them around. But God is a creative actor; He is the Creator of things with all their powers, strengths, and properties; and those powers and properties act in the same manner in all cases.

For example, God creates fire, water, and electricity, while man, by forging a sort of artificial link, makes use of existing water, fire, and electricity. He creates this artificial link in such a way that he uses it in one moment or instance in which it is useful for him (for example by turning on the electricity), and in another moment when it is not useful for him he doesn't make use of it (for example, by turning off the electricity). But God is the Creator and Originator of these affairs with all their properties and effects. The corollary of the existence of fire is that it warms or burns. The corollary of electricity is that it gives light or creates motion. God did not create fire or electricity for a specific person, and it is meaningless for Him to have done so, for example for it to warm his cottage but not burn his clothes. God created fire, which has the property of burning. So in Terms of the infinite Divine wisdom, fire must be taken in view in its entirety in the order of being to see whether its being in the entire universe is beneficial and necessary, or extraneous and harmful-not in its particularity, as to whose house it warmed and whose storage area it burned.

In other words, in addition to the fact that goals must be considered the goals of God's action and not His essence, we should know that the goals of God's actions are universal goals, not particular ones, and they are necessary ones, not accidental.

4. For a thing to come into being, it is not enough for God's causality to be complete; the potentiality of the recipient is also necessary. The non-potentiality of the recipient is a cause for beings to remain deprived of certain gifts. Evils that are of the form of non-being, which were indicated earlier, such as inabilities, weaknesses, and ignorance, in terms of their relation to the Divine Essence-that is, in terms of the entirety of the system (not in terms of their relation to human beings, or the particular and accidental aspects of the order)-spring from deficiencies of potentiality.

5. God, just as He is necessarily existent by essence, is necessary from all aspects; thus, He is necessarily bountiful and necessarily existent. It is impossible for a being to have the possibility of existing or of reaching perfection, and for God not to show His bounty and bestow existence. In certain instances when it appears that a being has the potential for a

certain perfection but remains devoid of it, that is a possibility in accordance with particular and accidental causes, not a possibility in terms of the universal and necessary causes.

6. Evils are either non-beings or beings that are a source of non-being in other things, and they are evil inasmuch as they are sources of non-being.

7. The evilness of the second type of evils lies in their relational and relative being, not in their in-itself being.

8. That which actually exists, is created, and has a cause is real existence, not relational existence.

9. Evils are all created subordinately and figuratively, and not in actuality.

10. The universe is a single indivisible unit; removing some of its parts and keeping some of them is a false supposition and a game of the thought.

11. Evil and good are not two separate formations; they are mixed together. Non-beings and beings, relational beings and real beings are inseparable from one another.

12. Not only are non-beings inseparable from beings and relational beings from real beings, but real beings themselves are also linked and inseparable by virtue of the principle of the indivisibility of the universe.

13. Beings have one ruling in terms of their individuality and independence, and another ruling in terms of their being a part and member of a body.

14. Wherever the principle of linkage rules, individual and independent being is suppositional and derivational.

15. If not for evil and ugliness, there would be no meaning for good and beauty.

16. Evil and ugliness manifest good and beauty.

17. Evil is a source of good and adversities are a source of felicities.

Death

The Phenomenon of Death

One of the concepts which has always tormented man is the thought of death and termination of life. Man asks himself why have we come to the world and why do we die? What is the purpose of this construction and destruction? Is it not a futile and meaningless exercise?

The Master did himself these vessels frame,
Why should he cast them out to scorn and shame?
If he has made them well, why should he break them?
Yea, though he marred them, they are not to blame.[1]

Behold these cups! Can He who deigned to make them,
In wanton freak let ruin overtake them,
So many shapely feet and hands and heads
What love drives Him to make, what wrath to break them?[2]

There is a chalice made with wit profound,
With tokens of the Maker's favor crowned;
Yet the world's Potter takes his masterpiece,
And dashes it to pieces on the ground![3]

Anxiety about death is one of the causes for philosophical pessimism. The pessimistic philosophers view life and existence as purposeless and meaningless and devoid of any wisdom. This view has embroiled them in confusion and perplexity, and at times even induced them to suicide; they reason that if we are to die and leave, then we should not have come, but now that we have arrived without choice we can exercise at least this much choice that we do not allow this futility to continue; terminating this futility is in itself a wise act.

---

[1] Whinfield, quatrain 126.
[2] *Ibid*, quatrain 290.
[3] *Ibid*, quatrain 42.

I never would have come, had I been asked,
I would be happy not to go, if I were asked,
And, to be short, I would annihilate
All coming, being, going, were I asked![4]

Since all man's business in this world of woe
Is sorrow's pangs to feel, and grief to know,
Happy are they that never come at all,
And they that, having come, the soonest go![5]

Anxiety of Death

Before we discuss the issue of death and the objection, based on it and, levelled against the laws and order governing the universe, we ought to note the fact that fear and anxiety of death is a distinctly human characteristic. Animals do not think about death. What animals have is an instinct of flight from danger and self-preservation. Of course, the inclination for survival as expressed by the preservation of extant life is a necessary concomitant for life in general, but in humans, in addition to this, there is also an attention to the future and survival in the future. In other words, man also harbours a desire for eternity and perpetual life, and this yearning is specifically human. Desire is dependent on conceptualizing the future, and the desire for eternal life is dependent on conceptualizing eternity; the concept of which is uniquely human. Hence, Man's fear and apprehension of death which has always pre-occupied human thought is distinct from the instinct!' of flight from danger; the latter being an instantaneous and general reaction to dangers in animals. For, before the desire for eternity develops into a concept, even the human child avoids dangers based on the instinctive flight from danger.

Death anxiety is a product of desire for eternity, and since in the systems governing nature no inherent desire is created which is futile and purposeless, this desire can be taken as proof for man's survival after death. The fact that we are tormented by the thought of extinction is itself evidence that we will not become extinct. If like flowers and plants we

---

[4] Whinfield, quatrain 490
[5] *Ibid*, quatrain 387

were to have a limited and temporary life, the desire for eternity would not have emerged as a fundamental desire within us. The existence of thirst is evidence for the existence of water. Similarly, the existence of every fundamental potential and desire within us is evidence of the concrete existence of that perfection. It is as if every potential and capacity is a preconception and memory of the perfection toward which one ought to strive. The desire and anxiety about eternity and immortality which have always engaged the human mind are manifestations and expressions of the inextinguishable reality and being of man. The appearance of these desires and anxieties for a man are exactly like his dreams, which are the manifestations of human character traits and perceptions in his waking period. What appears in the dream world is the manifestation of things which have entered and sometimes taken root in our soul during our waking period. That which appears in our souls during the wakeful period in the form of a desire for immortality and eternity something totally incompatible with the temporary life of this world-is actually the manifestation and appearance of our immortal reality. We will endure. To quote Rumi:

> There must needs be the elephant, in order that,
>> when he sleeps supinely, he may dream of the land of Hindustan.
> The ass does not dream of Hindustan at all: The ass has never
>> journeyed from Hindustan to a foreign country.
> Because of desire the elephant remembers Hindustan; then by night
>> that remembrance of his takes form.[6]

These conceptions, ideas and desires are a reflection of that reality which was named by the philosophers and mystics as "alienation" (*ghurbat*) and "incommensurability" (*'adam e tajanus*) of man in this material world.

Death is Relative

The objection against death stems from the fact that they considered death as extinction whereas death is not the extinction of man; rather, it is a transformation and development, a demise in one realm but rising in

---

[6] Nicholson, vol. 4, p. 441, vr. 3068-9 and 3071

another. In other words, death is an extinction, but not an absolute extinction, rather a relative extinction, meaning an extinction from one realm but existence in another realm.

Man does not have an absolute death. It is abandoning one state and acquiring another state, and like all other transformations, the annihilation is relative. When soil changes to plant life, it is a death but not an absolute death; soil has abandoned its former form and characteristics and no longer has the appearance and manifestation it had as an inanimate entity; but it has died from one state and condition and acquired life in another state and condition.

> I died to the inorganic state and became endowed with growth, and
> (then) I died to (vegetable) growth and attained to the animal.
> I died from animality and became Adam (man); why, then, should I
> fear? When have r become less by dying?
> At the next remove I shall die to man, that I may soar and lift up my
> had amongst the angels;
> And I must escape even from (the state of) the angel; *everything is
> perishing except His Face*.[7]

The World is a Womb for the Soul

Transfer from this world to another world, is not dissimilar to the birth of a baby from the mother's womb. This analogy is complete in one sense but incomplete in another sense. It is incomplete in the sense that the difference between this world and the hereafter is much more profound and essential then the distinction between the womb and extra-uterine life. Both uterine and extra-uterine phases are parts of the material world and physical life, whereas the world here and hereafter are two different realms and worlds with fundamental distinctions. But this similitude is complete from another sense; the sense that reflects differences in conditions. The baby is nourished through the placenta and umbilical cord; but after birth, that route gets blocked, and it is instead nourished via the mouth and digestive tract. In the womb, the lungs are already formed but not functional, but after birth the lungs become functional.

---

[7] Nicholson, vol. 4, p., vr. 3068-9 and 3071

It is amazing that so long as the foetus is in the uterus it makes no use of the respiratory tract and lungs whatsoever, and if ever they were to function for even a moment, it would lead to death; this state continues till its last moment in the uterus, but the moment it steps into this world, the respiratory system immediately begins to function, and thereafter if it were to fail to function even for a moment, death would approach.

In this manner the system of life before birth transforms to another system after birth; the baby before birth lives in one life system and after birth in another life system.

Basically, the respiratory system though formed during uterine life, is not designed to function during that period; rather it is a prefiguration and preparation for extra-uterine life. The visual, auditory, olfactory and gustatory systems with all their complexity and expanse are not designed to function in the uterine phase; they are rather for the next phase of life.

This world in relation to the hereafter is like the womb in which all the bodies and mental systems are formed in preparation for life hereafter. The human psychic potential-its noncomposite and immaterial nature, the indivisibility and relative constancy of man's "I", his endless desires, his expansive and infinite thoughts, are all constituents of a much wider, expansive and longer, nay, an eternal, and endless life. These are the very realities which render man "alienated" and "incommensurate" with this temporary and ephemeral life. These are what have led man to be like the "reed" which has been separated from the "reed bed", from whose "tune both man and woman wail", and is always seeking a "heart which is torn to pieces from the separation", so that it may narrate the "details of the pain of love". These are the very realities which have caused man to view himself from the "lofty perspective of the King seated on the lotus throne", considering the world in relation to himself as the "*kunj mihnat abad*" or view himself as the "sweet celestial bird" and the world as "a snare of incidents".[8]

The glorious Qur'an declares:

$$أَفَحَسِبْتُمْ أَنَّمَا خَلَقْنَاكُمْ عَبَثًا وَأَنَّكُمْ إِلَيْنَا لَا تُرْجَعُونَ$$

---

[8] See Endnote 58

Did you suppose that We created you aimlessly, and that you will not
be brought back to Us?'

[Qur'an, 23:115]

If man furnished with all these systems and capabilities were to have
no return back to God, toward a world which is an expansive realm
commensurate with this well-equipped entity, it would be exactly like the
example of a foetus in the uterine life which had no extra-uterine life
ahead, and all foetuses were to become annihilated at the end of their
uterine phase of existence; all those elaborate visual, auditory, olfactory,
central and peripheral nervous systems, lungs and intestines which are of
no function in uterine life, and which are unnecessary for the vegetative
life there, would have been created without use and would have been
meaningless, futile and destroyed even before any use was ever made of
them.

Indeed, death is the termination of one phase of man's life and a
beginning for a new phase in it.

Death, in relation to this world, is death, but in relation to the next
world, is a birth, in as much as the birth of a newborn in relation to this
world is a birth but in relation to its previous life is a death.

World as a School for Man

This world in relation to the next world is a preparatory, training, and
perfecting phase for man. It is very much what a school or university is
for youth. In fact, we can even say that the entire world is really one big
school or training ground.

In the *Nahj al-Balagha*, under the section of short sayings, it is
narrated that a man came to the Leader of the Faithful Ali (a) and started
condemning the world, "The world is this and the world is that, the world
deceives man, the world corrupts man, the world is criminal and
cunning," and other words of this nature. This man had heard religious
leaders condemn the world, and mistook this condemnation as being
directed at the reality of this world-meaning that the world is inherently
evil. He failed to realize that what was actually evil was "love of the
world," and that what is evil is to hold a narrow view and limited

perspective *vis-a-vis* being-something that is fundamentally incompatible with man and man's felicity. Ali (a) explained to him:[9]

> You can be deceived by the world, but the world does not deceive anyone; you have committed a crime on the world, but the world has committed no crime against you ... the world is honest with whosoever deals with her honestly, and is a means of equilibrium for whosoever understands her; the world is a place of worship for the friends of God, a place of prayer for the angels of God, the destination for God's revelation, a trading place for the lovers of God.

Shaikh Farid ud Din al Attar has composed a poem about this incident.

> Nasir Khusraw addressing the world says:[10]
> O World, you may not have lasted more than
> the usual fourscore and ten for anyone, but still
> you are necessary. You may be as wretched as
> a thorn on the eye, but essentially you are
> as necessary as sight itself. You may have
> broken, but you have mended as well.
> Like a chameleon you take on the colour
> of corruption from the corrupt, but to the pure
> you are pure. To those who despise you
> say You have not known me.
> If you are modest and sedate, you'll find me
> modest and sedate as well. I gave you
> righteousness but you sought from me
> only ill. If you are wise you will be
> saved from me. Why hate that from which
> you 've been saved? God has given me
> to you as a thoroughfare-why do you
> loiter along the way? You are a branch
> of the tree God planted for your sake
> if you grow up crooked, you will end up
> in the fireplace-grow straight
> and you will be saved. Yes, crookedness

---

[9] See Endnote 59
[10] See Endnote 60

will land you in the flames, and no one
will ask if you were almond or pistachio.
You are the arrow of God to His enemies
why have cut yourself on your own point?[11]

The glorious Qur'an declares:

الَّذِي خَلَقَ الْمَوْتَ وَالْحَيَاةَ لِيَبْلُوَكُمْ أَيُّكُمْ أَحْسَنُ عَمَلًا

He, who created death and life that He may test you [to see] which of
you is best in conduct.

[Qur'an, 67:2]

Meaning that this world, which is a composite of life and death, is a
testing ground for the excellence in human conduct.

It should be noted that the Divine "test" is really to actualize potentials
and abilities. The actualization of a potential is to develop and perfect it.
This test is not designed to discover the secrets of beings, rather, it is to
actualize their hidden potentials. So, in this case, "disclosure" is an act of
creation and the Divine test "reveals" the human traits from the hidden
phase of potential and capability to the external and concrete phase of
actualization and perfection. The Divine test is not there to assess the
weight, rather it is there to increase the mass.

With this elaboration it becomes clear that the above-mentioned verse
reflects this truth that the world is a place for training and perfecting
human potentials.

Basis of the Objection

With the explanation of death we gave above, the groundless nature of
the objections is made apparent. In actual fact, these objections stem from
a lack of knowledge about man and the universe, or in other words, they
issue from an incomplete and sterile view of the world.

---

[11] Gholam-Reza Aavani and Peter Lamborn Wilson, *Fourty Poems from the Divan by
Nasir-i Khusraw* (London: Institute of Ismaili Studies).

Truly if death is the end of life, then the desire and longing for eternity will be extremely painful, and the face of death will become infinitely frightening to the human consciousness which.is awake.

That some humans consider life as meaningless is based on the fact that they harbour a longing for immortality but believe it cannot be achieved. If it were not for this desire and longing, they would not have considered life as futile and meaningless, -even if it all ended in utter non-existence. At least, they would have deemed it as a temporary fortune and an ephemeral kingdom. They never would have reckoned that non-existence is better than such an existence, since the presumption is that the defect of such an existence is its transience-its deficiency is that it is followed by non-existence. Thus, all defects stem from transience and non-existence, so how would it be better if non-existence were to replace even that small and limited amount of existence?

Indeed, we observe in ourselves a longing for immortality, and this yearning is dependent on conceptualizing it; that is, we have a notion of eternity and its beauty and appeal, and this appeal creates in us a tremendous desire for immortality, and for enjoying the bounties of life forever.

If a barrage of materialist notions were to overwhelm our mind, making us think that such ideas and desires are all futile and that there is no reality to eternity, then we would have every right to be worried and apprehensive. In this case, an immense sorrow and fear would develop in us and we would wish we had never come and had never faced such anguish and dread. Thus, the idea of existence being futile and meaningless is the consequence of the incompatibility between an inborn instinct and an acquired ideology. For, if it were not for that instinct, such an idea would not have developed; and with just as much reason, if the false materialistic ideas had not been propagated to us, we would not have developed such a concept.

Man's innate and inherent constitution is such that it creates the desire for immortality as a means for achieving the perfection whose potential he possesses. And since this constitution and the potentials it implies are beyond the scope of temporal earthly life, the assumption that existence is restricted to this worldly life would mean that all those potentials are futile and meaningless. The person who has no belief in eternal life finds incongruence between the constitution of his being on the one hand and his thoughts and longings on the other. Audibly and ostensibly he is heard to say, "the end of life is non-existence, all paths terminate in annihilation, thus life and existence is futile and meaningless", but existentially and in his heart of hearts he affirms, "there is no non-existence, there is an endless path ahead, if my life were limited I would not have been created with the potential for eternity and the longing for immortality."

Based on this, as mentioned earlier, the glorious Qur'an equates the denial of resurrection with belief in meaninglessness of creation:

$$\text{أَفَحَسِبْتُمْ أَنَّمَا خَلَقْنَاكُمْ عَبَثًا وَأَنَّكُمْ إِلَيْنَا لَا تُرْجَعُونَ}$$

Did you suppose that We created you aimlessly, and that you will not be brought back to Us?'

[Qur'an, 23:115]

Indeed, one who considers the world to be a school and place for perfection, and believes in life after death, will not raise such objections. He will not say that they should not have brought us into the world. Nor will he argue that now that they have brought us here, we ought not to die. To say this, is in a wise to say that either the child should not be sent to school or that if he has been sent to school, he should never leave school!

Khwaja Nasir al-Din Tusi's[12] teacher (or teacher's teacher) was a scholar by the name of Baba Afdal Kashani. He has expounded the philosophy of death in a profound poem. We can consider his quatrain to be a response to the famous quatrain by Khayyam. Perhaps it was composed for this very reason. The quatrain attributed to Khayyam is as follows:

Behold these cups! Can He who deigned to make them,
In wanton freak let ruin overtake them,
So many shapely feet and hands and heads
What love drives Him to make, what wrath to break them?[13]

---

[12] See Endnote 61
[13] Whinfield, quatrain 42.

178

Baba Afdal says:
> As the pearl (essence) of soul joined the shell of body,
> (Nourished by) the Water of Life it took the form of man.
> When the pearl was finished, when the shell was shattered
> It came to adorn the ear of the King (God).

In this quartet, man's body is equated with a shell which cultivates the precious pearl of a human soul in its centre. The breaking open of the shell, when the pearl is perfected, is necessary so that the precious pearl can be elevated from its lowly position to the lofty position of the human ear. Similarly, the philosophy of human death is to facilitate transfer from the prison of the material world to the free ranges of Paradise which span both the heavens and the earth-and take up position in the vicinity of the Omnipotent King and Majestic Lord, in whose proximity all perfection can be accomplished. This is the meaning of:

$$إِنَّا لِلَّـهِ وَإِنَّا إِلَيْهِ رَاجِعُونَ$$

'Indeed, we belong to Allah and to Him do we indeed return

[Qur'an, 2:156]

The objection 'why do we die?' and its response has been beautifully encapsulated in an anecdote of the Mathnawi of Rumi[14] says:

> Moses said, "O Lord of the Reckoning, Thou didst create the form: how didst Thou destroy it again?
> Thou hast made the form, male and female, that gives unto the spirit increase (of joy); and then Thou dost ruin it: why?"
> God said, "I know that this question of thine is not from disbelief and heedlessness and idle fancy;
> Else 1 should have corrected and chastised thee: I should have afflicted thee on account of this question.
> But (I know that) thou wishest to discover in My actions the wisdom and hidden meaning of (phenomenal) duration,

---

[14] See Endnote 62

That thou mayst acquaint the vulgar therewith and by this means
make every raw (ignorant) person to become cooked.

Then god spoke unto him, saying, "O thou who possessest the most
excellent (understanding), since thou have asked (the
question), come, hear the answer.

O Moses, sow some seed in the earth, that thou thyself mayst render
justice to this (question)."

When Moses had sown and the seed-com was complete (in growth)
and its ears had gained beauty and symmetry,

He took the sickle and was cutting that (crop); then a voice from the
Unseen reached his ear,

Crying, "Why dost thou sow and tend some seed corn and (now) art
cutting it when it has attained to perfection?"

He replied, "O Lord, I destroy and lay it low because straw is here
and (also) grain.

The grain is not suitable (to be stored) in the straw-barn; the straw
likewise is bad (for putting) in the com-barn.

'Tis not wisdom to mix these twains: it (wisdom) makes necessary
the separation (of them) in winnowing. "

He (God) said, "From whom didst thou gain this knowledge, so that
by means of the knowledge thou didst construct a threshing-
floor?"

He replied, "Thou, O God, gayest me discernment." He (God) said,
"Then how should I not have discernment?"

Amongst the created beings are pure spirits; there are (also) spirits
dark and muddy.

These shells are not in one grade: in one (of them) is the pearl and in
another the (worthless) bead.

It is necessary to make manifest (the difference between) this good
and evil, just as (it is necessary) to make manifest (distinguish)
the wheat from the straw.[15]

Death is an Extension of Life

In the discussion on death, we ought to pay attention to the fact that
the phenomenon of life and death creates a sequence in the realm of
creation. The death of some always creates the ground for the life others.

[15] Nicholson, vol. 4, p. 437, vr. 3001-6, 3015-27.

The carcass of an animal never remains unconsumed; plants and animals are nourished and invigorated by it. The shell breaks open and releases a shining pearl; then again from the same body and matter a new shell begins forming and another precious pearl develops in its core. The breaking of the shell and release of a pearl is a process that repeats over and over again, thereby extending the presence of grace and life through the span of time. If people living a thousand years ago were not to die, the opportunity would not have arisen for us living today; just as if humans alive today were not to die, there would be no possibility of life for those to come. If the flowers of the past year were not plucked, the fresh and new flowers of a new year would not have had the opportunity to blossom. The material realm has a limited capacity to accept life as far as space is concerned, but as far as time is concerned, it has unlimited capacity. It is interesting to note that in as much as the matter of the universe is expansive spatially, so too is it temporally-existence having an unparalleled extension in this dimension too.

Khayyam is one of those who have raised objections against death, (albeit they have been attributed to him). It just so happens that he has answered his own objections in one place:

> By suffering tribulations, is man set free;
> The drop imprisoned in a shell, a pearl shall be.
> If wealth will not last, in its stead life will withstand.
> The chalice now emptied, will once again filled be.

We should not be worried about the emptying of the chalice, the provider will refill it again. Khayyam'[16] also says:

> Lament not fortune's want of constancy,
> But up! and seize her favours ere they fee;
> If fortune always cleaved to other men,
> How could a turn of luck have come to thee?[17]

The poet attributes this to the undependability and lack of constancy of the world. Indeed, if only the person whose turn has come is the

---

[16] See Endnote 63
[17] Whinfield, quatrain 366.

measure, then this is betrayal. But if we consider the others who ought to come and also become fortunate then we would call it something else-instead of betrayal we would call it justice, fairness, and equal opportunity.

Here some may possibly interject that God's power is infinite, so what keeps Him from allowing those who are now living to live f9rever, and making provisions for those yet to come?

They do not realize that whatever can possibly be created, has been created, and is perpetually being granted Divine grace. Moreover, that which does not exist is what cannot possibly exist. Even supposing that there are other places, and assuming that the circumstances are favourable for the existence of other humans there, the objection would still remain [only having been transposed to a different scene] that their continued existence would preclude the possibility of the arrival and survival of future generations.

This last point is the completion of the response mentioned under the section 'Death is Relative.' The net result of both these points is that the matter of the universe, through a natural process and trans-substantial motion (*harakat e jawhari*), produces the shining pearls of human souls. The immaterial soul leaves its matter and material body and continues a more sublime and powerful life. The divorced matter takes on another project and proceeds to produce another pearl in her lap, so to speak. In such an order, there is nothing but perfection and expansion of life, and this expansion occurs through the process of transfer and transubstantiation.

The objection to the phenomena of death by comparing it to the shattering of a cup by its maker-insinuating whimsical desires in the Originator and Sustainer of creation-is so childish as to not merit any serious discussion. These notions are perhaps a poet's flight of fancy and subtle artistic nuances which may have nothing more to offer than their literary merit. In all probability the composer of these lines, attributed to Khayyam, had such ambitions or was influenced by a constrictive materialistic world-view. But all these objections are answered by the person who holds that, "in the same way as you fall asleep, so you die, and as you awaken from sleep, so also you will be resurrected." Such a person not only has no fear of death, but like Ali (a) longs for it, and considers it as felicity.

Mir Damad,[18] the eminent philosopher, says:

Do not fear the pain of death, for its pain is in its fear.

Suhrawardi.[19] the Islamic Illuminationist philosopher, says:

We do not hold a philosopher to be a true philosopher until he is able, at will, to disengage his soul from his body-so that such out-of-body experiences become an easy, ordinary, and habitual affair for him.

A similar quote has been reported from Mir Damad, the eminent philosopher and founder of the School of Isfahan.

This is the logic of those who have recognized the precious jewel which develops inside the body. But those who are imprisoned in restrictive and inadequate materialistic ideologies, suffer from anxiety of death, since death in their view is extinction. A person of this latter group is anguished that why should this body (which in his view encapsulates his whole identity and personality) be destroyed. Hence, the thought of death leads him to pessimism about the world. Such a person needs to review his vision of the world and must be made to realize that his objections are based on a misunderstanding of the same.

This discussion reminds me about a simple-minded bookseller in the Faydiyyah School:

In the years when I was engaged in studies in Qum, there used to be a simple-minded bookseller in the Faydiyyah School. This man used to spread out his collection of books and students would buy from him. Sometimes he would perform strange acts and say strange things, which would then be related by word of mouth and spread like a rumour. One of the students narrated an incident that occurred to him when he went to this seller to purchase a book one day: After checking the book, I enquired about its price. The bookseller said, "I won't sell". I asked, "Why not?" He said, "If I sell this then 1 must purchase another copy to replace it." I laughed at his response thinking, "If a bookseller does not constantly transact, buy and sell, he can't make profit and is not a bookseller."

---

[18] See Endnote 64
[19] See Endnote 65

It seems the bookseller was a follower of the school of the poet Khayyam who said:[20]

While Moon and Venus in the sky shall dwell,
None shall see aught red grape-juice to excel:
O foolish publicans, what can you buy
One half so precious as the goods you sell?[21]

He finds fault with the wine-seller as to why he sells wine? Of course, this objection is a poetic artifice, not a serious argument. In fact, its beauty and grace are based exactly on this aspect. But when we evaluate this logic with some measure of seriousness, we recognize how the wine drinker has mistaken the wine-seller's work with his own task. For the drinker, wine is the goal, but for the seller it is a means. The wine-seller's job is to buy and sell, and accrue profit, and repeat this cycle all over again. The person whose job is of this nature, will not be grieved by losing his merchandise, in fact, he will be happy since it is a part of his grand scheme and final goal. Hafiz says:[22]

Where's an *Arif* (mystic) who understandeth the lily's tongue?
That he may inquire: Why she went; and why she hath come back.[23]

Creation is like buying and selling. The world as market is a place to produce, sell, and make profit, and then to repeat this cycle all over again. The phenomena of life and death is the exchange process-facilitating the market's advancement and profit. The person who objects to this "exchange" in creation, has failed to recognize the law and goal of the world.

Whatever form your eye beholds, its essence subsists in no-place;
If the form goes, no worry, its archetype is eternally there.

---

[20] See Endnote 66
[21] Whinfield, quatrain 208.
[22] See Endnote 67
[23] Clarke, ghazal 174.

Retribution

Reward of Deeds

One of the issues that ought to be touched upon in any discussion on Divine justice is the issue of the compensation for deeds in the hereafter. Resurrection and the judgement of good and evil deeds-rewarding good-doers and punishing evildoers-are in themselves manifestations of Divine justice. One of the standard proofs presented for the validity of resurrection is that since God is all-wise and all-just, He does not abandon human deeds without reckoning and reward or punishment.

The Leader of the Faithful, Ali (a) says:

> It is possible that God grants respite to the oppressor but He never abandons him without punishment; He awaits him on his path of crossing, and will block him much like a bone stuck in the throat.[1]

Our aim in this section is not to establish the validity of resurrection through God's justice. On the contrary, our present discussion will address the objection and argument raised against Divine justice as regards the manner of punishment and retribution in the hereafter. It is claimed that the punishment in the hereafter, as it has been described to us, is contrary to Divine Justice! It is said that in the retribution of the hereafter, there is no correspondence between the crime and its punishment, and hence the retribution is meted out unjustly.

In this argument, the matter of retribution which is otherwise an evidence for Divine Justice, is presented as an objection against it, and as being contrary to wisdom. The idea which is at the root of the objection is that in the legislation of retributive laws, there ought to be a correspondence between the crime and retribution. For instance, if someone were to dump litter on a thoroughfare, justice demands that punitive action be taken against him. There is no doubt that the penalty for such an offence cannot be a heavy punishment, like execution or life

---

[1] *Nahj al-Balagha*, Sermon 96.

imprisonment. Based on the principle of correspondence between crime and punishment, the penalty for such an offence can be say a maximum of a week's imprisonment, and if such an offender is judged in a kangaroo court and punished by way of a firing squad, it would constitute injustice. To punish offences is necessary for justice, but if the principle of correspondence between crime and punishment is not observed, punishment would in itself be an act of injustice.

Sins like backbiting, lying, adultery, and manslaughter, are crimes which demand punishment, but are the punishments specified for them in the hereafter not excessive? The Qur'an specifies the punishment for manslaughter as an eternity in hell-fire. For backbiting, it is narrated that it constitutes the condiment for mongrels of hellfire.[2] Severe and unbearable punishments have been mentioned for other sins as well-chastisements which are qualitatively extremely intense and quantitatively very long. The objection is how does this incongruity be reconciled with Divine Justice?

In order to respond to this objection, we must discuss different types of punishments and point out the type that exists in the hereafter. This requires that we first study the order governing the realm of the hereafter and delineate the differences between it and the created order on the basis of what can be gleaned from reliable Islamic sources and logical proofs.

Differences between the Two Worlds

Do the same physical laws, rules and principles which govern this world also operate in the hereafter? Are there any differences between the life of this world and the hereafter? Is the realm of the hereafter the same as that of this world, the only difference being that one comes after the other in time?

Certainly, there are differences between the two worlds though there might be certain similarities; the existence of differences is definite.

These realms are two orders, two worlds, and two types of life with different laws. But do not be quick to judge, I do not mean to say that Divine Justice applies to this world but is not part of the laws of the hereafter-hence injustice is acceptable there but not here. No, this is not what I mean and I wish to say something else altogether, so bear with me.

---

[2] *Bihar al-Anwar*, vol. 15, p. 188

There is no easy and accessible paradigm to demonstrate the differences between these two types of life, since every paradigm that we may cite will be of this world and governed by earthly laws. But as an approximation we can use the analogy of life inside and outside a womb. We have used this example in another place and for another purpose.

The foetus in the womb has one type of life and after birth acquires another type of life. A common factor between these two lives is that in both there is nutrition, but the method of nutrition of the foetus differs from that of the newborn after birth. The foetus in the womb lives a vegetative life and takes nutrients from the mother's blood through the umbilical cord, much like a plant which absorbs nutrients from the soil through its roots. Both the lungs and intestines of the foetus are non-functional, but the moment it comes into this world its whole system of life is overhauled. It enters another realm and a different set of rules govern its new life in this "changed" world. In this world, it cannot survive even for a moment with the patterns and functions of its previous life. Here it must breathe and feed through its mouth. Before birth, if food were to have entered its intestines, and if air were to have filled its lungs, it would have died. But, now it is the opposite. Now, if even for a few moments air is kept from entering its lungs and food is prevented from reaching its intestines, it will suffer death. After birth, if someone wished to continue the previous life pattern for the newborn, for instance by placing him in an incubator and after closing his oral and nasal tracts provide him with blood through the umbilical cord, it would not be possible. The life pattern of the baby has changed altogether, and he must live by a new pattern and in a new system.

The world hereafter in relation to this world is similar to the example given above. The life pattern in the hereafter is different from that in this world. There is life in both, but not identical. The life there has specific rules and laws different from those of this world. In other words, this world and the hereafter are two different worlds and two realms of existence. In order to understand these differences, we must refer to the descriptions narrated in our sacred sources.

We will mention some of them in what follows:

A. Constancy and Change

There is change and motion in this world. The child becomes an adolescent, matures, grows senile, and finally dies. In this world, the young get old, the old pass away; but in the world of hereafter, there is no senility and old age, not even death prevails there. There is a world of eternity, and here is a world of ephemerality; there is a world of constancy and permanence, whereas here is a world of change and annihilation.

B. Pure and Tainted Life

The second difference is that in this world, life and death are mixed with each other, whereas the next world is purely life. Here there are inanimate and animate beings, each of which transforms to the other. The matter which is our body now and is alive was once dead and inanimate, and sometime in the future will again lose its life and revert to the inanimate state. In this world life and death are interwoven, unlike the next world; there it is pure life; the earth of the hereafter, its minerals and pebbles, its trees and fruits, all have life, even its fire is conscious and active.

The Holy Qur'an states:

$$وَإِنَّ الدَّارَ الْآخِرَةَ لَهِيَ الْحَيَوَانُ$$

…but the abode of the Hereafter is indeed Life

[Qur'an, 29:64]

The hereafter is a living entity, it is alive and animate.

The bodies and organs of this world have no perception or sensation, but in the hereafter, even the nails and skin have perception and will speak. During the resurrection, mouths will be sealed and every organ shall report by itself the acts it had performed.

The tongue shall not be asked as it could hide the truth by lying. Every member of the body will become articulate there, listing the acts it performed.

The Holy Qur'an states:

الْيَوْمَ نَخْتِمُ عَلَىٰ أَفْوَاهِهِمْ وَتُكَلِّمُنَا أَيْدِيهِمْ وَتَشْهَدُ أَرْجُلُهُم بِمَا كَانُوا يَكْسِبُونَ

Today We shall seal their mouths, and their hands shall speak to Us, and their feet shall bear witness concerning what they used to earn.

[Qur'an, 36:65]

Another verse refers to the dialogue and argument that takes place between men and their limbs and members of their bodies. After the eyes, ears, and other parts of the body bear witness against the sinners, they will say:

وَقَالُوا لِجُلُودِهِمْ لِمَ شَهِدتُّمْ عَلَيْنَا ۖ قَالُوا أَنطَقَنَا اللَّـهُ الَّذِي أَنطَقَ كُلَّ شَيْءٍ

They will say to their skins, 'Why did you bear witness against us?' They will say, 'We were given speech by Allah

[Qur'an, 41:21]

Indeed, the life in the hereafter is pure, unadulterated by death, with no trace of senility, aging, death, and annihilation; in the hereafter only, eternity governs supreme.

C. Sowing and Reaping

The third difference between this world and the hereafter is that here is the place of sowing and planting the seeds, and there is the place of reaping and benefiting from the produce. In the hereafter there is no scope for the performance of deeds, nor for their preparation-there is nothing but results and produce. Just like the day when examination results are announced. If the student pleads to be given respite to study at the hour of the exam, or if he asks to be tested at the time that the results are being announced, then the only answer he will hear is that the time for examination has finished, and now is the time for awarding grades. The reason prophets exhort: "O people! Engage in virtuous deeds and prepare provisions for your next abode," is that the time for acting and performing deeds is limited.

The Leader of the Faithful, Ali (a) says:

و إنَّ اليَومَ عَمَلٌ ولَا حسَابَ وغَداً حِسَابٌ وَلَا عَمَلَ

Today is [the time for] action, not reckoning; Tomorrow [will be the time] for reckoning, not action.[3]

And in another place he states:

عِبَادَ اللهِ، الآنَ فَاعلَمُوا، وَالأَلسُنُ مُطلَقَةٌ وَالأَبدَانُ صَحِيحَةٌ وَالأَعضَاءُ لَدْنَةٌ والمُنْقَلَبُ فَسِيحٌ

O servants of God! You must perform deeds now. Since, the tongues are free, the bodies healthy, the limbs obedient, and the opportunity abundant.[4]

Implying that the body is your means to perform deeds and actions, before it is taken from you and disintegrates, work with it, and do things which will be beneficial to you. When the time has elapsed, and the soul separates from the body by the omnipotent Lord's command, then it will be too late to act. At that time, whatever request you may make to return to perform any virtuous act, the only answer you will hear is: "Impossible." If it were possible for a fruit already separated from its tree to return back to the tree and regain its former position to ripen and sweeten as a fruit, then it would have been possible to return to this world, but the law of creation is otherwise.

What a beautiful statement has been spoken by the holy messenger of God (s) in this regard:

الدَّنيا مزرعة الآخرة

The world is a plantation for the hereafter.[5]

---

[3] *Nahj al-Balagha*, sermon 42
[4] *Nahj al-Balagha*, sermon 187 or 196
[5] *Kunz al-Haqa'iq*, Chapter "Dal": *'Awali al-La'ali*, p. 267

In this narration, the totality of man's existence has been compared to the annual cycle, wherein each of the world and the hereafter has been compared to one of two seasons, the world being the sowing season and the hereafter being the harvest season.

D. Individual and Collective Destiny

The fourth difference we are aware of between the systems of this world and hereafter is that the destinies in this world are to a large extent collective, but in the hereafter, everyone has a unique destiny. The purport is that worldly life is social, and social life is governed by unity and cooperation; the virtuous acts of good people affect the felicity of others, and the evil acts of wicked people have certain effects on society. It is for this very reason that there exists the idea of "shared responsibilities." The members of a society, like the limbs and organs of a body, must more or less endure each other's wrongs and stresses. Any problem in one limb, causes disease in other limbs; for instance, if the liver does not function well, it affects other organs in a harmful way.

It is due to the fact that individuals of a society have a collective destiny that it behoves them to restrain others when they want to commit sins. The Holy Prophet (s) explained the effect of sin on a community by way of a parable: A group of people had gone aboard a boat and set sail. One of the passengers began drilling a hole in the boat from where he was seated. The others refrained from restraining him with the excuse that he was only drilling on his part of the boat, and in conclusion the whole boat sank and its passengers drowned. But if they had restrained and stopped him, they would have saved themselves as well as the individual who did the deed.

In this world all colours are painted with a single brush. Dry tinder and green branches both either burn together in the fire or are saved from it. Likewise, in a society where there are both good-doers and evildoers, sometimes the evildoers benefit from the positive effects of the good, and sometimes innocent individuals have to suffer the negative consequences of the evildoers.

But the hereafter is not like this. There it is impossible for anyone to have any effect on another's deeds. Neither will a person enjoy the benefit of a good act if he had no role to play in it, nor will he suffer the punishment of the evil doers. The hereafter is an abode of separation and demarcation; it separates between good and evil, demarcates the good-doers from the evildoers. It declares to the sinners that:

$$وَامْتَازُوا الْيَوْمَ أَيُّهَا الْمُجْرِمُونَ$$

And 'Get apart today, you guilty ones!'

[Qur'an, 36:59]

In that world, father will be separated from son, and son from father; everyone will receive the reward for his own acts.

$$وَلَا تَزِرُ وَازِرَةٌ وِزْرَ أُخْرَىٰ$$

No bearer shall bear another's burden.

[Qur'an, 6:64, 17:15, 35:18, 39:7, 53:38]

This difference stems from the fact that the hereafter is a realm of pure actualization, whereas this world is a realm of motion and change-that is, a realm of a combination between potency and act. Pure actualizations neither accept any effect from each other, nor do they combine with each other; but mixed actualizations both accept effects and do combine with one another. Hence, in the world, societies are formed which are a kind of combination and congregation of individual humans; while in the hereafter, society has no meaning. In this world if someone mingles with the virtuous, he gets influenced by their company; and if he mingles with the wicked, he becomes misguided.

Rumi says:[6]

Good and hateful qualities pass from bosoms into bosoms by a hidden way;[7]

Firdawsi says:[8]

---

[6] See Endnote 68
[7] Nicholson, vol. 2, p. 294, vr. 1421
[8] See Endnote 69

If you pass the perfume seller's [shop], your vestments become all
   fragrant;
If you pass through [the shop of] the blacksmith; you will not get
   anything other than black.

But in the next world, if one were to eternally accompany the virtuous,
one's station would never be elevated, and if one were to eternally
accompany the sinners, one's station would not be demoted. There, being
in the company and presence of each other is not effective and nothing
has an effect on anything. In that realm, love and hate do not transfer
from heart to heart. Therein neither sitting in the company of perfume
sellers attracts the good scent, nor does accompanying the coal sellers
attract black dust. In that world, there is no mutual exchange, neither
natural exchange nor man-made exchange. These interactions and
exchanges are specific to this world only.

Of course, the fact that the life in the hereafter is not collective does
not imply that everyone will be isolated and lonely there, and that nobody
will see anyone else or have anything to do with them. Rather the
implication is that the interrelatedness, reciprocal influences,
cooperation, and contradiction that exist here, as well as the spiritual,
moral, and intellectual interactions which prevail and give shape to
society do not exist there. In other words, a real combination of
interacting individuals and destinies do not exist in the next world. But
there is collectiveness and mutual existence in both heaven and hell, with
this distinction that in the congregation: In of the virtuous, there is
friendship, intimacy, warmth, and honesty. For the Qur'an says:

إِخْوَانًا عَلَىٰ سُرُرٍ مُتَقَابِلِينَ

they are [intimate like] brothers, [they will be reclining] on couches,
facing one another

[Qur'an, 15:47]

On the other hand, in the congregation of the evildoers there is nothing
but disgust and enmity of each other.

كُلَّمَا دَخَلَتْ أُمَّةٌ لَعَنَتْ أُخْتَهَا

Every time that a nation enters [hell], it will curse its sister [nation]

[Qur'an, 7:38]

and abuse toward one another

إِنَّ ذَٰلِكَ لَحَقٌّ تَخَاصُمُ أَهْلِ النَّارِ

That is indeed a truth: the contentions of the inmates of the Fire

[Qur'an, 38:64]

The Correlation between the Two Worlds

From the above discussion, we came to understand the differences between the orders governing the two worlds. Now we will look into the basis of the inter-relationship between them.

There is no doubt in the fact that there is a relationship between this world and the hereafter. One might even call it a very intense affinity. The relationship of this world to the next is as two parts of one life, and two seasons of a year; in one season one must to sow and in the other season reap the harvest. To be precise, one is a sowing and the other is the produce itself-the first is the seed and the other the fruit. Hence, heaven and hell are created here. A narration has it:

أنّ الجَنَّةَ...قِيعَانٌ يَقَقٌ غَرسُهَا سُبحَانَ الله وَالحَمدُ لله وَلاَ إِلَهَ إِلَّا اللَّهُ وَاللَّهُ أكبَرُ وَلَا قُوَّةَ إِلَّا بِاللَّهِ

Verily, heaven is an empty desert, with no plantations or farms; Verily the incantations of *subhan allah*, *al-hamdu lilillah*, *allahu akbar* and *la hawla wa la quwwata illah billah*, are recited here but planted there.[9]

In another narration, the Holy Prophet (s) is reported to have said:[10]

---

[9] *Mustadrak al-Wasa'il*, vol. 5, p. 327.
[10] See Endnote 70

On the night of ascension, I entered Paradise. I saw angels busy in construction, a brick of silver and a brick of gold, and at times they would stop constructing. I asked them, "Why do you work sometimes and stop at other times?" They replied, "We wait for construction materials [to arrive]." I enquired, "What are these construction materials?" They said, "A believer's incantations which he recites in the world: *subhan allah, wal-hamdu lillah, wa la ilaha illallahu wallahu akbar*. Whenever they recite, we build, whenever they stop, we stop."[11]

In another narration, the Holy Prophet (s) is reported to have said,[12]

"Whoever recites *subhan allah*, God plants a tree for him in paradise, Whoever recites *alhamdu lillah*, God plants a tree for him in paradise, Whoever recites *la ilaha illa allah*, God plants a tree for him in paradise, Whoever recites *allahu akbar*, God plants a tree for him in paradise." A man from Quraish remarked, "Hence our trees in paradise are plenty." The Prophet cautioned, "Indeed, but be careful not to send fire to bum them up! And this is based on God's statement: 'O you who have faith! Obey God and obey the Apostle, and do not render your works void'".[13]

Implying that in as much as you create trees in paradise by your good acts, so also you ignite the hell fire by your evil deeds; and it is possible for this fire to destroy your good efforts.

In another narration, the Holy Prophet (s) is reported to have said:

$$\text{إِنَّ الْحَسَدَ لَيَأْكُلُ الْإِيمَانَ كَمَا تَأْكُلُ النَّارُ الْحَطَبَ}$$

Verily, envy consumes a person's faith like the fire consumes wood [and renders it into ash].[14]

From this we understand that hell, like heaven, is an empty desert; the fire and punishment are the embodiments of man's sins which are ignited and sent forth by man himself; serpents, scorpions, boiling water, and the

---

[11] *Wasa'il al-Shiah*, vol. 7, p. 189, tradition 9079.
[12] See Endnote 71
[13] *Wasa'il al-Shiah*, vol. 7, p. 187, tradition 9074.
[14] *Al-Kafi*, vol. 2, p. 307

food of hell (*zaqqum*), are all created from the wickedness and evil, in the same manner that houris, palaces, and the eternal pleasures of heaven are created from piety and virtuous acts. With regard to the inhabitants of hell fire, the Qur'an says:

$$\text{أُولَـٰئِكَ لَهُمْ عَذَابٌ مِّن رِّجْزٍ أَلِيمٌ}$$

for such is a painful punishment due to defilement

[Qur'an, 34:5]

Three Types of Retribution

The previous two discussions on 'the differences between the two worlds,' and the 'correlation between the two worlds,' were a preamble for the present discussion wherein we wish to study the various types of retribution. We want to prove in this section that the nature of retribution in the hereafter is different from the nature of retribution of this world, and that the answer to the objection of incongruity between crime and punishment depends on recognizing this difference. Punishments are of three types:

1. Conventional Punishments (warning and reprimand)

2. Punishments that have an existential and natural connection with sin (worldly consequence)

3. Punishments which are the very embodiment of the crime itself and inseparable from it (punishment of the hereafter or "Retribution")

Warning and Reprimand

The first type of punishment pertains to penalties and judicial measures legislated in human societies by either secular or religious authorities. The benefit of such measures is twofold. Firstly, they act as deterrents and prevent the repetition of the crime by the criminal himself or by others-for everybody fears being penalized. It is for this reason we can call such punishments "warnings." Secondly, they provide closure and relief to victims of the crime-this applying to the criminal cases of aggression and oppression against others.

The sense of revenge and wanting to get even is quite strong in humans. It appears that it was even stronger in earlier times and in more primitive societies. If criminals were not to be punished by law, a lot of corruption and destruction in society would follow. This feeling still persists in man today, the only difference being that in civilized societies it is attenuated or more hidden. An oppressed human develops a psychological complex, which if not resolved, can possibly, consciously or unconsciously, lead a person to commit crime himself. But if the criminal is punished in front of the victim, the latter's complex is resolved and his psyche is cleansed from hatred and discomfort.

The penal code is necessary and essential to reform the criminal and ensure order in society; nothing else can replace it. With regards to the proposal of certain individuals who hold that as an alternative to punishment, the criminal should be reformed, or that instead of prisons we should have disciplinary facilities, is actually a fallacy. Reform and disciplinary facilities are definitely necessary and essential, and undoubtedly such corrective measures will reduce crime levels. Likewise, social inequities are one of the causes of crime, and establishing social, economic, and cultural safety nets will also reduce crime rates. But none of these can be a substitute for the other. Correctional measures and an equitable social order cannot become a substitute for penalty and punishment. By the same token, penalties and reprimands cannot take the place of proper rehabilitation and justice in society.

No matter how good the rehabilitation and how just the social system, one will still find that rebellious criminals exist and for whom the only deterrence is the application of punishment which at times may need to be quite severe.

The crime rate can be reduced to a large extent through the strengthening of faith, proper rehabilitation, social reform, and by eliminating causes of crimes. All of these reductive methods should be employed, but the essential fact remains that the unique role of punishment cannot be denied and that none of the other methods can produce its effects. Man has not yet succeeded, and perhaps will never succeed, to reform people purely through admonishment, instruction, and all other educational and corrective means. What's more, there is no hope in the foreseeable future that the present civilization and materialistic mode of living will create a situation where no crimes will be committed.

The current civilization has not only failed to reduce crime rates, it has rather exacerbated and intensified the level of crime in many ways.

In olden times, theft used to take the form of petty theft, pick-pocketing, or highway robbery. But today it occurs in thousands of ways and forms, visible and invisible, overt and covert. Even the overt cases are not insignificant, for sometimes a whole ship or two is stolen from the seas in broad daylight.

Due to the reasons mentioned above, we are forced to conclude that human legislation of punishment and penalties is necessary and essential for human societies. But as was pointed out earlier, the legislators of the penal code need to maintain some form of congruity between the crime and punishment.

But an interesting point to note here is that such punishments cannot be envisaged in the hereafter. The reason is that, in that realm there is neither the question of deterrence from future crimes, nor of a need for revenge. The hereafter is not a realm for performing deeds, such that man ought to be punished to deter him from further crimes. Nor is it the case that the Lord, God forbid, has any sense of revenge and spite that He needs to resolve a psychological complex through retaliation. Similarly, the issue of assuaging the hurt feelings of the oppressed is not relevant there-especially if that oppressed is a saint and beloved of God, and a locus of universal Divine mercy. By all the more reason, others who are not saints, would also prefer the goodness, grace, and forgiveness of that realm to a world of revenge and vindication.

Furthermore, not all punishments are for a violation of people's rights, such that one may argue that Divine justice demands that the oppressed person's heart should be won through a retaliation aimed at the oppressor. A large portion of punishments are related to polytheism, hypocritical display of worship, neglecting God's worship, etc. These are Divine rights and not people's rights; and in such cases none of the two effects and characteristics of worldly punishment would apply.

Worldly Consequences

The second type of punishments are those that have a causal relationship with the crime. That is to say, they are the direct effects and natural consequences of the crime. These penalties are called the 'consequence of deeds' or 'natural effects of sins.' Many sins produce undesirable natural consequences in this world for the sinner. For instance, alcoholism, in addition to its social harms, does psychological and physical harm to the addict. Alcoholism causes nervous breakdown, arterial occlusion, liver damages. Sexual indiscretion can cause gonorrhea and syphilis.

These are natural effects of sin, not legal penalties, such that one could object that a correspondence between crime and punishment ought to be observed. If someone takes a deadly poison and ignores the advice of a well-wisher, he will die. Death is the natural consequence and direct effect of consuming poison. Such a careless individual will surely die, but it would be wrong for someone to argue that the poor fellow committed a crime of just say five minutes, so why should he have to suffer the penalty of death and lose his life? If someone is told not to jump off a cliff otherwise you will die, he has no right to object and say, "What is the relationship between my recklessness and such a severe punishment?" Here the laws of cause and effect apply. Falling off a cliff or consuming poison is the cause, and death its effect. That is the specific effect of the cause, and it cannot be otherwise.

The issue of congruity between crime and punishment is related to man-made punishments, wherein the relation between them and the crime is man-made, not natural and essential. But natural consequences are the results and necessary effects of actions. Now, as we mentioned in the second section of this book, everything in the universal causal chain has a special position and it is impossible for a real cause not to entail a real effect.

In the discussion on the differences between this world and the hereafter, we said that this world is the sowing ground, whereas the hereafter is the harvest. But at times, some deeds demonstrate their effects in this very world. In other words, the sowed seeds get harvested here and now. Of course, this acquisition of the results of deeds and reaping the produce of sowed seeds is a type of Divine retribution, though it is not a complete retribution. The final and detailed reckoning and the total retribution will take place in the hereafter. This world is an abode of deeds, and at times retribution can be seen here, but the hereafter is an absolute abode for retribution and reckoning, there being no scope for deeds whatsoever.

In the majority of the cases actions pertaining to God's creation, whether they involve good and humanitarian service to mankind, or evil and harm to people, will be rewarded or punished here in this world, without the retribution of the hereafter being reduced in any way whatsoever.

Doing evil to one's parents will be punished in this world, especially if that evil entails, God forbid, killing one's parents. Even if a person's parents are sinners or disbelievers, there also evil towards them will not go unpunished.

The Abbasid caliph Muntasir killed his father Mutawakkil, and after a short period of time he was killed himself - this despite the fact that Mutawakkil himself was a very wicked and evil person. In his gatherings of fun and frolic, Mutawakkil used to ridicule the Leader of the Faithful Ali (a). He would have his stooges dress up like that eminent personality and imitate him in jest, and degrade him in their poetry. It is said that upon hearing his father abuse the holy lady Fatimah (sa), Muntasir asked an elder what the punishment for it was? He was told that the punishment is certain death, but beware, whosoever kills his father, his own life will be shortened. Muntasir said I do not care that my life is shortened if it is for the sake of obedience to God. He killed his father and thereafter survived for only seven months.[15]

Ali (a), with regard to the consequences in this world to kindness and service to mankind, says:

وقال(ع) : لاَ يُزَ هِّدَنَّكَ فِي الْمَعْرُوفِ مَنْ لاَ يَشْكُرُهُ لَكَ، فَقَدْ يَشْكُرُكَ عَلَيْهِ مَنْ لاَ يَسْتَمْتِعُ بِشَيْءٍ مِنْهُ، وَقَدْ تُدْرِكُ مِنْ شُكْرِ الشَّاكِرِ أَكْثَرَ مِمَّا أَضَاعَ الْكَافِرُ وَاللهُ يُحِبُّ الْمُحْسِنِينَ

Sometimes you do an act of goodness to someone but he fails to appreciate it, (or perhaps is even ungrateful), but this should not discourage you from continuing doing good, for at times you will receive your reward multiple fold above your expectations, from someone to whom you had done no goodness at all. Anyway, the universe will pay you back-perhaps from a quarter you never expected it to come from.![16]

---

[15] *Safinat ul Bihar*, section *wkl* (وکل), *Bihar al-Anwar*, vol. 10, p. 296
[16] *Nahj al-Balagha*, saying 195

Mawlana Rumi in regard to action and reaction says:[17]

> This world is the mountain, and our action the shout: the echo of the shouts comes (back) to us.[18]
> Another poet speaks about retribution and worldly consequences thus:[19]
> I saw with my own eyes on the path, a chick taking the life of an ant.
> It had not yet finished downing its prey, when another bird of prey finished it off.
> So, if you do bad, do not feel safe from perils; for it is necessary for nature to punish.

Of course, we should never think that whenever an affliction befalls a person or a people, it is necessarily the consequence of their deeds; since afflictions in this world have other reasons too and we believe that in this world a certain degree of natural consequences also prevail.

Punishments of the Hereafter

The retribution of the next world has a stronger existential connection with sins. The relationship of deeds to their retribution in the hereafter is neither of the first type--conventional or man-made, nor is it of the second type-concrete and natural; rather, it is something higher than these two. Here the principle of 'unity' and 'identity' operates. *i.e.* the reward or punishment which will be meted out to good-doers or evil doers in the hereafter will be an embodiment of the act itself.

The Holy Qur'an states:

يَوْمَ تَجِدُ كُلُّ نَفْسٍ مَّا عَمِلَتْ مِنْ خَيْرٍ مُحْضَرًا وَمَا عَمِلَتْ مِن سُوءٍ تَوَدُّ لَوْ أَنَّ بَيْنَهَا وَبَيْنَهُ أَمَدًا بَعِيدًا

The day when every soul will find present whatever good it has done; and as for the evil, it has done, it will wish there were a far distance between it and itself

---

[17] See Endnote 72
[18] Nicholson, vol. 1, p. 15, vr. 215
[19] See Endnote 73

[Qur'an, 3:30]

In another place it declares:

وَوَجَدُوا مَا عَمِلُوا حَاضِرًا ۗ وَلَا يَظْلِمُ رَبُّكَ أَحَدًا

They will find present whatever they had done, and your Lord does not wrong anyone

[Qur'an, 18:49]

In another place it asserts:

يَوْمَئِذٍ يَصْدُرُ النَّاسُ أَشْتَاتًا لِّيُرَوْا أَعْمَالَهُمْ ﴿٦﴾ فَمَن يَعْمَلْ مِثْقَالَ ذَرَّةٍ خَيْرًا يَرَهُ ﴿٧﴾ وَمَن يَعْمَلْ مِثْقَالَ ذَرَّةٍ شَرًّا يَرَهُ ﴿٨﴾

On that day, mankind will issue forth in various groups to be shown their deeds. So, whoever does an atom's weight of good will see it, and whoever does an atom's weight of evil will see it

[Qur'an, 99:6-8]

In a verse which according to some commentators is the last verse to be revealed in the Qur'an, it is said:

وَاتَّقُوا يَوْمًا تُرْجَعُونَ فِيهِ إِلَى اللَّـهِ ۖ ثُمَّ تُوَفَّىٰ كُلُّ نَفْسٍ مَّا كَسَبَتْ وَهُمْ لَا يُظْلَمُونَ

And beware of a day in which you will be brought back to Allah. Then every soul shall be recompensed fully for what it has earned, and they will not be wronged.

[Qur'an, 2:281]

The Holy Qur'an refers to those who unjustly abuse the property of orphans as follows:

إِنَّ الَّذِينَ يَأْكُلُونَ أَمْوَالَ الْيَتَامَىٰ ظُلْمًا إِنَّمَا يَأْكُلُونَ فِي بُطُونِهِمْ نَارًا ۖ وَسَيَصْلَوْنَ سَعِيرًا

Indeed, those who consume the property of orphans wrongfully, only ingest fire into their bellies, and soon they will enter the Blaze.

[Qur'an, 4:10]

That is, consuming the property of orphans is actually consuming hell-fire, but since they are in this world, they fail to perceive it. Once the barrier of the body is removed by death, they will catch fire and burn.

The Holy Qur'an admonishes believers thus:

يَا أَيُّهَا الَّذِينَ آمَنُوا اتَّقُوا اللَّـهَ وَلْتَنظُرْ نَفْسٌ مَّا قَدَّمَتْ لِغَدٍ ۖ وَاتَّقُوا اللَّـهَ

O you who have faith! Be wary of Allah, and let every soul consider what it sends ahead for Tomorrow, and be wary of Allah

[Qur'an, 59:18]

It is an exceptionally stern and explicit tone, it commands thus: Everyone ought to consider what they have sent forth for their morrow. The message is about sending in advance meaning that you will get over there exactly what you send forth now from here. Hence, carefully observe what you send forth.

It is like the traveller who purchases some items and sends them in advance back to his hometown. Such a person must scrutinize and be careful, since when he returns from his journey and arrives back home, he will find exactly those things that he had previously packed and sent by post. It is not possible for a him to have sent one type of item and after returning home to find another type of item.

In this holy verse, the word *ittaqu allah* has been used twice between which there is a short phrase: *wal tandhur nafsun ma qaddamat lighadin*. Perhaps there is no similar verse in the Qur'an where after such a short gap the imperative of "God wariness" is repeated.

Again, the holy Qur'an states:

إِذَا الشَّمْسُ كُوِّرَتْ ﴿١﴾ وَإِذَا النُّجُومُ انكَدَرَتْ ﴿٢﴾ وَإِذَا الْجِبَالُ سُيِّرَتْ ﴿٣﴾ وَإِذَا الْعِشَارُ عُطِّلَتْ ﴿٤﴾ وَإِذَا الْوُحُوشُ حُشِرَتْ ﴿٥﴾ وَإِذَا الْبِحَارُ سُجِّرَتْ ﴿٦﴾ وَإِذَا النُّفُوسُ زُوِّجَتْ ﴿٧﴾ وَإِذَا الْمَوْءُودَةُ سُئِلَتْ ﴿٨﴾ بِأَيِّ ذَنبٍ قُتِلَتْ ﴿٩﴾ وَإِذَا الصُّحُفُ نُشِرَتْ ﴿١٠﴾ وَإِذَا السَّمَاءُ كُشِطَتْ ﴿١١﴾ وَإِذَا الْجَحِيمُ سُعِّرَتْ ﴿١٢﴾ وَإِذَا الْجَنَّةُ أُزْلِفَتْ ﴿١٣﴾ عَلِمَتْ نَفْسٌ مَّا أَحْضَرَتْ ﴿١٤﴾

When the sun is wound up, when the stars scatter, when the mountains are set moving, when the pregnant camels are neglected, when the wild beasts are mustered, when the seas are set afire, when the souls are assorted, when the girl buried-alive will be asked for what sin she was killed. When the [scrolls of the] scriptures are unrolled, when the sky is stripped off, when hell is set ablaze, when paradise is brought near, then a soul shall know what it has readied [for itself]

[Qur'an, 81:1-14]

That is, whatever man shall receive in that world, whether heavenly bounties or hellish punishment, all of it will be what he has readied and prepared for himself. The only thing is that in this world he is unable to perceive them, whereas in the hereafter he shall be fully conscious of them. This is the purport of many verses in the holy Qur'an--that on the Day of Resurrection God will inform you of what you did, implying that right now you are not fully aware of what you are doing, and it will only be on the Day of Resurrection that you shall be made aware of your deeds and fully conscious of your behaviour.

قُلْ إِنَّ الْمَوْتَ الَّذِي تَفِرُّونَ مِنْهُ فَإِنَّهُ مُلَاقِيكُمْ ثُمَّ تُرَدُّونَ إِلَىٰ عَالِمِ الْغَيْبِ وَالشَّهَادَةِ فَيُنَبِّئُكُم بِمَا كُنتُمْ تَعْمَلُونَ

Say, 'The death that you flee will indeed encounter you. Then you will be returned to the Knower of the sensible and the Unseen, and He will inform you about what you used to do.

[Qur'an, 62:8]

The retribution in the hereafter is the embodiment of the deeds done here. The rewards and punishments there are actually these very acts of goodness or evil and which will be revealed and manifested when the veils are lifted. The recitation of the Qur'an here, will become a beautiful entity there-a presence which will perpetually accompany the reciter. On the other hand, backbiting or hurting people will manifest as the gravy of the mongrels of hell.

In other words, our acts have an earthly dimension which is temporary and ephemeral-and that is the one which appears in this world as the spoken word or done deed; and they have another celestial dimension and appearance-which even "after" the deed is done, never disappears and is an inseparable effect and offspring of ours. Our deeds from that celestial dimension and unseen perspective are permanent, and one day we shall reach those deeds and will be able to perceive them in their celestial form and appearance. If they are beautiful and pleasing, it will be bounty and grace for us, and if they are ugly and unpleasant, it will be our fire and hell.

There is a narration that a woman of short stature received an audience with the Holy Prophet (s). After her departure, 'Aishah imitated her shortness with gestures. The Holy Prophet (s) said to her, "Pick your teeth". 'Aishah asked, "But have I eaten anything, O Prophet of God?" The Holy Prophet repeated, "Pick your teeth." 'Aishah used a toothpick and a piece of meat fell from her mouth.[20]

In reality, the Holy Prophet, by his control over the celestial realm, enabled 'Aishah to perceive in this world, the celestial and other-worldly reality of backbiting. The holy Qur'an explains backbiting thus:

$$\text{وَ لَا يَغْتَب بَّعْضُكُم بَعْضًا ۚ أَيُحِبُّ أَحَدُكُمْ أَن يَأْكُلَ لَحْمَ أَخِيهِ مَيْتًا فَكَرِهْتُمُوهُ}$$

And do not backbite one another. Will any of you love to eat the flesh of his dead brother? You would hate it.

[Qur'an, 49:12]

Qays ibn 'Asim was one of the companions of the Holy Prophet (s), He narrates that one day in the company of Bani Tamim, I entered the presence of the Holy Prophet (s), and I made the following request, "O Prophet of God! We live in the desert, and we rarely get an occasion to

---

[20] *Bihar al-Anwar*, vol. 15, part 4, p. 188

benefit from your presence, please admonish us." The Holy Prophet (s) gave us useful advice, some of which is as follows:

You will inevitably have a companion who will never separate from you; He will be buried with you, such that you will be dead but he will be alive. If your companion is honourable, he will honour you; and if he is ignoble, he will abandon you to the events. The companion will be resurrected with you, and you will be responsible for him, so take care in the choice of companion-that he should be good. For if he is good, he will provide you comfort, otherwise he will cause you distress. That companion is your deeds.

Qays ibn 'Asim said, "I would like your admonishments to be put into verse so as to make it easier to memorize them and treasure them as a source of pride for us. The Holy Prophet (s) instructed someone to summon Hassan ibn Thabit, but before Hassan could arrive, Qays who was enchanted by the guidance of the holy Prophet, himself composed the admonishment in the form of a poem and presented it to the holy Prophet. The poem was:

Choose for your behaviour a good companion, for a Man's escort in the grave is his action,

There is no option but to prepare, For the day when man shall be summoned

So, if you will preoccupy yourself with anything, let it not be in what displeases the Lord,

For man will not be accompanied after death, save by what he used to do,

Indeed, man is not but a guest amongst his people, he will tarry a little then depart.[21]

It is narrated in a tradition thus:

إنّما هي أعمالكم ترد إليكم

These punishments are your very actions and behaviors which are being returned to you. [22]

---

[21] Saduq, *Khisal*, section 3, number 93
[22] *Bihar al-Anwar*, vol. 3, p. 91.

Hats off to Sa'di who composed such sublime verses:[23]

Every moment a breath of life is spent, If I consider, not much of it
remains.

O thou, whose fifty years have elapsed in sleep, Wilt thou perhaps
overtake them in these five days?

Shame on him who has gone and done no work. The drum of
departure was beaten but he has not made his load.

Whoever had come had built a new edifice. He departed and left the
place to another

Send provision for thy journey to thy tomb. Nobody will bring it after
thee; send it before.

Life is snow, the sun is melting hot. Little remains, but the gentleman
is slothful still.

O thou who hast gone empty handed to the bazar, r fear thou wilt not
bring a towel filled.

Who eats the com he has sown while it is yet green, Must at harvest
time glean the ears of it.[24]

Reminiscences of a Teacher

I recall the incident of a dream whose narration will not be without
benefit here. It pertains to my teacher, the late eminent scholar, Aqa Haj
Mirza' Ali Aqa Shirazi (may God raise his station) who was one of the
greatest men I saw in my life, a true and living example of an ascetic,
worshipper, man of conviction, and a reminder of the pious predecessors
about whom we had studied in history.

In the summer of the year twenty-one and twenty-two (solar hijri
calendar) I travelled from Qum to Isfahan and was blessed with the
opportunity to meet and benefit from that great personality. This first
encounter later transformed into intense affection from my side, and a
fatherly teacher's love from that great personality's side. The
acquaintance developed to such an extent that later, when he visited Qum,
he put up in our hostel-room and the great scholars of the Hawza

---

[23] See Endnote 74
[24] Richard Francis Burton, *The Golestan of Sa'di*

'Ilmiyyah, all of whom had great affection for him, used to come and visit him there.

In the year twenty when I visited Isfahan for the first time, my Isfahani classmate of eleven years who is currently a teacher and mujtahid at the Hawza 'Ilmiyyah in Qum, suggested that we attend the lectures of a great scholar who is teaching *Nahj al-Balagha* at Madrasah-i Sadr. This invitation was difficult for me to accept. I thought, what is the need to attend a lecture on *Nahj al-Balagha* for a senior seminary student who is studying *Kifayat ul-Usul*? He could study *Nahj al-Balagha* by himself and solve all the academic difficulties with the research tools of *istishab* and *bara'ah*.

Since it was a holiday and I had no other engagements and because the suggestion was made by classmate, I accepted. I attended the lecture and soon discovered my great mistake. I discovered that I had not yet understood the *Nahj al-Balagha*, and not only did I feel the need for a teacher, but I came to admit that there weren't any appropriate teachers for the *Nahj al-Balagha*. Furthermore, in that lecture, I sensed I was face to face with a man of great piety and spirituality, who-in the language of us seminary students- "is one of those whom one ought to travel long distances to benefit from his presence" (*mimman yanbaghi an yushadd ilaihi rihaal*).

He was an embodiment of the *Nahj al-Balagha*-the admonishments of *Nahj al-Balagha* had penetrated the depths of his being. It was evident for me that the soul of this man was in contact and connected to the soul of the Leader of the Faithful (a). Truly, whenever I recount the past, my biggest spiritual treasure is having won the company of this great man-may the supreme pleasure of God be granted to him, and may he be resurrected in the company of his holy and pure Infallible Imams.

I have several anecdotes about this great man. One of them which relates to this discussion pertains to a dream which I will now relate.

One day during his lecture as tears were flowing down his white beard he narrated this dream, he said:

"I saw in a dream that my death has arrived; I saw dying in my dream the way it has been described to us; I saw myself separated from my body, and I observed my body being carried to the cemetery for burial. They carried me to the cemetery and buried me and left me. I was left alone and worried about what will befall me?! Suddenly I saw a white dog who entered the grave. In that state I felt that the dog is an embodiment of my hot temper which has come towards me. I became agitated. I was agitated when the Leader of martyrs arrived and told me: do not be worried, I will keep it away from you"[25]

In this anecdote there is a reference to intercession which we shall, with God's help, discuss in the next section.

Summary

The response to the objection of correspondence (or lack thereof) between crime and punishment can be summarized in that the necessity of correspondence applies to social manmade penalties. Of course, in such penalties, the legislator has to keep in mind the correspondence between crime and punishment. But in punishments which have an existential and ontological relationship with the act-meaning that they are the actual effects and real consequences of the act-or in retributions which have a unitive and identical relationship with the crime-meaning

---

[25] Marhum Mirza Ali Agha Shirazi (may God raise his station) had a strong relationship and an intense devotion to the Holy Prophet and his holy progeny (divine peace and blessings be on them). This man despite being a jurisprudent (at the level of *ijtihad*) philosopher, mystic, physician and literary master and in some fields, like ancient medicine and literature, was among the top experts, and taught the *Canon* of Abü Ali Sina, he was also amongst the servants of the holy court of he Lord of the Martyrs (a); he used to address from the pulpit and recite elegies. Few were those who would attend this pious sincere scholar's sermons and fail to be moved. During admonition and in struction on God and Hereafter the man himself would undergo a spiritual and internal upheaval; love for God and His prophet and progeny would fully pull him. With Divine remembrance he would be moved; he was embodiment of the divine verse:
"The faithful are only those whose hearts tremble [with awe] when God is mentioned, and when His signs are recited to them, they increase their faith, and who put their trust in their Lord" (*Sura al-Anfal*, v. 2)
When he would mention the Holy Prophet's (s) name or Leader of the Faithful (a) his tears would flow. One year the honorable Ayatullah Burujardi (may God raise his station) invited him home to address from the pulpit during the ten days of Ashura. His sermons were unique. Usually he would not speak other *than Nahj al-Balagha*. He would address from the pulpit in the honorable Ayatullah's home and the audience which was mainly theology scholars and students would be intensely moved to an extent that from the beginning till the end of his address one could only see tears flowing and shoulders shaking.

that they are in reality the act itself, there remain no grounds to even speak of the presence or absence of correspondence.

Bertrand Russell, who objects how can there be a God who punishes us severely for very minor crimes, has failed to appreciate that the relationship between this world and the hereafter is not of the social man-made or conventional sort.

The likes of Russell are far from and unaware of Islamic truths and sciences. They are even unfamiliar with the basic Divine truths. The likes of Russell are only familiar with the Christian world, and have not the least awareness of Islamic philosophy, theology, mysticism, and the other Islamic sciences. In the eyes of a person with even the most minimal awareness of Islamic teachings, and of the philosophical tradition of the East, Russell is not even at the level of a primary school student.

Islam has trained eminent men who, while living in this world, were aware of the hereafter, and could experience realities which were beyond the comprehension of Russell and his ilk.

The students of the Qur'anic school learn this truth well, that the reward of the hereafter is the actual act in the world here, not something separate from the act. Mawlawi has a poem which expresses this truth and it is appropriate to quote it here as a lesson for one and all.

Rumi[26] says:
> O thou that hast torn the coat of (many) Josephs, thou wilt arise from this heavy slumber (in the form of) a wolf.
> Thy (evil) dispositions, one by one, having become wolves will tear thy limbs in wrath.
> Wear, all the year round, (a garment) of that (cloth) which you are weaving; eat and drink, all the year round, of that (crop) which you are sowing.
> If you are wounded by a thorn, you yourself have sown; and if you are (clad) in satin and silk, you yourself have spun.
> When blows proceeded from your hand against the victim of injustice, they became a tree (in Hell): the *Zaqqum* grew from them.

---

[26] See Endnote 75

Your words resembling snakes and scorpions have become
    snakes and scorpions and are seizing your tail
    (assailing you from behind).[27]

* * * *

Rumi[28] also says:

The resurrection of the greedy vile eater of carrion
    (unlawful food) will be in the shape of a hog on the
    Day of Reckoning.

Adulteris (erit) foetor membri latentis; wine drinkers will
    have stinking mouths.

The hidden stench that was reaching (only) to (people's)
    hearts will become sensible and manifest at the
    Resurrection.

The being of Man is a jungle: be on our guard against this
    being, if you are of that (Divine) Breath.

In our being there are thousands of wolves and hogs; (there
    is) goodly and ungodly and fair and foul.

To the disposition that is preponderant belongs the decision
    (as to what you are): when the gold is more than the
    copper, it (the mixture) is gold.

The manner of acting that preponderates in your nature-in
    that same form you must needs rise (from the dead).[29]

Congratulations are in order to the Qur'an for such students. If it was
not for the Qur'an, Rumi, Hafiz, Sanai, Attar, Sa'di and their likes would
not have come into existence. Persian talent flourished with the
enlightenment of Islam and even this honour on its own is sufficient for
Iran that it managed to comprehend the Islamic truth better than other
peoples.

---

[27] Nicholson, vol. 4, vrs. 3662-3, vol. 5, vr. 3181, vol. 3, vrs. 3444, 3471, and 3475.
[28] See Endnote 76
[29] *Ibid*, vol. 2, p. 294, vrs. 1413-9.

Intercession

In the study of Divine Justice, one of the issues which ought to be raised, studied and analyzed is the issue of Intercession. Regarding intercession, there is much discussion and debate, which has especially intensified after the appearance of the Wahhabi sect. The Wahhabi sect is affiliated to Muhammad ibn 'Abd al-Wahhab and is currently the official religion in the Kingdom of Saudi Arabia. It is a sect which ostensibly claims to promote Divine Unity in worship-albeit in a superficial way, and thereby rejects many of the profound and lofty teachings of Islam. The *tawhid* promulgated by the Wahhabis, like the *tawhid* of Ash'arites, is in contradiction to many Islamic principles.

Objection and Question

The objections which are raised or can be raised against intercession are as follows:

1. Intercession is incompatible with Divine Unity (*tawhid*) of worship, and belief in it is a type of polytheism. This is the very objection raised by the Wahhabis and a pro-Wahhabi group among the Shias are enamoured by it also.

2. Intercession is not only incompatible with Divine Unity (*tawhid*) of worship but also with Divine Unity (*tawhid*) of Essence, since the logical necessity of belief in intercession is that the compassion and mercy of the intercessor is greater and more comprehensive than Divine mercy. For the presumption is that were it not for intercession, God would chastise the sinner.

3. Belief in intercession emboldens souls prone to sinning, in fact, encourages them to commit sins.

4. The glorious Qur'an falsifies and negates intercession. The Qur'an describes the Day of Resurrection in these words:

وَاتَّقُوا يَوْمًا لَّا تَجْزِي نَفْسٌ عَن نَّفْسٍ شَيْئًا وَلَا يُقْبَلُ مِنْهَا شَفَاعَةٌ وَلَا يُؤْخَذُ مِنْهَا عَدْلٌ وَلَا هُمْ يُنصَرُونَ

213

Beware of the day when no soul will compensate for another, neither any intercession shall be accepted from it, nor any ransom shall be received from it, nor will they be helped.

[Qur'an, 2:48]

5. Intercession is incompatible with the fundamental principle established in the Qur'an whereby the felicity of every individual is made dependent on his deeds. The Qur'an says:

وَأَن لَّيْسَ لِلْإِنسَانِ إِلَّا مَا سَعَىٰ

that nothing belongs to man except what he strives for.

[Qur'an, 53:39]

6. The logical necessity of the validity of intercession is that we believe God can be influenced by intercession and that His wrath can be transformed into pleasure, whereas, God is immutable, not given to change and no factor can exert any effect on Him; mutability is essentially incompatible with the Divine Essence.

7. Intercession is, in a way, making exceptions, a kind of discrimination and injustice. Whereas the Divine system allows no injustice. In other words, intercession is an exception in the Divine Law, whereas Divine laws are universal, immutable, and permit no exceptions:

وَلَن تَجِدَ لِسُنَّةِ اللَّـهِ تَبْدِيلًا

and you will never find any change in Allah's precedent.

[Qur'an, 48:23]

These are the objections that connect the discussion of intercession with Divine Justice, and form the basis for the inclusion of the issue of intercession in this book.

To elaborate: definitely, intercession does not encompass all criminals for in such a case, neither law nor intercession would have any meaning. But, the very nature of intercession is associated with discrimination and making exceptions giving rise to the objection that how can it be just a case of dividing criminals into two groups; a group which escapes punishment because of its affiliations to a party, and another group which is entrapped by punishments because it lacks such contacts?

We consider those human societies as corrupt, decadent, and unjust whose laws are suspended due to party affiliations; so how can we accept party politics in the Divine system? Any society which has intercession has no justice.

Weakness of the Law

An indicator of the impotence and weakness of law in any society is the importance and influence of money, partisan politics, and coercion in it. Obviously when the rule of law falters in this way, it cannot apprehend the strong and powerful, and its only show of strength applies to the weak. A weak law can only arrest weak criminals and bring them to court-being unable to apprehend powerful ones.

The Qur'an introduces Divine laws as powerful and effective, and categorically rejects the influence of money, partisanship, and coercion in the Divine court of justice. The Qur'an refers to these ideas by using the following terms: money is referred to as *adl* (derived either from the root word *udul*, since money given as a bribe causes deviation (literally '*udul*') from truth; or from the root word '*adl*' meaning equivalent or substitute), and party influence is called *shafa'ah*, and the recourse to external force is termed *nusrat*. Thus, we read in Surah al-Baqarah:

وَاتَّقُوا يَوْمًا لَّا تَجْزِي نَفْسٌ عَن نَّفْسٍ شَيْئًا وَلَا يُقْبَلُ مِنْهَا شَفَاعَةٌ وَلَا يُؤْخَذُ مِنْهَا عَدْلٌ وَلَا هُمْ يُنصَرُونَ

Beware of the day when no soul will compensate for another, neither any intercession shall be accepted from it, nor any ransom shall be received from it, nor will they be helped.

[Qur'an, 2:48]

215

That is, the system governing the world hereafter is unlike the system operating in human societies, wherein an individual can escape from justice by seeking recourse to money or influence, or occasionally solicit help from his tribe and ethnic group, who employ their force against the law-enforcing agents.

In the early history of Islam, the rule of law was effective. It even affected the close friends and relatives of the rulers. When Ali (a) learned that his daughter had borrowed a necklace from the public treasury (*bayt al-mal*), though she had placed collateral for it and used it only on 'Id day, he strongly reprimanded her and firmly stated:

لو كانت أخذت العقد على غير عارية مضمونة مردودة لكانت إذن أول هاشمية قطعت يدها فى سرقة

Had she had not borrowed it as other than a guaranteed item, then she would have been the first Hashimiyyah to have her hands cut off for theft.[1]

When his cousin and learned companion, Ibn 'Abbas committed an offence, he wrote a letter to him criticizing him severely. He wrote:[2]

If you do not refrain from your offence, I will discipline you with my sword! The same sword which I have never struck anyone with, but that he is relegated to the hell-fire! You know that my sword never falls on anyone but those who deserve hell, and this offence of yours has rendered you of the people of hell, deserving to be struck by my sword. I swear by God, even if Hasan and Husayn (a) were to commit this offence, I would not have spared them.[3]

This is from the early history of Islam and the law-enforcer is the Leader of the Faithful (a), hence it is not surprising or strange. If you want to appreciate the extent to which the system set up by the Holy Prophet (s) had progressed and what type people were dragged to the court of justice, consider the following incident:

---

[1] *Bihar al Anwar*, vol. 40, p. 338.
[2] See Endnote 77
[3] *Nahj al-Balagha*, letter 41.

Amr As was appointed governor of Egypt by Umar. One day the son of Amr As slapped a citizen's face. The aggrieved carried his complaint to Amr As who ignored it.

This chivalrous person travelled to Madina to lodge his complaint with Umar in person. 'Umar summoned Amr As and his son and took them to task. In this sentencing, a historical statement has been quoted from Umar. He addressed Amr As and his son saying:

متى استعبدتم النّاس وقد النّاس و قد ولدتهم أمّهاتهم أحرار

Since when have you enslaved people to yourselves whereas their mothers have given them birth as free individuals?'

Saying this, he issued the order for retaliation.

Umar dealt even with his son in a similar fashion. When it was proven that his son had consumed alcohol, he executed the Divine penalty on him.

This was the justice taught to the Muslims by the Holy Prophet (s), and the Muslims had not yet forgotten it. In other words, it was a machinery set into motion by God's messenger, which more and less, kept its momentum going.

Types of Intercession

In reality, *shafa'ah* is of several types, some of which are false, unjust and have no presence in the Divine scheme of things, whereas other types are true and just and do exist. The false *shafa'ah* (intercession) is against the Law and disrupts it, whereas the true *shafa'ah* supports and protects the law. The false type of *shafa'ah* is when a person wishes to use party influence to obstruct the path of justice. Based on such a perspective of *shafa'ah*, the criminal acts in contrary to the lawmaker's desire and in opposition to the aims of legislation. By invoking the help and influence of a certain party, he overcomes the legislator's wish and goal of legislation. This type of *shafa'ah* is injustice in this world and impossible in the world hereafter. The objections levelled against *shafa'ah* are actually aimed against this type of *shafa'ah*, which in any case is the type rejected by the Qur'an.

217

The other type of *shafa'ah* is the true one, which does not have any exceptions or discrimination, nor does it contravene any law or entail over-riding the legislators wishes. The Qur'an clearly supports this type of *shafa'ah*. Even the true *shafa'ah* has several types, as we shall soon elaborate.

Violation of Law

The false type of *shafa'ah*, which is refuted by both rational and religious proofs, lies in a sinner using a means through which he can block the implementation of a Divine sentence and decree. This is similar to the backroom influences which transpire in corrupt human societies and courts.

Many common people consider this to be the type of *shafa'ah* practiced by prophets and Imams (a). They believe that the holy Prophet (s), the Leader of the Faithful (a), the holy Lady Fatimah (sa), and the infallible Imams (a) especially Imam Husayn (a)-are influential beings who can exert control in the Divine kingdom, alter the Divine Will, and contravene His law.

The Arabs of the pre-Islamic era who associated partners with God, believed in a similar type of *shafa'ah* for their idols. They claimed that creation is by God, with no deity having any partnership role in it, but in the governing of the world, the idols are His partners. The pre-Islamic Arabs' polytheism was not in relation to God as "Creator," rather it was with respect to His station of "Lordship" and role as the Nourisher or Guardian of the world.

We know from human examples that sometimes a person can establish an institute but entrust its administration to another, or run it in joint partnership with others. This was the belief held by polytheists about God and the universe and the governing of the universe.

The Qur'an vigorously opposed this belief and repeatedly declared that there is no partner with God, neither in creation nor in administration. He alone is the Creator of the Universe, and He exclusively governs it. The kingdom and dominion of the world belongs to Him alone and He is the Lord of the worlds.

The polytheists who believed that governance of the universe is divided between God and other deities, did not see it as necessary upon themselves to strive to attain God's pleasure and acceptance. They claimed that we can win this pleasure and acceptance via the other deities, by offering sacrifices and through the ritual worship of idols, even though it may displease God, the Almighty. If we win the satisfaction of these gods and goddesses, so they thought, they will sort out the matter themselves with the Almighty God.

If someone amongst the Muslims were also to hold such a belief that besides God's kingdom there is a parallel dominion working alongside it, that would be tantamount to polytheism. If someone were to assume that one way is to attain Divine pleasure and acceptance and another way entail winning the approval and pleasure of, say Imam Husayn (a), and that each of these two ways can independently ensure man's salvation, then he has fallen prey to serious misguidance. In this incorrect belief, it is held that God is pleased with one set of things, whereas Imam Husayn (a) with another. God is pleased with the performance of compulsory acts like prayers, fasting, pilgrimage, Jihad, charity, truthfulness, righteousness, service to mankind, benevolence to parents, etc. And He is also pleased by refraining from sins like lying, injustice, backbiting, consumption of alcohol, adultery, etc. But, in contrast, Imam Husayn (a) is not concerned with such things, his pleasure instead is attainable through the likes of mourning and weeping or at least feigning to cry-for his youthful son Ali Akbar. Hence, the what is at issue with Imam Husayn (a) is distinct from those things that concern God, the Almighty. As a logical conclusion to such a distinction, the attainment of Divine pleasure is difficult since it entails performing many tasks to win His approval; whereas winning the approval of Imam Husayn (a) is relatively easy-only mourning and chest beating are required. And once Imam Husayn (a) is satisfied, he will use his influence in the Divine kingdom through intercession and mend one's affairs. All the prayers, fasts, pilgrimage, Jihad, charity in God's way, etc. which we failed to perform will be forgiven, and sins we committed will be instantaneously wiped out.

Such a conception of *shafa'ah* is not only false and incorrect, but is also polytheism or shirk in God's Lordship, and an insult to the holy status of Imam Husayn (a), whose greatest source of pride was his total submission and devotion to God. In the same way that his noble father used to be extremely angered by the allegations made by the fanatics with respect to himself, and Imam Husayn (a) will also seek God's refuge from their exaggerated claims. Imam Husayn (a) was not martyred so that, God forbid, he could set up a system parallel to the Divine kingdom, or against his grandfather's *shafa'ah*, and thereby propose a means to escape God's laws. His martyrdom was not to attenuate the practical program of Islam or the Qur'anic laws. On the contrary, he sacrificed himself for the sake of reviving prayers, charity, and all other Islamic precepts.

He clarified his purpose of uprising thus:

إِنِّي لم أخرج أشرًا ولا بطرًا و لا مفسدًا ولا ظالمًا وإنَّما خرجت لطلب الإصلاح في أمّة جدي
(ص) أريد أن آمر بالمعروف وأنهى عن المنكر

I have not made my uprising neither for ulterior motives nor for seeking power, rather my uprising is to seek to reform my grandfather's community, to enjoin good and prohibit evil.[4]

We address him in the *ziyarat* in the following words:

أَشهَدُ أَنَّك قَد أَقَمتَ الصَّلاةَ وَ آتَيتَ الزَّكاةَ وَأَمَرتَ بِالمَعروفِ وَ نَهَيتَ عَنِ المُنكَرِ وَ جَاهَدتَ فِي
سَبيلِ اللَّهِ حَتَّى أَتَاك اليَقِينُ

I testify that you established prayers, gave charity, enjoined good, prohibited evil, and strove in the way of God in its true sense, and acted upon His book and implemented His prophet's traditions [5]

Safeguarding the Law

Let us now examine what the right type of *shafa'ah* is? The right kind of *shafa'ah* which supports the law and safeguards the system, and whose existence is established by many proofs from Qur'anic verses and Prophetic traditions, mentioned in both Sunni and Shia sources, is of two types:

1. *Shafa'ah* of leadership or *shafa'ah* by action

2. *Shafa'ah* of forgiveness or *shafa'ah* by grace

---

[4] *Manaqib*, Ibn Shahr Ashub, *Bihar al-Anwar*, vol. 44, p. 329.
[5] *Al-Kafi*, vol.4, p. 578.

The first type, is *shafa'ah* which entails salvation from perdition, reward of good deeds, and even attainment of higher stations. Whereas the second type is a *shafa'ah* whose effect is to ward off punishment and bring about forgiveness of sins the most it can possibly achieve is getting rewards and benefits, but it does not enable attainment of higher stations. This latter type is referred to by the Prophet (s):

قال رسول الله (ص): إنّما شفاعتي لأهل الكبائر من أمّتي، فأمّا المحسنون فما عليهم من سبيل

I have stored my intercession for the members of my community who commit major sins; as for the virtuous, they shall not be punished.[6]

Intercession of Leadership

In order to clarify this type of intercession, we need to recapitulate an issue discussed under "retribution in the hereafter" earlier on. We explained in that earlier discussion that behaviour and actions of humans in this world will be manifested and embodied in the world hereafter where its true reality will appear in full. Now we add that, in the world hereafter, not only will actions be embodied, but even relationships will be personified. Spiritual relationships which are established in this world between people will achieve a celestial and real form in the hereafter. When an individual becomes the means of guidance for another, the relationship between leader and follower will appear in its real form after resurrection, whereby the giver of guidance will manifest as leader and guide and the beneficiary as the follower and guided one. The same applies with misguidance and deviation.

The glorious Qur'an states:

يَوْمَ نَدْعُو كُلَّ أُنَاسٍ بِإِمَامِهِمْ

The day We shall summon every group of people along with their imam

[Qur'an, 17:71]

---

[6] *Wasa'il al-Shiah*, vol. 15, p.336.

That is, every individual shall be resurrected with his own guide, who inspired him and was his role model.

Referring to the embodiment of Pharaoh's leadership of his people, it states:

يَقْدُمُ قَوْمَهُ يَوْمَ الْقِيَامَةِ فَأَوْرَدَهُمُ النَّارَ

On the Day of Resurrection, he will lead his people and conduct them into the Fire.

[Qur'an, 11:98]

Pharaoh who in this world was misguided and a leader of the misguided, and the misguided of his community followed in his footsteps, will be embodied in the hereafter as their guide and leader. So, in reality we can say that Pharaoh was the intercessor and intermediary for his people both in the world here and in hereafter-an intercessor who caused others to sin and be misguided and who will be the medium for their entry into the hellfire in that world. His role in being a means to leading his people to hellfire is actually the embodiment of his being a means of their misguidance in this world.

The interesting point to be noted in the expression used in the Qur'an is that it states Pharaoh will lead his people to the hellfire. With such a statement, the Qur'an alludes to the embodiment of the effect of Pharaoh's misguidance, stating that in as much as he led them in this world to misguidance, so he will lead them to hellfire in the hereafter; in fact, leading them into hellfire in the hereafter is a clear manifestation and embodiment of leading them to deviation in this world.

Of course, it is obvious that in as much as righteous and misguided leadership in this world has many types and varieties, so also will be the case in the next world. For instance, all those who have been enlightened by the Prophet's (s) light of guidance and have benefited from that blessed personality's *shafa'ah*, will be under his leadership as he, may our souls be ransomed for him, will be the doyen of the virtuous, holding the *liwa al hamd* (the Banner of Praise) on the day of resurrection.

It is in this sense of *shafa'ah* that the holy Prophet (s) will be the intercessor for the Leader of the Faithful (a) and the holy Lady Fatima (sa), who in turn will be the intercessors for Hasanayn (a). In this way, every Imam will be the intercessor for the succeeding Imam and of his own followers and students. The hierarchy will be maintained for whatever it is that the other infallibles have, they receive it through the holy prophet.

In the same way, even the scholars will intercede on behalf of those who received their guidance and instructions. This process creates a multi-faceted linked chain wherein the smaller groups link to larger ones and the head of the chain is the holy personality of the honourable Prophet (s).

> Intercessor, obeyed, prophet, gracious,
> Bountiful, majestic, affable, marked with the seal of God.[7]

* * *

> Surging forward and all hearts follow,
> The hands of all spirits cling to his cloak. [8]

* * *

Rumi:[9]

> He is the intercessor in this world and in the yonder world-in this world (for guidance) to the (true) religion, and yonder (for entrance) to Paradise.

> In this world he says, "Do Thou show unto them the Way," and in yonder world he says, "Do Thou show unto them the Moon."

> It was his custom in public and in private (to say), "Guide my people: verily they know not."

---

[7] Richard Francis Burton, Trans. *The Golestan of Sa'di*, Introduction
[8] Unknown poet.
[9] See Endnote 78

By his breath (powerful intercession) both the Gates were opened: in both worlds his prayer is answered.

He has become the Seal (of the prophets) for this reason that there never was anyone like him in munificence nor ever shall be.

A hundred thousand blessings on his spirit and on the advent and cycle of his sons!

Those fortunate Caliph-born sons of his are born of the substance of his soul and heart.

Whether they be of Baghdad or Heart or Rayy, they are his progeny without admixture of water and earth.

Wherever the rose-bough blossoms, 'tis still the (same) rose; wherever the wine-jar bubbles, 'tis still the (same) wine.

If the sun uplifts its head (rise) from the west, 'tis the same sun, not anything else.[10]

The reason why the traditions state that Imam Husayn (a) will intercede on behalf of a large number of people is that his movement, more than any other in this world, led to the revival of religion and the guidance of mankind.

As was mentioned earlier, the intercession by Imam Husayn (a) will not be in the sense that he will ask anything from God contrary to the Divine Will and pleasure. His intercession will be of two types: one type will be this same guidance created by him in this world, which will be embodied and personified in the hereafter; the other type will be explained later.

Imam Husayn (a) will be the intercessor for those who have been guided by his school, and he will not be the intercessor for those who have misused his school to misguide.

We should not overlook the fact that in as much as some have been guided by the holy Qur'an and others misguided, so also some have been enlightened by the school of Imam Husayn (a), while others have been misled, depending on the people themselves.

---

[10] Nicholson, vol. 6, p. 266, vrs. 167-171, 175-179.

Referring to parables, the Qur'an asserts:

$$\text{يُضِلُّ بِهِ كَثِيرًا وَيَهْدِي بِهِ كَثِيرًا ۚ وَمَا يُضِلُّ بِهِ إِلَّا الْفَاسِقِينَ}$$

Thereby He leads many astray, and thereby He guides many; and He leads no one astray thereby except the transgressors.

[Qur'an, 2:26]

Rumi has illustrated this matter using a profound and beautiful allegory:[11]

Beseech God continually that you may not stumble over these deep sayings and that you may arrive at the (journey's) end,

For many have been led astray by the Qur'an: by (clinging to) that rope a multitude have fallen into the well.

There is no fault in the rope, O perverse man, inasmuch as you had no desire for (reaching) the top.[12]

"*Rasan*" (in the Persian text of the poem) means rope. With a rope can one can either ascend out of the well or descend into the depths of the well, depending on what choice we make.

The Qur'an and the school of Imam Husayn (a) are ropes which have the capacity to elevate man out of the abyss of damnation to the pinnacle of salvation; one is a rope from God (*habl min allah*) and the other is a rope from man (*habl min allah*). But if one were to misuse these two Divine ropes, the ropes would not be to blame, rather we would say that the individual never had the intention of elevating himself; and undoubtedly such people would be "led" by the Qur'an and the Husayni school to the abyss of hell. This reality would manifest itself in the hereafter in such a fashion that it would be by the order of the Qur'an and the Imams that these misled individuals would be relegated to hellfire. And this is the true explanation of [the Imam] being the Divider or Distributor of heaven and hell (*qasim al jannah wa al-nar*).

It has been narrated from the holy Prophet:

---

[11] See Endnote 79

[12] Nicholson, vol. 3, 235, vrs. 4209-11

فَعَلَيْكُمْ بِالْقُرْآنِ فَإِنَّهُ شَافِعٌ مُشَفَّعٌ وَماجِلٌ مُصَدَّقٌ

The Qur'an is an intercessor whose intercession is approved, And a
prosecutor whose truthfulness is accepted[13]

This is a truly amazing statement. He says: the glorious Qur'an is an
intercessor for the believers and the virtuous mediating their way to the
Paradise of eternal felicity, and it is also a prosecutor for the disbelievers
and evil-doers-leading them to hellfire. For the first lot it is a gateway to
heaven, and for the second a stepping stone to hell.

It is appropriate to name such an intercession as *shafa'ah* of leadership
or *shafa'ah* by action, since the fundamental factor which determines
salvation or damnation is the action of the individual.

Obviously, none of the objections raised against intercession apply to
this type of *shafa'ah* as was explained above. And it is also abundantly
clear that this type of *shafa'ah* is not only not incompatible with Divine
justice, but rather it supports it.

Intercession of Forgiveness

The second type of *shafa'ah* is intercession for the forgiveness and
clemency of sins. This is the sense of *shafa'ah* which has been the target
of attacks and objections by critics and opponents, but with the
explanation that will be forwarded in this book, by God's will, it shall
become clear that not only is no objection valid against it, on the contrary,
it is one of the lofty and profound teachings of Islam.

Precedence of Mercy

In the beginning we should recognize the fact that in order to attain
salvation, in addition to deeds and acts performed by man himself, there
has always been another universal phenomenon in operation, namely, the
precedence of Divine mercy. The religious texts mention:

---

[13] *Al-Kafi*, vol. 2, p. 599.

يا مَن سَبَقَت رَحمَتُهُ غَضبَهُ

He whose mercy precedes His wrath.[14]

Hafiz in a famous ghazal says:[15]

> The green expanse of sky, I beheld; and the sickle (the
> crescent) of the new moon;
> To me, recollection came of my own sown-field; and of the
> time of reaping (the judgment-day)
> I said: "O fortune! Thou hast slept; and appeared hath the
> sun:"
> He said: "Despite all this, hopeless of the past, be not.[16]

What Hafiz meant by "past"- *shafa'ah* -is the precedence of Divine
mercy over His wrath, though he could also have meant something else
which has been alluded to in the verse:

إِنَّ الَّذِينَ سَبَقَتْ لَهُم مِّنَّا الْحُسْنَىٰ أُولَٰئِكَ عَنْهَا مُبْعَدُونَ

Indeed, those to whom there has gone beforehand [the promise of] the
best reward from Us will be kept away from it.

[Qur'an, 21:101]

In any case, that which is fundamental in the scheme of creation is
mercy, salvation, and felicity; disbelief, disobedience, and evil being
accidental and non-fundamental. That which is accidental will be
overcome by God's mercy, whenever possible. One of the evidences for
the precedence of Divine mercy over Divine wrath is the felt presence of
succour and support from the unseen realms. Divine forgiveness and
effacement of the effects of sins is another proof for the precedence of
Divine mercy and compassion over wrath and anger.

---

[14] *Bihar al-Anwar*, vol. 95, p. 232.
[15] See Endnote 80
[16] Clarke, ghazal 407

The Principle of Purification

In the created order, one of the manifestations of Divine mercy is what might be called the "process of purification." The created order is characterized by purification and cleansing. One of the instances of purification is the absorption of carbon dioxide by plants and oceans, thus cleansing the air. If the air which is polluted by the respiration of living beings and burning of fossil fuels were not to be purified by the plant and ocean refinery, the earth's atmosphere would soon lose its ability to sustain life and breathing would become impossible. The disintegration of animal carcasses and the catalysis of excreta from living beings is another example of cleansing and purification in creation.

Just as manifestations of purification and cleansing exist in the physical and natural world, they also exist in the spiritual world. Forgiveness and the effacement of the effects of sins belong to this category. Forgiveness means a cleansing of hearts and souls-to the extent that they can be purified-from the effects and consequences of sins.

Of course, some hearts lose the receptivity to be purified, to this extent that no celestial cleanser whatsoever can cleanse them. It is as if they become inherently polluted entities. When disbelief and shirk get established in a heart, it disables the hearts capacity to be purified. In the Qur'an, the consolidation of disbelief in the heart is referred to as "the closing of the heart" or "God's sealing."

The Principle of Equilibrium

Another proof for the precedence of Divine mercy over wrath in the realm of creation is the fact that health and equilibrium is the rule, whereas disease and sickness is the exception. In the constitution of every living being, there is an inherent power or faculty active in maintaining the health and equilibrium of that being for its survival. One example is the presence of white blood corpuscles with their amazing defensive capabilities. Another example is the ability of living bodies to heal and repair themselves. Thus, bone fractures, cuts, wounds, and nutritional deficiencies are repaired and restored to a healthy state by this faculty.

From the religious point of view there is the concept of the *fitrah* (original nature or creation). Every child is born in this world with a pure fitrah

كلّ مولود يولد على الفطرة حتى يكون أبواه يهودانه و ينصرانه

Every newborn is born with the *fitrah*, but his parents convert him either to Judaism or Christianity.[17]

Inherent in every being who has deviated from its original path, there is a propensity toward returning to its primordial state. In philosophical terms, in every nature that suffers from an impediment (*qasr*), there exists an inclination to revert to its original natural state. *i.e.* there always exists in the universe a force to escape from disequilibrium and move toward health and equilibrium. These are proofs of the precedence of mercy over wrath. Forgiveness also stems from this same principle.

Universal Mercy

The principle of forgiveness is not an exception, rather a universal formula and a consequence of the predominance of mercy in the realm of creation. From this it becomes clear that Divine forgiveness is universal and embraces all existent beings to the extent of their possibility and receptivity. This principle is effective in the attainment of salvation and the escape from damnation for all successful beings; hence, the Qur'an states:

مَّن يُصْرَفْ عَنْهُ يَوْمَئِذٍ فَقَدْ رَحِمَهُ

Whoever is spared of it on that day, He has certainly been merciful to him

[Qur'an, 6:16]

Thus, if there were to be no Divine mercy, none would be saved from chastisement.

The Holy Prophet (s) referred to this fact in a sermon delivered to the Muslims towards the end of his noble life. in this sermon he emphasized that two things are crucial for salvation: action and compassion. An extract from the sermon is as follows:

أَيّها النّاس إنّه ليس بين الله و بين أحد نسب ولا أمر يؤتيه به خيرًا أو يصرف عنه شرًّا إلّا العمل. ألا لا يدّعينّ مدّع و لا يتمنّينّ متمنّ، والّذى بعثنى بالحقّ لا ينجى إلا عمل مع رحمة و لو عصيت لهويت. اللّهمّ قد بلّغت

_____

[17] *Bihar al-Anwar*, vol. 3, p. 281.

O people! Verily there is neither any kinship between God and anyone nor any other relationship whereby one is entitled to receive goodness or ward off evil except through deeds. Beware! Let no claimant make any claim, let none harbour lofty expectations. I swear by the One who has raised me as a righteous messenger, there is no salvation save through deeds coupled with Divine mercy, even if I were to sin, I would perish. O Lord! Have I conveyed?[18]

The secret behind the seeking of forgiveness by the Holy Prophet (s), as well as by the rest of the prophets and the infallible guides (a), is this very principle of universal and all-embracing mercy. In fact, one can assert that, the nearer one is (to the all-perfect Being) the more he benefits from this principle. As a general rule, the more proximity one enjoys, the more one is enlightened by the *asma al husna*, *i.e.* the perfect Divine attributes. The Prophet (s) has declared:

إنّه لَيُغانُ على قلبي وإنّي لأستغفر الله في كلّ يوم سبعين مرّة

Effects of pollution appear on my heart and every day I seek forgiveness from my Lord seventy times.[19]

Connection between Intercession and Mercy

What is the relationship between Divine pardon and intercession?

Divine forgiveness, like all other types of mercy, has a special order and scheme. In the second section of the book, we discussed in detail the fact that the universe has a system, and we explained that the necessity of a hierarchy is due to the differences between living beings. What's more, the differences between creatures is neither arbitrary nor created, rather it is inseparably inherent in them; specifically, it is their core identity and manner of existence. Hence, absence of these differences is tantamount to their non-existence, and positing their existence is incompatible with absence of differences.

From the above explanation it becomes clear that it is impossible that any of the manifestations of Divine mercy can be actualized without a hierarchy. A hierarchically organized universe in its turn requires that

---

[18] Ibn Abi al-Hadid, Shahr *Nahj al-Balagha*, vol.10, p. 184
[19] Tabatabai, *al-Mizan*, vol. 18, p. 245. *Mustadrak al-Wasail*, vol.5, p. 321, tradition 5987

Divine forgiveness flow through the certain conduits to reach the sinners at the bottom-these conduits and mediums being none other than prophets and saints. By the same reason that the grace of revelation is not granted without an intermediary and all people are not raised and inspired to become prophets, no other Divine mercy descends without an intermediary. This implies that the mercy of forgiveness and pardon also cannot possibly descend without an intermediary.

Supposing that we had no access to proofs for intercession from traditional sources, we would be compelled to believe in it by logical and conclusive rational proofs, like the proof of the hierarchically organized universe (*mikan-i ashraf*).

If one accepts the existence of Divine forgiveness, authoritative logical proofs will compel him to believe that Divine forgiveness must flow through the Logos or perfect soul-a soul which holds the status of Universal Sainthood (*wilayah kulliyyah*). It is impossible for Divine grace to flow in creation without a certain order and account in place.

Fortunately, the Qur'an has guided us on this issue too. It, in conjunction with Islamic traditions-specifically keeping in mind all that has been narrated in the reliable corpus of Shia traditions about the Universal Sainthood (*walayah*) of the messenger of God (s) and the infallible Imams (a) as well as the lower levels of *walayah* proper to lower levels of faith-leads us to infer that the mediation for Divine forgiveness is not just a single universal Spirit, but universal souls and particular human spirits with an hierarchy between them; each having a specific role in intercession. This is one of the most significant and profound Islamic and Qur'anic teachings, and one which has been properly expounded only in the Shia school of thought by the infallible Imams (a) and their prominent students. It is to be considered as an achievement of this sect.

Conditions for Intercession

At its base, intercession is Divine forgiveness. When it is attributed to God who is the source of all goodness and grace, it is named as forgiveness. But when it is attributed to the intermediaries through whom the grace flows, it is named as intercession. It now becomes crystal clear that the preliminary and requisite conditions for forgiveness must also apply in the case of intercession. From the logical point of view, there is no prerequisite for forgiveness save the worth and merit of the recipient. If someone is denied Divine forgiveness, it due to his own disqualification, and is not related to, God forbid, the restrictiveness and limitation of Divine mercy. Unlike bank reserves, Divine mercy is not limited. The reserves of Divine grace are unlimited, but the merits of recipients vary, some may be devoid of all merits and thus incapable of benefiting from Divine grace.

According to religious sources, this much is certain that disbelief and polytheism are impediments to Divine grace. The Qur'an states:

$$\text{إِنَّ اللَّـهَ لَا يَغْفِرُ أَن يُشْرَكَ بِهِ وَيَغْفِرُ مَا دُونَ ذَٰلِكَ لِمَن يَشَاءُ}$$

Indeed, Allah does not forgive that any partner should be ascribed to Him, but He forgives anything besides that to whomever He wishes.
[Qur'an, 4:116]

For man to lose faith is to totally severe this connection to forgiveness, after which it is impossible for him to benefit from this immense grace. When the heart is sealed with disbelief, it becomes like the closed vessel which cannot allow any water in, even if it were to be dipped into all the great oceans of the world. The being of such a person becomes like the infertile soil wherein the water of Divine grace can only cause thorns to grow instead of flowers.

Rain in whose munificence there is no doubt,
Enables the growth of flowers in a garden and thorns in infertile soil.

If a flower fails to grow in the salty soil, it is not due to deficiency in rain, but due to the inadequacy of the soil.

The Qur'an explains this all-embracing Divine grace through the words of the bearers of the Divine Throne:

$$\text{الَّذِينَ يَحْمِلُونَ الْعَرْشَ وَمَنْ حَوْلَهُ يُسَبِّحُونَ بِحَمْدِ رَبِّهِمْ وَيُؤْمِنُونَ بِهِ وَيَسْتَغْفِرُونَ لِلَّذِينَ آمَنُوا رَبَّنَا}$$
$$\text{وَسِعْتَ كُلَّ شَيْءٍ رَّحْمَةً وَعِلْمًا فَاغْفِرْ لِلَّذِينَ تَابُوا وَاتَّبَعُوا سَبِيلَكَ وَقِهِمْ عَذَابَ الْجَحِيمِ}$$

Those who bear the Throne, and those who are around it, celebrate the praise of their Lord and have faith in Him, and they plead for forgiveness for the faithful: 'Our Lord! You embrace all things in mercy and knowledge. So, forgive those who repent and follow Your way and save them from the punishment of hell.

[Qur'an, 40:7]

We can infer from this verse both the infinite nature of Divine mercy, and the necessary qualifications required to entitle someone to receive Divine pardon.

One can deduct from the Qur'anic verses that faith is a necessary but not sufficient condition for attaining forgiveness and intercession. No one can enumerate with certainty all the necessary requirements, God alone knows them all. In the verse that promises forgiveness of all sins other than polytheism, the restriction of to whomever He wishes is mentioned, and in the verses on intercession the restriction of

وَلَا يَشْفَعُونَ إِلَّا لِمَنِ ارْتَضَىٰ

and they do not intercede except for someone He approves of

[Qur'an, 21:28]

is mentioned, both of which imply the same sense. Apparently, the Qur'an did not expound clearly all the conditions required for intercession, it thus retained the heart between the states of fear and hope. From this we can understand that the objection against the belief in intercession, to the effect that it emboldens one to sin, is invalid.

Intercession Belongs to God Alone

The fundamental distinction between true intercession from false intercession is that true intercession originates from God and ends with the sinner, whereas in the false intercession the reverse is true.

In true intercession, the source of intercession, namely, God the Almighty activates the intermediary. Whereas in false intercession, the recipient, namely the sinner is the activator. In the false variety, whose examples abound in the world, the intercessor acquires his intermediary status from the criminal, because he is the one who instigates the intermediary to intercede on his behalf. That is to say, the sinner is the one who appoints the intermediary to his role. However, in true intercession, which can be correctly attributed to the prophets, imams, and those enjoying Divine proximity, the intermediary role of the intercessor is bestowed by God; God is the One who grants the intermediary his role.

In other words, in false intercession, the intercessor is influenced by the interceded one (the sinner) and the intercessor then influences the One who accepts the intercession (Final authority); whereas in true intercession, the reverse is true; the One who accepts the intercession (the Final authority, God) is the cause who influences the intercessor, and the intercessor under His influence and by His Will, is effective on the sinner. In the false type of intercession, the one who sets the process into motion is the sinner, whereas in the true type of intercession, it is God the almighty.

Mulla Sadra in his commentary on Surah al-Hadid, has a subtle and scholarly explanation on the distinction between the true and false types of intercession, and why it is that the false type of intercession exists in this world but does not exist in the hereafter; in fact it is impossible for it to exist therein.

By expanding the scope of the discussion, he touches upon essential and accidental causes as well as essential and accidental ends. He asks how it is sometimes possible that in this world-meaning not just the human realm-accidental causes sometimes specify the destiny of a thing or keep a thing from reaching its essential end; allowing it to reach only its accidental end. The hereafter is not like this and in that realm accidental causes and ends do not apply.

Since the discussion is quite profound, we will withhold from explaining and commenting on it here and will instead refer scholars to the details as explained by Mulla Sadra himself in various places in his commentary.

The verses in the holy Qur'an which assert the impossibility of intercession without Divine permission allude to this fact. There is a particularly amazing and very interesting expression in this regard:

$$\text{قُل لَّـِّهِ الشَّفَاعَةُ جَمِيعًا}$$

Say, 'All intercession rests with Allah.

234

[Qur'an, 39:44]

This verse unequivocally and explicitly affirms intercession and intermediation, and explicitly attributes all intercession to God exclusively, since it is God who renders the (human) intercessor as an (effective) intercessor. This verse could possibly be alluding to the intercession that will transpire after the resurrection, and in philosophical terminology, may be referring to the arc of ascent. Or it could possibly be referring to all intermediaries and the mediation of Divine mercy, which would then be the arc of descent. In other words, it could possibly include the entire universal sequence of cause and effects. Anyway, as far as it relates to intercession in the hereafter, it implies that without Divine permission, the criminal cannot activate the intercessor and likewise, without Divine authorization, the intercessor cannot affect anything.

The logical proof for this reality is that it is established in philosophy that the Necessary existent, is also necessarily existent in all aspects and modalities. To explain, as the necessarily existent Being is not an effect of any other being in its essence, by the same reason, it cannot be under the influence of any other causative entity with respect to its attributes and efficiency. It is exclusively and agent, accepting no effect or influence whatsoever from any other entity.

Tawhid and *Tawassul*

From our past discussion an important and profound fact emerges about unity in worship. That fact is that when seeking assistance and intercession of the sacred souls and saints, one must first ascertain that the one who is solicited and through whom one seeks help has been appointed by God as an intermediary. The holy Qur'an states:

يَا أَيُّهَا الَّذِينَ آمَنُوا اتَّقُوا اللَّـهَ وَابْتَغُوا إِلَيْهِ الْوَسِيلَةَ

O you who have faith! Be wary of God, and seek the means of recourse to Him. [Qur'an, 5:35]

As a general principle, to seek recourse to means and to use mediums is not in any way polytheism since God has created the means, and God is the one who has fashioned them to be effective mediums. What's more, it is God who has asked us to make use of these mediums and means-so all of this is nothing other than pure Divine Unity (*tawhid*). In this context, there is no difference whatsoever between material and spiritual mediums, between exoteric and esoteric means, between mediums of this world or the hereafter. Albeit, the material means can be recognized and identified through scientific and empirical methods, whereas the spiritual means can be discovered through religious guidance, based on Divine revelation-the Book and traditions of Prophet and infallible ones.

Secondly, when an individual seeks recourse to means or seeks intercession, he must focus attention on God, and from God towards the means and intercessor, since, as we explained above, the true intercession is one wherein the source of intercession activates the intercessor to effect intercession, and since God approves and grants permission, the intercessor can intercede. In contrast to this is the case of false intercession, wherein the original attention is directed toward the intercessor to influence the source of intercession. Hence, the criminal's attention is focused all the time on the intercessor, expecting the latter to exert his power and influence on the source of intercession and win his approval. Thus, if one's attention is directed primarily toward the intercessor rather than being subordinate to or resulting from attention toward God, then it will constitute polytheism in worship.

Divine acts have a coherent order. If someone wants to neglect this order in creation, then he is misguided. It is for this reason that God the Almighty has instructed the sinners to seek recourse to the Holy Prophet (s), and, in addition to praying for forgiveness by themselves, also ask that sublime personality to pray for their forgiveness. The Qur'an states:

وَلَوْ أَنَّهُمْ إِذ ظَّلَمُوا أَنفُسَهُمْ جَاءُوكَ فَاسْتَغْفَرُوا اللَّـهَ وَاسْتَغْفَرَ لَهُمُ الرَّسُولُ لَوَجَدُوا اللَّـهَ تَوَّابًا رَّحِيمًا

Had they, when they wronged themselves, come to you and pleaded to Allah for forgiveness, and the Apostle had pleaded for them [to Allah] for forgiveness, they would have surely found Allah all-clement, all-merciful. [Qur'an, 4:64]

Indeed, one cannot solely rely on virtuous deeds and piety; as the Prophet (s) himself declared towards the end of his noble earthly life: "There is no salvation save through deeds coupled with Divine mercy "

Response to the Objections

With the explanation we gave of the intercession of forgiveness, the objections against intercession can be answered thus:

1. Intercession is neither incompatible with unity of worship nor with unity of Divine essence, since the mercy of the intercessor is nothing but a manifestation of Divine mercy, and the intercession and mercy originates from the Lord. (response to the first and second objections)

2. In as much as belief in Divine forgiveness does not embolden anyone, rather only creates hope, so also belief in intercession does not encourage anyone to sin. Keeping in mind the fact that the pre-requisite condition for receiving forgiveness and intercession is Divine will and approval, it becomes clear that the effect of this belief is to the extent of saving hearts from despair and hopelessness, and retaining them in a state that lies between hope and fear. (response to the third objection)

3. Intercession is of two types: false and true. The reason why in some verses, intercession has been refuted whereas in others it has been approved of is this occurrence of two conceptions about intercession. The holy Qur'an sought to guide attention away from the false toward the true type of intercession. (response to the fourth objection)

4. Intercession is not incompatible with the principle of actions; since, actions are of the status of the passive cause whereas Divine mercy is in the position of the active cause (response to the fifth objection).

5. In the true intercession, there is no room for the concept that God can be influenced by any factor; since, true intercession comprises a process that starts at the top and works its way down. (response to the sixth objection).

6. In intercession, as in forgiveness, there exists no injustice or Exceptions-Divine mercy being infinite. Anyone who is denied it is due to his total loss of receptivity towards it. *i.e.* denial is the result of the recipient's deficiency (response to the seventh objection).

Good Deeds of Non-Muslims

Outline of the Discussion

One of the issues that are discussed regarding "Divine Justice" is the issue of the good deeds performed by non-Muslims.

Today, the issue of whether the good deeds of non-Muslims are accepted by God or not is under discussion among the different classes, whether learned or unlearned, literate or illiterate. If they are accepted, what difference does it make if a person is Muslim or not; the important thing is to do good in this world. If a person is not a Muslim and practices no religion, he or she has lost nothing. And if their actions are not acceptable and are altogether void, with no reward or recompense from God, how is that compatible with Divine Justice?

This same question can be asked from a Shia perspective within the bounds of Islam: Are the actions of a non-Shia Muslim acceptable to God, or are they null and void? If they are acceptable, what difference does it make if a person is a Shia Muslim or a non-Shia Muslim? What is important is to be Muslim; a person who is not a Shia and doesn't believe in the wilayah (Divinely-appointed guardianship) of the Ahlul-Bayt (a) has not lost anything. And if the actions of such a person are not acceptable to God, how is that compatible with Divine justice?

In the past, this issue was only discussed by philosophers and in books of philosophy. However, today it has entered the minds of all levels of society; few people can be found who have not at least broached the subject for themselves and in their own minds.

Divine philosophers would discuss the issue from the aspect that if all people who are outside the fold of religion are to face perdition and Divine punishment, it necessarily follows that in the universe, evil and compulsion are preponderant. However, the fact that felicity and good have primacy in the universe not evil and wretchedness-is an accepted and definitive principle.

Humanity is the greatest of all of creation; everything else is created for it (of course, with the correct conception of this idea that is

239

understood by the wise, not the conception that the shortsighted commonly possess). If humanity itself is to be created for the Hell-fire-that is, if the final abode of the majority of humanity is to be Hell-then one must grant that the anger of God supercedes His mercy. This is because the majority of people are strangers to the true religion; and even those who are within the fold of the true religion are beset by deviation and digression when it comes to practicing. This was the background of the discussion among the philosophers.

It has been nearly half a century that, as a result of easier communication among Muslim and non-Muslim nations, an increase in the means of communication, and greater interaction among nations, the issue of whether being a Muslim and a believer is a necessary condition for the acceptability of good deeds is being discussed among all levels of society, especially the so-called intellectuals.

When these people study the lives of inventors and scientists of recent times who weren't Muslim but who performed valuable services for humanity, they find such people worthy of reward. On the other hand, since they used to think that the actions of non-Muslims are altogether null and void, they fall into serious doubt and uncertainty. In this way, an issue which for years was the exclusive domain of the philosophers has entered the general conversations of people and has taken the form of an objection with regard to Divine Justice.

Of course, this objection is not directly related to Divine justice; it is related to Islam's viewpoint about human beings and their actions, and becomes related to Divine Justice inasmuch as it appears that such a viewpoint regarding human beings, their actions, and God's dealing with them is in opposition to the standards of Divine Justice.

In the interactions that I have and have had with students and the youth, I have frequently been faced with this question. Sometimes they ask whether the great inventors and scientists, with all the worthy services they have done for humanity, will go to Hell. Will the likes of Pasteur and Edison go to Hell while indolent holy people who have spent their lives idly in a corner of the mosque go to Heaven? Has God created Heaven solely for us Shias?

I remember that once an acquaintance from my city who was a practicing Muslim came to Tehran to visit me, and he raised this issue.

This man had visited a lepers' hospital in Mashhad and had been stirred and deeply affected by the sight of the Christian nurses who were sincerely (at least in his view) looking after the leprosy patients. At that time, this issue came up in his mind and he fell into doubt.

You are aware that looking after a patient of leprosy is a very difficult and unpleasant task. When this hospital was established in Mashhad, few doctors were willing to serve there, and similarly, no one was willing to care for the patients. Advertisements for the employment of nurses were taken out in the newspapers; in all of Iran, not a single person gave a positive answer to this invitation. A small group of so-called ascetic Christian girls from France came and took charge of nursing the lepers.

This man, who had seen the humanitarianism and loving care of those nurses towards lepers who had been abandoned by even their own parents, had been strongly affected by them.

He related that the Christian nurses wore long, loose clothes, and apart from their face and hands, no part of their body was visible. Each of them had a long rosary-which had perhaps a thousand beads-and whenever they would find free time from work, they would busy themselves in their recitations on the rosary.

Then the man would ask with a troubled mind and in a disturbed tone whether it was true that non-Muslims would not enter Heaven?

Of course, right now we are not concerned with the motives of those Christian ladies. Was it truly for God, in God's way, and out of pure humanitarianism that they did what they did, or was another motive in play? Certainly, we don't want to be pessimistic, just as we are not overly optimistic; our point is that these incidents and events have introduced our people to a serious question.

Several years ago, I was invited to an association to give a speech. In that association, in accordance with their tradition, the participants were requested to write down any questions they had so they could be answered at the appropriate time. Those questions had been recorded in a notebook, and that notebook had been given to me so I could choose the topic of my speech from among those topics. I noticed that the question that had been repeated more than any other was whether God will send all non-Muslims to Hell. Will Pasteur, Edison, and Koch be among those who will be punished in the Hereafter?

It was from that time that I realized the importance of this issue inasmuch as it had attracted people's thoughts.

Now, in this part of the book, we will discuss this issue. But before we begin, we clarify two points in order for the topic at hand to become completely clear.

1. The General Aspect of the Discussion

The purpose of this discussion is not to clarify the status of individuals, for example to specify whether Pasteur will go to Heaven or Hell. What do we know about his true thoughts and beliefs? What were his true intentions? What were his personal and moral traits? And in fact, what was the sum of all his actions? Our familiarity with him is limited to his intellectual services, and that is all.

And this doesn't apply only to Pasteur. As a matter of principle, the status of individuals is in the hands of God; no one has the right to express an opinion with certainty about whether someone will go to Heaven or Hell. If we were to be asked, "Is Shaykh Murtada al-Ansari (may God have mercy on him), in view of his known asceticism, piety, faith, and deeds, definitely among the inhabitants of Heaven?" our answer would be, "From what we know of the man, in his intellectual and practical affairs we haven't heard of anything bad. What we know of him is virtue and goodness. But as to saying with absolute certainty whether he will go to Heaven or Hell, that isn't our prerogative. It is God who knows the intentions of all people, and He knows the secrets and hidden things of all souls; and the account of all people's actions is also with Him. We can only speak with certainty about those whose final outcome has been made known by the religious authorities."

Sometimes people discuss and debate among themselves about who was the most virtuous and excellent among the 'ulama in terms of nearness to God. For example, was it Sayyid ibn Tawus, or Sayyid Bahr al ulum? Or Shaykh al Ansari? Or sometimes they ask about the most eminent among the descendants of the Imams. For example, is Sayyid 'Abd al Azim al-Hasani superior in God's view, or Sayyida Fatima al Ma'suma?

Once, one of the mujtahids was asked whether' Abbas ibn Ali (a) was superior or Ali al-Akbar (a). And in order to give the question the form of a practical issue so the mujtahid would be compelled to answer it, they asked, "If someone vows to sacrifice a sheep for the most superior of the Imams' descendants, what is his duty? Is Abbas ibn Ali superior, or Ali al Akbar?"

It is obvious that such discussions are improper, and answering such questions is neither the duty of a *faqih* (scholar of Islamic law), nor of anyone else. Specifying the rank of God's creation is not our responsibility. It should be left to God, and no one has any knowledge about the matter except through God himself.

In the early era of Islam, there were instances when people expressed such unjustified opinions, and the Prophet (s) forbade them from doing so.

When Uthman ibn Maz'un died, a woman of the Ansar named Umm Ala', who apparently was the wife of the man in whose house Uthman ibn Maz'un was staying and whose guest he was, addressed his bier in the presence of the Prophet (s) and said, "May Heaven be pleasant for you!"

Although 'Uthman ibn Maz'un was an eminent man, and the Prophet cried heavily at his funeral and threw himself over the bier and kissed him, the inappropriate statement of that woman displeased him. He turned to her and with an unhappy look said, "How did you know? Why did you make a statement out of ignorance? Have you received a revelation, or do you know the accounts of God's creation?" The woman replied, "O Messenger of God, he was your companion and brave warrior!" The Noble Messenger (s) answered her with interesting words that are worthy of attention. He said,

إِنِّي رَسولُ اللهِ وَ مَا أُدري مَا يُفعَلُ بِي

I am the messenger of God, yet I don't know what will be done with me.[1]

This sentence is the exact purport of a verse of the Qur'an:

---

[1] *Usd al-Ghaba*, under Uthman Ibn Maz'un

قُلْ مَا كُنتُ بِدْعًا مِّنَ الرُّسُلِ وَمَا أَدْرِي مَا يُفْعَلُ بِي وَلَا بِكُمْ

Say, 'I am not a novelty among the apostles, nor do I know what will
be done with me, or with you.'"!

[Qur'an, 46:9][2]

A similar incident has also been related regarding the death of Sa'd
ibn Muadh. In that instance, when the mother of Sa'd said a similar
sentence over his coffin, the Messenger (s) said to her, "Be silent; don't
make a decision with certainty in God's affairs (لا تحتمي على الله).[3]

2. No religion except Islam is accepted

The other point that must be made clear before beginning the
discussion is that the topic of the non-Muslims' good deeds can be
discussed in two ways and in reality, is two discussions: First, is any
religion other than Islam acceptable to God, or is Islam the only
acceptable religion? That is, is it necessary only for a person to have
some religion or at most follow a religion associated with one of the
Divine prophets, without it then making a difference which religion that
is, for example, whether one be a Muslim, Christian, Jew, or even a
Zoroastrian? Or is there only one true religion in each era?

---

[2] The objection may come to mind that the purport of this verse is contrary to what is
accepted by Muslims as established fact, meaning that the Prophet (s) informed of his
praiseworthy place on the Day of Judgment and of his intercession for various sinners,
and is rather contrary to the purpose of various verses, like "and verily your Lord will
grant you until you are pleased" and "for God to forgive that which has passed of your
mistake and that which is to come."

The answer is that the purport of the verse, as is also understood from the preceding
tradition, is that the end result of a person's actions are not known with certainty by
anyone; only God has certain knowledge of the final result, and if others come to know,
it is only by Divine revelation. So the verse that negates knowledge of the final end
relates to the Prophet (s) or someone else making a forecast relying on his or her own
actions; and the verses that the verses that indicate that the Prophet (s) has knowledge
of his own or other people's final end are through Divine revelation."

[3] *Bihar al-Anwar,* vol. 3. p. 165

After we have accepted that the true religion in each era is only one, the other discussion is 'whether a person who doesn't follow the true religion but performs a good deed, one that is actually good and is also sanctioned by the true religion, is worthy of reward or not? In other words, is faith in the true religion a condition for one's good deeds to merit reward?

What will be discussed here is the second issue.

With respect to the first issue, we can say briefly that there is only one true religion in each era, and all are obligated to believe in it.

The idea that has recently become common among some so-called intellectuals to the effect that all Divine religions have equal validity in all eras is a fallacious one.

Of course, it is true that there is no disagreement or contradiction among the prophets of God. All of the prophets of God call towards a single goal and the same God. They have not come to create mutually contradicting groups and sects among humanity.

But this doesn't mean that in every era there are several true religions, and thus people in each era can then choose whichever religion they want. To the contrary, it means that a person must believe in all of the prophets and affirm that each prophet would give tidings of the prophet to come, especially the final and greatest of them; and likewise, each prophet would affirm the previous one. Thus, the necessary consequence of believing in all of the prophets is to submit in every era to the religion of the prophet of the time. And of course, it is necessary that in the final era we act on the final commands that have been revealed by God to the final prophet. And this is what necessarily follows from Islam, that is, submission to God and acceptance of the missions of His messengers.

Many people in our day have subscribed to the view that it is sufficient for a person to worship God and be affiliated with and practice one of the Divine religions that were revealed by God; the form of the commandments is not that important. Isa (a) was a prophet, Muhammad (s) was also a prophet; if we follow the religion of Isa (a) and go to church once a week, that is fine, and if we follow the religion of the final messenger (s) and pray five times a day, that is also correct.

These people say that what is important is for a person to believe in God and practice one of the Divine religions.

George Jordac, author of the book[4] on Imam Ali (a), Gibran Khalil Gibran, the well-known Lebanese Christian author; and others like them have such a view.[5] These two individuals speak of the Prophet and Amir al-Mu'minin and especially Amir al-Mu'minm -just as a Muslim would.

Some people ask how these people, in spite of their belief in Amir al-Mu'minin (a) and the Prophet (s), are still Christian. If they were truthful, they would have become Muslims, and since they haven't done so, it is clear there is something behind the curtain. They are being deceptive, and they aren't sincere in their expression of love and belief in the Prophet and Ali (a).

The answer is that they are not without sincerity in their expression of love and belief in the Prophet and Amir al-Mu'minin (a). However, they have their own way of thinking regarding practicing a religion.

These individuals believe that human beings are not held to a particular religion; any religion is sufficient. Thus, at the same time that they are Christians, they consider themselves admirers and friends of Ali (a), and they even believe that he himself held their view. George Jordac says, "Ali ibn Abi Talib declines to compel people to necessarily follow a particular religion."

However, we consider this idea void. It is true that there is no compulsion in religion:

----

[4] *The Voice of Human Justice*

[5] George Jordac's words about the Prophet (s) indicate he believed in his prophecy and receiving Divine revelation, and he also believed firmly that Ali (a) was a man of God and regarded him as being like 'Isa (a), but at the same time he did not abandon Christianity. Gibran Khalil Gibran says of Ali (a): "In my view, Ali was the first Arab to have contact with and converse with the universal soul [of the world]"

He expresses greater love for Ali than even the Prophet. He has unusual statements about Ali; for example, he says, "He died while prayer was between his two lips." And he also says of Ali, "Ali was before his time, and I don't know the secret of why destiny sometimes brings people to the world before their time."

Incidentally, this point is the meaning of one of Ali's (a) own statements; he says, "Tomorrow you will see my days and my secrets will be exposed to you, and you will know me after my space has become empty and others take my place."

لَا إِكْرَاهَ فِي الدِّينِ

There is no compulsion in religion. [Qur'an, 2:256]

But this doesn't mean that there is more than one religion in every age that is acceptable to God, and we have the right to choose anyone we please. This is not the case; in every age, there is one true religion and no more. Whenever a prophet was sent by God with a new religion, the people were obligated to avail themselves of his teachings and learn his laws and commandments, whether in acts of worship or otherwise, until the turn of the Seal of the Prophets came. In this age, if someone wishes to come near God, he or she must seek guidance from the precepts of the religion he brought.

The Noble Qur'an says:

وَمَن يَبْتَغِ غَيْرَ الْإِسْلَامِ دِينًا فَلَن يُقْبَلَ مِنْهُ وَهُوَ فِي الْآخِرَةِ مِنَ الْخَاسِرِينَ

Should anyone follow a religion other than Islam, it shall never be accepted from him, and he will be among the losers in the Hereafter.
[Qur'an, 3:85]

If someone were to say that the meaning of "Islam" in this verse is not our religion in particular; rather, the intent is the literal meaning of the word, or submission to God, the answer would be that without doubt Islam means submission and the Islamic religion is the religion of submission, but the reality of submission has a particular form in each age. And in this age, its form is the same cherished religion that was brought by the Seal of the Prophets. So, it follows that the word Islam (submission) necessarily applies to it alone.

In other words, the necessary consequence of submission to God is to accept His commandments, and it is clear that one must always act on the final Divine commandments. And the final commandment of God is what His final messenger has brought.

Good deeds without faith

It has become clear that, first of all, our discussion has a general aspect, and we don't want to pass decisions about individuals.

Second, our discussion is not about whether the true religion is one or several; rather, we have accepted that the true religion is one and that all are obligated to accept it.

Third, our discussion is this: if a person, without accepting the true religion, performs a deed which the true religion considers good, does that person receive a reward for that good deed or not?

For example, the true religion has emphasized doing good to others. This includes cultural services like establishing schools, places of learning, writing, and teaching; health services like medicine, nursing, establishing sanitary establishments, and so forth; social services such as mediating disputes, helping the poor and disabled, supporting the rights of the exploited, fighting the exploiters and oppressors, assisting the deprived, establishing justice which is the aim and goal of the prophets' mission, providing the means of satisfaction for the broken-hearted and misfortunate, and such like. Every religion and every prophet has enjoined these things. In addition, the reasoning and conscience of each individual rules that these things are good and worthy.

Now, we ask whether a non-Muslim is rewarded if he or she performs such services. The true religion says to be trustworthy and not lie; if a non-Muslim acts in accordance with this principle, will he or she be rewarded or not? In other words, is it equal with respect to a non-Muslim to be trustworthy or treacherous? Are adultery and prayers equal with respect to him or her (سواء صلّى أم زنى)? This is the issue that we wish to discuss.

Two ways of thinking

Normally, those with an intellectual inclination say with certainty that there is no difference between a Muslim and non-Muslim, and even between a monotheist and non-monotheist; whoever performs a good deed, a service like establishing a charitable organization or an invention or something else, deserves recompense from God.

They say that God is Just, and a God who is Just does not discriminate among His servants. What difference does it make for God whether His servant recognizes Him or not or believes in Him or not? Certainly, God will not ignore the good deeds or waste the reward of a person simply because that person doesn't have a relationship of familiarity and love with Him. And even more certainly, if a person believes in God and does good deeds, but does not recognize His messengers and thus does not have a relationship of familiarity and covenant of friendship with them, God will not cancel out and nullify his or her good deeds.

Directly opposite to these people are those who consider almost all people worthy of punishment and believe in a good end and accepted actions with respect to only a few. They have a very simple standard; they say that people are either Muslim or non-Muslim. Non-Muslims, who are about three-fourths of the world's population, shall go to Hell because they are non-Muslims. The Muslims in their turn are either Shia or non-Shia. The non-Shias, who are about three-fourths of all Muslims, will go to Hell because they are non-Shias. And of the Shias, too, a majority-about three-fourths-are only Shia in name, and it is a small minority that is familiar with even the first obligation, which is to perform "*taqlid*" of a *mujtahid* (follow the religious rulings of a particular scholar), let alone their remaining obligations, and the correctness and completeness of those obligations depends on this obligation. And even those who perform taqlid are for the most part non-practicing. Thus, there are very few who will achieve salvation.

This is the logic of the two sides: the logic of those who, it can almost be said, are absolute conciliation, and the logic of those who we can say are a manifestation of Divine anger, giving anger precedence over mercy.

The Third Logic

Here there is a third logic, which is the logic of the Qur'an. In this issue the Qur'an gives us a concept that is different from the previous two ideas and that is peculiar to it. The Qur'an's view accords with neither the nonsensical idea of our so-called intellectuals, nor with the narrow-mindedness of our holier than-thou pious people. The Qur'an's view is rooted in a special logic that everyone, after learning of it, will admit is the correct position in this matter. And this fact increases our faith in this astonishing and remarkable book and shows that its lofty teachings are independent of the worldly thoughts of human beings and have a celestial source.

Here we present the proofs of both disputing groups (the so-called intellectuals and the so-called pious) and investigate them so that by critiquing them we can slowly arrive at the third logic in regard to this issue, that is, the logic and particular philosophy of the Qur'an.

The so-called Intellectuals

This group brings two types of proofs for their view: rational and narrational.

1. Rational proof. The rational demonstration that says that good deeds entail their reward no matter who performs them is based on two premises:

The first premise: God has an equal relation to all existent beings. His relation to all times and places is the same; just as God is in the East, He is in the West, and just as He is above, He is below. God is in the present and past and future; the past, present, and future have no difference for God, just as above and below and East and West are the same for Him. Similarly, His servants and creation are also the same for Him; He has neither family ties nor a special relationship with anyone. Thus, God's showing grace or showing anger towards people is also the same, except when there are differences in the people themselves.[6]

---

[6] Of course, this does not mean that all things have the same relation to God and deserve the same treatment. The relation of things to God is not the same, but the relation of God to things is the same. God is equally close to all things, but things are different in their closeness and distance from God. There is an interesting sentence in *Du'a al-Iftitah* in this regard: Text in Arabic on page 272. In this sentence, God has been described thus: "Who is distant and thus cannot be seen and Who is near and thus witnesses all conversations." In fact, it is we who are far from Him, while He is close to us. This is an enigma; how is it possible for two things to have a different relation with each other in terms of closeness and distance? But yes, such is the case here; God is close to things, but things are not close to God-that is, they have varying states of closeness and distance. The interesting point in this sentence is that when it describes God as being "far" it mentions an attribute of His creations as evidence, which is the attribute of sight. "None can see Him." And when it describes God as being near, it mentions an attribute of God as evidence, which is the attribute of Divine presence and awareness. When speaking of our state, we use the attribute of distance, for God, and when speaking of His state, we use the attribute of "closeness".

As a result, no one is dear to God without reason, and no one is lowly or outcast without justification. God has neither ties of kinship nor of nationality with anyone; and no one is the beloved or chosen one of God.

Since God's relation to all beings is the same, there remains no reason for a good deed to be accepted from one person and not from another. If the actions are the same, their reward will also be the same, since the assumption is that God's relation to all people is the same. So, justice demands that God reward all those who do good-whether Muslims or non-Muslims-in the same way.

The second premise: The goodness or badness of actions is not based on convention, but on actual reality. In the terminology of scholars of theology and the science of principles of jurisprudence, the "goodness" or "badness" of actions is *dhati*, or innate. That is, good and bad deeds are differentiated by their essence; good deeds are good by their essence, and bad deeds are bad by their essence. Honesty, virtue, doing good, helping others, and so forth are good by their essence; and lying, stealing, and oppression are bad by their essence. The goodness of "honesty" or badness of "lying" is not because God has mandated the former and forbidden the latter. To the contrary, it is because "honesty" is good that God has obligated it and because "lying" is bad that God has forbidden it. In short, God's commanding or forbidding is based on the goodness or badness of actions in their essence, and not the other way around.

From these two premises, we conclude that since God does not discriminate, and since good deeds are good from all people, whoever does a good deed will definitely and necessarily be rewarded by God.

It is exactly the same way with regard to evil deeds since there is no difference between those who commit them.

2. Narrational proof. The Qur'an affirms in many verses the principle of non-discrimination among people in rewarding good deeds and punishing evil deeds-which was mentioned in the above rational proof. The Qur'an strongly opposed the Jews, who believed in such discrimination. The Jews believed-and still believe-hat the Jewish race

---

Sa'di says, "He is a Friend closer to-me than myself, and amazing it is that I am far from Him. what to do: who can I tell that the Friend is by my side, and I am forsaken!"

is chosen by God; they would say, "We are the sons and friends of God. Supposing God sends us to Hell, it will not be for more than a limited time." The Qur'an calls such ideas wishes and untrue thoughts and has strongly combated them. The Qur'an also points out the error of Muslims who have fallen prey to such deception. Here are some of the verses in this regard:

1.

وَقَالُوا لَن تَمَسَّنَا النَّارُ إِلَّا أَيَّامًا مَّعْدُودَةً ۚ قُلْ أَتَّخَذْتُمْ عِندَ اللَّهِ عَهْدًا فَلَن يُخْلِفَ اللَّهُ عَهْدَهُ ۖ أَمْ تَقُولُونَ عَلَى اللَّهِ مَا لَا تَعْلَمُونَ ﴿٨٠﴾ بَلَىٰ مَن كَسَبَ سَيِّئَةً وَأَحَاطَتْ بِهِ خَطِيئَتُهُ فَأُولَٰئِكَ أَصْحَابُ النَّارِ ۖ هُمْ فِيهَا خَالِدُونَ ﴿٨١﴾ وَالَّذِينَ آمَنُوا وَعَمِلُوا الصَّالِحَاتِ أُولَٰئِكَ أَصْحَابُ الْجَنَّةِ ۖ هُمْ فِيهَا خَالِدُونَ ﴿٨٢﴾

And they say, 'The Fire shall not touch us except for a number of days.' Say, 'Have you taken a promise from Allah? If so, Allah will never break His promise. Do you ascribe to Allah what you do not know?' Certainly, whoever commits misdeeds and is besieged by his iniquity—such shall be the inmates of the Fire, and they will remain in it [forever]. And those who have faith and do righteous deeds—they shall be the inhabitants of paradise; they will remain in it [forever].

[Qur'an, 2:80-82]

2. In another place, the Qur'an says in answer to the conjecture of the Jews:

وَغَرَّهُمْ فِي دِينِهِم مَّا كَانُوا يَفْتَرُونَ ﴿٢٤﴾ فَكَيْفَ إِذَا جَمَعْنَاهُمْ لِيَوْمٍ لَّا رَيْبَ فِيهِ وَوُفِّيَتْ كُلُّ نَفْسٍ مَّا كَسَبَتْ وَهُمْ لَا يُظْلَمُونَ ﴿٢٥﴾

and they have been misled in their religion by what they used to fabricate. But how will it be [with them] when We gather them on a day in which there is no doubt, and every soul shall be recompensed fully for what it has earned, and they will not be wronged?

[Qur'an, 3:24-25]

3. In another place, the Christians have been added to the Jews, and together they have been opposed by the Qur'an:

وَقَالُوا لَن يَدْخُلَ الْجَنَّةَ إِلَّا مَن كَانَ هُودًا أَوْ نَصَارَىٰ ۗ تِلْكَ أَمَانِيُّهُمْ ۗ قُلْ هَاتُوا بُرْهَانَكُمْ إِن كُنتُمْ صَادِقِينَ ﴿١١١﴾ بَلَىٰ مَنْ أَسْلَمَ وَجْهَهُ لِلَّهِ وَهُوَ مُحْسِنٌ فَلَهُ أَجْرُهُ عِندَ رَبِّهِ وَلَا خَوْفٌ عَلَيْهِمْ وَلَا هُمْ يَحْزَنُونَ ﴿١١٢﴾

And they say, 'No one will enter paradise except one who is a Jew or Christian.' Those are their [false] hopes! Say, 'Produce your evidence, should you be truthful.' Certainly, whoever submits his will to Allah and is virtuous, he shall have his reward from his Lord, and they will have no fear, nor shall they grieve.

[Qur'an, 2:111-112]

4. In Surah al-Nisa', the Muslims, too, have been added to the Jews and Christians. The Qur'an demolishes discriminatory thinking no matter who it is from. It is as though the Muslims had come under the effect of the thinking of the People of the Book, and in the face of they who without reason considered themselves superior, adopted such an opinion about themselves. The Qur'an says, refuting these immature fancies:

لَّيْسَ بِأَمَانِيِّكُمْ وَلَا أَمَانِيِّ أَهْلِ الْكِتَابِ ۗ مَن يَعْمَلْ سُوءًا يُجْزَ بِهِ وَلَا يَجِدْ لَهُ مِن دُونِ اللَّهِ وَلِيًّا وَلَا نَصِيرًا ﴿١٢٣﴾ وَمَن يَعْمَلْ مِنَ الصَّالِحَاتِ مِن ذَكَرٍ أَوْ أُنثَىٰ وَهُوَ مُؤْمِنٌ فَأُولَٰئِكَ يَدْخُلُونَ الْجَنَّةَ وَلَا يُظْلَمُونَ نَقِيرًا ﴿١٢٤﴾

It will be neither after your hopes nor the hopes of the People of the Book: whoever commits evil shall be requited for it, and he will not find for himself any guardian or helper besides Allah. And whoever does righteous deeds, whether male or female, should he be faithful— such shall enter paradise and they will not be wronged [so much as] the speck on a date-stone. [Qur'an, 4:123-124]

5. Leaving aside the verses that condemn baseless suppositions of honour and nearness to God, there are other verses that say that God does not waste the reward of any good deed.

These verses have also been taken as proof of the acceptance of the good deeds of all people, whether Muslim or non-Muslim. In Surah Zilzal, we read:

فَمَن يَعْمَلْ مِثْقَالَ ذَرَّةٍ خَيْرًا يَرَهُ ﴿٧﴾ وَمَن يَعْمَلْ مِثْقَالَ ذَرَّةٍ شَرًّا يَرَهُ ﴿٨﴾

So, whoever does an atom's weight of good will see it, and whoever does an atom's weight of evil will see it. [Qur'an, 99:7-8]

253

Elsewhere, God says:

$$إِنَّ اللَّهَ لَا يُضِيعُ أَجْرَ الْمُحْسِنِينَ$$

Indeed, Allah does not waste the reward of the virtuous.

[Qur'an, 9:120]

And in another place, He says:

$$إِنَّا لَا نُضِيعُ أَجْرَ مَنْ أَحْسَنَ عَمَلًا$$

Indeed, We do not waste the reward of those who are good in deeds.
[Qur'an, 18:30]

The wording of these verses makes them universal statements that are not given to exceptions.

The scholars of the discipline of the principles of jurisprudence (*usul al-fiqh*) say that certain universal statements do not accept exceptions; that is, the wording and tone of the universal is such that it resists any exceptions. When it is said, "We don't waste the reward of the doer of good," it means that God's divinity demands that He preserve good deeds; thus, it is impossible for God to disregard His divinity in one instance and waste a good deed.

6. There is another verse which is frequently referred to in this discussion, and it is said that it clearly points to the assertion of this group:

$$إِنَّ الَّذِينَ آمَنُوا وَالَّذِينَ هَادُوا وَالصَّابِئُونَ وَالنَّصَارَىٰ مَنْ آمَنَ بِاللَّهِ وَالْيَوْمِ الْآخِرِ وَعَمِلَ صَالِحًا فَلَا خَوْفٌ عَلَيْهِمْ وَلَا هُمْ يَحْزَنُونَ$$

Indeed, the faithful, the Jews, the Sabaeans, and the Christians—those who have faith in Allah and the Last Day and act righteously—they will have no fear, nor will they grieve. [Qur'an, 5:69]

In this verse, three conditions have been mentioned for salvation and safety from God's punishment: belief in God, belief in the Day of Judgment, and good deeds; no other condition is mentioned.

Some who are apparently intellectuals have gone one step further and said that the aim of the prophets was to call towards justice and goodness, and in accordance with the rule "Comply with the spirit and not the letter of the law" we should say that justice and goodness are accepted even from those who don't believe in God and the Day of Judgment. Thus, those who don't believe in God and the Day of Judgment but have made great cultural, medical, economical, or political contributions to humanity shall have a great reward.

Of course, these people can argue on the basis of verses like, "We don't waste the reward of one who does good," and "So whoever does an atom's weight of good shall see it," but verses like the one above contradict their assertion.

Below we take a look at the proofs of the other group.

The Rigid Group

In opposition to the supposed intellectuals who claim that good deeds are accepted by God from all people in all situations are the rigid pious ones; their position is directly opposite to the former group. They say that it is impossible for a non-Muslim's actions to be accepted. The actions of unbelievers and similarly those of non-Shia Muslims have absolutely no value. The non-Muslim and non-Shia Muslim himself is rejected and rebuffed; his actions are even more worthy of being rejected. This group also brings two proofs: rational and narrational.

1. Rational proof: The rational proof of this group is that if it is supposed that the actions of non-Muslims and non-Shia Muslims are to be accepted by God, what is the difference between Muslims and non-Muslims? The difference between them should be either for the good deeds of Muslims and Shias to be accepted to the exclusion of nonMuslims and non-Shia Muslims, or for the evil deeds of Muslims and Shias not to be punished, again to the exclusion of non-Muslims and non-Shia Muslims. But if we suppose that the good deeds of both groups entail reward and the evil deeds of both groups lead to punishment, what difference will there be between them? And what is the effect of being Muslim or Shia in such a case? The equality of Muslims and non-Muslims, and similarly Shias and non-Shias, in accounting for their actions means that in essence practicing Islam or Shiaism is unnecessary and without effect.

2. Narrational proof: In addition to the above reasoning, this group also argues from two Qur'anic verses and several traditions.

In a few verses of Qur'an, it has been clearly stated that the actions of unbelievers are not accepted; similarly, in many traditions it has been said that the actions of non-Shias-that is, those who do not have the *wilayah* (Divinely-ordained guardianship) of the Ahl al-Bayt (a)-are not accepted.

In Surah Ibrahim, God compares the actions of unbelievers to ashes which are scattered by a strong wind and lost:

مَّثَلُ الَّذِينَ كَفَرُوا بِرَبِّهِمْ ۖ أَعْمَالُهُمْ كَرَمَادٍ اشْتَدَّتْ بِهِ الرِّيحُ فِي يَوْمٍ عَاصِفٍ ۖ لَّا يَقْدِرُونَ مِمَّا كَسَبُوا عَلَىٰ شَيْءٍ ۚ ذَٰلِكَ هُوَ الضَّلَالُ الْبَعِيدُ

A parable of those who defy their Lord: their deeds are like ashes over which the wind blows hard on a tempestuous day: they have no power over anything they have earned. That is extreme error. [Qur'an, 14:18]

In a verse of Surah Nur, the actions of unbelievers have been likened to a mirage which appears to be water but upon being approached turns out to be nothing.

This verse says that great deeds that give people pause and, in the view of some simpleminded people, are greater than the services of even the prophets are all null and void if they are not coupled with belief in God. Their greatness is nothing but a fancy, like a mirage. The words of the verse are as below:

وَالَّذِينَ كَفَرُوا أَعْمَالُهُمْ كَسَرَابٍ بِقِيعَةٍ يَحْسَبُهُ الظَّمْآنُ مَاءً حَتَّىٰ إِذَا جَاءَهُ لَمْ يَجِدْهُ شَيْئًا وَوَجَدَ اللَّـهَ عِندَهُ فَوَفَّاهُ حِسَابَهُ ۗ وَاللَّـهُ سَرِيعُ الْحِسَابِ

As for the faithless, their works are like a mirage in a plain, which the thirsty man supposes to be water. When he comes to it, he finds it to be nothing; but there he finds Allah, who will pay him his full account, and Allah is swift at reckoning. [Qur'an, 24:39]

This is the parable of the good deeds of unbelievers, which appear outwardly to be good. So, woe upon their evil deeds! We read their parable in the following verse in these words:

أَوْ كَظُلُمَاتٍ فِي بَحْرٍ لُّجِّيٍّ يَغْشَاهُ مَوْجٌ مِّن فَوْقِهِ مَوْجٌ مِّن فَوْقِهِ سَحَابٌ ۚ ظُلُمَاتٌ بَعْضُهَا فَوْقَ بَعْضٍ إِذَا أَخْرَجَ يَدَهُ لَمْ يَكَدْ يَرَاهَا ۗ وَمَن لَّمْ يَجْعَلِ اللَّـهُ لَهُ نُورًا فَمَا لَهُ مِن نُّورٍ

Or like the manifold darkness in a deep sea, covered by billow upon billow, overcast by clouds; manifold [layers of] darkness, one on top of another: when he brings out his hand, he can hardly see it. One whom Allah has not granted any light has no light. [Qur'an, 24:40]

By adding this verse to the previous verse, we deduce that the good deeds of unbelievers, with all their deceptive appearances, are a mirage that lacks reality. And as for their evil deeds, alas! They are evil above evil, darkness upon darkness!

The above verses clarify the status of the deeds of unbelievers.

As for non-Shia Muslims, from the point of view of us Shias, the traditions that have reached us from the Ahl al-Bayt (a) clarify their position:

Many traditions have reached us on this topic. Those interested can refer to *al-Kafi*; vol. 1, "Kitab al-Hujja," and vol. 2, "Kitab al-Iman wal-Kufr"; *Wasa'il al-Shia*, vol. 1, "Abwab Muqaddamat al-Ibadat"; *Mustadrak al-Wasa'il*, vol. 1, "Abwab Muqaddamat al-Ibadat"; *Bihar al-Anwar*; "Discussions about Resurrection," chapter 17 (Chapter on the Promise, Threat, Invalidation of Actions, and Atonement), and vol. 7 of the old print, chapter 227, and vol. 15 of the old print, section on ethics, p. 187. As an example, we relate one tradition from *Wasa'il al-Shia*:

Muhammad ibn Muslim said, "I heard Imam Muhammad Baqir (a) say, 'Whoever worships God and tires himself in worship but doesn't recognize the imam (leader) God has appointed for him, his deeds are not accepted, and he himself is astray and lost, and God abhors his actions ... and if he dies in this state, he dies not in the state of Islam, but in a state of unbelief and hypocrisy. O Muhammad ibn Muslim, know that the leaders of oppression and their followers are outside the religion of God. They themselves went astray, and they led others astray. Their actions are like ashes which are caught in a strong wind on a stormy day, and they cannot reach anything out of what they have earned. That is the distant deviation.[7]

These are the proofs of those who say that the basis of salvation is faith and belief.

Occasionally, some from this group go to extremes and consider simply the claim of having faith, or in reality a simple affiliation, to be the criterion of judgment. For example, the Murji'i sect in the era of Banu Umayya would propagate this idea, and fortunately, with the decline of Banu Umayya, they also ceased to exist. In that age, the Shia position, inspired by the imams from the Ahl al-Bayt (a), was opposite to the Murji'i one, but unfortunately the Murji'is' view has lately taken hold in new clothing among some of the common Shias. Some simpleminded Shias consider mere apparent affiliation with Amir al-Mu'minin (a) to be sufficient for salvation, and this idea is the basic factor behind the Shias' poor state in the modem era. The dervishes and Sufis of the recent era malign good deeds in a different way and under a different pretext; they have made the issue of goodness of heart a pretext, even though true goodness of heart encourages and affirms deeds rather than conflicting with them.

As opposed to these groups, there are others who have raised the value of deeds to such a point that they say that one who commits a major sin is an unbeliever. Such a belief was held by the Kharijites. Some theologians considered the committer of major sins to be neither a believer nor unbeliever, and held that there is a "state between the two states (of belief and unbelief)."

Our task is to see which of these positions is correct. Should we believe in the primacy of belief or the primacy of action? Or is there a third path?

To begin, let us discuss the value of belief and faith.

---

[7] *Wasail al-Shia*, vol.1, part 1, p.90

Value of Belief

With regard to the value of belief, the discussion should proceed in three stages:

1. Is lack of belief in the principles of religion, such as the Oneness of God, Prophecy, and resurrection-and according to the Shia view, these three in addition to Divine justice and Imamate (succession)-always and necessarily cause for Divine punishment? Or is it possible for some unbelievers to be excused and not be punished for their unbelief?

2. Is belief a necessary condition for the acceptance of good deeds, such that no good deed of a non-Muslim or non-Shia is acceptable to God?

3. Do unbelief and rejection of the truth cause the invalidity of good deeds or not?

In the coming discussions, we will touch on each of these three stages.

Being Held Accountable for Unbelief

There is no doubt that unbelief is of two types: One is unbelief out of obstinacy and stubbornness, which is called the unbelief of repudiation; and the other is unbelief out of ignorance and unawareness of the truth. With regard to the former, definitive rational and narrational proofs indicate that a person who deliberately and knowingly shows obstinacy towards the truth and endeavours to reject it deserves punishment. But with regard to the latter, it must be said that if the ignorance and unawareness do not spring from negligence, they shall be forgiven and overlooked by God.

To explain this point, it is necessary to speak a bit about submission and obstinacy. The Qur'an says,

يَوْمَ لَا يَنفَعُ مَالٌ وَلَا بَنُونَ ﴿٨٨﴾ إِلَّا مَنْ أَتَى اللَّهَ بِقَلْبٍ سَلِيمٍ ﴿٨٩﴾

the day when neither wealth nor children will avail, except him who comes to Allah with a sound heart...

[Qur'an, 26:88-89]

259

Levels of Submission

The most basic condition of soundness of heart is to be submissive to the truth. Submission has three levels: submission of the body, submission of the intellect, and submission of the heart.

When two opponents face each other in combat and one of them feels likely to lose, he may surrender, or submit, to the other. In such surrender, normally the losing opponent puts his hands up as a sign of defeat and desists from fighting, coming under the sway of his opponent. That is, he acts in accordance with whatever command his opponent gives.

In this type of submission, the body submits, but the mind and reason do not; instead, they are constantly thinking of rebellion, incessantly contemplating how to get a chance to overcome the opponent once again. This is the state of his reason and thought, and as for his feelings and emotions, they too continuously denounce the enemy. This type of submission-that of the body-is the most that can be achieved by force.

The next level of submission is the submission of the intellect and reason. The power that can make the intellect submit is that of logic and reasoning. Here, physical force can't accomplish anything. It is absolutely impossible through physical force to make a student understand that the sum of the angles of a triangle is equal to two right angles. Mathematical propositions must be proven through reasoning and not through any other way. The intellect is forced to submit through thinking and reasoning. If sufficient proof exists and is presented to the intellect and the intellect understands it, it submits, even if all the powers of the world say not to submit.

It is well-known that when Galileo was tortured for his belief in the movement of the earth and centrality of the sun in the solar system, out of fear that they would bum him alive, he expressed repentance of his scientific view; in that condition, he wrote something on the ground. It is said that he wrote, "Galileo's repentance will not make the earth stand still."

Force can compel a person to recant his or her words, but the human intellect does not submit except when faced with logic and reasoning.

قُلْ هَاتُوا بُرْهَانَكُمْ إِن كُنتُمْ صَادِقِينَ

Say, 'Produce your evidence, should you be truthful.

[Qur'an, 27:64]

The third level of submission is the submission of the heart. The reality of faith is submission of the heart; submission of the tongue or submission of the thought and intellect, if not coupled with submission of the heart, is not faith. Submission of the heart is equal to submission of the entire existence of a person and the negation of every type of obstinacy and rejection.

It is possible that someone may submit to an idea as far as the intellect and mind are concerned, but not the spirit. When a person shows obstinacy out of prejudice or refuses to yield to the truth because of personal interests, his or her mind and intellect have submitted, but the spirit is rebellious and lacks submission, and for this very reason lacks faith, since the reality of faith is the submission of the heart and soul.

God says in the Qur'an:

يَا أَيُّهَا الَّذِينَ آمَنُوا ادْخُلُوا فِي السِّلْمِ كَافَّةً وَلَا تَتَّبِعُوا خُطُوَاتِ الشَّيْطَانِ

O you who have faith! Enter into submission, all together, and do not follow in Satan's steps. [Qur'an, 2:208]

That is, your soul should not be at war with your intellect; your feelings should not be at war with your perceptions.

The story of Shaytan that has come in the Qur'an is an example of unbelief of the heart even though the intellect has submitted. Shaytan recognized God, believed in the Day of Judgment, completely recognized the prophets and their legatees and admitted their position; at the same time, God calls him an unbeliever and says of him:

وَكَانَ مِنَ الْكَافِرِينَ

and he was one of the faithless. [Qur'an, 2:34]

The evidence that, in the view of the Qur'an, Shay tan recognized God is that the Qur'an explicitly says that he confessed that He is the Creator. Addressing God, he said:

خَلَقْتَنِي مِن نَّارٍ وَخَلَقْتَهُ مِن طِينٍ

'You created me from fire and You created him from clay.'

[Qur'an, 7:12]

And the evidence that he believed in the Day of Judgment is that he said:

أَنظِرْنِي إِلَىٰ يَوْمِ يُبْعَثُونَ

'Respite me till the day they will be resurrected'.

[Qur'an, 7:14]

And the evidence that he recognized the prophets and infallibles is that he said:

قَالَ فَبِعِزَّتِكَ لَأُغْوِيَنَّهُمْ أَجْمَعِينَ ﴿٨٢﴾ إِلَّا عِبَادَكَ مِنْهُمُ الْمُخْلَصِينَ ﴿٨٣﴾

He said, 'By Your might, I will surely pervert them, except Your exclusive servants among them.' [Qur'an, 38:82-83]

The meaning of the purified servants, who are pure not just in their actions, but whose entire existence is purified and free of all except God, is the friends of God and the infallibles; Shayt an recognized them, too, and believed in their infallibility.

The Qur'an, while describing Shaytan as knowing all these things, calls him an unbeliever. Thus, we come to know that mere recognition and knowledge, or the submission of the intellect and mind, is not sufficient for a person to be considered a believer. Something else is necessary as well.

In the Qur'an's logic, why has Shaytan been regarded as an unbeliever in spite of all his knowledge?

Obviously, it is because while his perception accepted reality, his feelings rose to battle it; his heart rose against his intellect; he showed arrogance and refused to accept the truth: he lacked submission of the heart.

True Islam and Regional Islam

Normally when we say so-and-so is Muslim or isn't Muslim, our view isn't toward the reality of the matter. Those who geographically live in a particular region and are Muslims through imitation and inheritance from their parents we call Muslims; and those who live under different conditions and are affiliated with another religion or have no religion altogether, again out of imitation of their parents, we call non-Muslims.

It should be known that this aspect does not have much value, neither the aspect of being a Muslim nor that of being a non-Muslim and an unbeliever. Many of us are imitative or geographical Muslims; we are Muslims because our mothers and fathers were Muslim and we were born and raised in a region whose people are Muslim. That which has value in reality is true Islam, and that is for a person to submit to truth in the heart, having opened the door of one's heart to the truth to accept and act on it, and the Islam that he or she has accepted should be based on research and study on the one hand, and submission and lack of prejudice on the other.

If someone possesses the trait of submission to the truth and for whatever reason the reality of Islam has remained hidden from him or her without that person being at fault, God will most certainly refrain from punishing him or her; he or she shall achieve salvation from Hell. God says

$$\text{وَمَا كُنَّا مُعَذِّبِينَ حَتَّىٰ نَبْعَثَ رَسُولًا}$$

We do not punish [any community] until We have sent [it] an apostle.
[Qur'an, 17:15]

That is, it is impossible for God, the Wise and Munificent, to punish someone for whom the proofs (of truth) have not been completed. The scholars of the principles of jurisprudence have termed the purport of this verse, which acts to confirm the dictate of reason, "the improperness of punishment without prior explanation." They say that until God has made clear a reality for a person, it is unjust for Him to punish that person.

To show the fact that it is possible to find individuals who possess the spirit of submission without being Muslims in name, Descartes, the French philosopher-according to his own words-is a good example.

In his biography, they have written that he began his philosophy from doubt; he doubted all that he knew and began from zero. He made his own thought a starting point and said, "I think, therefore I am."

After proving his own existence, he proved the spirit, and likewise the existence of body and God became definite for him. Gradually the issue of choosing a religion arose; he chose Christianity, which was the official religion of his country.

But he also says, "I don't say that Christianity is definitely the best religion that exists in the entire world; what I say is that among the religions that I currently know and that are in my reach, Christianity is the best religion. I have no conflict with the truth; perhaps there is a religion in other parts of the world that is superior to Christianity." Incidentally, he mentions Iran as an example of a country about which he lacks information and doesn't know the religion of; he says: "What do I know? Perhaps there is a religion in Iran that is better than Christianity."

Such people cannot be called unbelievers, since they have no obstinacy; they are not deliberately seeking unbelief. They are not involved in concealing reality, which is the essence of unbelief. Such people are "dispositional Muslims." Though they cannot be called Muslim, they also cannot be termed unbelievers, since the opposition between Muslim and unbeliever is not like the opposition between affirmation and negation or that between the existence and non-existence of a trait in a subject capable of possessing the trait (according to the terminology of logicians and philosophers). Instead, it is the opposition of *tadadd*; that is, it is the opposition of two existential things, not that of one existential and one non-existential thing.

Of course, the fact that we mentioned Descartes as an example was not to depart from the basic principle we explained earlier. We stipulated from the beginning that we were not to express opinions about individuals. Our intent in mentioning Descartes as an example is that if we suppose that what he said is true and he is as submissive to the truth as his words indicate, and on the other hand truly did not have more ability to research, then he is a dispositional Muslim.

Sincerity, the Condition for the Acceptance of Actions

The second of the issues that we raised regarding the value of faith is what influence faith can have in the acceptance of actions.

Previously, in relating the proofs of those who say that the good deeds of unbelievers are acceptable to God, we said that they say that the goodness and badness of actions is related to their essence. A good deed, whether of a believer or an unbeliever, is good by its essence and must inevitably be accepted by God, since good is good no matter who does it and bad is bad no matter who does it, and since God's relation to all people is the same.

Now, we would like to add that though what has been said in the above reasoning is correct, a basic point has been neglected in it. To explain this point, we must first explain another term from the subject of the principles of jurisprudence, which is that goodness and evil are of two types: action-related, and actor-related.

Every action has two aspects, and every one of the two aspects has a separate ruling with regard to goodness or badness. It is possible for an action to be good from one dimension and not be good from the other. Similarly, the reverse is possible; and it is also possible for an action to be good or bad from both dimensions.

The two dimensions consist of the action's beneficial or harmful effect in the external world and human society, and the action's association to its doer and that person's spiritual motivations which caused that action and the goal to which the doer aspired by performing it.

From the point of view of the former, one must determine the extent of the beneficial or harmful effect of the action. And from the point of view of the latter, one must determine what type of action the doer has performed in his or her mental and spiritual framework and what goal he or she has pursued.

Human actions, in terms of the trajectory of their beneficial and harmful effects, are recorded in books of history, and history passes judgment about them; it praises them or condemns them. But the aspect of attribution to the human soul is only recorded in the otherworldly books [of human deeds]. Books of history like great and influential actions and praise such actions; but the Divine otherworldly and celestial books, in addition to this aspect, are in search of actions that have spirit.

The Qur'an says,

الَّذِي خَلَقَ الْمَوْتَ وَالْحَيَاةَ لِيَبْلُوَكُمْ أَيُّكُمْ أَحْسَنُ عَمَلًا

He, who created death and life that He may test you [to see] which of you is best in conduct. [Qur'an, 67:2]

It refers to "the best deeds," not "the most deeds," since the important thing is for us to know that when we perform an action under the influence of spiritual motives, aside from the outward appearance of the action-which is a series of movements and has its own social effects and value-spiritually we actually move in a certain direction and traverse a certain path.

The issue is not so simple as to say, "All that exists is the 'action,' the work, the muscular energy that is spent. As for the thoughts and intentions, their value lies only in preparing for the action; they are no more than a mentality and preliminary. And whatever the preliminary may be, the main thing is the action itself." To the contrary, the importance of the thought and the intention is not less than that of the action. Such a way of thinking, which maintains the primacy of action rather than the primacy of the intention and belief, is a materialistic thought. Under the names "objectivity" and "subjectivity" it gives the belief and intention behind the action no more than preliminary value. Leaving aside the fact that the invalidity of this school is clear in its own right, what is certain is that the Qur'anic teachings cannot be interpreted on the basis of such ways of thinking.

In the view of the Qur'an, our true personality and self is our spirit, with every voluntary action, the spirit moves from potentiality to actuality and acquires an effect and an attribute commensurate to its own intention and aim. These effects and habits become a part of our personality and carry us to a world appropriate to themselves from among the realms of existence.

Thus, from the first dimension the goodness and evilness of actions depends on the external effect of those actions; and from the second dimension goodness and evilness depends on the manner in which that action was performed by its doer. In the first case, our position about an action is based on its external and societal outcome; and in the second case, it is based on the internal and mental effect of the action on its doer.

If a person establishes a hospital or performs some other charitable deed with respect to the cultural, health, or economic affairs of a country, without doubt from a societal point of view and in the view of history, that action is good. That is, it is an act that benefits God's creation. In this regard, it doesn't matter what the intention was of the person who established the hospital or other philanthropic institution. Whether the intention is to show off and fulfil one's selfish instincts or whether the intention is altruistic and unselfish, from a societal point of view a charitable institution has come into being. The ruling of history with regard to people's actions is always from this aspect and in view of this particular dimension. History has no concern with people's intentions. When the masterpieces of art or architecture in Isfahan are mentioned, no one is concerned with what intention or aim the maker of the Shaykh Lutfullah Mosque, the Shah Mosque, or the Thirty-Three Bridge had; history sees the outward form and calls the action a "good deed."

However, in ascertaining an action's actor-related goodness, our attention doesn't go to the societal and external effect of the action. Instead, from this aspect, we are concerned with how the action relates to its doer. In this reckoning, it is not enough for the action to be beneficial in order for it to be considered a "good deed." What counts is what the doer's intention was in performing the action, and what goal he or she wanted to attain. If the doer had a good intention and aim and performed the action with a good motive, that action is good-that is, it possesses actor-related goodness. The action itself is two-dimensional; that is, it proceeds in two dimensions: the historical and societal dimension, and the spiritual dimension. But if the doer performed the action to show off or to attract material benefit, the action is one-dimensional. It goes forward only in time and in history, and not in the spiritual dimension; and in Islamic terminology, the action does not ascend to the higher realm. In other words, in such instances, the doer has served society and raised its level but has not benefited him or herself, and may actually have committed treachery. Instead of ascending spiritually by performing the action, the doer's soul may have descended to a lower spiritual level.

Of course, our intent is not that the action-related goodness of an action is totally separate from its actor-related goodness, and that from a spiritual point of view a person should have nothing to do with actions that are beneficial to society. The intent is that a socially beneficial deed is only spiritually beneficial when the spirit, by performing that action, has travelled a spiritual path as well, having left the station of selfishness and pleasure-seeking and set foot on the station of sincerity and purity.

The relation between action-related goodness and actor related goodness is the relation of the body to the spirit. A living being is a combination of spirit and body. Likewise, the second type of goodness must be breathed into the body of an action possessing the first type of goodness for that action to come alive.

Thus, the rational proof of the so-called intellectuals is fallacious. This proof states that "God's relationship with all His creatures is equal, and the goodness or evilness of actions is innate to them. Thus, good deeds are equal for all people. And the corollary of these two equalities is that in the hereafter, the recompense of believers and unbelievers shall be the same." In this reasoning, the actions and the equality of the creatures before the Creator have been given attention; but the doer and his or her personality, aim, motive, and spiritual path-all of which necessarily cause actions to be dissimilar and cause a difference among them similar to the difference between the living and the dead-has been forgotten. They say, "What difference does it make for God whether the doer of a good deed recognizes Him or not or is familiar with Him or not? Whether he or she performed the action for His pleasure or with some other purpose, whether the intention be seeking nearness to God or not?"

The answer is that it makes no difference for God, but it makes a difference for that person him or herself. If the person doesn't recognize God, he or she will perform one type of spiritual action and another type if he or she is familiar with God. If one doesn't know God, one's action will be one-dimensional; the action will have only action-related and historical goodness. But if one knows God, one's action will be two-dimensional and will have actor-related and spiritual goodness. If one knows God, one's action and one's self will ascend towards God, and if one doesn't know God one will not ascend. In other words, it makes no difference for God, but it does make a difference for the action. In one case, the action will be a living, ascending action, and in the other case it will be a dead, descending action.

They say that God, who is Wise and Just, will certainly not nullify the good deeds of a person on account of not having a relationship of friendship with Him.

We too believe that God will not nullify them, but we must see whether a person who doesn't recognize God actually performs a good deed that is good both in its effect and its relation to its doer, good both from the aspect of the societal order as well as from the doer's spiritual aspect. The fallacy arises because we have supposed that for an action to be beneficial to society suffices for it to be considered a "good deed." To suppose the impossible, if a person doesn't know God and yet ascends toward God through his or her action, without doubt God will not send that person back. But reality is that a person who doesn't know God doesn't break the curtain to enter the spiritual realm, doesn't traverse any of the stations of the soul, and doesn't ascend towards God's spiritual realm in order for his or her action to acquire a spiritual aspect and a form that will be a source of pleasure, felicity, and salvation for him or her. The acceptance of an action by God is nothing other than for the action to possess these qualities.

One of the primary differences between Divine laws and human laws is this very point; Divine laws are two dimensional, and human laws are one-dimensional. Human laws have nothing to do with the spiritual order or spiritual advancement of the individual. When a government legislates taxes in the interests of the country, its goal is solely to obtain money and cover the country's expenses. The government has no concern with the intention of the taxpayer. Does he or she pay taxes freely and willingly out of love for the country and its government, or out of fear? The government's purpose is only to obtain money; even if the taxpayer curses the government under his or her breath, the government's purpose has been attained.

Similarly, when a government calls its armed forces to defend the country, it does not concern itself with the intention of the soldiers; it desires the soldiers to fight its enemies in war. It makes no difference to the government whether the soldier fights out of his free will and inclination or out of fear of the gun to his head; or whether his fighting is to show off, as a result of foolish prejudices, or in defense of truth and what is right.

However, Divine laws are not like that. In these laws, monetary dues and warriors are not wanted in absolute terms, but together with a pure intention and desire to seek nearness to God. Islam desires actions with a soul, not soulless actions. Thus, if a Muslim pays *zakat*, but with an element of showing off, it is not accepted; if he performs Jihad, but does it in order to show off, it is not accepted. The Divine law says that a coerced soldier is useless; I want a soldier who has the soul of a soldier, who has accepted the call, "Verily God has purchased from the believers their souls and their belongings in return for Paradise"[8] and answered it sincerely.

It has been related from the Messenger of Islam (s) in a consecutively-narrated tradition among both the Sunnis and Shias that he said

إنّما الأعمال بالنّيات

The value of deeds is based on the intention.

لكل امرىء ما نوى

Every individual shall have what he or she intended.

لا عمل إلا بنيّة

---

[8] [Qur'an, 9:111]

No deed is accepted without an intention.[9]

One tradition has been narrated in the following words:

إِنَّمَا الأَعْمَالُ بِالنِّيَّاتِ ، وَإِنَّمَا لِكُلِّ امْرِئٍ مَا نَوَى ، فَمَنْ كَانَتْ هِجْرَتُهُ إِلَى اللَّهِ وَرَسُولِهِ ،
فَهِجْرَتُهُ إِلَى اللَّهِ وَرَسُولِهِ ، وَمَنْ كَانَتْ هِجْرَتُهُ إِلَى دُنْيَا يُصِيبُهَا أَوْ إِلَى امْرَأَةٍ يَنْكِحُهَا ، فَهِجْرَتُهُ
إِلَى مَا هَاجَرَ إِلَيْهِ

The value of actions is in their intention, and a man shall only get that which he intended. So, whoever migrated for the sake of God and His messenger, his migration is towards God and His messenger; and whoever migrated for the sake of worldly wealth or a woman he wished to marry, his migration is towards that thing.[10]

Imam Sadiq (a) said, "Perform your actions for the sake of God and not people, because whatever is for God, (ascends) towards God, and whatever is for the people, does not ascend towards God."

The intention is the soul of the action, and just as the body of a human being is noble because of the human soul, so too does the nobility of a human being's action depend on its soul. What is the soul of an action? The soul of an action is sincerity. The Qur'an says:

وَمَا أُمِرُوا إِلَّا لِيَعْبُدُوا اللَّـهَ مُخْلِصِينَ لَهُ الدِّينَ

Though they were not commanded except to worship Allah,
dedicating their faith to Him. [Qur'an, 98:5]

Quality or Quantity?

From the above discussion, an interesting conclusion can be obtained, which is that in the reckoning of God, the value of actions is by their quality rather than their quantity. Inattention to this point has caused some people to make up fantastic stories regarding the extraordinarily valuable actions of holy personages when they see the societal dimension of those actions to be insignificant. For example, with regard to the ring that Imam Ali (a) bestowed on a beggar while bowing in prayer, about which a verse of Qur'an was revealed, they say that the value of that ring was equal to the revenue of greater Syria; and in order for people to believe that, they gave it the form of a tradition. In the view of these people, it was hard to believe that a great verse of

---

[9] This and the previous two traditions are in *Wasail sl-Shia*, vo.1, p.8
[10] *Sahih Muslim,* vol.6, p.48

Qur'an would be revealed about the bestowal of an insignificant ring. And since they were unable to believe such a thing, they created a story and raised the ring's material value. They didn't stop to think that a ring equal in value to the revenue of all of Syria would not, in the poor and indigent Madinah, be found on the finger of Imam Ali (a). Supposing such a ring was in Imam Ali's possession, he would not give it to just one beggar; instead, with such a ring he would make Madinah flourish and save all the city's needy.

The intellect of these fantasy-weavers hasn't understood that for God a great deed has a reckoning different from material reckonings. It is as if they have supposed that the value of the ring caught God's attention and compelled Him to praise Ali (a) for the great deed he did-God be exalted from such suppositions!

I don't know what these short-sighted people have thought up regarding the pieces of barley that Ali and his family (a) bestowed in charity and about which surah "Hal Ata"[11] was revealed. Perhaps they will say that the flour of that bread was not from barley, but from gold dust!

But in fact, that is not the case. The importance of Ali and his family's action (a) is not in the material aspect which attracts our attention; the importance of their action is that it was pure and entirely for God's sake; it was at a level of sincerity which it is beyond us even to conceive, a sincerity which was reflected in the highest realm and elicited Divine praise and glorification.

In the words of Shaykh Farid al-Din Attar,

It is beyond [the power] this world to describe his spear;
It is beyond that world to describe his three pieces of bread.

The importance of their action lies in what the Qur'an has quoted:

إِنَّمَا نُطْعِمُكُمْ لِوَجْهِ اللَّهِ لَا نُرِيدُ مِنكُمْ جَزَاءً وَلَا شُكُورًا

[saying,] 'We feed you only for the sake of Allah. We desire no reward from you, nor thanks. [Qur'an, 76:9]

---

[11] Also known as Surah Al-Insan, the 76th Surah of Holy Qur'an.

These are the words of their heart which God, the A ware, has made known; that is, with their selflessness and sacrifice, they desired from God naught but God Himself.

The fact that the Qur'an regards the actions of unbelievers to be like a mirage, hollow and devoid of reality, is because their actions have an adorned and misleading exterior, but since they are done for lowly material and individual motives and not for God, they have no spiritual aspect.

Zubayda, the wife of the Abbasid caliph Harun al-Rashid, caused a river to be dug in Makkah which has been used by visitors of God's sanctuary from that time until today. This action has a very righteous exterior. The resolve of Zubayda caused this river to flow to barren Makkah from the rocky land between Taif and Makkah, and it has been close to twelve centuries that the hot, thirsty pilgrims have been making use of it.

From a worldly perspective, it is quite a great deed; but how about from a spiritual perspective? Do the angels reckon as we do? Is their attention, like ours, drawn to the apparent magnitude of this act?

No, their reckoning is different. Using a Divine scale, they measure the other dimensions of the action. They take account of where Zubayda obtained the money for this act. Zubayda was the wife of an oppressive and tyrannical man who had control of the public treasury of the Muslims and would do as he pleased. Zubayda had no money of her own, and she didn't spend her own wealth in this charitable act; she spent the people's money on the people. The difference between her and other women in her position is that others would spend the public's money on their personal desires, and she spent a portion of this money on a project for the public good. Now, what was Zubayda's purpose in this action? Did she wish for her name to remain in history? Or did she truly have God's pleasure in her mind? Only God knows.

It is in this reckoning that it is said that someone saw Zubayda in a dream and asked her what God gave her for the river she ordered to be made. She replied that God had given the entire reward of that action to the original owners of that money.

The Mosque of Bahlul

It has been related that once a mosque was being constructed when Bahlul arrived and asked, "What are you doing?" They replied, "We are building a mosque." Bahlul asked, "What for?" They replied, "What kind of question is that? We are building it for God."

Bahlul wanted to show the doers of that charitable work their level of sincerity. Secretly, he had a stone engraved with the words, "The Bahlul Mosque," and at night he affixed it above the mosque's main gate. When the builders of the mosque came the next day and saw the sign, they became angry. They found Bahlul and beat him for portraying the toils of others as his own work. Bahlul retorted, "But didn't you say you built this mosque for God? Suppose that people mistakenly think it was I who built it; God won't make such a mistake!"

How many great deeds there are which are great in our eyes, but are worthless in the eyes of God! Perhaps many great buildings, whether mosques, mausoleums, hospitals, bridges, rest houses for travellers, or schools, have such an end; the account of such things is with God.

Belief in God and the Hereafter

The relation of this world to the hereafter is the relation between the body and the spirit, or the relation of the outer aspect to the inner aspect. This world and the next are not two wholly and entirely separate worlds; this world and the hereafter together are one unit, just as a sheet of paper has two pages and a coin has two sides. This same earth that exists in this world will appear in the hereafter in its otherworldly form. The plants and objects of this world will appear in the hereafter in their otherworldly aspect. Fundamentally, the hereafter is the celestial, or *malakuti*, form of the present world.

The condition for an action to acquire a good otherworldly aspect is for it to be performed with attention to God and in order to ascend to God's higher realm. If a person doesn't believe in the hereafter and isn't attentive to God, his or her action will not have an otherworldly aspect, and thus will not ascend to the higher realm. The otherworldly aspect is the higher aspect, and the worldly aspect is the lower aspect. As long as an action does not acquire illumination and purity through intention, belief, and faith, it cannot attain to the highest realm; only an action that has a spirit can attain that station. And the spirit of an action is its otherworldly aspect.

How beautiful are the words of the Qur'an:

$$\text{إِلَيْهِ يَصْعَدُ الْكَلِمُ الطَّيِّبُ وَالْعَمَلُ الصَّالِحُ يَرْفَعُهُ}$$

To Him ascends the good word, and He elevates righteous conduct.
[Qur'an, 35:10]

This verse can be understood in two ways, and both have been mentioned in books of exegesis. The first is that good deeds raise pure words and pure belief; the other is that pure words and pure belief raise good deeds and make them otherworldly. The two explanations-both of which are correct and possibly both are intended-together convey the principle that faith has an effect on the acceptance of actions and their ascent to God, and actions have an effect on the perfection of faith and on increasing the degree of faith. This principle is an accepted one in the Islamic teachings. Our reference to this verse is based on the second explanation, though as we indicated, in our view it is possible that the verse has intended both meanings at the same time.

In any case, it is a mistake for us to think that the actions of those who don't believe in God and the Day of Judgement ascend to God and acquire an otherworldly aspect.

If we are told that someone has taken the northbound highway from Tehran and continued to travel northward for several days, we will obviously not expect that person to reach Qum, Isfahan, or Shiraz (which lie south of Tehran); if someone were to entertain such a possibility, we would laugh and tell him that if that person wished to go to one of those cities, he or she would have to take the southbound highway from Tehran and travel on it.

It is impossible for someone to travel towards Turkistan, yet reach the Ka'bah.

Heaven and Hell are the two ends of a person's spiritual journey. In the next world, every person sees him or herself at his or her journey's final point; one above, and the other below; one the highest of the high, and the other the lowest of the low.

275

إِنَّ كِتَابَ الْأَبْرَارِ لَفِي عِلِّيِّينَ

the record of the pious is in Illiyun. [Qur'an, 83:18]

إِنَّ كِتَابَ الْفُجَّارِ لَفِي سِجِّينٍ

The record of the vicious is indeed in Sijjin. [Qur'an, 83:7]

How is it possible for a person not to travel towards a certain destination, or to travel in a direction opposite to it, yet still reach that destination? Moving towards the highest heaven (*illiyyin*) requires an intention and desire to reach it, and that in turn requires recognition and belief on the one hand, and facilitation and submission on the other. If a person has no belief in such a destination, or lacks the quality of facilitation and submission, and in short has neither any desire nor takes even the smallest step to reach it, how can one expect him or her to attain that destination? Without doubt, every path leads to its own destination. And unless God is that destination, the path does not lead to God.

The Qur'an says,

مَّن كَانَ يُرِيدُ الْعَاجِلَةَ عَجَّلْنَا لَهُ فِيهَا مَا نَشَاءُ لِمَن نُّرِيدُ ثُمَّ جَعَلْنَا لَهُ جَهَنَّمَ يَصْلَاهَا مَذْمُومًا مَّدْحُورًا ﴿١٨﴾ وَمَنْ أَرَادَ الْآخِرَةَ وَسَعَىٰ لَهَا سَعْيَهَا وَهُوَ مُؤْمِنٌ فَأُولَٰئِكَ كَانَ سَعْيُهُم مَّشْكُورًا ﴿١٩﴾

Whoever desires this transitory life, We expedite for him therein whatever We wish, for whomever We desire. Then We appoint hell for him, to enter it, blameful and spurned. Whoever desires the Hereafter and strives for it with an endeavour worthy of it, should he be faithful—the endeavour of such will be well-appreciated.

[Qur'an, 17:18-19]

That is, if a person's level of thinking is no higher than this world and he or she has no goal higher than this world, it is impossible for that person to attain the high target of the hereafter; but Our Divine grace and benevolence demand that We grant him or her something of the worldly goal he or she desired to achieve.

There is a subtle point here: this world is the world of nature and matter; it is the world of causes and reasons. Worldly causes are in conflict with each other, and constraints also exist in this material world.

Thus, for a person whose goal is this world, there is no guarantee that he or she will definitely attain that goal. The words the Qur'an has chosen to impart this point are as follows:

"We expedite for him therein whatever We wish, for whomever We desire."

However, one who has a higher goal in his or her spiritual makeup, has not given his or her heart to trifling goals, and who, moving forward with faith, takes steps towards a Divine object will certainly attain the goal, since God recognizes the value of good deeds; He accepts and rewards those good deeds that are presented to Him.

Here, effort and endeavour are necessary, since it is impossible for a person to move forward and attain the goal without taking a step.

Then in the next verse, the Qur'an says

كُلًّا نُّمِدُّ هَـٰٓؤُلَاءِ وَهَـٰٓؤُلَاءِ مِنْ عَطَاءِ رَبِّكَ ۚ وَمَا كَانَ عَطَاءُ رَبِّكَ مَحْظُورًا

To these and to those—to all We extend the bounty of your Lord, and the bounty of your Lord is not confined. [Qur'an, 17:20]

That is, Our bounty is limitless; whoever sows a seed, We bring it to fruit; whoever moves towards a goal, We convey him or her to that goal.

The Divine sages say that the Being who is necessarily existent by essence is necessarily existent from all aspects and dimensions. Thus, He is necessarily Bountiful (*Fayyaz*). As a result, whoever wishes something, God assists him or her. It is not the case that if someone seeks the world, God says to him or her, "You are misguided and have acted contrary to Our guidance and direction, so We will not assist you." That is not the case; the seeker of the world is also supported and assisted by God in seeking this world and benefits from His unhesitant bounty within the limits permitted by this world of causes, mutual exclusivity, and conflicting outcomes.

In other words, this world is a place appropriate for and given to planting, growing, increasing, and harvesting. It all depends on what seed a person chooses to grow and develop and what harvest he or she wishes to reap. Whatever seed he or she chooses is exactly what will grow and develop in the rich and fertile land of this world.

True, there is an exclusive assistance particular to the people of Truth, which is called the *rahimiyya* (exclusive) mercy; the seekers of this world are deprived of this mercy, since they do not seek it. But the *rahmaniyya* (general) mercy of God applies equally to all people and all paths. In the words of Sa'di,[12]

> The earth's surface is His all-encompassing table,
> From this table all partake, whether friend or foe.

From what has been said in this discussion, a portion of the issues under discussion are resolved.

We made clear that action-related goodness is not sufficient for reward in the hereafter; actor-related goodness is also necessary. Action-related goodness is similar to a body, and actor-related goodness is similar to its spirit and life. And we explained that belief in God and the Day of Judgement is a fundamental condition of actor-related goodness. This conditionality is not based on convention, but is instead an essential and actual conditionality, just like the conditionality of a particular path with respect to reaching a particular destination.

Here, it is necessary to clarify one point, which is that some will perhaps say that actor-related goodness does not necessarily require the intention of seeking nearness to God; if a person does a good deed because of one's conscience or out of a feeling of compassion or mercy, that is sufficient for his or her action to possess actor-related goodness. In other words, a humanitarian motive is sufficient for actor-related goodness; as long as a person's motive is other than the "self," actor-related goodness is present, whether the motive be "God" or "humanism."

This point is worthy of consideration. While we don't affirm the view that it makes no difference whether one's motive be God or humanism, and we can't enter this discussion in depth right now, we do truly believe that whenever an action is performed with the motive of doing good, serving others, and for the sake of humanity, it is not the same as an action that is performed solely with selfish motives. Without doubt, God will not leave such people without any reward. Several traditions indicate that on account of their good deeds, polytheists like Hatam al-Ta'i will not be punished or their punishment will be reduced, even though they were polytheists.

---

[12] See Endnote 81

We can understand this point from many traditions that we have before us.

1. Allamah Majlisi quotes from *Thawab al-A'mal* of Shaykh Saduq that Ali ibn Yaqtin narrated from Imam Musa Kazim (a) that he said, "Among the Banu Isra'il there was a believer whose neighbor was an unbeliever. That unbeliever would always show kindness and good conduct towards his believing neighbor. When he died, God made for him a house out of a type of mud which shielded him from the heat of the fire, and his sustenance would be given to him from outside his own environment, which was of fire. He was told, 'This is because of your kindness and good conduct towards your believing neighbor.'"[13]

Allamah Majlisi, after quoting this tradition, says: This tradition and others like it are evidence that the punishment of some unbelievers in Hell will be lifted, and the verses of Qur'an that say the punishment of the unbelievers shall not be lightened are with regard to those who have not performed such good deeds.

2. He also narrates from Imam Muhammad Baqir (a) that he said, "There was a believer who lived in the land of an oppressive king. That oppressor threatened the believer, and he fled to a non-Islamic land, arriving at the place of a polytheist man. The polytheist sat him beside himself and hosted him well. As soon as he died, God addressed him, 'I swear by My Honour and Glory that if there were a place in Heaven for a polytheist, I would put you in that place; but O' fire, make him fear, but don't harm him.'"

Then the Imam said, "Every morning and evening his sustenance is brought for him from outside that environment." The Imam was asked, "From Heaven?" He answered, "From where God wills."[14]

3. The Noble Messenger (s) said about Abdullah ibn Jadan, who was one of the well-known unbelievers in the Age of Ignorance and one of the chiefs of Quraysh, "The one who has the lightest punishment in Hell is Ibn Jadan." He was asked why, to which he replied, "He used to give people to eat."

---

[13] *Bihar al-Anwar*, vol.3, p. 377
[14] *Bihar al-Anwar*, vol.3, p. 382, from *al-Kafi*

4. And the Prophet (s) said with regard to several people who lived in the Age of Ignorance: "I saw in Hell, the possessor of the tunic and the possessor of the cane who would drive the pilgrims, and also the woman who had a cat which she had tied up and which she would neither feed nor set free so it could find its own food. And I entered Heaven and I saw there the man who saved a dog from thirst and gave it water.'?"[15]

Such people, who are found in more or less every age, will at least have their punishment lightened or else their punishment will be lifted altogether.

In my view, if there are individuals who do good to other people or even to another living being-whether a human being or animal-without any expectation, not even because they see themselves mirrored in the existence of the deprived (*i.e.*, fear that one day they may be in similar straits is not the moving factor in what they do), and instead the motive of doing good and serving others is strong enough in them that even if they know that no benefit will accrue to them and not even a single person will come to know of what they did or say so much as "God bless you" to them, yet they still do good deeds, and they are not under the influence of habit and such like, one must say that in the depths of their conscience there exists the light of recognition of God. And supposing they deny it with their tongues, they confess it in the depths of their conscience; their denial is in reality a denial of an imagined being which they have conceived in place of God, or a denial of another imagined thing which they have conceived in place of the return to God and the Day of Judgement, not a denial of the reality of God and the Resurrection.

Love of good and justice and doing good because it is good and just and worthy, without any other factor, is a sign of love of the Essence possessed of Absolute Beauty; therefore, it is not farfetched that such people actually will not be resurrected among the unbelievers, though by their tongues they are considered deniers. And God knows best.

---

[15] This and previous tradition are in *Bihar al-Anwar*, vol.3, p. 382, from *al-Kafi*

Belief in the Prophecy and Imamate

Now we will discuss another aspect of the issue, which is the position of those non-Muslims who are monotheists and believe in the Resurrection and perform their actions for God.

Among the People of the Book, people can be found who neither believe the Messiah nor Ezra to be the son of God; they are neither dualists nor fire-worshippers. They do not say, "The Messiah is the son of God," or "Uzayr is the son of God," nor that Ahriman is the god of evil; they also believe in the Day of Judgement. What is the outcome of the actions of such people?

Right now, our discussion is not about those inventors, innovators, and servants of humanity who are materialists and deny God's existence, and whose practical motives naturally do not transcend the material realm. From the preceding discussions, our view regarding them from the perspective of Islam was made clear. Our discussion in this section pertains to those good-doers who believe in Creation and in the Resurrection, and thus are able to have a higher motive in their actions and work towards a goal that goes beyond the material. It is said that Edison and Pasteur were such people, that they were religious people and had religious motives. That is, in their actions they, just like religious Muslims, worked for God's pleasure and with a Divine motive. In reality, these Christians are not Christian, because if they were true Christians and believed in the creeds of the existing Christianity, they would regard the Messiah as God, and naturally it would not be possible for them to be true monotheists; perhaps few of today's Christian intellectuals believe in the superstitions of the Trinity.

In order to answer this question, one must determine in what way faith in the Prophethood and Imamate are necessary, and why such faith is a condition for the acceptance of actions.

It appears that faith in the Prophets and friends of God is involved in the acceptance of actions for two reasons:

First, recognition of them goes back to recognition of God. In reality, recognition of God and His affairs is incomplete without recognition of His friends. In other words, recognition of God in a complete form is to recognize the manifestations of His guidance.

Second, recognition of the station of Prophethood and Imamate is necessary because without it, it is not possible to obtain the complete and correct program of action to achieve guidance.

The big difference between a Muslim good-doer and an unbelieving good-doer is that the unbeliever who does good deeds does not possess the proper program to achieve guidance and thus has only a negligible chance of success. In contrast, since the Muslim has submitted to a religion that has a comprehensive and proper program for guidance, he or she is assured of success if he or she implements that program correctly. Good deeds do not consist only of doing good to others; all obligatory, forbidden, recommended, and disliked actions form the part of the program of good deeds. The practicing Christian, who is outside the fold of Islam and lacks the correct program, is deprived of its great gifts, since he or she commits actions which are prohibited. For example, alcohol is forbidden, but he or she drinks it. We know that alcohol was prohibited because of its personal, societal, and spiritual harms, and naturally one who drinks alcohol will face its harms, similar to how a person who is deprived of the guidance of a doctor may do something which makes his or her heart, liver, or nerves prematurely sick and shortens his or her life.

In the program of Islam, there are some commands which it is conditional to act upon for spiritual perfection and development. It is obvious that a non-Muslim, no matter how unprejudiced and free of obstinacy, by virtue of being deprived of the complete program of human perfection, will also remain deprived of its features.

Such a person will naturally be deprived of great acts of worship, such as the five daily prayers, fasting during the month of Ramadan, and pilgrimage to the House of God. He or she is like someone who plants seeds without a systematic method of farming; in no way will the product such a person obtains be like that obtained by a person who sows the earth according to a comprehensive and proper program, plants at an appropriate time and weeds at the proper time, and in short performs all the necessary technical steps.

The difference between a Muslim and a non-Muslim good doer can be explained like this: the Muslim good-doer is like a sick person who is under the care and direction of an expert doctor; his or her food and medicine are all under the direction of the doctor. With regard to the type of medicine and food and its timing and amount, he or she acts entirely as directed. However, the non-Muslim good doer is like a sick person who has no such program and acts as he or she pleases; he or she eats whatever food or medicine comes into his or her hand. Such a sick person may occasionally consume a beneficial medicine and get a positive result, but it is just as likely that he or she will make use of a medicine that is harmful or even fatal. Similarly, it is possible he or she may eat a beneficial food, but by subsequent negligence or by eating the wrong food, may cancel the beneficial effect of the first food.

With this explanation, it becomes clear that the difference between a Muslim and a non-Muslim who believes in God is that the Muslim is a theist who possesses a proper program, while the non-Muslim theist performs his or her actions without a correct program. In other words, the Muslim has been guided, and the non-Muslim, though he or she believes in God, is misguided. In this very regard the Qur'an says,

فَإِنْ أَسْلَمُوا فَقَدِ اهْتَدَوا

If they submit, they will certainly be guided [Qur'an, 3:20]

From all that we have said in the last two sections, it has become clear that all non-Muslims are not equal in terms of being rewarded for good deeds; there is a great difference between a non-Muslim who doesn't believe in God and the Resurrection and one who believes in God and in the Day of Judgement but is deprived of the gift of faith in the Prophethood. For the first group, it is not possible to perform an action acceptable to God, whereas for the second it is possible. It is possible for this group to go to Heaven under certain conditions, but for the first group it is not possible. Apparently, the reason that Islam differentiates between polytheists and the People of the Book in its laws of interaction-in that it doesn't tolerate the polytheist but tolerates the People of the Book, it forces the polytheist to abandon his or her belief but doesn't force the People of the Book-is that the polytheist or atheist, by virtue of his or her polytheism or denial, forever closes the gate of salvation for him or herself and is in a condition of having deprived him or herself of crossing the material world and ascending to the higher world and eternal Paradise. However, the People of the Book are in a condition in which they can perform good deeds, even if in a deficient manner, and with certain conditions can attain the results of those actions.

The Qur'an says, addressing the People of the Book:

تَعَالَوْا إِلَى كَلِمَةٍ سَوَاءٍ بَيْنَنَا وَبَيْنَكُمْ أَلَّا نَعْبُدَ إِلَّا اللَّـهَ وَلَا نُشْرِكَ بِهِ شَيْئًا وَلَا يَتَّخِذَ بَعْضُنَا بَعْضًا أَرْبَابًا مِّن دُونِ اللَّـهِ

Come to a common word between us and you: that we will worship no one but Allah, that we will not ascribe any partner to Him, and that some of us will not take some others as lords besides Allah. [Qur'an, 3:64]

The Noble Qur'an has given the People of the Book such a call, but has absolutely not given and does not give such a call to polytheists and atheists.

Affliction

The third issue that deserves attention in relation with the value of faith is the negative value of unbelief and obstinacy. That is, do unbelief and obstinacy cause a good deed to become null and void and lose its effect, making it go bad as an affliction does? In other words, if a person performs a good deed with all the conditions of action-related and actor-related goodness, and yet on the other hand that person shows obstinacy with respect to truth, especially a truth that is one of the principles of religion, in this situation, does this deed-which in and of itself is good, otherworldly, and luminous and free of defect from the Divine and celestial dimension-become null and void because of this stubbornness and obstinacy or other devious spiritual condition? Here the question of affliction comes about.

It is possible for an action to have both action-related and actor-related goodness, and in other words to have both the proper body and a sound soul and spirit, to be good both from the worldly and from the otherworldly point of view, but at the same time to be destroyed and become null from the otherworldly point of view through affliction, just like a sound seed that is planted in fertile ground and even gives fruit, but which falls prey to an affliction before it can be used, and is destroyed, for example, by locusts or lightening. The Qur'an calls this affliction "habt' (invalidation).

Such affliction is not exclusive to unbelievers; it can take place with respect to the good deeds of Muslims as well. It is possible that a believing Muslim may give alms to a deserving needy person for God's sake and for that deed to be accepted by God, but for him or her to later destroy that good deed and make it void by lording it over the other person or some other form of mental torment.

The Qur'an says,

يَا أَيُّهَا الَّذِينَ آمَنُوا لَا تُبْطِلُوا صَدَقَاتِكُم بِالْمَنِّ وَالْأَذَىٰ

O you who have faith! Do not render your charities void by reproaches and affronts. [Qur'an, 2:264]

Another of the afflictions of good deeds is jealousy, as has been said,

إنَّ الحسد ليأكل الحسنات كما تأكل النَّار الحطب

Verily jealousy eats away good deeds just as fire destroys wood.'[16]

Another affliction is *juhud* (denial), or a condition of fighting with the truth. Denial means that a person perceives the truth but at the same time opposes it. In other words, denial is when one's mind has submitted through reason and logic and truth has become clear to one's intellect and power of thinking, but the spirit and its selfish and arrogant feelings rebel and refuse to submit. The essence of unbelief is opposition and resistance to truth while recognizing what it is. Previously, when we discussed the levels of submission, we gave some explanation regarding this condition. Here, we provide some further explanations relevant to the discussion of afflictions.

Imam Ali (a) says, defining Islam:

الإسلام هو التَّسليم

Islam is submission.[17]

That is, when personal interest, prejudice, or habit conflicts with truth and reality, for a person to submit to truth and turn away from all that isn't truth is Islam.

Denial means a condition of willful unbelief, the condition that Abu Jahl possessed. He knew that the Noble Messenger (s) was truthful in his claim of being a prophet, but because he had a condition of wilful unbelief, he didn't believe in him. Sometimes people can be heard to say things like, "We're willing to go to Hell, but not to do such-and-

---

[16] *Bihar al-Anwar*, vol.15, part 3, p. 132-133

[17] *Nahj al-Balagha*, saying 125.

such a thing." That is, even if that action is the truth, we still are not willing to accept it. Other expressions, such as to be a mule, to be intractable, and such like all describe this quality of denial. The Qur'an has excellently described the presence of this quality in some people where it says

$$وَإِذْ قَالُوا اللَّهُمَّ إِن كَانَ هَذَا هُوَ الْحَقَّ مِنْ عِندِكَ فَأَمْطِرْ عَلَيْنَا حِجَارَةً مِّنَ السَّمَاءِ أَوِ ائْتِنَا بِعَذَابٍ أَلِيمٍ$$

And when they said, 'O Allah, if this be the truth from You, rain down upon us stones from the sky, or bring us a painful punishment.
[Qur'an, 8:32]

What a picture the Qur'an has painted! By narrating one sentence, it indicates the sick mentality of some people.

The obstinate person whose words have been quoted in this verse, instead of saying, "O' God, if this be the truth from You, then make my heart ready to accept it," says, "If this be the truth, send upon me a punishment and annihilate me, because I haven't the strength to remain alive and face the truth."

This condition is a very dangerous one, even if it be in small matters. And it may well be that many of us are suffering from it-God forbid! Suppose that an eminent doctor, or *mujtahid*, or some other specialist who has a worldwide reputation makes a determination and expresses an opinion in an issue related to his or her specialization; then, some unknown, a doctor or a young student, expresses a conflicting opinion in the same issue and even presents definitive proofs, and that eminent personality him or herself affirms in his or her heart the truth of what that person is saying, but other people remain unaware as they were before, and in view of the reputation of that eminent person, accept his or her view. In this situation, if that famous expert submits to the opinion of that young doctor or student, that is if he or she submits to reality and admits his or her own mistake, he or she is truly a "Muslim," because "Islam is submission," and in a way it can be said this is an example of the verse "Rather, one who submits himself to God."[18] Such a person is free of the impure trait of denial. But if he or she engages in

---

[18] Qur'an, 2:112

denial and opposes the truth to save his or her standing and fame, he or she is willfully seeking unbelief and is in a state of *juhud*.

If that doctor, for example, is not entirely unfair, he or she may not take back his or her words, but may change in practice; and if he or she is very unfair, he or she will not change in practice, either, and will give the same prescription and perhaps kill the patient, then say that the patient was beyond treatment. And the same goes for any other eminent intellectual. The opposite of this condition also occurs frequently. There is a tradition in *al-Kafi* that sheds light on this reality:

Muhammad ibn Muslim narrated that he heard Imam Muhammad Baqir (a) say

كلّ شيء يجرّه الإقرار والتّسليم فهو الإيمان، و كل شيء يجره الإنكار والجحود، فهو الكفر

"Everything that results from confession and submission is faith, and everything that results from denial and rejection is unbelief."[19]

They say that the late Ayatullah Sayyid Husayn Kuhkamari, may God be pleased with him, who was one of the students of the author of *Jawahir al-Kalam* and a prominent and well-known mujtahid and recognized teacher, would go daily at an appointed time, as was his pattern, to one of the mosques of Najaf and teach.

As we know, the post of teaching the level of "*kharij*" of jurisprudence and its principles is the grounds for leadership and religious authority. Leadership and religious authority for a seminary student mean to go suddenly from zero to infinity, since a student is nothing as long as he is not a religious authority (*marji*), and his opinion and belief are not given the least importance, and usually he lives a meagre life. But as soon as he becomes a religious authority, all of a sudden, his view is obeyed and no one has anything to say in the face of his opinion. Financially as well as intellectually, he has full discretion without being held accountable to anyone. Thus, a scholar who has a chance of becoming a religious authority passes through a sensitive stage; the late Sayyid Husayn Kuhkamari was in such a stage.

One day he was returning from somewhere, perhaps from visiting someone, and no more than half an hour remained until his class. He

---

[19] *Al-Kafi*, vol.2, p.387

thought to himself that if he were to return home in that short time, he wouldn't have time to accomplish anything, so it was better to go to the appointed place and wait for his students. He went and saw that none of his students had come yet, but he saw that in a corner of the mosque a humble looking shaykh was seated and lecturing to a group of students. The late Sayyid listened to his words, and with great surprise he realized that the shaykh's discourse was very scholarly. The next day, he was motivated to deliberately come early and listen to the words of that shaykh. So, he came and listened, and his conviction from the previous day became stronger. This was repeated for several days, and the late Sayyid Husayn became sure that the shaykh was more learned than he himself and that he could benefit from his lectures, and if his own students were to attend the shaykh's lectures, they would benefit more.

Here it was that he saw himself as being offered a choice between submission and obstinacy, between faith and unbelief, between the hereafter and this world.

The next day when his students came and gathered, he said, "Friends, today I want to tell you something new. The shaykh who is sitting in that corner with a few students is more deserving to teach than I am, and I myself benefit from his lectures, so let us all go together to his lecture. From that day, he joined the circle of students of that humble shaykh who's eyes were slightly swollen and in whom the signs of poverty were visible.

This austere shaykh was the same scholar who later became famous as Shaykh Murtada al-Ansari, earning the title "teacher of the latter-day scholars."

Shaykh Ansari at that time had just returned from a trip of several years to Mashhad, Isfahan, and Kashan, and he had acquired much knowledge from this trip, especially from the presence of the late Hajj Mulla Ahmad Naraqi in Kashan.

Whoever this condition is found in is an example of the verse "one who submits himself to God."

Thus, unbelief and denial mean to willfully stand in the face of the truth and show obstinacy. Later, we will mention that in the view of the Qur'an, the unbeliever has been called an unbeliever because he or she is in a state of denial and obstinacy while at the same time perceiving the truth; and it is this state that causes nullification and is considered an affliction of good deeds. This is why God says about the actions of those who disbelieve that they are like ashes which a strong wind blows upon and destroys:

مَثَلُ الَّذِينَ كَفَرُوا بِرَبِّهِمْ ۖ أَعْمَالُهُمْ كَرَمَادٍ اشْتَدَّتْ بِهِ الرِّيحُ فِي يَوْمٍ عَاصِفٍ

A parable of those who defy their Lord: their deeds are like ashes over which the wind blows hard on a tempestuous day.. [Qur'an, 14:18]

Suppose that Pasteur performed his intellectual research, which led to the discovery of bacteria, for God and that his intention was to serve humanity and seek nearness to God. That is not sufficient for him to be rewarded by God in the end. If he possessed qualities like denial and such like and was prejudiced in favour of his own beliefs without doubt all his actions are null and void, since in this case, he is in a state of denying the truth, and this state of opposing the truth destroys all a person's efforts. This would be the case if, for example, it were said to him, "Christianity is a regional and an ancestral faith for you; have you researched whether there is a better and more complete religion than Christianity or not?" and he were to reject those words and-without being ready to study and search-say, "The best religion is Christianity." A person's actions, in such a case, are like ashes subject to ruin by a swift wind.

We only mentioned Pasteur as an example; we don't mean to say that Pasteur was like this. God alone knows that. If we, too, are obstinate towards to the truth, we fall into this general rule. O Lord! Protect us from the state of unbelief, obstinacy, and opposition to the truth.

Apart from what has been mentioned, there are also other afflictions that befall good deeds. Perhaps one of these afflictions is apathy and indifference in defending truth and righteousness. One must not only avoid denial and rejection of truth, one must also not be neutral, and instead must defend the truth. The people of Kufah knew that truth was with Husayn ibn Ali (a), and they had even admitted this fact, but they were neglectful in supporting and defending the truth. They didn't show resolve and perseverance. Not to support the truth is to deny the truth in practice.

Lady Zaynab (a), in her famous address to the people of Kufah, rebukes them for their negligence in coming to the defense of the truth and for oppressing and sinning against it. She said:

يا أهلَ الكوفَةِ يا أهلَ الخَتلِ والغَدرِ أتَبكونَ، ألا فَلا رَقأتِ العَبرَةُ وَلاهَدأتِ الزَّفرَةُ إنَّما مَثَلُكُم كَمَثَلِ التِى نَقَضَت غَزلَها مِن بَعدِ قُوَّةٍ أنكاثاً

O' people of deception treachery and disloyalty, do you weep? So, let your tears not dry, and your cries not cease! Your parable is that of the woman who undid her weaving after having made it firm." [20]

Another of the afflictions that can befall actions is conceit and vanity.

Boasting about one's deeds, like jealousy and conceit and denial, destroys actions. There is a tradition that says:

"Sometimes a person performs a good and worthy deed, and his or her action finds a place in the '*illiyyin*, but later he or she mentions that action in public and boasts of it. This causes the action to descend. If he or she mentions it again, it descends further. When it is mentioned a third time, it is destroyed altogether, and sometimes is converted into an evil deed."

Imam Muhammad Baqir (a) said,

الإبقاءُ عَلى العَمَلِ أشَدُّ مِن العَمَلِ ، قالَ (الرّاوي) : و ما الإبقاءُ عَلى العَمَلِ ؟ قالَ : يَصِلُ الرَّجُلُ بِصِلةٍ و يُنفِقُ نَفَقَةً لِلهِ وَحدَهُ لا شَريكَ لهُ فَتُكتَبَ لَهُ سِرّاً ، ثُمَّ يَذكُرُها فَتُمحى فَتُكتَبُ لَهُ عَلانِيَةً ، ثُمَّ يَذكُرُها فَتُمحى و تُكتَبُ لَهُ رِياءً

"Preserving a deed is harder than the deed itself." The narrator asked what preserving a deed meant. The Imam replied, "A person does a good deed and gives something in the way of God, and it is recorded for him as an act done in secret. Then he mentions it, so it is erased and recorded as an act done in public. Then he mentions it, so it is erased and recorded as an act done to show off."[21]

Below the Zero point

So far, our discussion has been of the acceptance and nonacceptance of acts of worship and good and positive deeds of non-Muslims, and in other words the above discussion was about what is above the zero

[20] *Nafs al-Mahmum*, p. 393
[21] *Wasail al-Shia*, vol.1, p.55

point; the discussion was whether their good deeds cause them to ascend or not.

Now let us see what is the state of what is below the zero point, that is, what happens to the sins and evil deeds of non-Muslims. Are they all alike from the aspect of our discussion, or is there a difference? In addition, in these actions that are evil and bring a person down, is there a difference between Muslims and non-Muslims, and similarly between Shias and non-Shias? Does a Muslim, and especially a Shia Muslim, have a sort of protection with regard to such actions, or not?

In the preceding matter, it became clear that God only punishes people when they commit wrong deeds out of culpability (*taqsir*), that is, when they do so deliberately and with knowledge, not out of incapacity (*qusur*). Previously, we translated and explained the verse of Qur'an from which scholars of the principles of jurisprudence derive the rule that says "It is evil to punish one without having explained his or her duty." Now, to clarify the situation of non-Muslims with respect to actions that fall below the zero point and to study their punishment and retribution for the evil deeds they commit we have no choice but to broach another issue that is touched upon in Islamic sciences and is rooted in the Noble Qur'an; and that is the issue of "incapacity" and "powerlessness" (*istid'af*). Here, we begin our discussion under this heading.

The Incapable and the Powerless

The scholars of Islam make use of two terms; they say that some people are "powerless" (*mustad'af*), or are "awaiting the command of God" (*murjawn li-amrillah*). "Powerless" refers to the unfortunate and unable; "those awaiting the command of God" denotes people whose affairs and status are to be regarded as being with God and in His hands; God Himself shall deal with them as His wisdom and mercy dictate. Both terms have been taken from the Qur'an.

In surah al-Nisa, verses 97-99, we read

إِنَّ الَّذِينَ تَوَفَّاهُمُ الْمَلَائِكَةُ ظَالِمِي أَنفُسِهِمْ قَالُوا فِيمَ كُنتُمْ ۖ قَالُوا كُنَّا مُسْتَضْعَفِينَ فِي الْأَرْضِ ۚ قَالُوا أَلَمْ تَكُنْ أَرْضُ اللَّهِ وَاسِعَةً فَتُهَاجِرُوا فِيهَا ۚ فَأُولَٰئِكَ مَأْوَاهُمْ جَهَنَّمُ ۖ وَسَاءَتْ مَصِيرًا ﴿٩٧﴾ إِلَّا الْمُسْتَضْعَفِينَ مِنَ الرِّجَالِ وَالنِّسَاءِ وَالْوِلْدَانِ لَا يَسْتَطِيعُونَ حِيلَةً وَلَا يَهْتَدُونَ سَبِيلًا ﴿٩٨﴾ فَأُولَٰئِكَ عَسَى اللَّهُ أَن يَعْفُوَ عَنْهُمْ ۚ وَكَانَ اللَّهُ عَفُوًّا غَفُورًا ﴿٩٩﴾

And those whose souls the angels take while they are oppressive of themselves; they say, 'What state were you in?' They say, 'We were weak in the land.' They say, 'Was not God's earth wide, that you may migrate in it?' So, the abode of those people is Hell, and evil an abode it is, except the powerless among the men, women, and children who neither have access to any means nor are guided to anyway; so perhaps God may pardon them, and God is Ever Forgiving, Ever-Pardoning.

In the first verse, mention is made of the interrogation of some people by the Divine appointees (in the grave). The angels ask them, "What state were you in in the world?" They forward the excuse: "We were unfortunate, our means were inadequate (and we were unable change our state)." The angels will say, "You were not powerless, since God's earth was spacious and you could have migrated from your homeland and gone to an area where you had greater opportunity; thus, you are culpable and deserving of punishment."

In the second verse, the state of some people is mentioned who are truly powerless; whether they be men, women, or children. These are people who had no means and no way out.

In the third verse, the Qur'an gives tidings and hope that God may show forgiveness towards the second group.

In his commentary of the Qur'an, *al-Mizan*; our most esteemed teacher, Allamah Tabatabai, has this to say regarding these very verses:

"God considers ignorance of religion and every form of preventing the establishment of the signs of religion to be oppression, and Divine forgiveness does not encompass this. However, an exception has been made for the powerless who did not have the ability to move and change the environment. The exception has been mentioned in such a way that it is not exclusive to when powerlessness takes this form. Just as it is possible for the source of powerlessness to be an inability to change the environment, it is possible for it to be because a person's mind is not aware of the truth, and thus remains deprived of the truth."[22]

---

[22] *Al-Mizan*, vol.5, p.51

Many traditions have been narrated in which those people who for various reasons have remained incapable have been counted among the "powerless."[23]

In verse 106 of surah al Tawbah, God says,

وَآخَرُونَ مُرْجَوْنَ لِأَمْرِ اللَّهِ إِمَّا يُعَذِّبُهُمْ وَإِمَّا يَتُوبُ عَلَيْهِمْ ۚ وَاللَّهُ عَلِيمٌ حَكِيمٌ

[There are] others waiting Allah's edict: either He shall punish them, or turn to them clemently, and Allah is all-knowing, all-wise.

The term *murjawn li-amrillah* (those awaiting God's command) has been taken from this verse.

It has been narrated that Imam Muhammad Baqir (a) said about this verse:

"Verily there was a people in the early era of Islam who were once polytheists and committed grave misdeeds; they killed Hamzah and Ja'far and people like them from among the Muslims. Later, they became Muslims; abandoning polytheism for monotheism, but faith did not find its way into their hearts for them to be counted among the believers and become deserving of Heaven, while at the same time they had forsaken denial and obstinacy, which was the cause of their being (deserving of) punishment. They were neither believers, nor unbelievers and deniers; these then are the *murjawn li-amrillah*, whose affair is referred to God."[24]

In another tradition, is has been narrated that Humran ibn A'yan said, "I asked Imam Sadiq (a) about the powerless." He replied, "They are neither of the believers nor of the unbelievers; they are the ones whose affair is referred to God's command."[25]

Though the purport of the verse regarding those whose affair is referred to God's command is that one should say only that their affair is with God, still, from tone of the verse regarding the powerless, a hint of Divine forgiveness and pardon can be deduced.

What is understood in total is that those people who in some way were incapable and not blameworthy will not be punished by God.

---

[23] Refer to *al-Mizan*, vol. 5, p. 56-61, 'Discussion of the Traditions'

[24] *al-Mizan*, vol. 9, p. 405, from *al-Kafi*

[25] *al-Mizan*, vol. 9, p. 407, from *Tafsir al-Ayyashi*

In *al-Kafi*, there is a tradition from Hamzah ibn Tayyar who narrated that Imam Sadiq (a) said,

> "People are of six groups, and in the end are of three groups: the party of faith, the party of unbelief, and the party of deviation. These groups come into being from God's promise and warning regarding Heaven and Hell. (That is, people are divided into these groups according to their standing with respect to these promises and warnings.) Those six groups are the believers, the unbelievers, the powerless, those referred to God's command, those who confess their sin and have mixed good deeds with evil deeds, and the people of the heights (*a'raf*).[26]

Also in *al-Kafi*, it is narrated from Zurarah that he said,

> I visited Imam Baqir (a) with my brother Humran, or with my other brother Bukayr. I said to the Imam, "We measure people with a measuring tape: Whoever is a Shia like ourselves, whether among the descendants of Ali or otherwise, we forge a bond of friendship with him (as a Muslim and one who will achieve salvation), and whoever is opposed to our creed, we dissociate from him (as a misguided person and one who will not achieve salvation)." The Imam said, "Zurarah! God's word is more truthful than yours; if what you say is correct, then what about God's words where He says, 'Except the powerless among the men, women, and children who find no way out nor find a path?' What about those who are referred to God's command? What about those regarding whom God says, 'They mixed good deeds and other, evil deeds?' What happened to the people of the heights? Who, then, are the ones whose hearts are to be inclined?"

Hammad, in his narration of this event from Zurarah, narrates that he said,

> "At this point the Imam and I began to argue. Both of us raised our voices, such that those outside the house heard us."

Jamil ibn Darraj narrates from Zurarah in this event that the Imam said,

---

[26] *Al-Kafi*, vol.2, '*Kitab al-Iman wa al-Kufr*", section *Asnaf an-Nas*, p.31.

"Zurarah! [God has made it] incumbent upon Himself that He take the misguided (not the unbelievers and deniers) to Heaven."[27]

Also in *al-Kafi*, it is narrated from Imam Musa Kazim (a) that he said,

"Ali (a) is a gate among the gates of guidance; whoever enters from this gate is a believer, and whoever exits from it is an unbeliever; and one who neither enters from it nor exits from it is among the party whose affair is referred to God."

In this tradition, the Imam clearly mentions a party who are neither among the people of faith, submission, and salvation, nor among the people of denial and annihilation.[28]

Also in *al-Kafi*, it is narrated from Imam Sadiq (a)

لو أنّ العباد إذا جهلوا وقفوا ولم يجحدوا، لم يكفروا

If only people, when they are ignorant, pause and don't reject, they will not be unbelievers."[29]

If one ponders the traditions which have come down from the pure Imams (a) and most of which have been collected in the sections "Kitab al-Hujjah" and "Kitab al-Iman wa al-Kufr" in *al-Kafi*, he or she will realize that the Imam's (a) position was that whatever [punishment] befalls a person is because truth was presented to him or her, and he or she showed prejudice or obstinacy towards it, or at the very least was in a position where he or she should have researched and searched, but didn't do so. And as for people who, out of incapacity of understanding and perception, or because of other reasons, are in a position where they are not in denial or negligent in researching, they are not counted among the deniers and adversaries. They are counted among the powerless and those referred to God's command. And it is understood from the traditions that the pure Imams (a) view many people to be of this category.

---

[27] *Ibid*, p.382. The last sentence of the tradition is (text in Arabic) translated as above. But in some texts it is as follows: (text in Arabic), which would mean that the Imam (a) changed his opinion and accepted the view al-Zurarah. Obviously. this isn't correct, but based on this reading another meaning is possible, which is that the Imam (a) may have intended that these people will not be punished, but they will also not go to heaven.

[28] *Ibid*, p.388

[29] *Ibid*, p.388

In *al-Kafi*, in the section "Kitab al-Hujjah," Kulayni narrates several traditions to the effect that:

كلّ من دان الله عزّ وجلّ بعبادة يجهد فيها نفسه و لا إمام له من الله فسعيه غير مقبول

"Whoever obeys God with an act of worship in which he exhausts himself, but doesn't have an Imam appointed by God, his effort is not accepted.'[30]

Or that:

لا يقبل الله أعمال العباد إلا بمعرفته

"God does not accept the actions of His servants without recognition of him (the Imam)."[31]

At the same time, in that same "Kitab al-Hujjah" of *al-Kafi* it is narrated from Imam Sadiq (a):

من عرفنا كان مؤمنًا، و من أنكرنا كان كافرًا، و من لم يعرفنا و لم ينكرنا كان ضالًّا حتّى رجع الى الهدى الَّذى افترض الله عليه من طاعتنا، فان يمت على ضلالته يفعل الله ما يشاء

"Whoever recognizes us is a believer, and whoever denies us is an unbeliever, and whoever neither recognizes nor denies us is misguided until he or she returns to the guidance of our obedience which God enjoined upon him or her. So, if he or she dies in the state of misguidedness, God shall do what He pleases."[32]

Muhammad ibn Muslim says,

> I was with Imam Sadiq (a). I was seated to his left, and Zurarah to his right. Abu Basir entered and asked, "What do you say about a person who has doubts about God?" The Imam replied, "He is an unbeliever." "What do you say about a person who has doubts about the Messenger of God?" "He is an unbeliever." At this point the Imam turned towards Zurarah and said, "Verily, such a person is an unbeliever if he or she denies and shows obstinacy.'?"[33]

---

[30] *al-Kafi,* vol.1, p.183
[31] *al-Kafi,* vol.1, p.203
[32] *al-Kafi,* vol.1, p.187
[33] *al-Kafi,* vol.1, p.399

Also, in *al-Kafi*, Kulayni narrates that Hashim ibn al-Barid (Sahib al-Barid) said:

> Muhammad ibn Muslim, Abu al-Khattab, and I were together in one place. Abu al-Khattab asked, "What is your belief regarding one who doesn't know the affair of Imamate?" I said, "In my view he or she is a unbeliever." Abu al-Khattab said, "As long as the evidence is not complete for him or her, he or she is not a unbeliever; if the evidence is complete and still he or she doesn't recognize it, then he or she is a unbeliever." Muhammad ibn Muslim said, "Glory be to God! If he or she doesn't recognize the Imam and doesn't show obstinacy or denial, how can he or she be considered an unbeliever? No, one who doesn't know, if he doesn't show denial, is not an unbeliever." Thus, the three of us had three opposing beliefs.

> When the hajj season came, I went for hajj and went to Imam Sadiq (a). I told him of the discussion between the three of us and asked the Imam his view. The Imam replied, "I will reply to this question when the other two are also present. I and the three of you shall meet tonight in Mina near the middle *Jamarah*."

> That night, the three of us went there. The Imam, leaning on a cushion, began questioning us.

> "What do you say about the servants, womenfolk, and members of your own families?

> Do they not bear witness to the unity of God?"

> I replied, "Yes."

> "Do they not bear witness to the prophecy of the Messenger?"

> "Yes."

> "Do they recognize the Imamate and *wilayah* (Divinely-appointed authority) like yourselves?"

> "No."

> "So, what is their position in your view?"

> "My view is that whoever does not recognize the Imam is an unbeliever."

"Glory be to God! Haven't you seen the people of the streets and markets? Haven't you seen the water-bearers?"

"Yes, I have seen and I see them."

"Do they not pray? Do they not fast? Do they not perform hajj? Do they not bear witness to the unity of God and the prophethood of the Messenger?"

"Yes."

"Well, do they recognize the Imam as you do?"

"No,"

"So, what is their condition?"

"My view is that whoever doesn't recognize the Imam is an unbeliever."

"Glory be to God! Do you not see the stat of the Ka'bah and the circumambulation of these people? Don't you see how the people of Yemen cling to the curtains of the Ka'bah?"

"Yes."

"Don't they profess monotheism and believe in the Messenger? Don't they pray, fast, and perform hajj?"

"Yes."

"Well, do they recognize the Imam as you do?"

"No."

"What is your belief about them?"

"In my view, whoever doesn't recognize the Imam is an unbeliever."

"Glory be to God! This belief is the belief of the Kharijites."

At that point the Imam said, "Now, do you wish me to inform you of the truth?"

Hashim, who in the words of the late Fayd al-Kashani, knew that the Imam's view was in opposition to his own belief, said, "No."

The Imam said, "It is very bad for you to say something of your own accord that you have not heard from us."

Hashim later said to the others:

"I presumed that the Imam affirmed the view of Muhammad ibn Muslim and wished to bring us to his view."[34]

In *al-Kafi*, after this tradition, Kulayni narrates the well-known tradition of the discussion of Zurarah with Imam Muhammad Baqir (a) in this regard, which is detailed.

In *al-Kafi* at the end of "Kitab al-Iman wa al-Kufr," there is a chapter eutitled, "No action causes harm with belief, and no action brings benefit with unbelief.'?"[35]

But the traditions that have come under this heading do not affirm this heading. The following tradition is among them: Ya'qub ibn Shu'ayb said, I asked Imam Sadiq (a) :

هل لأحد على ما عمل ثواب على الله موجب إلّا المؤمنين؟ قال: لا

"Does anyone aside from the believers have a definite reward from God?" He replied, "No."[36]

The purport of this tradition is that God has given a promise of reward to none but the believers, and without doubt He will fulfil His promise. However, aside from the believers, God has not given any promise for Him to have to fulfil of necessity. And since He has not given any promise, it is up to Him Himself to reward or not to reward.

With this explanation, the Imam wishes to convey that the non-believers are counted with the powerless and those whose affair is referred to God's command in terms of whether God will reward them or not; it must be said that their affair is with God, for Him to reward or not to.

At the end of this chapter of *al-Kafi* there are some traditions which we will mention later under the heading, "The Sins of Muslims."

Of course, the relevant traditions are not limited to those mentioned here; there are other traditions as well. Our deduction from all of these

---

[34] *al-Kafi*, vol.2, chapter on deviation (*zalal*) p.401

[35] *al-Kafi*, vol.2, p.463

[36] *al-Kafi*, vol 2, p.464

traditions is what we have mentioned above. If someone deduces something else and doesn't affirm our view, he or she may explain his or her view with its evidence, and perhaps we can benefit from it as well.

From the View of the Islamic Sages

Islamic philosophers have discussed this issue in a different way, but the conclusion they have reached in the end corresponds with what we have deduced from the verses and traditions. Avicenna says,

> People are divided into three groups in terms of soundness of body or physical beauty: one group is at the stage of perfection in soundness or beauty, another is at the extreme of ugliness or illness. Both of these groups are in a minority. The group that forms the majority are the people who in the middle in terms of health and beauty; neither are they absolutely sound or healthy, nor do they, like the deformed, suffer from deformities or permanent sickness; neither are they extremely beautiful, nor ugly. Similarly, from the spiritual point of view, people fall into the same categories; one group is in love with truth, and another is its stubborn enemy. The third group consists of those in the middle; and they are the majority, who are neither in love with truth like the first group, nor its enemies like the second. These are people who have not reached the truth, but if they were shown the truth, they wouldn't refuse to accept it.

In other words, from the Islamic perspective and from a jurisprudential viewpoint, they are not Muslims, but in real terms, they are Muslims. That is, they are submissive to truth and have no stubbornness toward it.

Avicenna says, after this division

واستوسع رحمة الله

"Believe God's mercy to be encompassing."[37]

---

[37] *Al-Isharat,* towards the end of the seventh section (namat)

In the discussions of good and evil of *al-Asfar*, Mulla Sadra mentions this point as an objection:

> How do you say that good overcomes evil even though, when we look at the human being, which is the noblest creation, we see that most people are caught in evil deeds in terms of their practice, and stuck in unsound beliefs and compound ignorance in terms of their beliefs? And evil deeds and false beliefs destroy their position on the Day of Judgment, making them worthy of perdition. Thus, the final outcome of humanity, which is the best of creation, is wretchedness and misfortune.

Mulla Sadra, in answering this objection, points to the words of Avicenna and says,

> In the next life, people are the same as they are in this life in terms of their soundness and felicity. Just as the extremely sound and exceedingly beautiful, and likewise the very ill and exceptionally ugly, are a minority in this world, while the majority is in the middle and is relatively sound, so too in the next world the perfect, who in the words of the Qur'an are *al-sabiqun*, or "the foremost ones," and similarly the wretched, who in the words of the Qur'an are *ashab al-shimal*, or "the people of the left," are few, and the majority consists of average people, whom the Qur'an calls *ashab al-yamin*, or "the people of the right."

After this, Mulla Sadra says,

فلأهل الرّحمة والسّلامة غلبة في النّشأتين

"Thus, the people of mercy and soundness are predominant in both worlds."

One of the latter sages, perhaps the late Aqa Muhammad Rida Qumshi'i, has some unique verses of poetry about the vastness of the Lord's mercy; in these verses, he reflects the belief of the sages, and rather the broadness of the *'arifs'* (mystics') stand. He says,

> Consider all to be Gods', accepted and non-accepted,
> From mercy it commenced and to mercy it will return.
> From mercy the created ones came, and to mercy they go,

This is the secret of love, which baffles the intellect.
All of creation was born with the innateness of Divine Unity,
This polytheism is incidental, and the incidental subsides.
Says wisdom: Keep hidden the secret of truth;
What will the prying intellect do with love, which pulls aside
    the curtains?
Consider the story of what was and what will be to be a dot,
This dot sometimes ascends and sometimes descends.
None but I strove to keep the trusts,
Whether you call me oppressive or call me ignorant.

The discussion of the sages pertains to the minor premise of an argument, not the major premise. The sages don't discuss what the criterion of a good deed or the criterion of a deed's acceptance are; their discussion is about the human being, about the idea that relatively speaking, in practice the majority of people-to differing extents-are good, remain good, die good, and will be resurrected good.

What the sages wish to say is that although those who are blessed to accept the religion of Islam are in a minority, the individuals who possess *fitri* (innate) Islam and will be resurrected with innate Islam are in a majority.

In the belief of the supporters of this view, what has come in the Qur'an about the Prophets interceding for those whose religion they approve of is in reference to the innate religion, and not the acquired religion, which, through incapacity, they haven't reached, but towards which they show no obstinacy.

The Sins of Muslims

As for the sins of Muslims, this issue has the exact opposite form of first issue (the good deeds of non-Muslims) and is the completion of the previous discussion. The issue is whether the sins committed by Muslims are similar to the sins of non-Muslims with regard to punishment or not.

Broaching the previous issue was necessary from the aspect of its being a matter of intellectual belief; but broaching this issue is a practical necessity, because one of the factors in the fall and ruin of Muslim societies in the present age is the undue pride which in the latter days has come into being in many Muslims, and also in many Shias.

If these individuals are asked whether the good deeds of non-Shias are acceptable to God, many of them answer, "No." And if they are asked what ruling the evil deeds and sins of Shias have, they answer, "They are all forgiven."

From these two sentences, it is deduced that actions have no value; they have neither positive nor negative value. The necessary and sufficient condition for felicity and salvation is for a person to name him or herself Shia, and that's it.

Normally, this group argues as follows:

First, if our sins and those of others are to be accounted for in the same way, what difference is there between Shias and non-Shias?

Second, there is a well-known tradition:

حبّ عليّ بن أبي طالب حسنة لاتضر معها سيئة

"Love of Ali ibn Abi Talib (a) is a good deed with which no evil deed can bring harm."

In answer to the first argument, it must be said that the difference between Shias and non-Shias becomes apparent when a Shia acts on the program his or her leaders have given him or her and the non-Shia also acts on the teachings of his or her own religion. In such a case, the precedence of the Shia, both in this world and in the other, will become clear. That is, the difference should be sought in the positive side, not the negative side. We shouldn't say that if the Shia and non-Shia put the teachings of their religion under their feet, there must be some difference between them-and if there is no difference in that case, then what difference is there between Shias and non-Shias?

This is exactly as if two patients were to refer to a doctor, one referring to an expert doctor and the other to a doctor with less expertise, but when they receive the doctor's prescription, neither of them acts in accordance with it. Then the first patient complains, saying, "What difference is there between me and the patient who referred to the non-expert doctor? Why should I remain sick like him, even though I referred to an expert doctor and he referred to a non-expert doctor?"

Just as in the example of the two patients, it is not correct for us to differentiate between Ali (a) and others by saying that if we don't act according to his commands, we will see no harm, but for them, whether they act according to the words of their leader or not, they will be in loss.

One of the companions of Imam Sadiq (a) said to the Imam that some of your Shias have gone astray and consider forbidden actions to be permissible, saying that religion is recognition of the Imam and no more; thus, once you have recognized the Imam, you may do whatever you want. Imam Sadiq (a) said:

> Verily we belong to God and to Him shall we return. These unbelievers have interpreted that which they don't know according to their own ideas.

> The proper statement is, "Acquire recognition [of the Imam] and do whatever good deeds you want, and they will be accepted of you, for God does not accept actions without recognition."[38]

Muhammad ibn Marid asked Imam Sadiq (a): "Is it true that you have said, 'Once you have recognized (the Imam), do what you please'?" The Imam (a) replied, "Yes, that is correct." He said, "Any action, even adultery, theft, or drinking wine?!" The Imam (a) replied:

> Verily we belong to God and to Him shall we return. I swear by God, they have wronged us. We [the Imams] ourselves are responsible for our actions; how can responsibility be lifted from our Shias? What I said is that once you have recognized the Imam, do what you wish of good deeds, for they will be accepted from you."[39]

As for the tradition that says, "Love of Ali (a) is a good deed with which no evil deed will cause harm," we must see what its interpretation is. One of the eminent scholars-I think it was Wahid Bihbahani has interpreted this tradition in a noteworthy way. He says that the meaning of the tradition is that if one's love of Ali (a) is true, no sin will bring harm to a person. That is, if one's love of Ali (a)-who is the perfect example of humanity, obedience, servitude, and ethics-is sincere and not out of self-centeredness, it will prevent the committing of sins; it is like a vaccine that brings immunity and keeps sickness away from the vaccinated person. Love of a leader like Ali (a), who is the

---

[38] *Mustadrak al-Wasail*, vol.1, p.24.
[39] *al-Kafi*, vol.2, p. 464.

personification of good deeds and piety, causes one to love Ali's character; it chases the thought of sin from one's mind, with the condition, of course, that one's love be true. It is impossible for one who recognizes Ali (a)-his piety, his tearful prayers, his supplications in the heart of the night-and one who loves such a person, to act in opposition to his command, he who always commanded others to be pious and do good deeds. Every lover shows respect to the wishes of his or her beloved and respects his or her command. Obedience to the beloved is a necessary result of true love; thus, it is not exclusive to Ali (a); true love of the Prophet (s) is the same way. Thus, the meaning of the tradition:

حبّ عليّ عبادة لا يضرّ معها سيئة

Love of Ali (a) is a good deed with which no evil deed can cause harm"

is that love of Ali (a) is a good deed that prevents evil deeds from bringing harm; that is, it prevents their occurrence. It doesn't indicate the meaning that the ignorant have understood, which is that love of Ali (a) is something alongside of which no sin you may commit will have an effect.

Some dervishes on the one hand claim to love God and on the other hand are more sinful than all other sinners; these, too are false claimants. Imam Sadiq (a) said:

هذا لعمري في الفعال بديع	تعصي الإله و أنت تظهر حبّه
إنّ المحبّ لمن يحبّ مطيع	لو كان حبك صادقًا لأطعته

You disobey God while claiming to love Him,
This by my life is an incredible deed.
If your love were true, you would obey Him;
Verily the lover shows obedience to the beloved.

The true friends of Amir al-Mu'minin (a) would always abstain from sins; his patronage (wilayah) would protect from sin, not encourage it.

Imam Baqir (a) said:

ما تنال ولايتنا إلّا بالعمل والورع

"Our patronage is not attained except through deeds and piety."[40]

Now, some traditions in support of this point:

1. Tawus al-Yamani says:

    > I saw Ali ibn Husayn (a) circumambulating the House
    > of God and busying himself in worship from the time
    > of 'Isha prayers until the last part of the night. When he
    > found himself alone, he looked toward the sky and
    > said, "O God! The stars have disappeared in the
    > horizon and the eyes of the people have slept, and Your
    > gates are open to those who seek ..."

Tawus narrated many sentences in this regard from the humble and worshipful supplications the Imam (a), saying, "Numerous times in the course of his supplication, he wept." He said:

> Then he fell to the earth and prostrated on the ground.
> I approached and, putting his head on my knees, wept.
> My tears flowed and fell on his face. He rose, sat, and
> said: "Who has busied me from the remembrance of
> my Lord?" I said: "I am Tawus, O son of the
> Messenger of God. What is this agitation and disquiet?
> We, who are sinners and full of shortcomings, should
> do thus. Your father is Husayn ibn Ali, your mother is
> Fatima Zahra, and your grandfather is the Messenger
> of God (a)-that is, with such a noble ancestry and lofty
> link, why are you in discomfort and fear?" He looked
> to me and said,

هيهات هيهات يا طاووس دع عنّي حديث أبي وأمّي وجدّي ، خلق الله الجنة لمن أطاعه
وأحسن و لو كان عبدًا حبشيًّا ، و خلق النَّار لمن عصاه و لوكان ولدًا قرشيًّا. أما سمعت
قوله تعالى: " فإذا نفخ فى الصّور فلا أنساب بينهم يومئذ و لا يتساءلون". والله، لا
ينفعك غدًا إلّا تقدمة تقدّمها من عمل صالح.

> Not at all, O Tawus, not at all! Leave aside talk of my
> ancestry. God created Heaven for those who obey Him
> and do good, even if he be an Abyssinian slave, and
> He created Hell for those who disobey him, even if he
> be a Qurayshi lad. Have you not heard the words of

God: "so when the trumpet shall be blown, there will be no relations among them, nor shall they ask one another?" By God, nothing shall benefit you tomorrow except what good deeds you send forth.[41]

2. The Messenger of God (s), after the conquest of Makkah, ascended the hill of Safa and called out: "O sons of Hashim! o sons of Abd al-Muttalib!" The descendants of Hashim and Abd al-Muttalib assembled; when they came together, the Messenger (s) addressed them:

إِنِّي رَسُولُ اَللَّهِ إِلَيْكُمْ وَ إِنِّي شَفِيقٌ عَلَيْكُمْ لاَ تَقُولُوا إِنَّ مُحَمَّداً مِنَّا فَوَاللَّهِ مَا أَوْلِيَائِي مِنْكُمْ وَ لاَ مِنْ غَيْرِكُمْ إِلاَّ اَلْمُتَّقُونَ فَلاَ تَأْتُونِي يَوْمَ تَحْمِلُونَ اَلدُّنْيَا رِقَابِكُم وَ يَأْتِي اَلنَّاسُ يَحْمِلُونَ اَلْآخِرَةَ أَلاَ وَ إِنِّي قَدْ أَعْذَرْتُ فِيمَا بَيْنِي وَ بَيْنَكُمْ وَ فِيمَا بَيْنَ اَللَّهِ عَزَّ وَ جَلَّ وَ بَيْنَكُم وَ إِن لِي عَمَلِي و لَكُم عَمَلُكم

Verily I am God's messenger to you; verily [am your well-wisher. Don't say that Muhammad is from among us, for I swear by God, my friends from among you and from among others are only the pious ones. So do not let me see you come to me on the Day of Judgment carrying the world on your shoulders, while the people come carrying the Hereafter. Aye, I have left no excuse between myself and you, and between God the Exalted and you. Verily, for me are my deeds and for you are your deeds.'[42]

3. Books of history have written that the Noble Messenger (s), in the last days of his life, went out alone at night to the Baqi graveyard and sought forgiveness for those buried in it. After that, he said to his companions, "Each year Jibra'il would show the Qur'an to me once, and this year he recited it for me twice. I think this is a sign that my death has approached." The next day he went to the pulpit and declared, "The time of my death has approached. Whoever I have made a promise to, let him come forward so that I may fulfil it, and whoever is owed something by me, let him come forward so that I may give it."

---

[41] *Bihar al-Anwar,* vol. 11, p.25, "Chapter on the Nobel Morals of Imam Zain al Abedin (a).

[42] *Bihar al-Anwar,* vol. 21, p.111, from *Attributes of Shia* by Shaykh Sadduq.

Then he continued his words thus:

أيّها النّاس إنّه ليس بين الله و بين أحد نسب و لا أمر يؤتيه به خيرًا أو يصرف عنه شرًّا
إلا العمل ، ألا لا يدّعين مدّع و لا يتمنين متمنّ . والّذي بعثني بالحقّ لا ينجي إلا عمل
مع رحمة ، و لو عصيت لهويت . اللهم هل بلّغت ؟

> O people! Verily there is no kinship between God and
> any person, nor is there anything on account of which
> He will do good to a person or cast away evil from him
> except deeds. Aye, let no one claim or wish (otherwise).
> I swear by Him Who sent me with the truth, nothing will
> give salvation save (good) deeds along with mercy, and
> if [even] I were to disobey, I would perish. O God! I
> have conveyed."[43]

4.   Imam Ali al-Rida (a) had a brother known as Zayd al-Nar. The
character of this brother of the Imam (a) was not very pleasing to
the Imam. One day, during the time that the Imam was in Marw,
Zayd was present in a gathering in which there was a large group of
people who were speaking to each other. While the Imam was
speaking, he noticed that Zayd was talking to a group of people and
speaking of the station of the Messenger's family, and in a proud
manner would constantly saying, "we this" and "we that." The
Imam (a) cut short his own words and said, addressing Zayd:

> What are these things that you are saying? If what you
> say is correct and the descendants of the Messenger of
> God (s) have an exceptional status; that is, if God is not
> to punish their evildoers and will reward them without
> their doing good deeds, then you are more honourable
> near God than your father Musa ibn Jafar (a), because
> he would worship God until he attained the stations of
> Divine proximity, whereas you think that without
> worship you can attain the station of Musa ibn Jafar (a).

The Imam (a) then turned to Hasan ibn Musa al-Washsha', one of the
scholars of Kufah who was present in that gathering, saying,

How do the scholars of Kufah recite this verse:

قَالَ يا نوحُ إنَّهُ لَيسَ مِن أهلِك إنَّهُ عَمَلٌ غَيرُ صالِحٍ

---

[43] *Nahj al-Balagha, Sharh Ibn Abil Hadid*, vol.2, p.863.

"O Nuh! Verily he is not of your family; he is a (doer) of unworthy deeds."

He replied: They recite it thus:

إِنَّهُ عَمَلُ غَيْرُ صالحٍ

That is, he is not your son and is not from your seed; he is the son of an unrighteous man.

The Imam (a) said, "Such is not the case. They recite the verse incorrectly and interpret it incorrectly. The verse is thus

إِنَّهُ عَمَلُ غَيْرُ صالحٍ

That is, your son himself is unworthy. He was actually the son of Nuh; he was driven away from God and drowned because he himself was unrighteous, even though he was the son of Prophet Nuh (a).

Thus, being descended from and related to the prophet or imam has no benefit; good deeds are required."[44]

Creational Conditions and Conventional Conditions

Usually, people compare the Divine rules in creation, reward and punishment, and salvation and perdition to human societal rules, even though these affairs are in accordance with creational and actual conditions and are a portion of them, whereas social conditions and rules follow conventional, manmade rules. Social rules can follow conventional conditions, but the rules of creation, and among them Divine reward and punishment, cannot follow these conditions, and instead follow creational conditions. To clarify the difference between a creational system and a conventional system, we present an example:

We know that in social systems, every country has its own particular rules and laws. Social rules, in some issues, differentiate between two people who are equal in physical and creational conditions, but different with respect to conventional conditions.

For example, when they wish to hire someone in Iran, if an Iranian and an Afghani apply to for the job and both are equal in terms of creational conditions, it is possible that the Iranian will be hired rather

---

[44] *Bihar al-Anwar*, vol. 10, p.65

than the Afghani, simply because he is not an Iranian. In this case, if the Afghani says that I am completely equal in terms of physical conditions to the Iranian who was hired-if he is healthy, I too am healthy, if he is young, so am I, if he is a specialist in such-and-such a field, so am I-he will be given the answer that administrative rules do not permit us to hire you.

Based on a conventional and man-made decision, the position of this same Afghani individual can change and become like others; that is, he can apply for and receive Iranian citizenship. It is obvious that citizenship papers have no effect on his actual personality; but from the view of social rules, he has become another person. Normally, the observance of conventional conditions is concurrent with a lack of observance of equality in actual and creational conditions.

But in issues that do not follow social and conventional rules and instead follow only creational conditions, the case is different.

For example, if God forbid, an illness or an epidemic comes to Iran, it will not differentiate between a citizen of Iran and that of another country. If an Iranian and an Afghani are equal with respect to temperamental, environmental, and all other conditions, it is impossible for the bacteria that cause illness to discriminate and say that since the Afghani is not a citizen of Iran, I have nothing to do with him. Here, the issue is of creation and nature, not society and societal conventions; the issue pertains to creation, not to legislation and rule-making.

The Divine rules with respect to reward and punishment and salvation and perdition of individuals are subject to actual and creational conditions. It is not the case that if someone claims, "Since my name is recorded in the register of Islam and I am Muslim by name, I must have special treatment," it will be accepted of him or her.

Let there be no confusion; here we are concerned with the discussion of reward and punishment, salvation and perdition, and the conduct of God with His servants; we are not talking about the laws that Islam has legislated in the Muslims' social life.

There is no doubt that the laws of Islam, like all other legislations of the word, are a series of conventional laws, and a series of conventional conditions has been observed in them. And in these laws which are related to their worldly life, human beings of necessity must follow a set of conventional conditions.

But the actions of God, and the operation of Divine will in the system of creation-including the granting of salvation and leading to perdition of individuals and rewarding and punishing them-do not follow social rules, and instead are of another type altogether. God, in carrying out His absolute will, does not act on the basis of conventional rules. Conventional matters which naturally have a major effect on social systems have no role in the creational will of God.

From the viewpoint of the rules Islam has legislated that pertain to the social conduct of human beings, whenever a person recites the two testimonies, he or she will be recognized as a Muslim and will benefit from the advantages of Islam. But with regard to the rules of the hereafter and from the viewpoint of God's conduct, the laws of

فَمَن تَبِعَني فَإِنَّهُ مِنِّي

Whoever follows me, is from me… [Qur'an, 14:36]

And

إنَّ أكرَمَكم عِندَ اللهِ أتقاكُم

Verily the most honourable of you near God is the most pious of you."
[Qur'an, 14:36]

prevail.

The Messenger of God (s) said,

أيّها النّاس إن أباكم واحد، وإنّ ربّكم واحد، كلكم لآدم وآدم من تراب، لا فخر لعربيّ على عجميّ إلا بالتّقوى

"O people! Verily your father is one, and your Lord is One. All of you are from Adam, and Adam was from dust. There is no pride for an Arab over a non-Arab, except through piety."[45]

Salman al-Farsi, who strove to reach truth, reached such a station that the Noble Messenger (s) said of him,

سلمان منّا أهل البيت

---

[45] *Tarikh al-Yaqubi*, vol.2, p.110.

Salman is one of us, the People of the House.

There are some who have come under the influence of satanic whisperings and have contented themselves with the thought, "Our name is among the names of Ali ibn Abi Talib's (a) friends. However, we may be, we are considered his subjects. Or we will make a will that a large sum out of the money that we have acquired through wrong means or that we should have spent in our lifetime in good causes-but didn't-should be given to the caretakers of one of the holy shrines in order for us to be buried near the graves of God's saints, so that the angels don't dare punish us." Such people should know that they have been blinded and the curtain of negligence has covered their eyes. Their eyes will open when they will find themselves drowned in Divine punishment and they will suffer from such regret that if it were possible to die, they would do so a thousand times. So, let them awake from the slumber of carelessness today, repent, and make up for what has passed.

وَأَنذِرْهُمْ يَوْمَ الْحَسْرَةِ إِذْ قُضِيَ الْأَمْرُ وَهُمْ فِي غَفْلَةٍ وَهُمْ لَا يُؤْمِنُونَ

Warn them of the Day of Regret, when the matter will be decided, while they are [yet] heedless and do not have faith. [Qur'an, 19:39]

From the point of view of the Qur'an and the Islamic traditions, it is definite that the sinner, even if Muslim, will be punished by God. True, since he or she has faith, he or she will in the end achieve salvation and liberty from Hell, but it may be that this salvation will only come after years of hardship and punishment. Some people's account of sins will be cleansed by the hardships of dying; another group will pay the penalty for their sins in the grave and *barzakh* (intermediary realm between this world and the next); another group will get their retribution in the horrors of Resurrection and difficulties of accounting for their deeds; and yet others will go to Hell and linger for years in punishment. It has been narrated from the sixth Imam, Imam Ja'far Sadiq (a) that the verse

لَّابِثِينَ فِيهَا أَحْقَابًا

to reside therein for ages, [Qur'an, 78:23]

pertains to those who will attain salvation from Hell.[46]

---

[46] *Bihar al-Anwar*, vol. 3, p.376-7

Here we mention some examples of traditions that talk of the punishments of the time of death and after death so that they may help us take notice, awaken, and prepare ourselves for the daunting and dangerous stations we have ahead of us.

1. Shaykh Kulayni narrates from Imam Sadiq (a) that Ali (a) was once suffering from pain in the eye. The Prophet (s) went to visit him at a time when he was crying out from the pain. He said, "Is this cry from impatience, or because of the severity of pain?" Amir al-Mu'minin (a) replied, "O Messenger of God, I have not suffered any pain like this until today." The Prophet (s) began to narrate the terrifying account of what happens to unbelievers when they die. Upon hearing this, Ali (a) sat up and said, "Messenger of God, please repeat this account for me, for it made me forget my pain." Then he said, "O Messenger of God! Will anyone from your community face such a death?" He replied, "Yes: a ruler who oppresses, and one who usurps the property of an orphan, and one who bears false witness."[47]

2. Shaykh Saduq narrates in *Man la Yahd uruhu al-Faqih* that when Dharr, the son of Abu Dharr al-Ghifari, died, Abu Dharr stood by his grave, put his hand on the grave, and said:

> "God have mercy on you; I swear by God that you were good to me and now that you have left me I am pleased with you. I swear by God that I am not worried because of your leaving; nothing has been diminished from me, and I am in need of none but God. And were it not for the fear of the time of notification, I would wish that I had gone in your place. But now I wish to compensate for what has passed and prepare for the next world, and verily my grief for your sake has prevented my grief over you. [That is, I am absorbed in thinking about doing something that could benefit you, and so I have no time to grieve at being separated from you.] I swear by God that I have not wept on account of your separation, but I have cried thinking about how you are and what you have gone through. I wish I knew what you said and what was said to you! O God! I have

---

forgiven the rights that You had made obligatory on my son for me, so You too forgive him Your rights over him, for magnanimity and generosity are more befitting of You." [48]

3. Imam Sadiq (a) narrates from his noble ancestors that the is (s) said, "The squeezing in the grave for a believer is an atonement for the shortcomings he or she has committed."[49]

4. Ali ibn Ibrahim narrates from Imam Sadiq (a) regarding the verse

وَمِن وَرَائِهِم بَرْزَخٌ إِلَىٰ يَوْمِ يُبْعَثُونَ

and beyond them is a barrier until the day they shall be resurrected. [Qur'an, 23:100]

that he said,

والله ما أخاف عليكم إلا البرزخ فأمّا إذا صار الأمر إلينا فنحن أولى بكم

I swear by God, I fear nothing for you except *barzakh*; as for when the affair is committed to us, we are more worthy of you."[50]

That is, our intercession is related to after *barzakh*; there is no intercession in *barzakh*.

In general, there are so many Qur'anic verses and clear traditions regarding the punishment for sins like lying, backbiting, false accusation, treachery, oppression, usurping other's property, drinking, gambling, tale bearing, defaming, abandoning prayer, abandoning fasting, abandoning pilgrimage, abandoning jihad, and so forth that it is beyond reckoning; none of them is exclusive to unbelievers or non-Shias. In the tradition of the *m'iraj* (Prophetic ascent to Heaven), we find many examples where the Prophet (s) says: I saw various groups of my community, men and women, in different forms of punishment, who were being punished on account of various sins.

---

[48] *Ibid.* p. 24-25

[49] *Bihar al-Anwar*, vol. 3, p.153, from *Thawab al-A'mal* and *Amali* of Shaykh Sadduq.

[50] *Bihar al-Anwar*, vol. 3, p.151, from *Tafsir Ali ibn Ibrahim*.

Summary and Conclusion

From all that has been said in this section about the good and bad deeds of Muslims and non-Muslims, the following conclusions can be reached:

1. Both salvation and perdition have degrees and levels; neither the people of salvation are all at the same level, nor are those of perdition. These levels and differences are called *darajat* "levels of ascent" with regard to the people of Heaven and *darakat* "levels of descent" with regard to the inhabitants of Hell.

2. It is not the case that all of the dwellers of Heaven will go to Heaven from the beginning, just as all of the people of Hell will not be in Hell for eternity. Many dwellers of Heaven will only go to Heaven after suffering very difficult periods of punishment in *barzakh* or the hereafter. A Muslim and a Shia should know that, assuming he or she dies with sound faith, if God forbid he or she has committed sins, injustices, and crimes, he or she has very difficult stages ahead, and some sins have yet greater danger and may cause one to remain eternally in Hell.

3. Individuals who don't believe in God and the hereafter naturally don't perform any actions with the intention of ascending towards God, and since they don't perform good deeds with this intent, by necessity they do not embark on a journey towards God and the hereafter. Thus, they naturally don't ascend towards God and the higher realm and don't reach Heaven. That is, because they were not moving towards it, they don't reach that destination.

4. If individuals believe in God and the hereafter, perform actions with the intention of seeking nearness to God, and are sincere in their actions, their actions are acceptable to God and they deserve their reward and Heaven, whether they are Muslims or non-Muslims.

5. Non-Muslims who believe in God and the hereafter and do good deeds with the intention of seeking nearness to God, on account of being without the blessing of Islam, are naturally deprived of benefiting from this Divine program. That proportion of their good deeds is accepted which is in accordance with the Divine program, such as forms of favours and services to God's creation. But invented acts of worship that without base are naturally unacceptable, and a series of deprivations

resulting from unavailability of the complete program apply to and include them.

6. Accepted good deeds, whether of Muslims or otherwise, have certain afflictions which may come about afterwards and corrupt them. At the head of all of these afflictions is rejection, obstinacy, and deliberate unbelief. Thus, if non-Muslim individuals perform a great amount of good deeds with the intention of seeking nearness to God, but when the truths of Islam are presented to them show bias and obstinacy and set aside fairness and truth-seeking, all of those good deeds are null and void, "like ashes caught in a strong wind on a stormy day."

7. Muslims and all other true monotheists, if they commit indecencies and transgressions and betray the practical aspect of the Divine program, are deserving of long punishments in *barzakh* and the Day of Judgment, and occasionally because of some sins, like intentionally murdering an innocent believer, may remain in eternal punishment.

8. The good deeds of individuals who don't believe in God and the Day of Judgment and perhaps may ascribe partners to God will cause their punishment to be lessened and, occasionally, be lifted.

9. Felicity and perdition are in accordance with actual and creational conditions, not conventional and man-made conditions.

10. The verses and traditions that indicate that God accepts good deeds do not look solely to the action-related goodness of actions; in Islam's view, an action becomes good and worthy when it possesses goodness from two aspects: action-related, and actor-related.

11. The verses and traditions that indicate that the actions of those who deny Prophethood or Imamate are not acceptable are with a view to denial out of obstinacy and bias; however, denial that is merely a lack of confession out of incapacity (*qusur*) -rather than out of culpability (*taqsir*}-is not what the verses and traditions are about. In the view of the Qur'an, such deniers are considered mustad'af (powerless) and *murjawn li'amr illah* (those whose affair is referred to God's command).

12. In the view of the Islamic sages such as Avicenna and Mulls Sadra, the majority of people who haven't confessed to the truth are incapable and excusable rather than culpable; if such people do not know God they will not be punished though they will also not go to

Heaven-and if they believe in God and the Resurrection and perform pure good deeds with the intention of seeking nearness to God, they will receive the recompense for their good deeds. Only those will face perdition who are culpable, not those who are incapable.

O God! Seal (our fate) for us with goodness and felicity, and cause us to die as Muslims, and join us with the righteous, Muhammad and his noble progeny, upon whom be peace.

Endnotes

1. Sayyid Ruhullah al-Musawi al-Khumayni (1902-1989), known as Imam Khumayni was the mystic, philosopher, jurisprudent, and the most outstanding Islamic political figure in contemporary history. He lived at a time when Islam (and Shi'ism) found itself on the far periphery of the political and military paradigm established by the West and, being culturally weakened, was on the verge of internal collapse. Witnessing this state of affairs, Imam Khumayni ardently applied himself to learning and acquiring the Islamic sciences in a comprehensive manner by embarking upon the path-in all of its mystical, moral and practical dimensions. He activated and became the very embodiment of the Islamic and Shi'i heritage that he carried. In his capacity as the *Marja'* (Supreme Religious Authority) of the Shi'ahs of his time, and making use of the potentials that existed in the Shi'ah culture of Iran, he guided the Islamic Revolution of Iran to its eventual victory and thus introduced the Islamic world as a new player on the scene and as a pole of civilization to the West. Some of his mystical writings include *Misbah al-Hidiyah fi sharh al-Khilafah wa al-Wilayah, Sharh e Du'a al-Sahr, Asar al-Salat* and marginal notes on both the *Fusus al-Hikam of Ibn 'Arabi* and *Misbah al-Uns* of *Ibn Fannari*. His *Kitab al-Bay'*, in five volumes, is one of his works on jurisprudence. His lessons on jurisprudence and the principles of jurisprudence have also been published.

2. Abu Ali Ibn Sina (980-1037), known in the West as Avicenna, was the foremost philosopher in the Islamic world. In his philosophical methodology he was greatly influenced by Farabi and though he mainly commented on the Aristotelian tradition, his penetrating inquiries led to new conclusions. While Ibn Sina's fame is mostly due to his achievements in philosophy and medicine, he was also a master in such fields as methodology, formal logic, mathematics and astronomy. His written works include *Kitib al-Shifa, Kitab al-Isharat wa al-Tanbihat,* and *Qanun fi al-Tibb*.

3. *Tawhid* is the fundamental principle and fort of the Islamic tradition. It includes the idea of the unicity of the Godhead as well as the principal unity of all Being in both its transcendental and immanent modalities. There is no exact equivalent for this term in English. "Monotheism" will be used to refer to *tawhid* in some cases but in general the word will be left in its transliterated form.

لو شق عن قلبي يرى وسطه ⠀⠀سطران قد خُطّا بلا كاتب.4

5. Jalal al-Din Rumi (1205-1273), also called *Mawlana*, the most important Persian Sufi thinker, metaphysician and poet of all times. His *Diwan* of *Shams-i Tabrizi* and the *Mathnawi* have been translated into many languages and are widely known the world over.

6. Ali ibn Abi Talib (600-661), upon him be peace, the first man to believe in the Prophet, upon him and his progeny be peace. The prophet called him the gate of knowledge and chose him to be his trustee. Ibn Arabi held that the Imam was the closet of all people to the prophet, the pinnacle of the universe and the esoteric reality of all the prophets of God- Ibn Sina wrote about him saying that he was amidst the companions of the prophet just as the intellect is amongst sensible things. Ibn Abi al-Hadid traces all the fields of knowledge in the Islamic world back to the Imam. The book, *Nahj al-Balaghah*, contains some of the Imam's letters, speeches and words of wisdom. This book, being a great source of knowledge of the unicity of God as well as of sociological matters, comes second to only the Qur'an in its effects upon Islamic culture. All Muslims are united in acknowledging the Imam's position and worthiness as a caliph and successor to the Prophet; they are not united however in the case of others and are divided into the two main sects of Sunni and Shi'ah.

7 Sadr al-Din Shirazi (1571-1641), known as Mulla Sadra, philosopher, *muhaddith* (transmitter of traditions), and exegete who, drawing upon the peripatetic and Illuminationist (*ishraqi*) philosophical traditions and making full use of the mystical heritage of the Islamic world, inaugurated a synthesis and a new point of convergence in the history of Islamic philosophy at a time when philosophy in the west strayed farther away from discussions on ontology and metaphysics (*mabahith e wujudi*) and, in so doing, laid the foundations of modern Civilization. Mulla Sadra intensified Islamic philosophy's connection with these fields. He was the originator of doctrine of trans-substantial motion (*harakat al-jawhari*) and the belief that the soul was contingent in body and eternal in spirit. His school of philosophy came to be distinguished from the peripatetic and the Illuminationist schools and, under the name of "Transcendental philosophy" (*Hikmat al-Mutaliyyah*), it slowly but surely gained wide acceptance. This school was particularly effectual in shaping the social and cultural movements inside Iran during the latter's initial contacts with the west. He was the author of more than fifty books. His *Asfar al-Arba'ah* and, *Shawahid al-Rububiyyah* have become standard texts of philosophy. His other works include *Sharh Usul al-Kafi* and *Tafsir al-Qur'an*.

8. Khwajah Nasir al-Din al-Tusi (1201-1274), well-known philosopher, theologian, mathematician and astronomer who expounded and revived philosophy at a time when it was under attack by Ash'ari theologians. In his commentary on the *Kitab al-Isharat wa al-Tanbihat*, he aptly responded to Fakhr al-Razi's criticism of philosophical thought and went on to accept most of Shaykh al-Ishraq's original ideas. He was instrumental in the establishment and progress of the observatory at Maragha. His works include *Awsaf al-Ashraf* which was written in the style of the mystics, and *Tajrid al-I'tiqad* which expounded the theological doctrine of the Shi'ah and became the theological text *par excellence* of the entire Muslim world. Tusi was also active in the political realm. At the time of the Mongol invasion of Iran, he played a prominent role in the defense and promulgation of Islamic thought and culture.

9. Abu Hamid Muhammad ibn Muhammad al-Tusi al-Ghazali (1058-1111), theologian and mystic whose great work, *Ihya' Ulum al-Din* ("The Revival of the Religious Sciences"), made Sufism an acceptable part of orthodox Islam.

10. Shams al-Din Muhammad Hafiz (1317-1392), also called *lisan al-ghayb*. Persian scholar, thinker, and the greatest Persian Sufi poet who has expounded the most profound Divine mysteries in his poetry.

11. چشمم از آینه داران خط و خالش گشت   لبم از بوسه ربایان بر و دوش باد.

12. روی خوبت آیتی از لطف بر ما کشف کرد   زین سبب جز لطف و خوبی نیست در تفسیر ما

مرا به کار جهان هرگز التفات نبود   رخ در نظر من چنین خوشش آراست

13. Ghiyath al-Din Abul al-Fath 'Umar ibn Ibrahim al-Khayyam (1048-1131) Persian poet, mathematician, and astronomer. Known in the west through the translation of some of his quatrains by Edward FitzGerald entitled *The Rubaiyat of Omar Khayyam* (1859) in which the author appears as an impious sceptic given to sensual abandon and ephemeral pleasures.

14. Abu al-'Ala' Ahmad ibn 'Abd Allah ibn Sulayman al-Ma'arri (973-1058), famous Arabic poet and ascetic who took up celibacy and a vegetarian life-style. Unlike other poets, he was sober to the extreme and was known for his virtuosity and for the pessimism of his vision.

عارف از پرتوی می در طمع خام افتاد.15   عکس روی تو چو آینه در جام افتاد

این همه نقش در آینه او وهام افتاد   حسن روی تو به یک جلوه که در آینه کرد

یک فروغ رخ ساقی است که در جام افتاد   این همه عکس می و نقش و نگارین که نمود

تا کدامین را تو باشی مستعد.16   از جهان دو بانگ می آید به ضد

و آن دگر بانگش نفور اشقیا   آن یکی بانگش نشور اتقیا

17. For a detailed treatment of "Satan", see Sayyid Muhammad Husayn Tabatabai's, *Tafsir al-Mizan*, vol.8, pp.34-58, exegesis of verse 7:1 and the author's book, *Mutual Services of Islam and Iran*.

18. Friedrich Nietzsche (1844-1900), German philosopher and critic of culture, who became one of the most influential of all modem thinkers. His attempts to unmask the motives that underlie conventional Western religion, morality, and philosophy deeply affected generations of philosophers, psychologists, poets, novelists, and playwrights. He thought through the consequences of the triumph of the Enlightenment's secularism, expressed in his observation that "God is dead," in a way that determined the agenda for many of Europe's most celebrated intellectuals after his death.

19. Arthur Schopenhauer (1788-1869), German philosopher, often called the "philosopher of pessimism," who held the centrality of the will in human experience. As the demands of the will cannot be ever fully met, he affirmed the idea of resignation to the endless cycle of suffering.

20. Refer to the author's book, *Mutual Services of Islam and Iran*, seventh print, after the section on "The Philosophical Services of Iranians for Islam."

ز اشتیاق روی تو جوشد چنان.21   باده کاندر خم همی جوشد نهان

وی همه هستی!چه می جویی عدم؟   ای همه دریا!چه خواهی کردنم؟!

تو چرا منت باده کشی؟   تو خوشی و خوب و کان هر خوشی

طوق اعطیناک آویز برت   تاج کرمنا است بر فرق سرت

ذوق جویی تو ز حلوای سبوس؟   علم جویی از کتبهای فسوس؟!

تا تو جویی زان نشاط و انتفاع؟   می چه باشد یا جماع و یا سماع!

زهره ای از خمره کی شد جام خواه؟   آفتاب از ذره کی شد وام خواه؟

ای عجب من عاشق این هر دو ضد.22   عاشقم بر لطف و بر جدش به جد

23. كان أبو طلحة يحبّ ابنه حبًّا شديدًا فمرض فخافت أمّ سليم على أبي طلحة الجزع حين
قرب موت الولد فبعثه إلى النّبي صلّى الله عليه و اله فلمّا خرج أبو طلحة من داره توفّى الولد
فسجّته أمّ سليم بثوب وعزلته فى ناحية من البيت ثمّ تقدّمت إلى أهل بيتها و قالت لهم: لا
تخبروا أبا طلحة بشيء ثمّ انّها صنعت طعامًا ثمّ مسّت شيئًا من الطّيب و فى نقل آخر ثم
تصنّعت له أكثر ممّا كانت تتصنّع له من قبل ذلك فجاء أبو طلحة من عند رسول الله صلى الله
عليه و اله فقال: ما فعل ابني فقالت له: هدأت نفسه آخر قالت: ثم قال: هل لنا ما نأكل؟ فقامت
فقرّبت إليه الطّعام ثم تعرّضت له فوقع عليها فلما اطمأن قالت له: يا أبا طلحة أتغضب من
وديعة كانت عندنا فرددناها إلى أهلها. فقال: سبحان الله لا، فقالت: ابنك كان عندنا وديعة
فقبضه الله تعالى قال أبو طلحة: فأنا أحق منك بالصبر ثم قام من مكانه فاغتسل و صلّى
ركعتين ثم انطلق الى رسول الله صلى الله عليه و اله: فأخبره بصنيعتها فقال رسول الله صلى
الله عليه و اله: بارك الله لكما فى وقعتكما ثم قال رسول الله صلى الله عليه و اله: الحمد لله
الذي جعل فى أمّتي مثل صابرة بني إسرائيل.

24. اجرام که ساکنان این ایوان اند   اسباب تردد خردمندان اند

هان تا سر رشته خرد گم نکنی   کانان که مدبرند سرگردان اند

افلاک که جز غم نفزاید دگر   ننهند بجا تا نربایند دگر

نا آمدگان اگر بدانند که ما   از دهر چه می کشیم ناﻳند دگر

چون حاصل آدمی در این شورستان   جز خوردن غصه نیست تا کندن جان

خرم دل آنکه زین جهان زود برفت   و آسوده کسی که خود نیامد به جهان

ای چرخ فلک خرابی از کینه توست   بیداد گری شیوه دیرینه توست

ای خاک اگر سینه تو بشکافند   بس گوهر قیمتی که در سینه توست

25. The correct explanation of this tradition is that to complain and put blame on Time (or the ages; destiny), is to put blame on the total world order and consequently on God (or Providence). Some scholars claim that this tradition was fabricated by a sect of the Majus called the "Zarwaniyya", who actually believed that God is destiny.

26. دارنده که ترکیب طبایع آراست   از بهر چه افکنش اندر کم و کاست

گر نیک آمد، از بهر چه بود؟   ور نیک نیامد این صور، عیب که راست؟

ترکیب پیاله ای که در هم پیوست   بشکستن آن روا نمی دارد مست

چندین قد سرونازنین و سر و دست   از بهر چه ساخت وز برای چه شکست؟

جامی است که عقل آفرین می زندش   صد بوسه ز مهر بر جبین می زندش

این کوزه گر دهر چنین جام لطیف   می سازد و باز بر زمین می زندش

27. Abu Mu'in Nasir ibn Khusraw ibn Harith al-Qubadhiyani (1004-1072), known as *Nasir e Khusraw*, Persian poet, philosopher, and noted traveler. His *Diwan* and *Safar Nama*, are two of his best known works, while his *Jami' al-Hikmatayn* is a philosophical text which attempts to reconcile religion with peripatetic philosophy.

28. بار خدایا اگر ز روی خدایی   طینت انسان همه جمیل سرشتی

چهره رومی و صورت حبشی را   مایه خوبی چه بود و علت زشتی؟

طلعت هند و روی ترک چرا شد   همچو دل دوزخی و روی بهشتی؟

از چه سعید اوفتاد و از چه شقی شد   زاهد محرابی و کشیش کنشتی؟

چیست خلاف اندر آفرینش عالم   چون همه را دایه و مشاطه تو گشتی؟

گیرم دنیا،ز ی محلی دنیا   بر گرهی خربط و خسیس بهشتی

نعمت منعم چراست دریا دریا؟   محنت مفلس چراست کشتی کشتی؟

29. همه جور من از بلغاریان است   کز آن آهم همی باید کشیدن

گنه بلغاریان را نیز هم نیست   بگویم گر تو بتوانی شنیدن

خدایا راست گویم فتنه از توست   ولی از ترس نتوانم چغیدن

لب و دندان ترکان ختارا   نباید چنین خوب آفریدن

که از دست لب و دندان ایشان   به دندان دست و لب باید گزیدن

به آهو می کنی غوغا که بگریز   به تازی می زنی هی بر دویدن

30. Abu Nasr Muhammad al-Farabi (870-950), considered the founder of Islamic philosophy, he became known as the "second teacher", the first being Aristotle. Though he figured prominently in the choice of the intellectual elements of Hellenic thought that Islam would adopt, he was not just a transmitter of Greek philosophy. By way of original thought and penetrating metaphysical insights, he attempted a synthesis of the opinions of Plato and Aristotle. In working out his own philosophical system, Farabi attempted to detail the status of Revelation and explain its relation to the different levels of Intellect. In "practical philosophy"- or what might be called social science-he formulated the perfect state and wrote *Al-Madinah al-Fadilah.* His philosophical writings were usually short treatises on chosen topics. The Peripatetic, Illuminations, and Transcendental schools of philosophy in Islam can be said to be elaborations and developments of Farabi's philosophy.

31. Rene Descartes (1596-1650), French mathematician. scientist, and philosopher who has been called the father of modem philosophy. He radically distinguished between the mind, which he perceived as indubitable, and the body (or matter in general), which he explained on the basis of purely mechanistic principles. The axiom *Cogito, ergo sum* (I think, therefore I am) is his most famous formulation.

32. پیر ما گفت خطا بر قلم صنع نرفت   آفرین بر نظر پاک خطا پوشش باد.

33. This principle holds that the One only produces unity or the one. The One cannot create the many. It is a logical conclusion of peripatetic philosophy which is best explained, ironically enough, by their antagonists. the mystics.

34. Literally, "There is no effective agent in existence other than God."

35. Literally, "The act is God's act, and it is [in the same instance] our act."

36. Refer to the section, "The Shia Intellectual School" in the Introduction for a discussion on the tradition which was the source of this principle.

37. من می خورم و هرکه چو من اهل بود   می خوردن من به نزد او سهل بود.

می خوردن من ز حق زازل می دانست   گر می نخورم علم خدا جهل بود

38. علم ازلی علت عصیان کردن   نزد عقلا ز غایت جهل بود.

39. زهرمار،آن مار را باشد حیات   لیک آن،مر آدمی را شد ممات.

پس بد مطلق نباشد در جهان   بد به نسبت باشد این را هم بدان

40. گر بر فلکم دست بدی چون یزدان   برداشتمی من این فلک را ز میان.

از نو فلکی چنان همی ساختمی   کازاده به کام دل رسیدی آسان

41. حق،جان جهان است و جهان همچو بدن اصناف ملائک چو قوای این تن.

افلاک و عناصر و موالید،اعضاء توحید همین است و دگرها همه فن

42. Georg Hegel (1770-1831), German idealist philosopher who developed a dialectical scheme that emphasized the progress of history and ideas from thesis to antithesis and thence to a higher and richer synthesis. He is quoted as having said, "The rational is the real."

43. Karl Marx (1818-1883), German philosopher, economist, historian and revolutionary. With the help of Friedrich Engels, he wrote *The Communist Manifesto* (1848) and *Das Kapital* (1867 -1894).

۴۴. در این چمن گل بی خار کس نچید آری   چراغ مصطفوی با شرار بولهبیست

۴۵. در کارخانه عشق از کفر ناگزیر است   آتش که بسوزد گر بولهب نباشد

۴۶. زندگی در مردن و در محنت است   آب حیوان در درون ظلمت است

۴۷. همه عمر تلخی کشیده است سعدی   که نامش برآمد به شیرین زبانی

۴۸. آمد از آفاق،یاری مهربان   یوسف صدیق را شد میهمان
کاشنا بودند وقت کودکی   بروساده آشنایی متکی
یاد دادش جور اخوان و حسد   گفت او زنجیر بود و ما اسد
عار نبود شیر را ز سلسله   ما نداریم از قضای حق گله
شیر را بر گردن از زنجیر بود   بر همه زنجیر سازان میر بود
گفت چون بودی در زندان وچاه   گفت همچون در محاق و کاست ماه
در محاق ار ماه تو گردد دو تا   نی در آخر بدر گردد بر سماء؟
گرچه در دانه به هاون کوفتند   نور چشم و دل شد و رفع گزند
گندمی را زیر خاک انداختند   پس ز خاکش خوشه ها بر ساختند
بار دیگر کوفتندش ز آسیا   قیمتش افزون شد و نان شد جان فزا
باز نان را زیر دندان کوفتند   گشت عقل و جان و فهم سودمند
باز آن جان چون که محو عشق گشت   یعجب و الزراع آمد بعد کشت

۴۹. هست حیوانی که نامش اسغر است   کو به زخم چوب،زفت و لمتر است
تا که چوبش می زنی به می شود   او از زخم چوب فربه می شود
نفس مومن اسغری آمد یقین   کوبه زخم رنج زفت است و سمین
زین سبب بر انبیا رنج و شکست   از همه خلق جهان افزون تر است
تا ز جان ها جانشان شد زفت تر   که ندیدند آن بلا قومی دگر

50. پوست از دارو بلاکش می شود   چون ادیم طائفی خوش می شود

ورنه تلخ و تیز مالیدی در او   گنده گشتی ناخوش و نا پاک بو

آدمی را نیز چون آن پوست دان   از رطوبت ها شده زشت و گران

تلخ و تیز و مالش بسیار ده   تا شود پاک و لطیف و بافره

ور نمی تانی رضا ده ای عیار   که خدا رنجت دهد بی اختیار

که بلای دوست تطهیر شماست   علم او بالای تدبیر شماست

51. قالوا حبست فقلت لیس بضائر   حبسی وأي مهند لا یغمد؟

أو ما رأیت اللیث ینلف غیلة   کبرا وأوباش السّباع تردد؟

والنّار فی أحجارها مخبوءة   لا تصطلي ما لم تثرها الأزند

والحبس ما لم تغشه لدینة   شنعاء نعم المنزل المستورد

52. کوتاه دیدگان همه راحت طلب کنند   عارف، بلا، که راحت او در بلای او است

بگذار هرچه داری و بگذر هر چه که نیست   این پنج روز عمر که مرگ از قفای اوست

هر آدمی که کشته شمشیر عشق شد   گو غم مخور که ملک ابد خون بهای اوست

از دست دوست هرچه ستایی شکر بود   سعدی رضای خود مطلب چون رضای اوست

53. چون صفا بیند بلا شیرین شود   خوش شود دارو چو صحت بین شود

برد بیند خویش را در عین مات   پس بگوید اقتلونی یا ثقات

54. گوهر قیمتی از کام نهنگان آرند   آن که اورا غم جان است به دریا نرود.

55. آن یکی می گفت در عهد شعیب   که خدا را از من بسی دیده است عیب.

چند دید از من گناه و جرم ها   وز کرم یزدان نمی گیرد مرا

حق تعالی گفت در گوش شعیب   در جواب او فصیح از راه غیب

که بگفتی چند کردم من گناه   وز کرم نگرفت در جرم م اله

327

عکس می گویی و مقلوب ای سفیه   ای رها کرده ره و بگرفته تیه

چند چندت گیرم و مقلوب ای سفیه   در سلاسل مانده ای پا تا به سر

زنگ تو برتوست ای دیگ سیاه   کرد سیمای درونت را تباه

بر دلت زنگار بر زنگار ها   جمع شد تا کور شد ز اسرار ها

56. Jean Jacques Rousseau (1112-1778), French philosopher and writer whose treatises and novels inspired the leaders of the French Revolution and the Romantic generation. His written works include *The Social Contract* and the novel *Emile* (both 1762). Rousseau was the least academic of modem philosophers and perhaps the most influential. His thought marked the end of the Age of Reason.

گنج و مار و گل و خار و غم شادی بهمند.57

58. These expressions are allusions to the first few couplets of Rumi's *Mathnawi*,

> Listen to the reed how it tells a tale, complaining of separations –
>
> Saying, "Ever since I was parted from the reed-bed,
>
> > my lament hath caused man and woman to moan.
>
> I want a bosom torn by severance, that I may
>
> > unfold (to such a one) the pain of love-desire.
>
> Everyone who is left far from his source wishes back,
>
> > back the time when he was united with it.

59. وَ قَالَ (عليه السلام) : وَ قَدْ سَمِعَ رَجُلًا يَذُمُّ الدُّنْيَا أَيُّهَا الذَّامُّ لِلدُّنْيَا الْمُغْتَرُّ بِغُرُورِهَا الْمَخْدُوعُ بِأَبَاطِيلِهَا أَ تَغْتَرُّ بِالدُّنْيَا ثُمَّ تَذُمُّهَا أَنْتَ الْمُتَجَرِّمُ عَلَيْهَا أَمْ هِيَ الْمُتَجَرِّمَةُ عَلَيْكَ مَتَى اسْتَهْوَتْكَ أَمْ مَتَى غَرَّتْكَ أَ بِمَصَارِعِ آبَائِكَ مِنَ الْبِلَى أَمْ بِمَضَاجِعِ أُمَّهَاتِكَ تَحْتَ الثَّرَى كَمْ عَلَّلْتَ بِكَفَّيْكَ وَ كَمْ مَرَّضْتَ بِيَدَيْكَ تَبْتَغِي لَهُمُ الشِّفَاءَ وَ تَسْتَوْصِفُ لَهُمُ الْأَطِبَّاءَ غَدَاةَ لَا يُغْنِي عَنْهُمْ دَوَاؤُكَ وَ لَا يُجْدِي عَلَيْهِمْ بُكَاؤُكَ لَمْ يَنْفَعْ أَحَدَهُمْ إِشْفَاقُكَ وَ لَمْ تُسْعَفْ فِيهِ بِطَلِبَتِكَ وَ لَمْ تَدْفَعْ عَنْهُ بِقُوَّتِكَ وَ قَدْ مَثَّلَتْ لَكَ بِهِ الدُّنْيَا نَفْسَكَ وَ بِمَصْرَعِهِ مَصْرَعَكَ إِنَّ الدُّنْيَا دَارُ صِدْقٍ لِمَنْ صَدَقَهَا وَ دَارُ عَافِيَةٍ لِمَنْ فَهِمَ عَنْهَا وَ دَارُ غِنًى لِمَنْ تَزَوَّدَ مِنْهَا وَ دَارُ مَوْعِظَةٍ لِمَنِ اتَّعَظَ بِهَا مَسْجِدُ أَحِبَّاءِ اللَّهِ وَ مُصَلَّى مَلَائِكَةِ اللَّهِ وَ مَهْبِطُ وَحْيِ اللَّهِ وَ مَتْجَرُ أَوْلِيَاءِ اللَّهِ اكْتَسَبُوا فِيهَا الرَّحْمَةَ وَ رَبِحُوا فِيهَا الْجَنَّةَ فَمَنْ ذَا يَذُمُّهَا وَ قَدْ آذَنَتْ بِبَيْنِهَا وَ نَادَتْ بِفِرَاقِهَا وَ نَعَتْ نَفْسَهَا وَ أَهْلَهَا فَمَثَّلَتْ لَهُمْ بِبَلَائِهَا الْبَلَاءَ وَ شَوَّقَتْهُمْ بِسُرُورِهَا إِلَى السُّرُورِ رَاحَتْ بِعَافِيَةٍ وَ ابْتَكَرَتْ بِفَجِيعَةٍ تَرْغِيباً وَ

تَرْهِيباً وَ تَخْوِيفاً وَ تَحْذِيراً فَذَمَّهَا رِجالٌ غَداةَ النَّدامَةِ وَ حَمِدَها آخَرُونَ يَوْمَ الْقِيامَةِ ذَكَّرَتْهُمُ الدُّنْيَا فَتَذَكَّرُوا وَ حَدَّثَتْهُمْ فَصَدَّقُوا وَ وَعَظَتْهُمْ فَاتَّعَظُوا.

60. جهانا چه در خورد و بایسته ای   اگر چند با کس نپایسته ای

به ظاهر چو در دیده خس،ناخوشی   به باطن چو دو دیده بایسته ای

اگر بسته ای را گهی بشکنی   شکسته نیز هم بسته ای

چون آلوده بینندت آلوده ای   و لیکن سوی شستگان،شسته ای

کسی که تو را می نکوهش کند   بگویش:هنوزم ندانسته ای

ز من رسته ای تو اگر بخردی   چه بنکوهی آن را کزان رسته ای

به من بر،گذر داد ایزد تو   را تو در رهگذر،پست چه نشسته ای

ز بهر تو ایزد درختی بکشت   که تو شاخی از بیخ او جسته ای

اگر کژ بر او رسته ای سوختی   وگر راست بر رسته ای رسته ای

بسوزد بلی،هرکسی چوب کژ   نپرسد که بادام یا پسته ای

تو نیز خدایی سوی دشمنش   به تیرش چرا چرا خویشتن خسته ای

62. گفت موسی ای خداوند حساب   نقش کردی،باز چون کردی خراب؟

نر و ماده نقش کردی جانفزا   وانگهی ویران کنی آن را،چرا؟

گفت حق:دانم که این پرسش تو را   نیست از انکار و غفلت وز هوی

ورنه تنذیب و عنابت کردمی   بهر این پرسش تو را آزردمی

لیک می خواهی که در افعال ما   از جویی حکمت و سرقضا

تا از آن واقف کنی مر عام را   پخته گردانی بدین هر خام را

پس بفرمودش خدا ای ذو لباب   چون بپرسیدی بیا بشنو جواب

موسیا تخمی بکار اندر زمین   تا تو خود وا دهی انصاف این

چون که موسی کشت و کشتش شد تمام   خوشه هایش یافت خوبی و نظام

داس بگرفت و مر آنها را برید   پس ندا از غیب در گوشش رسید

که چرا کشتی کنی و پروری   چون کمالی یافت آن را می بری؟

گفت یا رب زان کنم ویران و پست   که در این جا دانه هست و کاه هست

دانه لایق نیست در انبار کاه   کاه در انبار گندم،هم تباه

نیست حکمت این دو را آمیختن   فرق،واجب می کند در بیختن

گفت این دانش ز که آموختی؟   نور این شمع از کجا افروختی؟

گفت تمییزم تو دادی ای خدا   گفت پس تمییز چون نبود مرا؟

در خلایق روح های پاک هست   روح های تیره گلناک است

این صدفها نیست در یک مرتبه   در یکی در است و در دیگر شبه

واجب است اظهار این نیک و تباه   همچنان کاظهار گندمها ز کاه

۶۳.برخیز و مخور غم جهان گذران   بنشین و دمی به شادمانی گذران

در طبع جهان اگر وفایی بودی   نوبت به تو خود نیامدی از دگران

64. Mir Muhammad Baqir ibn Shams al-Din Muhammad al-Husayni al-Astarabadi (d. 1630), known as Mir Damad for short, philosopher, theologian, and leader in the cultural renascence of Iran during the Safavid dynasty. Mir Damad was the first to advance the notion of *huduth-e dahri* ("eternal origination") as an explanation of creation. *Al-Qabasat* is perhaps his most important work. He also wrote poetry under the pseudonym of Ishraq. As a measure of his stature, he was given the title *al-mu'allim althalith* (i.e., "third teacher"-the first two being Aristotle and al-Farabi)' His work was continued by his pupil Mulla Sadra, who became the most prominent Muslim philosopher of the 17th century.

65. Shahab al-Din Yahya Suhrawardi (1154-1191), commonly known as Shaykh al-Ishraq, is one of the most famous Muslim philosophers. Despite his short life, he introduced many novel ideas that starkly contrasted Avicennian doctrines. He kept to logical methods but, like Plato, also emphasized the role of intuition, inspiration and the direct vision of realities. Suhrawardi spent much effort in trying to prove the existence of the Imaginal world, a world that is situated between the world of intellects (i.e. the Platonic Ideas or Forms) and the natural order. His most important work is *Hikmat al-Ishraq.*

۶۶.تا زهره و مه در آسمان گشت پدید   بهتر ز می ناب کسی هیچ ندید

من در عجبم ز می فروشان کایشان   به زانچه فروشند چه خواهند خرید!؟

عارفی کو که کند فهم،زبان سوس   تا بپرسد که چرا رفت و چرا باز آمد؟.67

می رود از سینه ها در سینه ها   از ره پنهان صلاح و کینه ها.68

به عنبر فروشان اگر بگذری   شود جامه تو   همه عنبری.69

اگر بگذری سوی انگشت گر   از او جز سیاهی نیابی دگر

قَالَ رَسُولُ اَللَّهِ صَلَّى اَللَّهُ عَلَيْهِ وَ آلِهِ : لَمَّا أُسْرِيَ بِي إِلَى اَلسَّمَاءِ دَخَلْتُ اَلْجَنَّةَ فَرَأَيْتُ فِيهَا   .70
قِيعَان قِيعَاناً بَيْضَاءَ وَ رَأَيْتُ فِيهَا مَلاَئِكَةً يَبْنُونَ لَبِنَةً مِنْ ذَهَبٍ وَ لَبِنَةً مِنْ فِضَّةٍ وَ رُبَّمَا أَمْسَكُوا
فَقُلْتُ لَهُمْ مَا لَكُمْ رُبَّمَا بَنَيْتُمْ وَ رُبَّمَا أَمْسَكْتُمْ فَقَالُوا حَتَّى تَجِيئَنَا اَلنَّفَقَةُ فَقُلْتُ لَهُمْ وَ مَا نَفَقَتُكُمْ فَقَالُوا
قَوْلُ اَلْمُؤْمِنِ فِي اَلدُّنْيَا سُبْحَانَ اَللَّهِ وَ اَلْحَمْدُ لِلَّهِ وَ لاَ إِلَهَ إِلاَّ اَللَّهُ وَ اَللَّهُ أَكْبَرُ فَإِذَا قَالَ بَنَيْنَا وَ إِذَا
أَمْسَكَ أَمْسَكْنَا.

قَالَ رَسُولُ اَللَّهِ صَلَّى اَللَّهُ عَلَيْهِ وَ آلِهِ : مَنْ قَالَ سُبْحَانَ اَللَّهِ غَرَسَ اَللَّهُ لَهُ بِهَا شَجَرَةً فِي   .71
اَلْجَنَّةِ وَ مَنْ قَالَ اَلْحَمْدُ لِلَّهِ غَرَسَ اَللَّهُ لَهُ بِهَا شَجَرَةً فِي اَلْجَنَّةِ وَ مَنْ قَالَ لاَ إِلَهَ إِلاَّ اَللَّهُ غَرَسَ اَللَّهُ
لَهُ بِهَا شَجَرَةً فِي اَلْجَنَّةِ وَ مَنْ قَالَ اَللَّهُ أَكْبَرُ غَرَسَ اَللَّهُ لَهُ شَجَرَةً فِي اَلْجَنَّةِ فَقَالَ رَجُلٌ مِنْ قُرَيْشٍ
يَا رَسُولَ اَللَّهِ إِنَّ شَجَرَنَا فِي اَلْجَنَّةِ لَكَثِيرٌ قَالَ نَعَمْ وَ لَكِنْ إِيَّاكُمْ أَنْ تُرْسِلُوا عَلَيْهَا نِيرَاناً فَتُحْرِقُوهَا
وَ ذَلِكَ أَنَّ اَللَّهَ عَزَّ وَ جَلَّ يَقُولُ يَا أَيُّهَا اَلَّذِينَ آمَنُوا أَطِيعُوا اَللَّهَ وَ أَطِيعُوا اَلرَّسُولَ وَ لاَ تُبْطِلُوا
أَعْمَالَكُمْ.

این جهان کوه است و فعل ما ندا   باز آید سوی ما از که صدا.72

به چشم خویش دیدم در گذرگاه   که زد بر جان موری مرکی راه.73

هنوز از صید،منقارش نپرداخت   که مر دیگر آمد کار او ساخت

چو بد کردی مشو ایمن ز آفات   که واجب شد طبیعت را مکافات

هر دم از عمر می رود نفسی   چون نگه می کنم نمانده بسی.74

ای که پنجاه رفت و در خوابی   مگر این پنج روز دریابی

خجل آن کس که رفت و کار نساخت   کوس رحلت زدند و بار نساخت

عمر،برف است و آفتاب تموز   اندکی مانده،خواجه ره هنوز

هرکه آمد عمارتی نو ساخت   رفت و منزل به دیگری پرداخت

برگ عیشی به گور خویش فرست   کس نیارد ز پس تو پیش فرست

هرکه مزروع خود بخورد بخوید   وقت خرمنش خوشه باید چید

ای تهیدست رفته بازار   ترسمت برنیاوری دستار

ای دریده پوستین یوسفان   گرگ برخیزی از این خواب گران.75

گشته گرگان یک به یک خوهای تو   می درانند از ضب اعضای تو

زآنچه می بافی همه روزه بپوش   ز آنچه می کاری همه ساله بنوش

گر ز خاری خسته ای،خود کشته ای   ور حریر و قز دری،خود رشته ای

چون ز دستت زخم بر مظلوم رست   آن درختی گشت و ز آن قوم رست

این سخن های چون مار و کژ دمت   مار و کزدم می شود گیرد دمت

حشر پر حرص خس مردار خوار   صورت خوکی بود روز شمار.76

زانیان را گنده اندام نهان   خمر خواران را بود گنده دهان

گند مخفی کان به دل ها می رسید   گشت اندر حشر محسوس و پدید

بیشه ای آمد وجود آدمی   برحذر شو زین وجود ار آدمی

ظاهر و باطن اگر باشد یکی   نیست کس را در نجات او شکی

در وجود ما هزاران گرگ و خوک   صالح و ناصالح و خوب و خشوک

حکم،آن خو راست کان البتر است   چونکه زر بیش از مس آمد آن زر است

سیرتی کاندر وجودت الب است   هم بر آن تصویر،حشرت واجب است

فَاتَّقِ اللَّهَ وَ ارْدُدْ إِلَى هَؤُلَاءِ الْقَوْمِ أَمْوَالَهُمْ فَإِنَّكَ إِنْ لَمْ تَفْعَلْ ثُمَّ أَمْكَنَنِي اللَّهُ مِنْكَ لَأُعْذِرَنَّ إِلَى 77.
اللَّهِ فِيكَ وَ لَأَضْرِبَنَّكَ بِسَيْفِي الَّذِي مَا ضَرَبْتُ بِهِ أَحَداً إِلَّا دَخَلَ النَّارَ وَ اللَّهِ لَوْ أَنَّ الْحَسَنَ وَ الْحُسَيْنَ
فَعَلَا مِثْلَ الَّذِي فَعَلْتَ مَا كَانَتْ لَهُمَا عِنْدِي هَوَادَةٌ وَ لَا ظَفِرَا مِنِّي بِإِرَادَةٍ حَتَّى آخُذَ الْحَقَّ مِنْهُمَا وَ
أُزِيحَ الْبَاطِلَ عَنْ مَظْلَمَتِهِمَا

او شفیع است این جهان و آن جهان   این جهان در دین و آنجا در جنان.78

این جهان گوید که تو رهشان نما   آن جهان گوید که تو مه شان نما

پیشه اش اندر ظهور و در کمون   اهد قومی انهم لا یعلمون

باز گشته از دم او هر دو باب   در دو عالم دعوت او مستجاب

بهر این خاتم شده است او که به وجود   مثل او نی بود و نی خواهند بود

صدهزاران آفرین بر جان او   برقدوم و دور فرزندان او

آن خلیفه زادگان مقبلش   زاده انداز عنصر جان و دلش

گر ز بغداد و هری یا از ری اندر   بی مزاج آب و گل نسل وی اند

شاخ گل هرجا که می روید گل است   خل مل هرجا که می جوشد مل است

گر ز مرب برزند خورشید،سر   عین خورشید است نی چیز دگر

از خدا می خواه تا زین نکته ها   در نلزی و رسی در منتها.79

ز آنکه از قرآن بسی گمره شدند   زین رسن قومی درون چه شدند

مر رسن را نیست جرمی ای عنود   چون تو را سودای سر بالا نبود

مزرع سبز فلک دیدم و داس مه نو   یادم از کشته خویش آمد و هنگام درو.80

گفتم ای بخت بخسبیدی و خورشید دمید   گفت با این همه از سابقه نومید مشو

ادیم زمین سفر عام اوست   بر این خوان یغما چه دشمن چه دوست.81

Index